Yale French Studies

NUMBER 69

The Lesson of Paul de Man

Yale French Studies

Peter Brooks, Shoshana Felman, J. Hillis Miller,
    Special editors for this issue
Liliane Greene, *Managing editor*
Editorial board: Peter Brooks (Chairman), Alan
    Astro, Ellen Burt, Lauren Doyle-McCombs,
    Shoshana Felman, Richard Goodkin, Leonard
    Koos, Christopher Miller, Charles Porter
Staff: Peggy McCracken
Editorial office: 315 William L. Harkness Hall.
Mailing address: 2504A Yale Station, New Haven,
    Connecticut 06520.
Sales and subscription office:
    Yale University Press, 92A Yale Station
    New Haven, Connecticut 06520.
Published twice annually by Yale University Press.
Designed by James J. Johnson and set in Trump
    Medieval Roman by The Composing Room of
    Michigan, Inc.
Printed in the United States of America by The
    Vail-Ballou Press, Binghamton, N.Y.
ISSN 0044–0078
ISBN for this issue 0–300–03409–1

Foreword

"The Lesson of Paul de Man" represents but one among what will no doubt be many efforts over the coming years to bear witness to the legacy of an extraordinary critic, teacher, and colleague. We have chosen our title, and the contents of this issue, with a special attention to Paul de Man's pedagogical presence, which was so much a part of our experience of him since, in whatever context, he never was not teaching. Several of the contributors to this issue were students of Paul de Man's in the classroom sense of the term. Others learned from his collegial presence, whether at Yale or elsewhere, whether over the space of years or from a single lecture. However delivered, his lesson was essentially unforgettable. And all the contributors show that this lesson posed particularly acute challenges in their own work, demanding an unusually thoughtful response.

We suggested that contributors address themselves to Paul de Man's work, or to questions inspired by his work, or else to more personal evocations of the man and his lesson. We have included nine tributes spoken at the Memorial Service held in January, 1984, as a first response to Paul de Man's disappearance. We have also included a transcript of Paul de Man's Messenger Lecture at Cornell University, delivered during his last semester of active teaching. And then, following the essays, we have provided what we hope is a complete bibliography of Paul de Man's published work. It is in that work that the lesson now resides, and from which new directions for literary study will continue to emerge.

A number of colleagues and students at Yale responded to the spirit of this issue by remarkable contributions of time, energy, and talent, in the translation and editing of manuscripts, and the compilation of the bibliography. The Editors wish to express special thanks to: Vernon Chadwick, Cyrus Hamlin, William D. Jewett, Thomas Keenan, Robert Livingston, Peggy McCracken, Andrzej Warminski.

PETER BROOKS
SHOSHANA FELMAN
J. HILLIS MILLER

In Memoriam

The Following Tributes Were Offered at the Memorial Service for Paul de Man Held at the Yale University Art Gallery on January 18, 1984.

We have gathered here today to honor Paul de Man, his accomplishments and his influence. The ten friends, colleagues, and students of Paul de Man who will each say a few words about him can hardly be said to be "representative." Paul de Man would have smiled ironically at that idea and have murmured something about the aberrancy of synecdoche. Each of us speaks for herself or himself. After this ceremony is over there will be an informal reception in the Comparative Literature Library on the eighth floor of Bingham Hall for those who want to greet Mrs. de Man and one another.

I want to speak not about de Man's power as a teacher and as a writer, but about the extraordinary intellectual authority he exerted on his friends and colleagues, at least on me. Paul de Man much disliked words like "power," "force," or "authority," especially when applied to the academic world. He would have smiled ironically again and more than a little scornfully at the idea that he had what those words name, though obviously he did. What was the source of this authority? Though it was surely in part his extraordinary personal charm and his imperturbable good humor, a kind of radiant joy in the possession of intellectual mastery, these do not quite account for it. I suggest that Paul de Man's intellectual power sprang from a double orientation toward the situation of the reader which was fundamental to his thought. On the one hand he assumed and tirelessly demonstrated that most students of literature, even the most renowned or distinguished, are aberrant readers. Each of us most likely dwells in a wandering state of delusory belief in a whole set of interlocking mistakes about particular authors and about literary history. De Man was fascinated by the question of why this should be so. He saw it as related to the broadest questions of epistemology, aesthetics, ethics, the institutionalizing of knowledge, politics, the life and death of culture. As he said once to me this past fall, speaking of the current polemical situation in literary studies, "the stakes are enormous." On the other hand, this calm assumption of almost universal aberrancy was not only held in the name of an attainable truth but even held in the belief that all of us are in the truth, even speak the truth, without necessarily knowing it and yet without being able to do otherwise. As he says in one of his last and as yet unpublished essays, "Whatever truth may be fighting, it is not error but stupidity, the belief that one is right when one is

3

in fact in the wrong"[1] ("Anthropomorphism and Trope in the Lyric," p. 4). Far from holding, as he and his associates are sometimes said to do, that interpretations are free-floating, Paul de Man held that they are to be measured by a truth which is at least a possibility of "the negative knowledge of error."[2] Who would wish to be stupidly aberrant when one might at least know that one is in error? The other part of Paul de Man's authority, then, was his ability to persuade one to believe that one is in spite of everything, in the truth. Even the most naive paraphrase of a poem repeats the disruptions and discontinuities which are the truth of the text and which the paraphrase is intended to cover up. Far from placing authority in some will to power of the critic, as, once more, he and his colleagues are sometimes, quite falsely, said to do, Paul de Man placed the ultimate source of power and authority where in fact it is, in the words on the page. De Man's clearest statement of this is in the "Foreword" to Carol Jacobs' *The Dissimulating Harmony*. If I may dare to say so, the future of literary studies depends on reading Paul de Man as best we can, on being true to his example as a reader and as a continuator of the long tradition of literary study to which he belonged. Here are his words in a characteristically rigorous and elegant formulation: "Understanding is not a version of one single and universal Truth that would exist as an essence, a hypostasis. The truth of a text is a much more empirical and literal event. What makes a reading more or less true is simply the predictability, the necessity of its occurrence, regardless of the reader or of the author's wishes. 'Es ereignet sich aber das Wahre' (not *die Wahrheit*) says Hölderlin, which can be freely translated: 'What is true is what is bound to take place.' And, in the case of the reading of a text, what takes place is a necessary understanding. What marks the truth of such an understanding is not some abstract universal but the fact that it has to occur regardless of other considerations. . . . It is not a matter of choice to omit or to accentuate by paraphrase certain elements in a text at the expense of others. We don't have this choice, since the text imposes its own understanding and shapes the reader's evasions." This general confidence in our ability to get it right as readers, after all, was the other half of Paul de Man's authority over those he touched.

J. HILLIS MILLER

I imagine that over the past weeks many of us have been remembering the moment when we first "discovered" Paul de Man. For me, that discovery took place twenty-five years ago, when as a college senior I walked into a room in Sever Hall, in the Harvard Yard, to have a look at a course called "Valéry, Rilke, and Yeats." The class had already begun when I entered. The teacher was sitting at the desk, with Yeats's *Collected Poems* open before him, talking, and as he talked his hands would move upwards from the page, as in a gesture of

---

1. Paul de Man, "Anthropomorphism and Trope in the Lyric," *The Rhetoric of Romanticism* (New York: Columbia University Press, 1984).
2. Ibid.

unfolding or releasing, as if he were pulling things from the text and setting them loose. It was as if I had come into the presence of a magician, working the spells from some old *grimoire*, taking what turned out to be that peculiar early poem of Yeats, "The Wanderings of Oisin," and by the newest and least understandable of alchemies freeing from it the shape of a passionate and perplexing allegory of reading. To be given to understand that there was this kind of drama available in the reading of texts, that what was at stake in the study of literature was as difficult and demanding and unsettling as philosophy or any other mode of discourse—this was an enthralling revelation. I recall that during the year following that class with Paul de Man—when I was supposed to be reading history in England—I found myself puzzling over Mallarmé and Proust in a kind of muddled homage to what I construed to be the questions he had raised. I blame it on Paul that I decided to go back to Harvard for graduate study. Alas, when I got there he had moved on to Cornell.

It was not until another ten years had passed that I would make the still more important discovery of Paul as colleague and friend. The image of the magician didn't entirely disappear, but now the magic included that remarkable generosity, patience, and understanding, that gift for attentive kindness, that made any meeting with Paul—even the meeting of a committee that included Paul—full of moments of rare humor and warmth and fellowship. From the array of memories that come to mind on this occasion, I'll mention only one, which concerns a trip Paul and I made to the headquarters of a corporate foundation in New York, in search of a grant for the Literature Major. This potentially dismal venture became in Paul's company an improbable and festive outing. When at last we sat in an office high above Park Avenue, amidst the symbols of American corporate might, I found myself watching the face of the foundation officer, at once bemused and slightly alarmed, as Paul explained that it was entirely legitimate to consider the entire epistemology of the sciences of man to be founded in a lie superimposed upon an error, and then went on to instance the kind of error that the foundation officer would have committed had he named his son "Achilles" in the expectation that this would make him act like a lion. The outing had suddenly improvised a sumptuous intellectual picnic. And somehow even in this alien context the power of that mind and its unanswerable, unsettling logic made itself felt. We in fact got the grant.

Let me close by remembering for one more moment that course on Valéry, Rilke, and Yeats that marked my own discovery of Paul. I have not forgotten the poem he gave the class to explicate on the final exam; it was Yeats's "At Algeciras—A Meditation on Death," which, you may recall, ends with the lines:

> Greater glory in the sun,
> An evening chill upon the air,
> Bid imagination run
> Much on the Great Questioner;
> What He can question, what if questioned I
> Can with a fitting confidence reply.

Paul was himself eminently the great questioner. We who were privileged to be present at his questionings, and to feel the intellectual and the human warmth they generated against the chill air of their implications, can only feel how much we miss him.

PETER BROOKS

A tremendous light for humane life and learning is gone and nothing for us will ever be the same. I think of Paul de Man always in terms of lucidity, as a radiant presence. "Brilliance" is a word that takes on a special and full meaning when it is associated with him.

To find special and full meaning was Paul's profession and way of life. He had absorbed and not abandoned all that Europe could teach a spacious and effortless mind—all that literary culture and science and the upheavals of the twentieth century had to say, and then he saw, from his oblique and direct perspective, what more there was. He parsed complexity in all things to find the root of simplicity. He was impatient with easy complications. He wanted to find the beginning, where the light started.

He was a man who could never be surprised and yet who was never indifferent. He maintained the highest standards in all things and believed no task or chore was beneath doing with elegant dispatch. A university was his natural home; he and a university were instinctively congenial to each other. How fortunate we were that he was with us here, although he and Yale really held each other in trust for the benefit of those everywhere who cared for humane learning. His students were his public joy, the enduring human links to our common civilization. His family was the center of his life, and there his wisdom, his humor and his radical human touch shone brightest. He knew that of all the things that pass, and all things do, human affection lasts longest and sweetest.

I shall always see his shy and candid smile. It was luminous, and wordlessly encouraged us to be better.

A. BARTLETT GIAMATTI

A month has passed, but a month is nothing; and the wound that thought gives, that memory enforces, remains fresh. "The set is broken"—that phrase, Wordsworth's when he heard of his youngest brother's death, came involuntarily to my mind, so close did I feel to Paul; so close, I assume, everyone of his colleagues felt; and that he was the oldest, not the youngest, was only a semblance, for, in fact, we knew *him* to be the one who had most the resistance to time, a vigor, a vigilance, a stability that went far beyond what the emigré, the uprooted person, usually carries within.

So, in the space war of the theorists, he became the Yoda figure. From the beginning, those remarkable essays in *Critique,* which during the 1950s meant so much for us, expressed a sense that there were no sublime monuments, only perplexed readings, or that, as he put it with a poetic and aphoristic gift akin to a Hegel he was always seeking to disenchant: "Substance itself . . . is the abyss." Nevertheless, he viewed each essay in poetry or philosophy as a "supreme wager" within and against language, as if it could achieve a sort of clarity, at least a clearing in which the work of thought became a working thought rather than a consolation. It is that very clarity which, separated from Paul, we now need.

Nothing can console us except his writings, however unseduced and uncomforting they are. They have more of a personal stamp than we may presently see; and to claim them, to interpret them, is a natural form of grieving. They are so consistent, yet so unpredictable; in them every sentence goes to the mark, we see it and don't see it, like a curve ball right in over the plate.

Yet I cannot say at this moment that there is no bitterness, when one thinks of what was left unfulfilled. It is hard to believe that he and Pat—who was always a presence nearby—came to Yale less than fourteen years ago. It was Paul's intellectual passion that sustained the teaching of literature at Yale, and never allowed false polemics to divert attention from the pedagogical task. He had wit, he had judgment, the classical virtues; and he put them where they were needed—in the service of the Romantics, for instance, who had been mistaught, praised or despised, canonized or decanonized, for the wrong reasons. And perhaps it was no accident that he was drawn to writers who recognized "cold mortality" without ceasing to be, in Shelley's words, "a mirror of the fire for which all thirst."

If Paul's clairvoyance, his mirroring of that fire, was a trouble, it was so not only to others, but also to himself. He made his mind increasingly more severe, and those who remember him listening fixedly to lectures by students or visitors know he could always spot the vulnerable point which turned the monumental thesis into a mortal project. Yet, however uncompromising he seemed to be, he was the most gracious of persons, never dismissive, even if he knew "de Trut," the most considerate and engaged teacher, the most agreeable conversationalist. Who will forget his smile, which remained with him almost to the end?

The last time we taught conjointly was at the School of Criticism and Theory in the summer of 1982. He was already ill. Yet the day before his illness obliged him to return to New Haven, he saw every student in his seminar till late at night, to discuss their ideas, or simply to chat and so tide them over. We had come back from a platform performance a few days earlier, and these things etch themselves in the mind: someone there in the audience tried to break down Paul's gentle, unrelenting exclusion of self-reference, his version of Pascal's "Le Moi est haïssable." This challenger from the audience pointed triumphantly to Paul's own presence—why are you here, in person, if you believe as you do—and Paul's smile became a glint of steel, as he replied: the text matters, what you write matters, everything else is vanity. *His* text matters;

and I believe I am following his own lesson when I say that his example made a difference, that all who heard him, as teacher, friend, or colleague, changed their relation to the written word.

GEOFFREY H. HARTMAN

Wednesday afternoon—this very hour—was throughout the years the time reserved for Paul de Man's class. It is fitting that we should today recall him in *his teaching time*, for his teaching now recalls us, and will never cease to summon us.

Today—a Wednesday—Paul would spend the morning in the library, have lunch with a colleague, and in the afternoon, would take the elevator to the eighth floor of Bingham Hall, where a crowd of students would await him. (I remember: as his young colleague, I myself used to attend some of his classes, for I felt that through him, through his works and through his person, something extraordinary spoke.) He would come to class, put down on the table his always far too heavy brief-case, take out some books in English, German, French, and would invariably—in his self-effaced and unexpected manner— make a joke, make the waiting of the class explode with laughter; and his jokes would always be in some sophisticated manner joking at his own expense, pedagogically disclaiming, in a Nietzschean manner, his own authority:

> Verily, I counsel you: go away from me and resist Zarathustra! . . . Perhaps he deceived you. . . .
>
> One repays a teacher badly if one remains nothing but a pupil . . .
>
> You say you believe in Zarathustra? But what matters Zarathustra? You are my believers—but what matter all believers? . . .
>
> Now I bid you lose me and find yourselves; and only when you have all denied me will I return to you.[3]

Paul disclaimed his own authority, yet none had more authority than him. He did not seek leadership, yet he was naturally at once an intellectual leader and a human guide.

I remember having lunch with Paul de Man right after my father died; I remember Paul facing my silence, my incapacity to talk, and gently talking then to me, for the first time, about the people *he* had lost—about his own experience of surviving death—speaking of himself only so as to enable *me* to speak, to break out of my silence.

There couldn't be a more delicate means of telling me that the way death—or the loss of those we love—is inscribed in our life, even while it

---

3. Nietzsche, *Thus Spoke Zarathustra,* tr. Walter Kaufman (New York: The Viking Portable Library,) first Part, 3, 190.

disrupts our words, should also be *that out of which we talk:* that out of which we talk to one another.

As a friend, as a colleague, as a thinker, as an educator, Paul was an infinitely *giving* person. He was generous with his time; he was generous with his ideas; he was generous with his suffering; he was generous even with his own mortality.

When he learned he was terminally ill, his first concern was not so much about his own death as about *Yale's welfare.* I will never forget how, from his hospital bed in which he was recuperating from his first emergency operation, he addressed us (visitors, colleagues and friends) with the question: who should replace him? Who would be best for Yale after his departure?

I remember how I wanted to protest—because I was myself too plunged in his and my own pain, too overwhelmed with the grief of his mortality—I wanted to protest and say to him: just now, Paul, all I care about is you, just yet I couldn't care less about what will happen after you, who will replace you,—don't you see that a person like yourself, with this kind of generosity and courage even in the face of death, is *irreplaceable?*

But he was wiser, and his own concern was, as always, transcendent to his own pain, transcendent to his own anxiety and to his own self-centered interest: his own concern, then as always, was tied up with *life:* the life beyond his own; the work that would go on beyond and after him. *His* concern was— *our own survival.*

Such was the power of his extraordinary mind. Such was the power of his extraordinary heart: the liberating power of his generosity and courage; for in his thinking, in his teaching, in his being in the world, he was above all this: a liberator.

On his deathbed, he became, thus, all the more a giver, all the more a teacher: transforming his own death into a life-lesson.

He was teaching us how, even in the face of death, mortality can be experienced, consummated, and assumed in creativity, how life can be asserted in acts of intellectual and human kindness.

Thank you, Paul, for having taught us, even through the process of your loss of life, how life can triumph.

May we live up to your precious memory.

May we, through the loss of you, learn how to live *up to your triumph.*

SHOSHANA FELMAN

It feels strange to go against the grain of Paul de Man's own vocabulary, and to feel compelled to use, in speaking about him, the very words that he was most suspicious of—words like integrity, honesty, authenticity, generosity, even seductiveness. The last thing he probably would have wanted to be was a moral and pedagogical—rather than merely intellectual—example for generations of students and colleagues, yet it was precisely his way of *not* seeking those roles that made him so irreplaceably an exception, and such an inspiration. He never sought followers; people followed him in droves. He was ironic toward discipleship; the country is dotted with his disciples. His impact was so profound and so specific that it is possible to determine from people's work not only *that* he was their teacher but also *when* he was their teacher—what he was working on when they passed their time beside him. He was the implied reader driving literary critical pens in every university in the country. Yet when given an essay or a chapter of one's thesis or of one's life, he would respond as Melville describes Billy Budd responding to the chaplain's benediction: "He received, but did not appropriate. It was like a gift placed in the palm of an outreached hand upon which the fingers do not close." This left his students immeasurably free—free from the fear of embarrassing him or the desire to reflect him, free to make fools of themselves in their own way, free to differ from him without making an issue of it—free, but never without his support.

He lived and worked as much without waste as without haste, as much without compromise as without complacency. His unflaunted generosity and efficiency and singleminded pursuit of his own path were made possible, I think, because he spent so little time looking in the mirror. He did not try to charm away the consequences of the rigor and honesty of his thought, but neither did he glory in the resistance he encountered. Faced with systematic misinterpretation, he would say only, with ironic and moving pseudo-resignation, "I have all the fewer illusions about the possibility of countering these aberrations since such an expectation would go against the drift of my own readings." Reading, indeed, was the one imperative on which he unfailingly insisted—reading in the literal as well as in the broadest sense as the most taken for granted, the most difficult, the most urgent, and the most passionately resisted imperative of human life.

In a profession full of fakeness, he was real; in a world full of takers, he let others take; in a crowd of self-seekers, he sought the truth, and distrusted it. Although he will never be other than alive to those who have known him and loved him and learned from him, nothing can make up for our loss as we now face a world without Paul de Man.

BARBARA JOHNSON

Countless students owe their continued presence in the university, and the course that their career has taken, to the support and the teaching of Paul de Man. I was one of those students. On anyone who knew him, or took the time to read his work, he exercised a powerful fascination. On those of us who took his courses, who read him avidly, who sat for hours in his office, the fascination was particularly strong. It was first attached to the man—to his gait, to the shrug of the shoulders, the set of the head, the quizzical smile. But it had as its truer source a moral trait: what we sensed to be as complete a detachment from the claims of subjectivity or individual personality as was possible.

Such a divestment of personal stakes meant that he wielded an unparalleled strategic skill in the institution. He took each institutional encounter away from the murky plane of the personal, and made it appear to us in its proper light, as a practical question. Free from any hesitation born of the fear of others, he could engage upon and pursue a course of action without a backward glance. We all profited, both materially and by example, from his ability to call our attention away from the shadowy motives we imagined behind each turn of the cogs in the administrative process, or from the games of seduction played out in the classroom. Rather than seeking out the agents responsible for a problem, rather than retreating behind the rules or the deadlines, he asked himself instead whether a question required his intervention, how to give it most effectively. The issues were entirely pragmatic: how was a student to find the money to continue his or her studies? Which would be the proper place to send his letter of recommendation? How and where was a neophyte professor to be given his or her chance to profess? Would his intervention help or hinder? How and when should he intercede? His care was all the more eagerly sought by his students because it hid no suspect pity, voyeuristic kindness, or self-love: he did not need to care about us personally, we thought, because he cared for us, practically, professionally.

Women gained by his detachment especially, since in seeking to dispense with the level on which intersubjective dispute might occur, he was effectively seeking to dispense with the kinds of accusations to which they are customarily subject. He had himself no time to waste being seduced, disquieted, or threatened by women. And thus no time to waste vindictively barring them from effecting a full entry into the profession. He seemed to have no time to waste barring anyone from entering the profession. His time was devoted to giving us time, to work.

His detachment, and our fascination with it, made it possible for us to profit practically from his teaching too. We learned the tools of the trade from him because, as we could hear his detachment, his words could carry weight with us, could ring much truer than ours. If he said in an aside one day that we ought to read Hegel's *Aesthetics*, we read them, in order to understand why we must read them. If he said that the first draft of Rousseau's *Social Contract* was more interesting than the second and more polished draft, we spent weeks comparing them. We poured for hours over the little checks he made in the margins of the papers he returned to us. We waited, after a conference, for *his* question—and discussed it avidly, referred back to it for years. We were not foolish; we were fascinated, and we were learning how to interpret, how to go about gaining interpretative skills.

But while he was able so to divest himself of personal claims as to become an entirely effective teacher in these practical ways, the real *tour de force* was in the way he unmasked our fascination, explaining in his dryest and most impersonal manner, why his own detachment was necessary. —In the first place, no one can know with any certainty what others' intentions might be— that went almost without saying. But, and here he spoke more insistently, that first question hides another: in seeking to interpret intentions, he suggested, we are avoiding the question of whether intentions are determined by subjects, or by language as figures in texts. The stake of such a doubt was subjectivity, and subjectivity included the moral trait of detachment that we ascribed to him. We found the source of our fascination, his power to speak truth, dismissed by him as a strategy of our self-love. Our fascination was but one of the illusions he was systematically undoing. We wanted to attribute to him an authority equal to the knowledge that he brought us, an authority from which he was always, with irony, with a shrug of his shoulders, detaching himself.

Finally, what he taught us then was that we could not, fixing our eyes on him too closely, follow him, that we must divest ourselves of our personal investment, our studenthood, if we wished to understand him. But that means that, in a way, he was teaching us how to begin to lose him, how to begin to lose the man and his teacherly qualities: his strategic skill, his keen gift for speaking truth, his ear for the unspoken and unthought in our words, his willingness to give of his time, his intellectual rigor.

What he could not teach us is how to begin to accept the loss of his ironic stance, that ironic stance that he had achieved over and over toward his own eventual disappearance. Piety toward the work or toward the man capable of such strong irony seems as inevitable as it would be wrong. We ought, to be true to his spirit, to resist that piety as hard as some have resisted his theories. But how can we? How can we begin to mourn what we would need to have still—his irony—in order to mourn him properly?

E. S. Burt

Five years ago, I remember, in the course of giving an undergraduate lecture on Shelley's "The Triumph of Life" Professor de Man spoke at length about the words "thread" and "tread," and the importance of their difference to the poem. His reading was made considerably more difficult by the fact that he pronounced the two words exactly the same way—as "tread." After some fifteen minutes of tread and tread, he paused, somewhat nonplussed, to look at the audience: "My whole argument is based on the difference between tread and tread, and I can't say the difference." A moment—of "parabasis," he might have called it—due, one felt sure, not to any accident of birth, but to a necessity of language, words and their lack.

There is certainly no lack of words to say the difference his life made, especially for those of us who stayed, first in graduate school, then in the profession, simply because of him: his teaching and his reading. There is much to say about his teaching. Always pointing beyond himself, Professor de Man was one of those rare teachers who do not make their own limitations the limitations of the student—a teacher who thus puts the student in an all the more difficult position, for, after all, everyone wants to *be* such a teacher. "Be like me," says the double bind of such teaching, "but (like me) only in my difference from myself." Those who learned the lesson he had to teach learned not to read like *him* but like him to *read*. They learned to listen for and to reread a whole lexicon of new words, not the ones that now serve as the currency of academic journalism, nor just the names of tropes that came and went over the years like harried and somewhat dishevelled Greek gods—catachresis, chiasmus, parabasis, metalepsis, anacoluthon, prosopopoeia—but other, more invisible and yet more insistent words that were there from the beginning. On the one side, words like negativity, rigor, terror, aberrant—all the words serving to unmask the unwarranted claims of false immediacy and the easy totalizations of apocalyptic or utopian historicist schemes. On the other side, words like pathos, monumentalization, aesthetification, trivial, reassuring, comfortable—all the words that conjure up the spectacle of cheap imitations of Greek art or leave a sweet taste in the mouth.

But what kept these words from being generalized into a system and what kept his reading from being rigidified into a merely negative method was the word "death" which he used as often as, but differently from, the others: more like a punctuation mark or a syntactical break than a semantic unit of meaning. This is the word that kept the others honest, that allowed his reading both to demystify a lack of rigor and to account for the necessity of the mystification. This is the word that served as the mark of articulation between the rigor of reading on the one hand and the inevitable falling back into aesthetic monumentalization on the other. It is the word he taught us to read. But precisely because he taught us to read it, it is also the word that makes it so difficult to say the difference his death makes now. Here the word is particularly lacking. And yet this particular lack of a word presents a challenge to the understanding, as he would put it, that demands to be read in its turn and thus opens up a space in which we may work to come to terms with his absence—a space in which we may mourn him, however improperly, thanks to his forgiving rigor.

ANDRZEJ WARMINSKI

Pardonnez-moi de parler dans ma langue. C'est la seule que j'aie toujours parlée avec Paul de Man. C'est aussi celle dans laquelle il a beaucoup enseigné, écrit, pensé. Et je n'ai pas le coeur aujourd'hui de traduire ces quelques mots et d'y ajouter, pour vous et pour moi, la souffrance et l'éloignement d'un accent étranger. Nous parlons moins pour dire quelque chose, aujourd'hui, que pour

An English translation of this tribute will be found below, on pp. 323–26 nous assurer, par la voix et par la musique, que nous sommes ensemble dans la même pensée. Nous savons combien il est difficile de parler en un tel moment, quand une parole juste et décente devrait s'interdire de céder à aucun usage, toutes les conventions paraissant intolérables ou vaines.

Si nous avons, comme on dit en français, la mort dans l'âme, c'est d'être désormais voués à parler *de* Paul de Man au lieu de *lui* parler, voués à parler du maître et de l'ami qu'il reste pour tant de nous, alors que le désir le plus vivant, et en nous le plus cruellement meurtri, le plus interdit désormais, serait de parler encore à Paul, de l'entendre et de lui répondre. Non seulement en nous-mêmes, comme nous continuerons, comme je continuerai de le faire sans cesse, mais de lui parler et de l'entendre nous parler, lui, lui-même. C'est là l'impossible, et de cette blessure nous ne pouvons même plus prendre la mesure.

Parler est impossible, mais se taire le serait aussi, ou s'absenter ou refuser de partager sa tristesse. Simplement je vous demande de me pardonner si je n'ai aujourd'hui que la force de quelques mots très simples. Plus tard j'essaierai de mieux dire, et de façon plus sereine, l'amitié qui me lie à Paul de Man (elle fut et reste unique), ce que je dois, comme tant d'autres, à sa générosité, à sa lucidité, à la force si douce de sa pensée, depuis ce matin de 1966 où je l'ai rencontré à Baltimore, lors d'un colloque, à une table de petit-déjeuner où nous avons parlé, entre autres choses, de Rousseau et de l'*Essai sur l'origine des langues*, texte alors peu fréquenté dans l'université et sur lequel nous travaillions chacun de notre côté sans le savoir. Depuis, rien ne nous a jamais séparés, pas l'ombre d'un dissentiment. Ce fut comme la loi d'or d'une alliance, celle d'une amitié confiante et sans réserve, sans doute, mais aussi le sceau d'une affirmation secrète, une sorte de foi partagée dans quelque chose que, aujourd'hui encore, je ne saurai pas cerner, délimiter, nommer (et c'est bien ainsi). Vous savez que Paul était l'ironie même et que, parmi toutes les pensées vivantes qu'il nous laisse, qu'il laisse vivre en nous, il y a aussi une énigmatique pensée de l'ironie, et même, selon le mot de Schlegel qu'il lui était arrivé de citer, une "ironie de l'ironie". Au coeur de ce qui m'a toujours attaché à lui, il y a aussi, justement, un certain au-delà de l'ironie qui réfléchissait vers la sienne une lumière de tendresse, de générosité, de compassion souriante pour tout ce qu'il éclairait de son infaillible vigilance. Sa lucidité fut parfois terrible, sans concession ni faiblesse, mais elle n'eut jamais rien de cette assurance négative dans laquelle se complaît parfois la conscience ironique.

Plus tard, donc, j'essaierai de mieux parler de ce que son amitié sut donner à tous ceux qui eurent la chance d'être ses amis, ses collègues, ses étudiants; mais aussi de son oeuvre, de l'avenir surtout de son oeuvre, l'une sans doute des plus marquantes de ce temps.[4] Son oeuvre, c'est-à-dire son enseignement et ses

---

4. Jacques Derrida publiera prochainement un essai en hommage à Paul de Man (University of Minnesota Press) et un ouvrage sur l'oeuvre de Paul de Man (Columbia University Press), série de conférences prononcées à l'Université de Californie à Irvine en avril 1984 (note de la rédaction).

livres, ceux qui sont déjà publiés et ceux qui le seront bientôt, car jusqu'au dernier moment, avec une force, une ferveur et une gaieté admirables il a travaillé, multiplié les conférences, les projets de textes, il a étendu et enrichi encore les perspectives qu'il avait déjà ouvertes pour nous. On sait déjà, et on en prendra de mieux en mieux conscience, qu'il a transformé dans l'université et hors d'elle, aux Etats-Unis et en Europe, le champ de la théorie littéraire et fécondé tout ce qui l'irrigue. Il y a imposé, en même temps qu'un nouveau style d'interprétation, de lecture, d'enseignement, la nécessité du polylogue et de ce raffinement pluri-linguistique dont il avait le génie, celui des langues na- tionales, le flamand, le français, l'allemand, l'anglais, mais aussi celui des idiomes que sont les littératures et les philosophies, renouvelant la lecture de Pascal aussi bien que de Rilke, de Descartes et de Hölderlin, de Hegel et de Keats, de Rousseau et de Shelley, de Nietzsche et de Kant, de Locke et de Diderot, de Stendhal et de Kierkegaard, de Coleridge, Kleist, Wordsworth, Baudelaire, Proust, Mallarmé, Blanchot, Austin, Heidegger, Benjamin, Bakhtine, et tant d'autres, contemporains ou non. Il ne se contentait jamais d'ouvrir de nouvelles lectures, il donnait à penser la possibilité de la lecture— et parfois de sa paradoxale impossibilité; et ce qui fut son engagement reste désormais celui de ses amis et de ses étudiants, qui lui doivent et se doivent de poursuivre ce qui fut par lui et avec lui engagé.

Au-delà de ce qui nous est visible dans les textes publiés, les siens et ceux qui en appellent aux siens, je puis témoigner, comme tant d'autres, de ce qu'est aujourd'hui le rayonnement de sa pensée et de sa parole. Aux Etats-Unis d'abord où tant d'universités sont reliées entre elles et vitalisées par la grande communauté de ses disciples, la grande famille de ses anciens étudiants ou collègues qui sont restés ses amis; mais aussi en Europe dans toutes les univer- sités où j'ai eu, comme ici, à Yale, la chance et l'honneur de travailler avec lui, souvent grâce à lui qui m'y invitait: je pense d'abord à Zürich où tant de fois nous nous sommes retrouvés, avec Patricia, avec Hillis; je pense naturelle- ment à Paris, où il a vécu, publié, partagé des responsabilités éditoriales ou universitaires (par exemple celles de Johns Hopkins ou de Cornell à Paris—et ce fut pour nous l'occasion de tant de rencontres). Je sais aussi les empreintes qu'a laissées son passage dans les universités de Constance, de Berlin, de Stock- holm. Et je ne dirai rien de Yale, parce que vous le savez mieux que quiconque et parce que ma mémoire est trop endeuillée aujourd'hui de ce que je partage ici même avec lui depuis dix ans, des moments de la simple quotidienneté aux moments les plus forts du travail qui nous liaient tous deux et qui nous liaient à d'autres amis, étudiants et collègues qui le pleurent ici tout près de moi.

Je voulais seulement témoigner, comme le ferait cette sorte d'observateur admiratif que j'ai aussi été à ses côtés dans le monde académique américain et européen. Ce n'est pas le moment ou le lieu de céder à l'indiscrétion des confi- dences ou des souvenirs trop personnels. Je m'en abstiendrai donc, j'en ai trop, comme certains d'entre vous, et ils sont trop bouleversants pour que nous ne préférions pas nous enfermer avec eux. Mais permettez-moi d'enfreindre la loi de cette pudeur pour évoquer deux souvenirs, seulement deux parmi tant d'autres.

La dernière lettre que j'ai reçue de Paul, je ne sais pas encore comment lire la sérénité ou la gaieté dont il y faisait preuve. Je n'ai jamais su jusqu'à quel point il l'affectait dans un mouvement de noble et souveraine discrétion, pour consoler et épargner ses amis dans leur inquiétude ou leur désespoir; et jusqu'à quel point au contraire il avait réussi à transfigurer ainsi ce qui pour nous reste le pire. Les deux sans doute. Il m'y disait ceci, entre autres choses, que je me permets de lire parce que, à tort ou à raison, je l'ai reçu comme un message à moi confié pour ses amis dans la peine. Vous y entendrez une voix et un ton qui nous sont familiers: "Tout cela, comme je vous le disais [au téléphone] me semble prodigieusement intéressant et je m'amuse beaucoup. Je l'ai toujours su, mais cela se confirme: la mort gagne beaucoup, comme on dit, à être connue de plus près—ce 'peu profond ruisseau calomnié la mort'". Et après avoir cité de Mallarmé ce dernier vers du "Tombeau de Verlaine," il ajoutait: "J'aime quand même mieux cela que la brutalité du mot 'tumeur'"—et qui est en français, en effet, plus terrible et insinuant, menaçant que dans toute autre langue.

Le deuxième souvenir, je le rappelle parce qu'il dit quelque chose de la musique. Et seule la musique me paraît aujourd'hui supportable, consonnante, à la mesure de ce qui nous rassemble dans la même pensée. Je savais depuis longtemps, bien qu'il en parlât peu, la place que la musique occupait dans la vie et dans la pensée de Paul. Or cette nuit-là, c'était à Chicago en 1979, et encore à l'occasion d'un colloque, nous roulions en voiture après un concert de jazz. Mon fils aîné m'avait accompagné et il parlait de musique avec Paul, plus précisément d'instruments de musique; ils le faisaient tous deux en experts qu'ils étaient, en techniciens qui savent nommer les choses. Je me suis alors aperçu que Paul, qui ne me l'avait jamais dit, avait une expérience d'instrumentiste et que la musique avait aussi été pour lui une pratique. Et le mot qui me le fit savoir, ce fut le mot "âme", quand Pierre, mon fils, et Paul parlèrent familièrement de "l'âme" du violon ou de la basse et m'apprirent que "l'âme" de ces instruments, c'est en français le nom de la pièce de bois, petite et fragile, toujours très exposée, menacée, qu'on place dans le corps de l'instrument pour soutenir le chevalet et mettre en communication les deux tables. Je ne savais pas pourquoi j'en fus si bizarrement ému sur le moment même, obscurément bouleversé par la conversation à laquelle j'assistais—sans doute à cause du mot "âme," qui nous parle toujours à la fois de vie et de mort et nous fait rêver d'immortalité, comme l'argument de la lyre dans le *Phédon*. Et je regretterai toujours, parmi tant et tant d'autres choses, de n'en avoir jamais reparlé à Paul. Comment pouvais-je savoir qu'un jour, de ce moment, de cette musique et de cette âme je parlerai sans lui, devant vous, qui me pardonnerez de le faire si mal à l'instant où déjà tout fait mal, si mal?

JACQUES DERRIDA

YVES BONNEFOY

Paul de Man

La première rencontre, vers 1955, au Collège de philosophie qu'animait, à peu près seul, Jean Wahl qui fut un peu (sinon beaucoup) notre maître. La conférence portait sur "la poésie, le devenir". J'étais venu pour le sujet mais aussi parce que cela m'était presque une habitude, en ces années, d'être à six heures dans la salle poussièreuse de l'Institut de géographie, place Saint-Germain-des-Prés, pour écouter Massignon ou Pierre Jean Jouve, Lévi-Strauss ou Georges Bataille.—J'étais venu pour le sujet, et j'en repartis avec une amitié naissante, qui allait se faire bientôt admiration, affection.

Et pour cela il avait suffi de cette tête au front en avant, penché sur un grand sourire soudain, au dessus duquel filtrait le regard très bleu; d'une parole presque à voix basse qui, aux moments importants, baissait encore ou s'entrecoupait d'un petit rire.

Ce rire était malicieux, avec quelque chose de presque enfantin, en tout cas de très juvénile: il semblait proposer de ne plus penser à l'idée qui venait d'être avancée, à ce projet saugrenu qu'un jeune penseur mi-critique mi-philosophe (ce double choix était encore assez rare) s'était donné ce jour-là, d'avoir des idées à propos de la poésie. Mais ce n'était pas pour autant un rire de dérision, un de ceux où l'on sent la peur et où s'annonce le dogmatisme qui va faire suite à l'instant de doute. Je sentais dans ce brusque déni du sérieux de l'heure à la fois la joie de comprendre, profondément, et l'ironie qui naît de la perception lucide des limites, que ce soient celles de la philosophie tout entière ou plus immédiatement les difficultés d'une pensée personnelle encore fragile, malgré ses intuitions magnifiques. Et étincelaient aussi dans cet enjouement la nostalgie des années de jeu et la mémoire, pouvait-on croire, d'une douleur,—avec déjà ce détachement, déjà cette sérénité d'un esprit tout à son travail quelle forme qu'ait prise l'existence, que nous avons vu, quelques-uns, s'approfondir et mûrir, se faire ironie pure, et sagesse, pendant tout le reste de ce destin.

An English translation of this article will be found below, on pp. 327–30.

Paul de Man. Une présence s'annonçait là, avec tout le mystère qui accompagne ce qui mérite ce nom; c'était à l'horizon du problème qui m'importait, qui m'avait requis ce jour-là, une région tout d'un coup plus claire (pas la clarté d'une explication, cependant, ni même celle d'une méthode, plutôt celle d'un feu qu'on percevrait à distance, sur une plage, on sent que quelqu'un répare là-bas son filet, recout le ciel à la terre); et ce fut un bonheur pour moi, deux ou trois ans plus tard, quand je vins pour la première fois aux Etats-Unis, à Harvard, pour un de ces grands étés où l'on va en blanc comme en Inde dans l'humidité accablante, sur l'herbe silencieuse, de retrouver Paul, à Cambridge. Il vivait alors à Boston, Beacon Street, dans un petit appartement sous les toits, sa fille naissait. Je le revois à la première rencontre, approchant sur le yard la tête penchée, souriant de loin, la couleur étonnante du regard déjà répandue autour de lui, sous les arbres: il était midi, l'heure où s'effacent les ombres. Nous prîmes l'habitude de déjeuner dans les petits restaurants français de Harvard Square, ou de Berkeley Street à Boston. Mais ce n'était plus pour parler de la poésie et du devenir, tout au moins de façon suivie, Paul aimait trop l'activité poétique pour s'y référer trop directement et, en somme, s'y établir,— préférant, comme en ses écrits, évoquer plutôt les poètes que la poésie elle-même, et plutôt les critiques que les poètes. Ce n'était pas s'éloigner de l'essentiel, cette façon de marquer, cruellement, gentiment, les limites d'une méthode ou les insuffisances d'une lecture, c'était pratiquer, avec encore ce rire bref et comme lointain qu'il tournait aussi contre soi, une sorte imprévue de théologie négative.

Et surtout il me racontait l'Irlande, qu'il aimait, parce que, me dit-il une fois, on ne peut pas y distinguer un homme d'une bête ou d'une plante (sans doute parce que le langage n'y est pas séparé du sol, par la vertu des mythes et de l'admirable musique populaire), et il évoquait Gott Island où je regrette de n'avoir pu ni cette année-là ni d'autres le rejoindre. L'île est au large du Maine, elle n'avait que deux ou trois petites maisons, dans la lumière. Et elle fut dans la vie de Paul de Man, recommencée tard en Amérique, le centre qui avait si longtemps manqué, la justification, parfois le refuge: toujours en tout cas le preuve de l'existence, sinon de Dieu, du moins de cette force unifiante qui, par dessous les tristesses, les nostalgies, remonte, irrésistiblement chez certains, pour alléger leur angoisse, comme l'eau le fait sous celui qui plonge.

Paul aima en effet, aima passionnément le monde naturel comme il est, prairies et forêts, vagues qui bouillonnent parmi les pierres, ce monde de l'immédiat et de l'éternel dont il ne cessait pas de constater, avec joie au plus vif de son inquiétude, qu'il était et demeurerait inaccessible au langage et même d'ailleurs à la poésie. Lui qui travaillait sur la particule verbale de façon si intellectualisée, si médiatisée par la culture—disons, d'un mot: si "seconde", mais il est vrai qu'il ne touchait qu'à des fragments de parole chargés déjà de l'énergie poétique et métaphysique la plus intense, comme s'ils étaient les surgissements d'un feu de l'esprit aussi élémentaire et aveugle que celui qui mène les astres—il recherchait la grande plage déserte qui s'étend dans les choses de la nature entre nous et la lumière là-bas, dans l'évidence silencieuse. Il s'avançait vers cet horizon, à tous ses moments de solitude, c'est de là, quand la vie des villes le reprenait, qu'il revenait avec ce courage que nous avons admiré en lui, et capable dès lors de cette attention comme lavée du souci qu'il savait accorder au plus fugitif étudiant tout autant qu'aux pensées les plus difficiles. Et il n'aima, bien sûr, et avec raison, que les oeuvres de poésie où paraît, où est méditée—où manque, parfois, mais de façon reconnue par le poète, et douloureuse pour lui—cette lumière. Wordsworth, Hölderlin, Yeats. Et Mallarmé, aussi bien. La parole qui se porte dans des hymnes, les derniers de notre tradition religieuse, ou dans simplement des fragments, signes de notre misère, vers ce qui transcende la parole; et qui, s'élançant ainsi, dit peut-être autre chose, dans l'économie du langage, que ce qu'elle croit faire entendre, ce qui retint Paul, on le sait. Mais la plus grave erreur qu'on pourrait faire sur Paul de Man serait de penser qu'il aima pour elle-mêmes, par simple goût de la vérité, ces syncopes de la signification, ces ruptures qui sourdement retentissent dans le sens que de grands poètes ont tenté de donner au monde. Il suivait des yeux, à la surface diaprée des énoncés poétiques, le jeu des intuitions, des méconnaissances, longue houle jamais brisé où s'échangent sans fin—et pour qui, on ne sait, dans la dérive des siècles—la réalité, comme l'on dit, et le rêve. Il se portait, dans ces instants d'attention extrême, au coeur de ce rire de moine zen qu'il avait toujours eu par pressentiment qu'il n'est pas de Dieu, même au plus profond du langage. Mais s'il regardait ainsi se faire et se défaire l'écume autour des flottaisons qui viennent de l'amont du fleuve, qui glissent vers l'estuaire, c'est parce que ce qui brille dans les figures et les images quand on les prend ainsi par l'infini de leur signifiance dans la matière du texte, c'est la lumière toujours, l'indifférente et sainte lumière. C'est parce que regarder la dérive élargit le ciel, aussi vide demeure celui-ci.

Longue série de rencontres trop espacées, dérive—là encore—des projets, des empêchements, des chances soudain offertes, parfois saisies: écoulement des années qui passent en déplaçant les lieux où l'on se retrouve, Cambridge longtemps, Ithaca, Zurich, la Provence, le Connecticut, la Californie. Voiture qui s'arrête, très en retard, devant le Clark Institute, à Williamstown—c'est le musée le lieu choisi pour le rendez-vous, à cause du Piero della Francesca—et Paul et Patricia et les enfants en descendent, ce sont des jours de vacances qui vont se poursuivre ainsi, où? hors du temps, me semble-t-il maintenant, hors du monde. Autre voiture, incroyablement chargée de bagages qui, étonnée d'arriver dans ce lieu sans route, s'immobilise devant la maison de Valsaintes: et les enfants ont grandi, et dix minutes n'ont pas passé que nous descendons dans le ravin, sous la chaleur, Patricia toujours en avant par la vertu de son pas de chèvre. C'est dans le bureau de Paul, à Woodbridge, qu'une certaine petite fille, un dimanche, se risque soudain à aller debout. Quinze ans plus tôt, sur une plage du New Hampshire, Paul faisait un grand feu de bois d'épaves, y posait des pommes de terre et la viande, c'était déjà la nuit, je me défendais avec des brandons enflammés contre les assauts d'une épée semblable qu'un petit garçon de six ans agitait avec l'agilité gauche de l'enfance.

Et la dernière fois ce fut à Irvine, j'habitais pour quelques semaines une petite maison dans les dunes qui sont au bout du campus, et Paul qui était venu en Californie pour un colloque vint revoir ce lieu où il avait vécu l'année précédente lui-même, où il avait été heureux, je le voyais bien. Après quoi il y eut les deux ou trois rencontres—ici, au bord de la mer, là chez des gens qu'on ne connaît pas, c'est le soir, il y a un dîner dehors, on s'attarde à parler dans le jardin, sous des lampes—qui sont, sans qu'on le sache, la fin. J'avais écouté Paul, dans le colloque, évoquer Jauss, présenter sa pensée critique, mais comme de loin, comme s'il était dans un autre monde que ces discussions ou cette salle: tant il semblait retiré dans l'analyse de quelques mots d'un poème de Baudelaire qu'il ne suivait pas eux-mêmes jusqu'à l'extrémité de leur sens, rêvant ce sens, eût-on dit, si bien que j'avais pensé qu'il parlait là de lui-même, qu'il se parlait. "Je suis deux êtres distincts", me dit-il, à peu près, à la sortie de la conférence. Quand la visite prit fin, nous avons conduit, John Naughton et

Paul de Man with his daughter.

moi, notre ami au petit aéroport de Orange County. C'était une après-midi, il faisait très beau et très chaud, comme d'habitude. Et la dernière minute étant arrivée, ou presque, Paul a empoigné sa valise, nous ne sommes pas sortis de la voiture, c'est en silence, c'est invisiblement—comme si souvent—que la vie a fait tourner en cet instant-là un de ces grands praticables dont elle peut leurrer des années notre affection, notre rêve.

Last Lecture

PAUL DE MAN

"Conclusions" Walter Benjamin's "The Task of the Translator" Messenger Lecture, Cornell University, March 4, 1983

Editorial Note

What appears here is an edited transcript of the last of six Messenger Lectures delivered at Cornell in February and March of 1983. The text is based on a collation of three sets of tape recordings, supplemented with eight pages of manuscript notes. Aside from differences in detail, formulation, and emphasis, the notes diverge significantly from the tapes only on the last sheet, where de Man wrote: "Im Anfang war das Wort und das Wort war bei Gott/Dasselbe war bei Gott/ohne Dasselbe" (the last two words lined out)—the beginning of Luther's translation of St. John's gospel, which Benjamin quotes in Greek and to which de Man made reference in the question session following the Cornell lecture. This text retains traces of the context in which the lecture was delivered, notably in references to the three preceding lectures.*

Though the task of the transcriber—to give to an unwritten text the after life of canonicity—may be undertaken only by suspending the ideal of fidelity that underwrites it, I have tried wherever possible to resist the necessity of fixing or immobilizing passages which appeared to be still underway toward formulation. De Man's sometimes unnaturalized English has been preserved, with the exception of a few modifications attempted for the sake of coherence. Some sentences, and a few paragraphs, had to be rearranged. Solecisms and redundancies have been retained, however, where the possibility of foregrounding a gap between oral performance and printed text seemed to outweigh the likelihood of inconvenience; in this way I have tried to transmit some of the burden and risk of reconstruction on to the reader. Omissions and emendations are intended to conform to this principle. I have punctuated less with an eye to correct usage than with the aim of remaining faithful to the tentative nature of the act of transcription. Here it was my intention to reproduce the pace of oral delivery and to close off as few readings as possible, even when leaving ambiguities open may have been less true to de Man's intent than to a certain reluctance to compromise the instability of this

---

* "Hegel on the Sublime" (in Mark Krupuick, ed., *Displacement: Derrida and After*, Bloomington: University of Indiana Press, 1983), "Phenomenality and Materiality in Kant" (in Shapiro and Sica, *Hermeneutics: Questions and Prospects*, Amherst: University of Massachusetts Press, 1983), and "Kant and Schiller" (unpublished).

artifact. Paragraphing generally follows de Man's oral pauses and the repetitions of thesis statements with which he seemed to demarcate articulations in his argument; such breaks are to an extent reflected in the manuscript outline. Except for a few passages in which de Man adopts Harry Zohn's translation, quotations in this text reproduce de Man's own impromptu translations, which sometimes bear little resemblance to the available English translations cited in my notes.

The article is printed with the kind permission of the University of Minnesota Press to whom it had been promised.

WILLIAM D. JEWETT

I at first thought of leaving this last session open for conclusions and discussion; I still hope for the discussion, but I have given up on the conclusions. It seemed to me best, rather than trying to conclude (which is always a terrible anticlimax), just to repeat once more what I have been saying since the beginning, using another text in order to have still another version, another formulation of some of the questions with which we have been concerned throughout this series. It seemed to me that this text by Benjamin on "The Task of the Translator" is a text that is very well known, both in the sense that it is very widely circulated, and in the sense that in the profession you are nobody unless you have said something about this text. Since probably most of us have tried to say something about it, let me see what I can do, and since some of you may be well ahead of me, I look forward to the questions or suggestions you may have. So, far from concluding or from making very general statements, I want to stay pretty close to this particular text, and see what comes out. If I say stay close to the text, since it is a text on translation, I will need (and that is why I have all these books) translations of this text; because if you have a text which says it is impossible to translate, it is very nice to see what happens when that text gets translated. And the translations confirm, brilliantly, beyond any expectations which I may have had, that it is impossible to translate, as you will see in a moment.

Nevertheless, I have placed this within a kind of framework, a framework which is historical. Since the problems of history have come up frequently, I though it would be good to situate it within a historical or pseudohistorical framework, and then to move on from there. Therefore I start out with a recurrent problem in history and historiography, which is the problem of modernity. I use as an introduction into this a little essay by the German philosopher Gadamer, who in a collection called *Aspekte der Modernität* wrote, many years ago, interesting articles called "Die philosophischen Grundlagen des zwanzigsten Jahrhunderts" ["The Philosophical Foundations of the Twentieth Century"]. Gadamer asks the somewhat naive but certainly relevant question, whether what is being done in philosophy in the twentieth century differs essentially from what was being done before, and if it then makes sense to speak of a modernity in philosophical speculation in the twentieth century. He finds as the general theme, the general enterprise of contemporary philosophy, a critical concern with the concept of the subject. Perhaps one wouldn't say this now, which perhaps dates this piece a little, but it is still relevant. His question then is whether the way in which the critique of the concept of the subject is being addressed by present-day philosophy, differs essentially from the way it had been addressed by the predecessors of contemporary philosophy, in German Idealist philosophy—in some of the authors with whom we have been concerned, such as Kant, Hegel, and others. He writes the following sentence, which is our starting point:

> Is the critique of the concept of the subject which is being attempted in our century something else, something different from a mere repetition of what had been accomplished by German Idealist philosophy—and, must we not admit, with, in our case, incomparably less power of abstraction, and without the conceptual strength that characterized the earlier movement?[1]

Is what we are doing just a repetition? And he answers, surprise: "There is not the case." What we are doing really is something new, something different, and we can lay claim to being modern philosophers. He finds three rubrics in which we—contemporary philosophers—he, Gadamer—is ahead of his predecessors, and he characterizes these three progressions in terms of a decreased naiveté. To us now it seems, if we look back on Hegel or Kant, that there is a certain naiveté there which we have now grown beyond. He distinguishes between three types of naiveté, which he calls *Naivität des Setzens* (naiveté of positing), *Naivität der Reflexion* (naiveté of reflection), and *Navität des Begriffs* (naiveté of the concept).

Very briefly, what is meant by the first, by a certain naiveté of position, is a critique which we have been able to develop of pure perception and of pure declarative discourse, in relation to the problem of the subject. We are now ahead of Hegel in that we know better that the subject does not dominate its own utterances; we are more aware that it is naive to assume that the subject really controls its own discourse; we know this is not the case. Yet he qualifies this one bit: nevertheless, understanding is available to us to some extent, by a hermeneutic process in which understanding, by a historical process, can catch up with the presuppositions it had made about itself. We get a development of Gadamer, disciple of Heidegger, of the notion of a hermeneutic circle, where the subject is blind to its own utterance, but where nevertheless the reader who is aware of the historicity of that blindness can recover the meaning, can recover a certain amount of control over the text by means of this particular hermeneutic pattern. This model of understanding is ahead of the

---

1. The German text, which appeared in *Aspekte der Modernität* (Göttingen: Vanderhoeck & Ruprecht, 1965), 77–100, is most readily available in Gadamer's *Kleine Schriften* (Tübingen: J. C. B. Mohr, 1967), v. 1, 131–48. An English translation may be found in the collection *Philosophical Hermeneutics*, trans., David E. Linge, (Berkeley: University of California Press, 1976), 107–29. Cf. *Kleine Schriften*, v. 1, 141; *Philosophical Hermeneutics*, 119.

Hegelian model exactly to the same extent that one could say that the hermeneutics of Heidegger are ahead of the hermeneutics of Hegel, in Gadamer's sense.

He then speaks of the naiveté of reflection, and develops further what is already posited in the first; namely, he asserts the possibility now of a historicity of understanding, in a way that is not accessible to individual self-reflection. It is said that Hegel, in a sense, was not historical enough, that in Hegel it is still too much the subject itself which originates its own understanding, whereas now one is more aware of the difficulty of the relationship between the self and its discourse. Where in the first progression he refers to Heidegger's contribution, here he refers very much to his own contribution: historicizing the notion of understanding, by seeing understanding (as the later *Rezeptionsästhetik*, which comes from Gadamer to a large extent, will develop it) as a process between author and reader in which the reader acquires an understanding of the text by becoming aware of the historicity of the movement that occurs between the text and himself. Here Gadamer also makes a claim that something new is going on nowadays, and indeed, the stress on reception, the stress on reading, are characteristics of contemporary theory, and can be claimed to be new.

Finally, he speaks of the naiveté of the concept, in which the problem of the relationship between philosophical discourse and rhetorical and other devices which pertain more to the realm of ordinary discourse or common language were not, with Kant and Hegel, being examined critically. We alluded to an example of that yesterday when Kant raises the problem of *hypotyposis* and invites us to become aware of the use of metaphors in our own philosophical discourse. That type of question, which at least was mentioned by Kant, and was mentioned by Hegel much less, is now much more developed. Gadamer's allusion is to Wittgenstein, and also indirectly to Nietzsche. We no longer think, says Gadamer, that conceptual and ordinary language are separable; we now have a concept of the problematics of language which is less naive in that it sees to what extent conceptual philosophical language is still dependent on ordinary language, and how close it is to it. This is the modernity which he suggests, and which he details by these three indications.

Now although this is Kantian to some extent in its critical outlook, it is still very much a Hegelian model. The scheme or concept of modernity, as the overcoming of a certain nonawareness or naiveté by means of a critical negation, by means of a critical examination which implies the negation of certain positive relationships and the achieving of a new consciousness, allows for the establishment of a new discourse which claims to overcome or to renew a certain problematic. This pattern is very traditionally Hegelian, in the sense that the development of consciousness is always shown as a kind of overcoming of a certain naiveté and a rise of consciousness to another level. It is traditionally Hegelian, which does not mean that it is in Hegel, but it is in Hegel the way Hegel is being taught in the schools. Indeed, Gadamer ends his piece with a reference to Hegel:

> The concept of spirit, which Hegel borrowed from the Christian spiritual tradition, is still the ground of the critique of the subject and of the subjective spirit that appears as the main task of the post-Hegelian, that is to say modern, period. This concept of spirit (*Geist*), which transcends the subjectivity of the ego, finds its true abode in the phenomonon of language, which stands more and more as the center of contemporary philosophy.[2]

Contemporary philosophy is a matter of getting beyond Hegel in Hegelian terms, by focusing the Hegelian *démarche*, the Hegelian dialectic more specifically on the question of language. That is how modernity is here defined, as a Hegelianism which has concentrated more on linguistic dimensions.

If we compare the critical, dialectical, nonessentialist (because pragmatic to some extent, since an allowance is made for common language) concept of modernity which Gadamer here advances, with Benjamin's text on language in "The Task of the Translator," then at first sight, Benjamin would appear as highly regressive. He would appear as messianic, prophetic, religiously messianic, in a way that may well appear to be a relapse into the naivceté denounced by Gadamer; indeed, he has been criticized for this. Such a relapse would actually return to a much earlier stage even than that of Kant, Hegel, and idealist philosophy. The first impression you receive of Benjamin's text is that of a messianic, prophetic pronouncement, which would be very remote from the cold critical spirit which, from Hegel to Gadamer, is held up as the spirit of modernity. Indeed, as you read this text, you will have been struck by the messianic tone, by a figure of the poet as an almost sacred figure, as a figure which echoes sacred language. All references to particular poets in the text put this much in evidence. The poets who are being mentioned are poets one associates with a sacerdotal, an almost priestlike, spiritual function of poetry: this is true of Hölderlin, of George, and of Mallarmé, all of whom are very much present in the essay.

(Since I mention George, one is aware of the presence of George—a name which has now lost much of its significance, but which at that time in Germany was still considered the most important, central poet, although in 1923 or 1924 when this was written this was already getting toward its end. For example, Benjamin quotes Pannwitz, a disciple of George, at the end of the text. And he refers to George in a relevant way; in George there was a claim made for the poet again as some kind of prophet, as a kind of messianic figure— George doesn't kid around with that, he sees himself at least as Virgil and Dante combined into one, with still quite a bit added to it if necessary— therefore he has a highly exalted notion of the role of the poet, and incidentally

---

2. Cf. *Kleine Schriften*, v. 1, p. 148; *Philosophical Hermeneutics*, p. 128.

of himself, and of the benefits that go with it. But this tone hangs over the German academic discourse, and over a certain concept of poetry, which were then current. There are many echoes of it in the way Benjamin approaches the problem, at least seen superficially. The same is true of references to Hölderlin, who at that time was a discovery of George and of his group, where you find a certain messianic, spiritual concept of Hölderlin. Many echoes of this are still to be found in Heidegger, who after all dedicated his commentaries on Hölderlin to Norbert von Hellingrath, who was a disciple of George and a member of the George circle, and who was, as you know, the first editor of Hölderlin. I sketch in this little piece of background—it may be familiar to you, it may be entirely redundant—to show that the mood, the atmosphere in which this essay was written is one in which the notion of the poetic as the sacred, as the language of the sacred, the figure of the poet as somehow a sacred figure, is common, and is frequent.)

It is not just in the form of echoes that this is present in Benjamin, it almost seems to have been part of the statement itself. This notion of poetry as the sacred, ineffable language finds perhaps its extreme form already from the beginning, in the categorical way in which Benjamin dismisses any notion of poetry as being oriented in any sense, toward an audience or a reader. This passage has provoked the ire of the defenders of *Rezeptionsästhetik*, who analyze the problem of poetic interpretation from the perspective of the reader—Stanley Fish or Riffaterre in this country follow that line to some extent, but it is of course Jauss and his disciples who do this the most. For them, a sentence like the one which begins this essay is absolutely scandalous. Benjamin begins the essay by saying:

> In the appreciation of a work of art or an art form, consideration of the receiver never proves fruitful. Not only is any reference to a certain public or its representatives misleading, but even the concept of an "ideal" receiver is detrimental in the theoretical consideration of art, since all it posits is the existence and nature of man as such. Art, in the same way, posits man's physical and spiritual existence, but in none of its works is it concerned with his response. No poem is intended for the reader, no picture for the beholder, no symphony for the listener.[3]

He couldn't be more categorical than in this assertion at the beginning of the essay. You can see how this would have thrown them into a slight panic in Konstanz, a panic with which they deal by saying that this is an essentialist theory of art, that this stress on the author at the expense of the reader is pre-

---

3. Walter Benjamin, "The Task of the Translator," in *Illuminations*, trans., Harry Zohn, (New York: Schocken Books, 1969), 69. Quotations from the French translation of Maurice de Gandillac are taken from Walter Benjamin, *Oeuvres* (Paris: Editions Denoël, 1971). Page numbers referring to either of these versions are given in parentheses; translations not identified with a page number are the author's. Page numbers supplied with quotations in German refer to the paperback *Illuminationen* (Frankfurt, Suhrkamp, 2d ed., 1980).

Kantian, since already Kant had given the reader, the receptor, the beholder an important role, more important than the author's. This then is held up as an example of the regression to a messianic conception of poetry which would be religious in the wrong sense, and it is very much attacked for that reason.

But on the other hand, Benjamin is also frequently praised as the one who has returned the dimension of the sacred to literary language, and who has thus overcome, or at least considerably refined, the secular historicity of literature on which the notion of modernity depends. If one can think of modernity as it is described by Gadamer as a loss of the sacred, as a loss of a certain type of poetic experience, as its replacement by a secular historicism which loses contact with what was originally essential, then one can praise Benjamin for having re-established the contact with what had there been forgotten. Even in Habermas there are statements in that direction. But closer to home, an example of somebody who reads Benjamin with a great deal of subtlety, who is aware of the complications, and who praises him precisely for the way in which he combines a complex historical pattern with a sense of the sacred, is Geoffrey Hartman, who writes in one of his latest books as follows:

> This chiasmus of hope and catastrophe is what saves hope from being un-masked as only catastrophe: as an illusion or unsatisfied movement of desire that wrecks everything. The foundation of hope becomes remembrance; which confirms the function, even the duty of historian and critic. To recall the past is a political act: a "recherche" that involves us with images of peculiar power, images that may constrain us to identify with them, that claim the *"weak* Messianic power" in use (Thesis 2). These images, split off from their fixed location in history, undo concept of homogeneous time, flash up into or recon-stitute the present. "To Robespierre," Benjamin writes, continuing Marx's reflections in *The Eighteenth Brumaire*, "ancient Rome was a past charged with the time of now (*Jetztzeit*) which he blasted out of the continuum of history. The French revolution viewed itself as Rome incarnate" (Thesis 14).[4]

The reference here is to historical remembrance, to a historical concept which then dovetails, which injects itself into an apocalyptic, religious, spritual concept, thus marrying history with the sacred in a way which is highly seductive, highly attractive. It is certainly highly attractive to Hartman, and one can understand why, since it gives one both the language of despair, the language of nihilism, with the particular rigor that goes with that; but, at the same time, hope! So you have it all: you have the critical perception, you have the possibility of carrying on in apocalyptic tones, you have the particular eloquence that comes with that (because one can only really get excited if one writes in an apocalyptic mode); but you can still talk in terms of hope, and Benjamin would be an example of this combination of nihilistic rigor with sacred revelation. A

---

4. Geoffrey H. Hartman, *Criticism in the Wilderness: The Study of Literature Today* (New Haven: Yale University Press, 1980), 78.

man who likes a judicious, balanced perspective on those things, like Hartman, has reason to quote and to admire this possibility in Benjamin. The problem of the reception of Benjamin centers on this problem of the messianic, and very frequently it is this text on "The Task of the Translator" that is quoted as one of the most characteristic indicators in that direction.

We now then ask the simplest, the most naive, the most literal of possible questions in relation to Benjamin's text, and we will not get beyond that: what does Benjamin say? What does he say, in the most immediate sense possible? It seems absurd to ask a question that is so simple, that seems to be so unnecessary, because we can certainly admit that among literate people we would at least have some minimal agreement about what is being said here, allowing us then to embroider upon this statement, to take positions, discuss, interpret, and so on. But it seems that, in the case of this text, this is very difficult to establish. Even the translators, who certainly are close to the text, who had to read it closely to some extent, don't seem to have the slightest idea of what Benjamin is saying; so much so that when Benjamin says certain things rather simply in one way—for example he says that something is *not*—the translators, who at least know German well enough to know the difference between something *is* and something *is not*, don't see it! and put absolutely and literally the opposite of what Benjamin has said. This is remarkable, because the two translators I have—Harry Zohn, who translated the text in English, and Maurice de Gandillac, who translated the text in French—are very good translators, and know German very well. Harry Zohn, you may know; Maurice de Gandillac is an eminent professor of philosophy at the University of Paris, a very learned man who knows German very well, and who should be able to tell the difference between, for example, "Ich gehe nach Paris" and "Ich gehe nicht nach Paris". It is not more difficult than that, but somehow he doesn't get it.

An example which has become famous and has an anecdote is the passage near the end of Benjamin's essay, where Benjamin says the following: "Wo der Text unmittelbar, ohne vermittelnden Sinn," and so on, "der Wahrheit oder der Lehre angehört, ist er übersetzbar schlechthin" (62). "Where the text pertains directly, without mediation, to the realm of the truth and of dogma, it is, without further ado, translatable"—the text can be translated, *schlechthin*, so there is no problem about translating it. Gandillac?—I won't comment on this—translates this relatively simple, enunciatory sentence: "Là où le texte, immédiatement, sans l'entremise d'un sens . . . relève de la vérité ou de la doctrine, il est purement et simplement *in*traduisible" (275)—*un*translatable. What adds some comedy to this particular instance is that Jacques Derrida was doing a seminar with this particular text in Paris, using the French—Derrida's German is pretty good, but he prefers to use the French, and when you are a philosopher in France you take Gandillac more or less seriously. So Derrida was basing part of his reading on the "intraduisible," on the untranslatability, until somebody in his seminar (so I'm told) pointed out to him that the correct word was "translatable." I'm sure Derrida could explain that it was the same—

and I mean that in a positive sense, it *is* the same, but still, it is not the same without some additional explanation. This is an example, and we will soon see some other examples which are more germane to the questions which we will bring up about this text.

Why, in this text, to begin with, is the translator the exemplary figure? Why is the translator held up in relation to the very general questions about the nature of poetic language which the text asks? The text is a poetics, a theory of poetic language, so why does Benjamin not go to the poets? or to the reader, possibly; or the pair poet-reader, as in the model of reception? And since his is so negative about the notion of reception anyway, what makes the essential difference between the pair author-reader and the pair author-translator—since one's first, simple impression would be that the translator is a reader of the original text? There are, to some extent, obvious empirical answers one can give. The essay was written, as you know, as an introduction to Benjamin's own translation of the *Tableaux parisiens* of Baudelaire; it might just be out of megalomania that he selects the figure of the translator. But this is not the case. One of the reasons why he takes the translator rather than the poet is that the translator, per definition, fails. The translator can never do what the original text did. Any translation is always second in relation to the original, and the translator as such is lost from the very beginning. He is per definition under-paid, he is per definition overworked, he is per definition the one history will not really retain as an equal, unless he also happens to be a poet, but that is not always the case. If the text is called "Die Aufgabe des Übersetzers," we have to read this title more or less as a tautology: *Aufgabe*, task, can also mean the one who has to give up. If you enter the Tour de France and you give up, that is the *Aufgabe*—"er hat aufgegeben," he doesn't continue in the race anymore. It is in that sense also the defeat, the giving up, of the translator. The translator has to give up in relation to the task of refinding what was there in the original.

The question then becomes why this failure with regard to an original text, to an original poet, is for Benjamin exemplary. The question also becomes how the translator differs from the poet; and here Benjamin is categorical in asserting that the translator is radically unlike, differs essentially from the poet and from the artist. This is a curious thing to say, a thing that goes against common sense, because one assumes (and obviously it is the case) that some of the qualities necessary for a good translator are similar to the qualities neces-sary for a good poet. This does not mean therefore that they are doing the same thing. The assertion is so striking, so shocking in a way, that here again the translator (Maurice de Gandillac) does not see it. Benjamin says (in Zohn's translation), "Although translation, *unlike* art, cannot claim permanence for its products . . ." (75); Gandillac, the same passage: "Ainsi la traduction, en-core qu'elle ne puisse élever une prétention à la durée de ses ouvrages, et en cela elle *n'est pas sans ressemblance* avec l'art . . ." (267). The original is abso-lutely unambiguous "Übersetzung also, wiewohl sie auf Dauer ihrer Gebilde nicht Anspruch erheben kann und hierin *unähnlich der Kunst* . . ." (55). As you come upon it in a text, the statement is so surprising, goes so much against common sense, that an intelligent, learned, and careful translator cannot see it, cannot see what Benjamin says. It is remarkable. Zohn saw it—don't get the impression that Zohn gets it all right and Gandillac gets it all wrong—basically Gandillac is a little ahead of Zohn, I think, in the final analysis.

At any rate, for Benjamin there is a sharp distinction between them. It is not necessary for good translators to be good poets. Some of the best translators—he mentions Voss (translator of Homer), Luther, and Schlegel—are very poor poets. There are some poets who are also translators: he mentions Hölderlin, who translated Sophocles and others, and George, who translated Baudelaire—Dante also, but primarily Baudelaire, so Benjamin is close to George. But then, he says, it is not because they are great poets that they are great translators, they are great poets *and* they are great translators. They are not purely, as Heidegger will say of Hölderlin, *Dichter der Dichter*, but they are *Übersetzer der Dichter*, they are beyond the poets because they are also translators.

> A number of the most eminent ones, such as Luther, Voss, and Schlegel, are incomparably more important as translators than as creative writers; some of the great among them, such as Hölderlin and Stefan George, cannot be simply subsumed as poets, and quite particularly not if we consider them as translators. As translation is a mode of its own, the task of the translator, too, may be regarded as distinct and clearly differentiated from the task of the poet. [76]

Of the differences between the situation of the translator and that of the poet, the first that comes to mind is that the poet has some relationship to meaning, to a statement that is not purely within the realm of language. That is the naiveté of the poet, that he has to say something, that he has to convey a meaning which does not necessarily relate to language. The relationship of the translator to the original is the relationship between language and language, wherein the problem of meaning or the desire to say something, the need to make a statement, is entirely absent. Translation is a relation from language to language, not a relation to an extralinguistic meaning that could be copied, paraphrased, or imitated. That is not the case for the poet; poetry is certainly not paraphrase, clarification, or interpretation, a copy in that sense; and that is already the first difference.

If it is in some fundamental way unlike poetry, what, in Benjamin's text, does translation resemble? One of the things it resembles would be philosophy, in that it is critical, in the same way that philosophy is critical, of a simple notion of imitation, of philosophical discourse as an *Abbild* (imitation, paraphrase, reproduction) of the real situation. Philosophy is not an imitation of the world as we know it, but it has another relationship to that world. Critical philosophy, and the reference would be specifically to Kant again, will be critical in the same way of the notion of the imitative concept of the world.

Um das echte Verhältnis zwischen Original und Übersetzung zu erfassen, ist eine Erwägung anzustellen, deren Absicht durchaus den Gedankengängen analog ist, in denen die Erkenntniskritik die Unmöglichkeit einer Abbildstheorie zu erweisen hat. [53]

In order to seize upon the real relationship between the original and its translation, we must start reflection of which the intent is in general similar to the modes of thought by means of which a critical epistemology—there's Kant, *Erkenntniskritik*—demonstrates the impossibility of a theory or simple imitation.

Kant indeed would be critical of a notion of art as imitation; this would be true of Hegel to some extent too, because there is precisely a critical element that intervenes here and which takes this image, this model, away, which destroys, undoes this concept of imitation.

Translation is also, says Benjamin, more like criticism or like the theory of literature, than like poetry itself. It is by defining himself in relation to Friedrich Schlegel and to German Romanticism in general that Benjamin establishes this similarity between literary criticism (in the sense of literary theory) and translation; and this historical reference to the Jena Romanticism here gives to the notion of criticism and literary theory a dignity which it does not necessarily normally have. Both criticism and translation are caught in the gesture which Benjamin calls ironic, a gesture which undoes the stability of the original by giving it a definitive, canonical form in the translation or in the theorization. In a curious way, translation canonizes its own version more than the original was canonical. That the original was not purely canonical is clear from the fact that it demands translation; it cannot be definitive since it can be translated. But you cannot, says Benjamin, translate the translation; once you have a translation you cannot translate it any more. You can translate only an original. The translation canonizes, freezes, an original and shows in the original a mobility, an instability, which at first one did not notice. The act of critical, theoretical reading performed by a critic like Friedrich Schlegel and performed by literary theory in general—by means of which the original work is not imitated or reproduced but is to some extent put in motion, de-canonized, questioned in a way which undoes its claim to canonical authority—is similar to what a translator performs.

Finally, translation is like history, and that will be the most difficult thing to understand. In what is the most difficult passage in this text, Benjamin says that it is like history to the extent that history is not to be understood by analogy with any kind of natural process. We are not supposed to think of history as ripening, as organic growth, or even as a dialectic, as anything that resembles a natural process of growth and of movement. We are to think of history rather in the reverse way; we are to understand natural changes from the perspective of history, rather than understand history from the perspective of natural changes. If we want to understand what ripening is, we should understand it from the perspective of historical change. In the same way, the relationship between the translation and the original is not to be understood by analogy with natural processes such as resemblance or derivation by formal analogy; rather we are to understand the original from the perspective of the translation. To understand this historical pattern would be the burden of any reading of this particular text.

All these activities that have been mentioned—philosophy as critical epistemology, criticism and literary theory (the way Friedrich Schlegel does it), or history understood as a nonorganic process—are themselves derived from original activities. Philosophy derives from perception, but it is unlike perception because it is the critical examination of the truth-claims of perception. Criticism derives from poetry because it is inconceivable without the poetry that precedes it. History derives from pure action, since it follows necessarily upon acts which have already taken place. Because all these activities are derived from original activities, they are singularly inconclusive, are failed, are aborted in a sense from the start because they are derived and secondary. Yet Benjamin insists that the model of their derivation is not that of resemblance or of imitation. It is not natural process: the translation does not resemble the original the way the child resembles the parent, nor is it an imitation, a copy, or a paraphrase of the original. In that sense, since they are not resemblances, since they are not imitations, one would be tempted to say they are not metaphors. The translation is not the metaphor of the original; nevertheless, the German word for translation, *übersetzen*, means metaphor. *Übersetzen* translates exactly the Greek *meta-phorein*, to move over, *übersetzen*, to put across. *Übersetzen*, I should say, *translates* metaphor—which, asserts Benjamin, is not at all the same. They are not metaphors, yet the word means metaphor. The metaphor is not a metaphor, Benjamin is saying. No wonder that translators have difficulty. It is a curious assumption to say *übersetzen* is not metaphorical, *übersetzen* is not based on resemblance, there is no resemblance between the translation and the original. Amazingly paradoxical statement, metaphor is not metaphor.

All these activities—critical philosophy, literary theory, history—resemble each other in the fact that they do not resemble that from which they derive. But they are all interlinguistic: they relate to what in the original belongs to language, and not to meaning as an extralinguistic correlate susceptible of paraphrase and imitation. They disarticulate, they undo the original, they reveal that the original was always already disarticulated. They reveal that their failure, which seems to be due to the fact that they are secondary in relation to the original, reveals an essential failure, an essential disarticulation which was already there in the original. They kill the original, by discovering that the original was already dead. They read the original from the perspective of a pure language (*reine Sprache*), a language that would be entirely freed of the illusion of meaning—pure form if you want; and in doing so they bring to light a dismembrance, a de-canonization which was already there in the original from the beginning. In the process of translation, as Benjamin understands it—which has little to do with the empirical act of translating, as all of us practice it on a daily basis—there is an inherent and particularly threatening danger. The emblem of that danger is Hölderlin's translations of Sophocles:

> Confirmation of this as well as of every other important aspect is supplied by Hölderlin's translations, particularly those of the two tragedies by Sophocles. In them the harmony of the languages is so profound that sense is touched by language only the way an aeolian harp is touched by the wind. . . . Hölderlin's translations in particular are subject to the enormous danger inherent in all translations: the gates of a language thus expanded and modified may slam shut and enclose the translator with silence. Hölderlin's translations from Sophocles were his last work, in them meaning plunges from abyss to abyss until it threatens to become lost in the bottomless depths of language. [81–82]

Translation, to the extent that it disarticulates the original, to the extent that it is pure language and is only concerned with language, gets drawn into what he calls the bottomless depth, something essentially destructive, which is in language itself.

What translation does, by reference to the fiction or hypothesis of a pure language devoid of the burden of meaning, is that it implies, in bringing to light what Benjamin calls "die Wehen des eigenen"—the suffering of what one thinks of as one's own—the suffering of the original language. We think we are at ease in our own language, we feel a coziness, a familiarity, a shelter in the language we call our own, in which we think that we are not alienated. What the translation reveals is that this alienation is at its strongest in our relation to our own original language, that the original language within which we are engaged is disarticulated in a way which imposes upon us a particular alienation, a particular suffering. Here too the translators, with considerable unanimity, cannot see this statement. Benjamin's text is, ". . . dass gerade unter allen Formen ihr als Eigenstes es zufällt, auf jene Nachreife des fremden Wortes, auf die Wehen des eigenen zu merken" (54). The two translators—I guess they didn't correspond with each other, they did this *d'un commun accord*—translate *Wehen*, pains, as "birth pangs," as being particularly the pains of childbirth. Gandillac is very explicit about it, he calls it "les douleurs obstétricales" (266) in the most literal, clinical way; Zohn says "birth pangs" (73). Why they do this is a mystery. *Wehen* can mean birth pangs, but it does mean any kind of suffering, without necessarily the connotation of birth and rebirth, of resurrection, which would be associated with the notion of birth pangs because you suffer in producing something,—and this is a magnificent moment, you'd be willing to suffer (especially easy for us to say). Benjamin has just been speaking of the "*Nachreife* des fremden Wortes," translated by Zohn as "maturing process," which again is wrong. *Nachreife* is like the German word *Spätlese* (a particularly good wine made from the late, rotten grape), it is like Stifter's novel *Nachsommer* ("Indian Summer")—it has the melancholy, the feeling of slight exhaustion, of life to which you are not entitled, happiness to which you are not entitled, time has passed, and so on. It is associated with another word that Benjamin constantly uses, the word *überleben*, to live beyond your own death in a sense. The translation belongs not to the life of the original, the original is already dead, but the translation belongs to the afterlife of the original, thus assuming and confirming the death of the original. *Nachreife* is of the same order, or has to do with the same; it is by no means a maturing process, it is a looking back on a process of maturity that is finished, and that is no longer taking place. So if you translate *Wehen* by "birth pangs," you would have to translate it by "death pangs" as much as by "birth pangs," and the stress is perhaps more on death than on life.

The process of translation, if we can call it a process, is one of change and of motion that has the appearance of life, but of life as an afterlife, because translation also reveals the death of the original. Why is this? What are those death pangs, possibly birth pangs, of the original? It is easy to say to some extent what this suffering is not. It is certainly not subjective pains, some kind of pathos of a self, a kind of manifestation of a self-pathos which the poet would have expressed as his sufferings. This is certainly not the case, because, says Benjamin, the sufferings that are here being mentioned are not in any sense human. They would certainly not be the sufferings of an individual, or of a subject. That also is very hard to see, for the translators. Zohn, confronted with that passage (I will stop this game of showing up the translators, but it is always of some interest), translates: "if they are referred *exclusively* to man" (70). Benjamin very clearly says, "wenn sie nicht . . . auf den Menschen bezogen werden" (51), if you *do not* relate them to man. The stress is precisely that the suffering that is mentioned, the failure, is not a human failure, it does not refer therefore to any subjective experience. The original is unambiguous in that respect. This suffering is also not a kind of historical pathos, the pathos that you heard in Hartman's reference to Benjamin as the one who had discovered the pathos of history; it is not this pathos of remembrance, or this pathetic mixture of hope and catastrophe and apocalypse which Hartman captures, which is present certainly in Benjamin's tone, but not so much in what he says. It is not the pathos of a history, it is not the pathos of what in Hölderlin is called the "dürftige Zeit" between the disappearance of the gods and the possible return of the gods. It is not this kind of sacrificial, dialectical, and elegiac gesture, by means of which one looks back on the past as a period that is lost, which then gives you the hope of another future that may occur.

The reasons for this pathos, for this *Wehen*, for this suffering, are specifically linguistic. They are stated by Benjamin with considerable linguistic structural precision; so much so that if you come to a word like "abyss" in the passage about Hölderlin, where it is said that Hölderlin tumbles in the abyss of language, you should understand the word "abyss" in the non-pathetic, technical sense in which we speak of a *mise en abyme* structure, the kind of structure by means of which it is clear that the test itself becomes an example of what it exemplifies. The text about translation is itself a translation, and the untranslatability which it mentions about itself inhabits its own texture and will inhabit anybody who in his turn will try to translate it, as I am now trying, and failing, to do. The text is untranslatable, it was untranslatable for the translators who tried to do it, it is untranslatable for the commentators who talk about it, it is an example of what it states, it is a *mise an abyme* in the technical sense, a story within the story of what is its own statement.

What are the linguistic reasons which allow Benjamin to speak of a suffering, of a disarticulation, of a falling apart of any original work, or of any work to the extent that that work is a work of language? On this Benjamin is very precise, and offers us what amounts in very few lines to an inclusive theory of language. The disjunction is first of all between what he calls "das Gemeinte," what is meant, and the "Art des Meinens," the way in which language means; between logos and lexis, if you want—what a certain statement means, and the way in which the statement is meant to mean. Here the difficulties of the translators are a little more interesting, because they involve philosophical concepts that are of some importance. Gandillac, a philosopher who knows phenomenology and who writes in a period when phenomenology is the overriding philosophical pressure in France, translates by "visée intentionelle" (272). The way we would now translate in French "das Gemeinte" and "Art des Meinens" would be by the distinction between *vouloir dire* and *dire*: "to mean," "to say." Zohn translates by "the intended object" and the "mode of intention" (74). There is a phenomenological assumption here, and Gandillac has a footnote which refers to Husserl: both assume that the meaning and the way in which meaning is produced are intentional acts. But the problem is precisely that, whereas the meaning-function is certainly intentional, it is not a priori certain at all that the mode of meaning, the way in which I mean, is intentional in any way. The way in which I can try to mean is dependent upon linguistic properties that are not only [not] made by me, because I depend on the language as it exists for the devices which I will be using, it is as such not made by us as historical beings, it is perhaps not even made by humans at all. Benjamin says, from the beginning, that is not at all certain that language is in any sense human. To equate language with humanity—as Schiller did, as we saw yesterday—is in question. If language is not necessarily human—if we obey the law, if we function within language, and purely in terms of language—there can be no intent; there may be an intent of meaning, but there is no tent in the purely formal way in which we will use language independently of the sense or the meaning. The translation, which puts intentionality on both sides, both in the act of meaning and in the way in which one means, misses a philosophically interesting point—for what is at stake is the possibility of a phenomenology of language, or of poetic language, the possibility of establishing a poetics which would in any sense be a phenomenology of language.

How are we to understand this discrepancy between "das Gemeinte" and "Art des Meinens," between *dire* and *vouloir dire*? Benjamin's example is the German word *Brot* and the French word *pain*. To mean "bread," when I need to name bread, I have the word *Brot*, so that the way in which I mean is by using the word *Brot*. The translation will reveal a fundamental discrepancy between the intent to name *Brot* and the word *Brot* itself, in its materiality, as a device of meaning. If you hear *Brot* in this context of Hölderlin, who is so often mentioned in this text, I hear *Brot und Wein* necessarily, which is the great Hölderlin text that is very much present in this—which in French becomes *Pain et vin*. "Pain et vin" is what you get for free in a restaurant, in a cheap restaurant where it is still included, so *pain et vin* has very different connotations than *Brot und Wein*. It brings to mind the *pain français, baguette, ficelle, bâtard*, all those things—I now hear in *Brot* "bastard". This upsets the stability of the quotidian. I was very happy with the word *Brot*, which I hear as a native because my native language is Flemish and we say *brood*, just as in German, but if I have to think that *Brot* [*brood*] and *pain* are the same thing, I get very upset. It is all right in English because "bread" is close enough to *Brot* [*brood*], despite the idiom "bread" for money, which has its problems. But the stability of my quotidian, of my daily bread, the reassuring quotidian aspects of the word "bread," daily bread, is upset by the French word *pain*. What I mean is upset by the way in which I mean—the way in which it is *pain*, the phoneme, the term *pain*, which has its set of connotations which take you in a completely different direction.

This disjunction is best understood (to take it to a more familiar theoretical problem) in terms of the difficult relationship between the hermeneutics and the poetics of literature. When you do hermeneutics, you are concerned with the meaning of the work; when you do poetics, you are concerned with the stylistics or with the description of the way in which a work means. The question is whether these two are complementary, whether you can cover the full work by doing hermeneutics and poetics at the same time. The experience of trying to do this shows that it is not the case. When one tries to achieve this complementarity, the poetics always drops out, and what one always does is hermeneutics. One is so attracted by problems of meaning that it is impossible to do hermeneutics and poetics at the same time. From the moment you start to get involved with problems of meaning, as I unfortunately tend to do, forget about the poetics. The two are not complementary, the two may be mutually exclusive in a certain way, and that is part of the problem which Benjamin states, a purely linguistic problem.

He states a further version of this when he speaks of a disjunction between the word and the sentence, *Wort* and *Satz*. *Satz* in German means not just sentence, in the grammatical sense, it means statement—Heidegger will speak

of *Der Satz vom Grund; Satz* is the statement, the most fundamental statement, meaning—the most meaningful word—whereas word is associated by
Benjamin with *Aussage*, the way in which you state, as the apparent agent of
the statement. *Wort* means not only the agent of the statement as a lexical
unit, but also as syntax and as grammar. If you look at a sentence in terms of
words, you look at it not just in terms of particular words but also in terms of
the grammatical relationships between those words. So the question of the
relationship between word and sentence becomes, for Benjamin, the question
of the compatibility between grammar and meaning. What is being put in
question is precisely that compatibility, which we take for granted in a whole
series of linguistic investigations. Are grammar (word and syntax) on the one
hand, and meaning (as it culminates in the *Satz*) on the other hand—are they
compatible with each other? Does the one lead to the other, does the one
support the other? Benjamin tells us that translation put that conviction in
question because, he says, from the moment that a translation is really literal,
wörtlich, word by word, the meaning completely disappears. The example is
again Hölderlin's translations of Sophocles, which are absolutely literal, word
by word, and which are therefore totally unintelligible; what comes out is
completely incomprehensible, completely undoes the sentence, the *Satz* of
Sophocles, which is entirely gone. The meaning of the word slips away (as we
saw, a word like *Aufgabe*, which means task, also means something completely different, so that the word escapes us), and there is no grammatical way
to control this slippage. There is also a complete slippage of the meaning when
the translator follows the syntax, when he writes literally, *wörtlich*. And to
some extent, a translator has to be *wörtlich*, has to be literal. The problem is
best compared to the relationship between the letter and the word; the relationship between word and sentence is like the relationship between letter and
word, namely, the letter is without meaning in relation to the word, it is *a-
sēmos*, it is without meaning. When you spell a word you say a certain number
of meaningless letters, which then come together in the word, but in each of
the letters the word is not present. The two are absolutely independent of each
other. What is being named here as the disjunction between grammar and
meaning, *Wort* and *Satz*, is the materiality of the letter: the independence, or
the way in which the letter can disrupt the ostensible stable meaning of a
sentence and introduce in it a slippage by means of which that meaning disappears, evanesces, and by means of which all control over that meaning is lost.

So we have, first, a disjunction in language between the hermeneutic and
the poetic, we have a second one between grammar and meaning, and finally,
we will have a disjunction, says Benjamin, between the symbol and what is
being symbolized, a disjunction on the level of tropes between the trope as such
and the meaning as a totalizing power of tropological substitutions. There is a
similar and equally radical disjunction, between what tropes (which always
imply totalization) convey in terms of totalization and what the tropes accom-
plish taken by themselves. That seems to be the main difficulty of this particu-

lar text, because the text is full of tropes, and it selects tropes which convey the illusion of totality. It seems to relapse into the tropological errors that it denounces. The text constantly uses images of seed, of ripening, of harmony, it uses the image of seed and rind (*l'écorce et le noyau*)—which seem to be derived from analogies between nature and language, whereas the constant claim is constantly being made that there are no such analogies. In the same way that history is not to be understood in terms of an analogy with nature, tropes should not be based on resemblances with nature. But that is precisely the difficulty, and the challenge of this particular text. Whenever Benjamin uses a trope which seems to convey a picture of total meaning, of complete adequacy between figure and meaning, a figure of perfect synecdoche in which the partial trope expresses the totality of a meaning, he manipulates the allusive context within his work in such a way that the traditional symbol is displaced in a manner that acts out the discrepancy between symbol and meaning, rather than the acquiescence between both.

One striking example of that is the image of the amphora:

> Fragments of a vessel which are to be glued together must match one another in the smallest details, although they need not be like one another. In the same way, a translation, instead of resembling the meaning of the original, must lovingly and in detail incorporate the original's mode of significatio, thus making both the original and the translation recognizable as fragments of a greater language, just as fragments are part of a vessel. For this very reason translation must in large measure refrain from wanting to communicate. . . . [78]

According to this image, there is an original, pure language, of which any particular work is only a fragment. That would be fine, provided we could, through that fragment, find access again to the original work. The image is that of a vessel, of which literary work would be a piece, and then the translation is a piece of that. It is admitted that the translation is a fragment, but if the translation relates to the original as a fragment relates, if the translation would reconstitute as such the original, then—although it does not resemble it, but matches it perfectly (as in the word *symbolon*, which states the matching of two pieces or two fragments)—then we can think of any particular work as being a fragment of the pure language, and then indeed Benjamin's statement would be a religious statement about the fundamental unity of language.

Benjamin has told us, however, that the symbol and what it symbolizes, the trope and what it seems to represent, do not correspond. How is this to be made compatible with a statement like the one made here? An article by Carol Jacobs called "The Monstrosity of Translation," which appeared in *Modern Language Notes*, treats this passage in a way which strikes me as exceedingly precise and correct. First, she is aware of the Kabbalistic meaning of the text, by referring to Gershom Scholem, who in writing about this text relates the figure of the angel to the history of the *Tikkun* of the Lurianic Kabbalah:

> Yet at the same time Benjamin has in mind the Kabbalistic concept of the *Tikkun,* the messianic restoration and mending which patches together and

restores the original Being of things, shattered and corrupted in the "Breaking of Vessels," and also [the original being of] history.

Carol Jacobs comments,

> Scholem might have turned to "Die Aufgabe des Übersetzers," where the image of the broken vessel plays a more direct role. . . . Yet whereas Zohn suggests that a totality of fragments are brought together, Benjamin insists that the final outcome is still "a broken part."[5] [763, note 9]

All you have to do, to see that, is translate correctly, instead of translating like Zohn—who made this difficult passage very clear—but who in the process of making it clear made it say something completely different. Zohn said, "fragments of a vessel which are to be glued together must match one another in the smallest detail." Benjamin said, translated by Carol Jacobs word by word: "fragments of a vessel, in order to be *articulated* together"—which is much better than *glued* together, which has a totally irrelevant concreteness— "must *follow* one another in the smallest detail"—which is not at all the same as *match* one another. What is already present in this difference is that we have *folgen*, not *gleichen*, not to match. We have a metonymic, a successive pattern, in which things follow, rather than a metaphorical unifying pattern in which things become one by resemblance. They do not match each other, they follow each other; they are already metonyms and not metaphors; as such they are certainly less working toward a convincing tropological totalization than if we use the term "match".
  But things get even more involved, or more distorted, in what follows.

> So, instead of making itself similar to the meaning, to the *Sinn* of the original, the translation must rather, lovingly and in detail, in its own language, form itself according to the manner of meaning (*Art des Meinens*) of the original, to make both recognizable as the broken parts of the greater language, just as fragments are the broken parts of a vessel.

That is entirely different from saying, as Zohn says:

> in the same way a translation, instead of resembling the meaning of the original, must lovingly and in detail incorporate the original's mode of signification, thus making both the original and the translation recognizable as fragments of a greater language, just as fragments are part of a vessel.

"Just as fragments are part of a vessel" is a synecdoche; "just as fragments," says Benjamin, "are the *broken* parts of a vessel": as such he is not saying that the fragments constitute a totality, he says the fragments are fragments, and that they remain essentially fragmentary. They follow each other up, metonymically, and they will never constitute a totality. I'm reminded of an example I heard given by the French philosopher Michel Serres—that you find out about

---

5. Carol Jacobs, "The Monstrosity of Translation," *Modern Language Notes*, v. 90 (1975), 763, note 9.

fragments by doing the dishes: if you break a dish it breaks into fragments, but you can't break the fragments any more. That's an optimistic, a positive synec-dochal view of the problem of fragments, because there the fragments can make up a whole, and you cannot break up the fragments. What we have here is an initial fragmentation; any work is totally fragmented in relation to this *reine Sprache,* with which it has nothing in common, and every translation is totally fragmented in relation to the original. The translation is the fragment of a fragment, is breaking the fragment—so the vessel keeps breaking, con-stantly—and never reconstitutes it; there was no vessel in the first place, or we have no knowledge of this vessel, or no awareness, no access to it, so for all intents and purposes there has never been one.

Therefore the distinction between symbol and symbolized, the nonade-quation of symbol to a shattered symbolized, the nonsymbolic character of this adequation, is a version of the others, and indicates the unreliability of rhetoric as a system of tropes which would be productive of a meaning. Meaning is always displaced with regard to the meaning it ideally intended—that mean-ing is never reached. Benjamin approaches the question in terms of the aporia between freedom and faithfulness, the question which haunts the problem of translation. Does translation have to be faithful, or does it have to be free? For the sake of the idiomatic relevance of the target language, it has to be free; on the other hand, it has to be faithful to some extent to the original. The faithful translation, which is always literal, how can it also be free? It can only be free if it reveals the instability of the original, and if it reveals that instability as the linguistic tension between trope and meaning. Pure language is perhaps more present in the translation than in the original, but in the mode of trope. Ben-jamin, who is talking about the inability of trope to be adequate to meaning, constantly uses the very tropes which seem to postulate the adequation be-tween meaning and trope; but he prevents them in a way, displaces them in such a way as to put the original in motion, to de-canonize the original, giving it a movement which is a movement of disintegration, of fragmentation. This movement of the original is a wandering, an *errance,* a kind of permanent exile if you wish, but it is not really an exile, for there is no homeland, nothing from which one has been exiled. Least of all is there something like a *reine Sprache,* a pure language, which does not exist except as a permanent disjunction which inhabits all languages as such, including and especially the language one calls one's own. What is to be one's own language is most displaced, the most alienated of all.

Now it is this motion, this errancy of language which never reaches the mark, which is always displaced in relation to what it meant to reach, it is this errancy of language, this illusion of a life that is only an afterlife, that Benjamin calls history. As such, history is not human, because it pertains strictly to the order of language; it is not natural, for the same reason; it is not phenomenal, in the sense that no cognition, no knowledge about man, can be deprived from a history which as such is purely a linguistic complication; and it is not really temporal either, because the structure that animates it is not a temporal structure. Those disjunctions in language do get expressed by temporal metaphors, but they are only metaphors. The dimension of futurity, for example, which is present in it, is not temporal, but is the correlative of the figural pattern and the disjunctive power which Benjamin locates in the structure of language. History, as Benjamin conceives it, is certainly not messianic, since it consists in the rigorous separation and the acting out of the separation of the sacred from the poetic, the separation of the *reine Sprache* from poetic language. *Reine Sprache*, the sacred language, has nothing in common with poetic language; poetic language does not resemble it, poetic language does not depend on it, poetic language has nothing to do with it. It is within this negative knowledge of its relation to the language of the sacred that poetic language initiates. It is, if you want, a necessarily nihilistic moment that is necessary in any understanding of history.

Benjamin said this in the clearest of terms, not in this essay but in another text called "Theological and Political Fragment,"[6] from which I will quote a short passage in conclusion. He said it with all possible clarity, it seemed to me, until I tried to translate that particular passage, and found that English happens to have a property which makes it impossible to translate. Here is the passage:

> Only the messiah himself puts an end to history, in the sense that it frees, completely fulfills the relationship of history to the messianic. Therefore, nothing that is truly historical can want to relate by its own volition to the messianic. Therefore the kingdom of God is not the *telos* of the dynamics of history, it cannot be posited as its aim; seen historically it is not its aim but its end.

That is where I have a great deal of trouble with English, because the English word for "aim" can also be "end." You say "the end and the means," the aim and the means by which you achieve it. And the English word "end" can mean just as well *Ziel* as it can mean *Ende*. My end, my intention. So that if we want to use that idiom, the translation then becomes: "seen historically it is not its end but its end," its termination—it would be perfect English. But it would indicate that the separation which is here undertaken by Benjamin is hidden in this word "end" in English, which substitutes for "aim" the word "end," the two things which Benjamin asks us to keep rigorously apart.

> It cannot be posited as its aim, seen historically it is not its aim but its end, its termination; therefore the order of the profane cannot be constructed in terms of the idea of the sacred. Therefore theocracy does not have a political but only a religious meaning.

---

6. Cf. *Illuminationen* op. cit., 262. An English translation of the "Theologico-Political Fragment" may be found in *Reflections*, Edmund Jephcott, trans., Peter Demetz, ed. (New York: Harcourt Brace Jovanovich, 1978), 312–13.

And Benjamin adds:

> To have denied the political significance of theocracy, to have denied the politi-
> cal significance of the religious, messianic view, to have denied this with all
> desirable intensity is the great merit of Bloch's book *The Spirit of Utopia*.

Since we saw that what is here called political and historical is due to
purely linguistic reasons, we can in this passage replace "political" by "poetical," in the sense of a poetics. For we now see that the nonmessianic, non-
sacred, that is the *political* aspect of history is the result of the *poetical* structure of language, so that political and poetical here are substituted, in opposition to the notion of the sacred. To the extent that such a poetics, such a
history, is nonmessianic, not a theocracy but a rhetoric, it has no room for
certain historical notions such as the notion of modernity, which is always a
dialectical, that is to say an essentially theological notion. You will remember
that we started out from Gadamer's claim to modernity, in terms of a dialectic
which was explicitly associated with the word "Spirit," with the spirituality in
the text of Hegel. We have seen, and it is for me gratifying to find, that Hegel
himself—when, in the section of the *Aesthetics* on the sublime, he roots the
sublime in this same separation between sacred and profane—is actually
much closer to Benjamin in "The Task of the Translator" than he is to Gadamer. I will end on that note, and I will be glad to answer questions if you want.
Thank you very much.

Reading de Man

SHOSHANA FELMAN

Postal Survival, or the Question of the Navel

> I love you, gentlest law, through which we yet
> were ripening while with it we contended,
> you great homesickness we have not transcended,
> you forest out of which we never wended,
> you song that from our silence has ascended,
> you somber net
> where feelings taking flight are apprehended.
> —Rilke quoted by Paul de Man, in *Allegories of Reading*[1]

> And to read is to understand, to question, to know, to forget, to
> erase, to deface, to repeat—that is to say, the endless
> prosopopeia by which the dead are made to have a face and a
> voice which tells the allegory of their demise and allows us to
> apostrophize them in our turn.
> —Paul de Man, *The Rhetoric of Romanticism*[2]

I

HOMESICKNESS

If to read is, indeed, "to understand, . . . to forget, . . . to repeat," how can we repeat de Man's unforgettable lesson of reading? How can we account for the lesson of this extraordinary teacher for whom reading was a true vocation, a genuine *profession*, but whose way of professing reading, whose "profession de foi"—or "allegory of reading"[3]—was, paradoxically enough, the statement that "the impossibility of reading should not be taken too lightly" (*AR*, 245)? If to read is, on the other hand, to evoke "the endless prosopopeia by which the dead are made to have a face and a voice which tells the allegory of their demise and allows us to apostrophize them in our turn," how can we not yield to the desire to apostrophize de Man, to read in him, with him, the "great homesickness we have not transcended," the "somber net/where feelings taking flight are apprehended"? But how, through such apostrophe, can we engage in our turn in an allegory of reading which, while endowing de Man with a face

---

1. Quoted in *Allegories of Reading* (New Haven and London: Yale University Press, 1979), 28–29. Quotations from this book will hereafter be signaled in the body of the text by the abbreviation *AR*, followed by the page number.

2. *The Rhetoric of Romanticism* (New York: Columbia University Press, 1984), 122. Quotations from this book will hereafter be signaled in the body of the text by the abbreviation *RR*, followed by the page number.

3. De Man's analysis of Rousseau's *Profession de foi* is entitled "Allegory of Reading (Profession de foi)." In *Allegories of Reading*, 221–45.

and a voice which tells the allegory of his own demise, will also teach us, once again, in his own voice, how to read in new and unexpected ways, how to contend with the impossibility of reading?

II

THE PATHOS OF A TEACHING

In 1975, welcoming Jacques Lacan's presence at Yale, Paul de Man pronounced, in honor of the guest, a few words of introduction, which described so vehemently and laconically what was crucially important in his eyes, that I asked him, afterwards, to let me read again this introduction. He had no intent of saving these purloined words and gave the page to me. Rereading it today, I find it too beautiful, too rich not to seize here the opportunity of first publishing it in its entirety.

L'université de Yale est honorée par la présence, parmi nous, du Dr. Jacques Lacan, Directeur et maître de la pensée de l'Ecole freudienne de Paris.

Jacques Lacan, c'est avant tout et parmi beaucoup d'autres choses, un enseignement et une lecture, l'enseignement d'une lecture.

Il se présente lui-même dans une phrase prise dans l'écrit de 1967 intitulé "Raison d'un échec":

"Le pathétique de mon enseignement, c'est qu'il opère à ce point. Et c'est ce qui, dans mes Ecrits, *dans mon histoire, dans mon enseignement, retient un public au-delà de toute critique. Il sent que quelque chose s'y joue dont tout le monde aura sa part"[4].*

La phrase est vraie dans l'ordre littéral des faits. Le Séminaire parisien dont le Dr. Lacan ne s'est absenté que pour venir nous parler, s'adresse à un public toujours croissant. Le volume intitulé Ecrits, *qui réunit ses travaux proprement théoriques, est un succès de librairie tout autant qu'une prose inaccessible à quiconque refuse le labeur d'une pensée qui se refuse à toute forme de repos.*

Les psychanalystes, les linguistes, les philosophes, les historiens, y ont, comme il dit, trouvé leur part. En tant que représentant d'un département littéraire, je dirai que nous n'avons pas encore commencé à soupçonner la part de ce qui, dans cet enseignement, revient à la littérature. Comme Freud, comme Nietzsche, Jacques Lacan est un de ceux qui connaissent l'insolite puissance qu'a la langue de refuser la vérité que pourtant il ne cesse d'exiger. Il nous a enseigné ce mélange de rigueur, de pathos et de suspicion qui doit guider quiconque se hasarde à un véritable acte de lecture. Les conséquences pour l'enseignement de la lecture, c'est à dire pour les départements de littérature, en sont incalculables.

Le Dr. Lacan nous disait l'autre jour que sa décision de réunir ses publica-

---

4. Jacques Lacan, "Raison d'un échec," in *Scilicet* (Paris: Seuil, 1976), 47.

*tions en volume (*Ecrits*) avait été prise après son dernier voyage aux Etats Unis qui remonte à près de dix ans. Que son présent séjour puisse conduire à un semblable déni de l'échec, c'est là notre plus fervent désir.*

Yale university is honored by the presence, among us, of Dr. Jacques Lacan, Director and intellectual leader of The Freudian School of Paris.

Jacques Lacan is, first and foremost and among many other things, a teaching and a reading: the teaching of a reading.

Lacan presents himself as follows in a sentence taken from his 1967 piece entitled, "The Reason for a Failure":

"The pathos of my teaching is that it operates at this point. And this is what, in my *Ecrits*, in my history, in my teaching, retains an audience beyond all criticism: an audience which feels that something is played out there of which everybody will have a share."

The sentence is true in the literal order of facts. The Parisian Seminar from which Dr. Lacan has accepted to absent himself only so as to come here to talk to us, is given to an ever-increasing audience. The volume entitled *Ecrits*, which assembles his theoretical works, is a commercial success at the same time that its prose is inaccessible to whoever refuses the labor of a thought that denies any form of rest.

The psychoanalysts, the linguists, the philosophers, the historians, have, as he puts it, found their share in it. As the representative of a literature department, I would say that we have not yet begun to suspect the extent to which this teaching partakes of literature. Like Freud, like Nietzsche, Jacques Lacan is one of those who know language's uncanny power to refuse the truth that nonetheless it never stops demanding. He has taught us this mixture of rigor, pathos and suspicion which ought to guide whoever takes the chance of a genuine act of reading. The consequences for the reaching of reading, that is for the literature departments, are incalculable.

Dr. Lacan told us the other day that his decision to assemble his publications in a volume (*Ecrits*) had been made after his last trip to the United States which took place more than ten years ago. May his present visit lead to a similar negation of failure: that is our most fervent desire.[5]

I would like to attempt to analyze, now, the subtlety of detail and complexity of pronouncements of this page, which describes de Man as much as it describes Lacan, pointing out the way in which the introducer recognizes in the introduced the tenor of his own life work and of his own professional and personal commitment:

Jacques Lacan is, first and foremost, . . . a teaching and a reading—the teaching of a reading.

It is well known that de Man resisted the discourse of psychoanalysis. And yet, he resisted it as one who was extremely close to it, as one who in a way

5. My translation.

knew all about it, but chose to say that knowledge in the form not so much of a denial as of a *refusal*, a refusal actively repeated, reasserted, paradoxically enough, not out of blindness to, but out of insight into, the importance of psychoanalysis. I would like to meditate here on this refusal, which I take to be nothing other than a complex dialogue with psychoanalysis: a lifelong dialogue engaged, in de Man's writing and in the process of his readings, between de Man's emotional proximity to, and simultaneous critical distance from, the psychoanalytic discourse. The presentation of Lacan is, indeed, unique in that it is the only text in which de Man implicitly acknowledges his closeness to, rather than—as is usually the case—explicitly states his distance from, psychoanalysis. It is the inner tension between this closeness and this distance which, in my view, determines de Man's particular conception of the act of reading.

Jacques Lacan is, then, "a teaching and a reading," in much the same way that de Man is. Reading, for de Man as for Lacan, is about a reform of understanding, about the necessity—and the trauma—of a cognitive revolution. This reform of understanding is, however, somehow, somewhere, bound to fail, and to fail the expectation its occurrence triggers. The cognitive revolution needs to be repeated, reenacted, re-begun in every reading. The reform is itself marked, as a reform, by a point of failure, a point of faltering Which is structurally built into it. In the text significantly entitled "The Reason for a Failure," Lacan writes:

> I have dedicated myself to a reform of understanding imposed by a task of which it is an act to commit others. In as little as the act *falters*, it is the analyst who becomes the true analysand, as any analyst will realize more surely, the nearer he is to being at a level with the task. The pathos of my teaching is that it operates at this point.[6]

It is the pathos of this point which de Man resonates to, underscores, by quoting from Lacan's "Reason for a Failure," as emblematic of what Lacan is all about, the following elliptical lines:

> The pathos of my teaching is that it operates at this point. And this is what, in my *Writings*, in my history, in my teaching, retains an audience beyond all criticism: an audience which feels that something is played out there of which everybody will have a share.

The "teaching of a reading" is thus an utterly personal and an utterly impersonal matter: an impersonal commitment of the personal which concerns everybody, "of which everybody will have a share." What is of personal concern to de Man is not Lacan the reader but the reading, not Lacan the teacher but the teaching, the way the teaching of a reading "plays out some-

---

6. Lacan, op. cit., 47. Emphasis mine. As a rule, in the quoted texts, the emphases are mine unless otherwise indicated.

thing"—something which is very personal—at a level which commits it to an impersonality "of which everybody will have a share."

> The pathos of my teaching is that it operates at this point. And this is what, in my *Writings*, in my history, in my teaching, retains an audience beyond all criticism.

What de Man subscribes to in Lacan's psychoanalytic stance, what, specifically, *suspends de Man's own criticism*, escapes his own critique of psychoanalytic discourse, is Lacan's awareness—and acknowledgement—of the point of failure or of faltering at which the teaching, and the commitment to the teaching, operate.

This awareness is explicitly inscribed in de Man's teaching as well. Thus, the opening of the essay entitled "The Resistance to Theory," introducing the special *Yale French Studies* issue entitled *The Pedagogical Imperative*, reads:

> This essay was not originally intended to address the question of teaching directly, although it was supposed to have a didactic and an educational function—which it *failed* to achieve. . . .
>
> I found it difficult to live up, in minimal good faith, to the requirements of this program and could only try to explain, as concisely as possible, why the main theoretical interest of literary theory consists in the impossibility of its definition. . . .
>
> For it is better to *fail* in teaching what should not be taught than to succeed in teaching what is not true.[7]

Not only is the point of failure actually built into the teaching, in de Man as well as in Lacan. It constitutes, for both, the very level at which the pedagogical imperative is experienced not just as an epistemological but as an ethical imperative: the very limit point out of which the commitment to the teaching paradoxically derives. De Man writes:

> It may well be . . . that the development of literary theory is itself overdetermined by complications inherent in its very project and unsettling with regard to its status as a scientific discipline. . . . To claim that this would be a sufficient reason not to envisage doing literary theory would be *like rejecting anatomy because it failed to cure mortality.* [*RTT*, 12]

In every reading, there is a certain attempt to live through death, and a certain failure to cure mortality. It is to the extent that reading (teaching literary theory, psychoanalyzing) operates at this level of necessity/impossibility that everybody is concerned by it—has a share in it.

This is also, for de Man, the story of all texts: all texts narrate the impos-

---

7. Paul de Man, "The Resistance to Theory," in *Yale French Studies* 63, "The Pedagogical Imperative," ed. Barbara Johnson (New Haven: Yale University Press, 1982), 12. This text will hereafter be abbreviated as *RTT*, followed by the page number of the *Yale French Studies* edition.

sibility of reading as the point of failure *out of which* they *demand to be read*, out of which they inscribe a paradoxical imperative to read.

> Do we have to interpret the genitive in the title of Keats' unfinished epic *The Fall of Hyperion* as meaning "Hyperion's fall," *the case story of the defeat* of an older by a newer power, . . . or as "Hyperion falling," the much less specific but more disquieting evocation of an *actual process of falling*. . . . The narrative context suits neither and both at the same time, and one is tempted to suggest that the fact that Keats was unable to complete either version manifests the impossibility, for him as for us, of reading his own title. One could then read the word "Hyperion" in the title *The Fall of Hyperion* . . . intertextually, as referring not to the the . . . mythological character but as referring to the title of Keats' own earlier text (Hyperion). But are we then telling *the story of the failure* of the first text as the success of the second, the Fall of *Hyperion* as the Triumph of *The Fall of Hyperion?* Manifestly yes, but not quite, since the second text also *fails* to be concluded.
>   Or *are we telling the story of why all texts, as texts, can always be said to be falling?* Manifestly yes, but not quite, either. . . . The undecidability involves the figural or literal status of the proper name Hyperion as well as of the verb *falling*. . . . In "Hyperion's Fall," the word "fall" is . . . the representation of a *figural fall*, and we, as readers, read this fall standing up. But in "Hyperion falling," this is not so clearly the case, for if Hyperion can be Apollo and Apollo can be Keats, then he can also be us and *his figural (or symbolic) fall becomes his and our literal falling as well.* [*RTT*, 16–17]

To read is to participate in the process of the faltering of meaning, to attempt to take control of, or to come to terms with, *our own fall inside language*. Those whose life and thought have revolutionized "the teaching of a reading," those whose teaching has been dedicated to the reform of understanding which is constitutive of what de Man calls reading, give us insight into the variety of ways in which language makes us fall, fails the expectations it erects.

> Like Freud, like Nietzsche, Jacques Lacan is one of those who know language's uncanny power to refuse the truth that nonetheless it never stops demanding. He has taught us this mixture of rigor, pathos and suspicion which ought to guide whoever takes the chance of a genuine act of reading.

LANGUAGE'S UNCANNY POWER, OR
THE IMPERATIVE TO IRONY

None suspected language more than Paul de Man, whose extraordinary reading lesson is indeed, very like the psychoanalytic one, a lesson of suspicion. And yet, with de Man's mixture of suspicion, of self-denying pathos and of impassioned rigor, none inquired more intensely and relentlessly into the dynamics of "language's uncanny power to refuse the truth that nonetheless it never stops demanding"; none investigated more persistently, in language, "this perpetual error that we call, precisely, life."[8]

De Man called "rhetoric" the object of this lucid and impassioned inquiry. To study rhetoric is to understand how life, through language, fools us; but also, to understand how this very understanding unwittingly repeats the process of our being fooled, of saying—doing—more than we know, of not quite knowing what it is we say or do. To read is then to read, specifically, the *difference* between life and language. The *necessity* of reading stems from the *discrepancy* between thought and life, between act and understanding, between the urge for freedom and the bondage in which language keeps us.

Reading is an attempt to cancel this discrepancy, to set ourselves free of the signifying chain—of our entrapment in linguistic structures, to catch up with, and cancel out, the foolishness unwittingly exhibited by living. Catching up, however, is impossible, because the act of catching up itself *repeats the difference* it attempts to read and cancel out. The attempt to catch up stumbles, thus, again, on the impossibility of reading, which de Man transforms into something like a philosophical imperative to irony.

> The naïve historical question from which we started out—should the *Profession de foi* be called a theistic text?—must remain unanswerable. The text both is and is not the theistic document it is assumed to be. *It is not the simple negation of faith it seems to proclaim*, since it ends up accounting in a manner that cannot be refuted for the necessary occurrence of this faith. *But it also denounces it as aberrant.* A text such as *Profession de foi* can literally be called *"unreadable"* in that it leads to a set of assertions that radically exclude each other. Nor are these assertions mere mental constatations; they are exhortative performatives that require the passage from sheer enunciation to action. They compel us to choose while destroying the foundations of any choice. They tell the allegory of a judicial decision that can be neither judicious nor just. As in the plays of Kleist, the verdict repeats the crime it condems. If, after reading the *Profession de foi*, we are tempted to convert ourselves to "theism," *we stand convicted of foolishness in the court of the intellect. But if we decide that belief*, in the most extensive use of the term (which must include all possible forms of idolatry and ideology) *can once and forever be overcome* by the enlightened mind, then *this twilight of the idols will be all the more foolish* in not recognizing itself as the first victim of its occurrence. One sees from this that the impossibility of reading should not be taken too lightly. [*AR*, 245]

---

8. "Cette erreur perpétuelle qu'on appelle, précisément, la vie." This sentence from Proust's *A la recherche du temps perdu* is quoted by de Man as the epigraph to the first edition to his book, *Blindness and Insight; Essays in the Rhetoric of Contemporary Criticism* (New York: Oxford University Press, 1971), v.

III

THE KNOT OF FRIENDSHIP AND OF INFLUENCE

As a living reading lesson, we all experienced Paul de Man as more than a colleague, a friend, a teacher: he was, both in his works and in his person, the unique event of an encounter: the encounter with an extraordinary reader whose contact *revolutionized* one's thought; the encounter with the unusual generosity and the unusually creative and subversive insight of an impassioned disbeliever, whose iconoclastic, unexpected ways of reading and of thinking constantly surprised one's life, opened up new ways of seeing one's own work, compelled one into a rethinking, a re-reading of everything one took for granted, including one's own habits of thinking and of reading.

In the preface to his *Allegories of Reading,* Paul de Man writes, by way of acknowledging the intellectual indebtedness of his book: "I feel unable . . . to disentangle the part of friendship from the part of influence" (*AR*, x). In coming to acknowledge, in my turn, my own indebtedness to Paul de Man, I would like not so much to try to disentangle the human from the intellectual indebtedness, the part of friendship from the part of influence, as, on the contrary, to say something about the unique involvement of the friendship with the influence, to speak about, precisely, the inextricable *knot* of friendship and of influence that his extraordinary presence has inscribed in my own life and work.

He professed nothing else than reading, and he did what he professed: he read his authors; he read his students; he read us—friends and colleagues. As a reader, he both supported and challenged, always addressing the work read with a surprise—an unexpected question—which made a difference. If his reading lesson kept contending with, and insisting on, the impossibility of reading, this impossibility—the point of failure built into his teaching—became, quite literally, something of which everybody had a share. Of that impossibility of reading which was his own, de Man made, in that way, a gift to others: a gift of reading.

To analyze the way in which de Man was *about reading:* about reading as at once a lesson and a gift, I want to show not merely what it means to read de Man, but what it means *to be read by him,* by reproducing, here, our last exchange of texts—of readings.

De Man's last letter to me, about four months before his death, responded to a text of mine he had just read. I would like to reproduce here, first, an excerpt of my text (which would account for his letter), and then, an excerpt of his letter (which I will analyze).

A DIALOGUE OF READINGS

My own text can be said to be about a certain form of the impossibility of reading, and to that extent it indirectly bears witness to de Man's impact on my work, to the way in which my work (unconsciously) resonated with de Man's preoccupations. To the extent, however, that my text deals with psychoanalysis, a subject that de Man shunned, his own supportive and challenging response, within the knot of friendship and of influence, speaks to *his difference*, in defining, subtly and elliptically, at once our personal and intellectual encounter and what separates us, our difference of position with respect to Freud's momentous insights. De Man's dialogue with me is also, then, at the same time, his intimate—but differential—dialogue with psychoanalytic discourse, shedding light, once more, both on his empathic closeness to, and on *the nature of his critical distance* from, that discourse.

My text is an analysis of Freud's "Irma dream," reported in chapter 2 of *The Interpretation of Dreams:* the very first dream Freud submits to detailed interpretation and from which he derives the psychoanalytic theory of dreams. Freud's text is thus a narrative not just of a dream but of the very discovery of his theory. The Irma dream is crucial, in my eyes, in that it is *the very dream from which psychoanalysis proceeds.* Since the dream discusses, on the other hand, Freud's relationships with various women, my own specific focus of interpretive attention is on the way the dream—and the discovery—also reflect upon Freud's encounter (as yet unconscious) with the crucial psychoanalytic question of femininity, a question that Freud, later, will articulate as *the very question that psychoanalysis leaves answerless:*

> The great question that has never been answered and which I have not been able to answer, despite my thirty years of research into the feminine soul, is *"what does a woman want?"*[9]

The thrust of my interpretive endeavor is to articulate, indeed, *the dream from which psychoanalysis proceeds* with *the question that psychoanalysis leaves answerless.* My reading of the dream, in other words, attempts to read in an anticipated manner how the dream articulates, from an unconscious place, at once Freud's later question and its answerlessness. The textual point of the answerlessness (the point of failure built into Freud's teaching) is formulated, in the way I read it, by Freud himself in a footnote to the dream, a footnote that becomes, thereby, quite crucial to my reading, and on which my analysis will indeed linger:

> There is [writes Freud] at least one spot in every dream at which it is unplumbable—a navel, as it were, that is its point of contact with the unknown.[10]

---

9. S. Freud, letter to Marie Bonaparte, quoted in Ernst Jones, *The Life and Work of Sigmund Freud* (New York: Basic Books, 1955), v. 1, 421.

10. S. Freud, *The Interpretation of Dreams,* in *The Standard Edition of the Complete Psychological Works of Sigmund Freud,* translated from the German under the General Editorship of James Strachey (London: The Hogarth Press and the Institute of Psychoanalysis, 1964), v. 4, 111, footnote 1. Quotations from Freud will refer to this edition, hereafter indicated, in the body of the text, only by volume number followed by page number.

De Man's response attached itself specifically to Freud's figure of the navel and to my analysis of it. "My only question," writes de Man, "arises, if I dare say, at the level of the navel. . . ."

I would like now to present (however fragmentary and incomplete) the most relevant excerpt of my text, in view of analyzing, later on, at once the content and the terms of de Man's response. The dialogue of texts—of readings—which will henceforth engage between my text on Freud and de Man's letter, will thus explicitly revolve and implicitly evolve around three questions: 1. What does a woman want? 2. What is a navel—in Freud, in my own reading of him, in de Man's reading of both? 3. What does it mean, indeed, to *pose a question at the level of the navel?*

Here then is the fragment of my text on which de Man will comment.

IV

THE STORY OF FREUD'S DREAM

The evening before the dream was dreamed (July 23–24, 1895), Freud met a colleague and friend, Otto, who had just returned from a summer resort where he had met a young woman called Irma who was Freud's patient. The treatment of this patient was crowned by partial success: she was cured of hysterical anxiety but not of certain somatic symptoms. Before going on vacation Freud had offered Irma an interpretation—a "solution"—of the riddle of her symptoms, but Irma had been unwilling or unable to accept it; and the symptoms persisted. To Freud's question about how Otto had found the patient in that summer resort, Otto replied: "better, but not quite well," words in which Freud detected a reproach. So as to justify himself, Freud, that evening, wrote out an explanation of his views on Irma's illness, in the form of a case history addressed to Dr. M., the leading figure in the medical circle at the time and a common friend of Otto's and of Freud's. These circumstances were followed by the dream:

> A large hall—numerous guests, whom we were receiving.—Among them was Irma. I at once took her on one side, as though to answer her letter and to reproach her for not having accepted my 'solution' yet. I said to her: 'If you still get pains, it's really only your fault.' She replied: 'If you only knew what pains I've got now in my throat and stomach and abdomen—it's choking me—I was alarmed and looked at her. She looked pale and puffy. I thought to myself that after all I must be missing some organic trouble. I took her to the window and looked down her throat, and she showed signs of recalcitrance, like women with artificial dentures. . . . She then opened her mouth properly and on one side I found a big white patch. . . . I at once called in Dr. M., and he repeated the examination and confirmed it. . . . My friend Otto was now standing beside her as well, and my friend Leopold was percussing her through her bodice and saying: 'She has a dull area low down on the left.' He

also indicated that a portion of the skin on the left shoulder was infiltrated. (I noticed this, just as he did, in spite of her dress.) . . . M. said: 'There's no doubt it's an infection, but no matter; dysentery will supervene and the toxin will be eliminated.' . . . We were directly aware, too, of the origin of the infection. Not long before, when she was feeling unwell, my friend Otto had given her an injection of a preparation of propyl, propyls . . . propionic acid . . . trimethylamin (and I saw before me the formula for this printed in heavy type). . . . Injections of that sort ought not to be made so thoughtlessly. . . . And probably the syringe had not been clean. [4, 107]

The pragmatic interpretation of the dream—through the chain of associations it evokes in Freud—is oriented toward the pathbreaking theoretical conclusion posited, at the end, as the basic thesis of Freud's book: that dreams do have a meaning, and that their meaning is the fulfilment of a wish: "The dream acquitted me of the responsibility for Irma's condition." (4, 119).

Apparently, Irma is the only female figure in the dream. But as the chain of associations reveals, Irma is in fact the condensation of three different women representing, with respect to Freud, three different sorts of feminine relations.

1) *The first female figure: the young, recalcitrant woman patient: Irma herself.*

Irma, a young widow, is characterized in the dream by her complaint (her pains), and her resistance, her unwillingness to accept Freud's solution. Through her "recalcitrance" she is doubled, however, by the image of another young woman patient, a governess who "seemed a picture of youthful beauty, but when it came to opening her mouth she had taken measures to conceal her plates" (4, 109).

The feature of the masculine medical examination of female cavities, unveiling and penetrating female secrets, can be related to the later part of the dream, in which Irma is examined and percussed by a group of male doctors, and her symptoms—this time an infection, an "infiltration" in the shoulder—are perceived and diagnosed through, "in spite of her dress."

2) *The second female figure behind Irma: the ideal, fantasmatic woman patient: Irma's friend.*

"The way in which Irma stood by the window" reminds Freud of a woman friend of Irma, whom Freud suspects of also being a hysteric, and wishes to have as a patient:

I now recollected that I had often played with the idea that she too might ask me to relieve her of her symptoms. I myself, however, had thought this unlikely, since she was of a very reserved nature. She was *recalcitrant*, as was shown in the dream. . . . Irma seemed to me foolish because she had not accepted my solution. Her friend would have been wiser, that is to say she would have yielded sooner. She would have *opened her mouth properly*, and have told me more than Irma. [4, 110]

3) *The third female figure behind Irma: Freud's wife.*

There still remained a few features that I could not attach either to Irma or to her friend: *pale; puffy; false teeth.* . . . I then thought of someone else to whom these features might be alluding.

The text does not spell out the identity of this "someone else"; but a footnote at the bottom of the page reads: "The person in question was, *of course*, my own wife". In the footnote, too, another unexplained *complaint* of Irma finds explanation (it is, in fact, the wife's complaint):

[1]The still unexplained complaint about *pains in the abdomen* could also be traced back to this third figure. The person in question was, of course, my own wife; the pains in the abdomen reminded me of one of the occasions on which I had noticed her bashfulness.

What Freud omits to tell us, here, is the crucial fact that his wife is, at the time of the dream, *pregnant*; a predicament which can perhaps better explain her "complaint" of "pains in the abdomen and in the stomach."

THE SUBJECT OF COMPLAINT, OR WHAT DO WOMEN WANT?

The dream is entirely focused on two features which insistently recur in all the female figures of the dream: resistance, on the one hand (resistance to solutions, recalcitrance to treatment); and on the other hand, suffering, pain, "complaint." It would not be inappropriate to see the entire Irma dream as a dream, specifically, about *female resistance*, and about *female complaint*. Freud is indeed obsessed, not just with Irma's nonacceptance of his solution, but, even more importantly, with her pain. Thus, the wish-fulfilment discovered in— and accomplished by—the dream is expressed in terms of the negation of responsibility for Irma's pain:

I was not to blame for *Irma's pains*, since she herself was to blame for them. . . . *I* was not concerned with *Irma's pains*, since they were of an organic nature. . . . *Irma's pains* could be satisfactorily explained by her widowhood. . . . *Irma's pains* had been caused by Otto. . . . *Irma's pains* were the result of an injection. . . . I noticed, it is true, that all these explanations of *Irma's pains* were not entirely consistent with one another. . . . The whole *plea*—for the dream was nothing else—reminded one . . . of the *defence*. . . . [4, 119]

The drama of the dream consists, thus, in a peculiar sexual relation between a plea and a complaint. "The whole plea—for the dream was nothing else"—is a male plea responding to a crucial female pain which the defense, in the same movement, strives at once to hear and not to hear; a male plea answering a feminine complaint which the male dreamer knows he misses, but which the dream, precisely, strives to comprehend.

How, then, does Freud's wife enter this picture of the confrontation between Freud and Irma, between the plea and the complaint?

It is, indeed, as an agent of resistance and as a *subject of complaint* that the wife emerges from behind the female patient: as a subject, more specifically, of a rhetorically repressed complaint whose centrality is relegated to the marginality of a footnote. Since, out of the footnote, the wife emerges as *a secret sharer in the feminine complaint* of the hysteric, the feminine complaint as such unfolds as more complex than it first seemed, in that it now appears to be articulated from different structural positions. It is from the dynamic play between the similarities and the dissimilarities between Irma and the wife that the full scope of the complaint emerges.

A. *Obvious Similarities*

1) The wife, like Irma, does not measure up to "the standard of the good and amenable patient." Both are resistant, recalcitrant to treatment. Speaking of his wife, as yet unnamed, Freud says, in the course of the associations: "she again was not one of my patients, nor should I have liked to have her as a patient, since I had noticed that she was bashful in my presence, and I could not think she would make an amenable patient" (110)

2) Irma has been infected, "infiltrated" by a male intervention: the injection of a "solution" from an unclean syringe. Metaphorically, the wife has been impregnated, fecundated by another male injection of another contaminating male solution.

B. *Obvious Dissimilarities*

1) "Irma's pains could be satisfactorily explained by her widowhood" (152). The complaint is coincident with the absence of a husband, in Irma's case, and with the presence of a husband, in the wife's case.

2) Freud's (pregnant) wife embodies female fertility. The hysteric patient embodies female sterility: that is why she is said to be, etymologically, "hysteric": "suffering from the womb."

C. *Paradoxical Similarities* (despite the dissimilarities)

Both the sterile hysteric (widowed) and the pregnant wife (husbanded, happily married) are *suffering from the womb.*

D. *Paradoxical Implications of the Interpenetration of Complaints*

According to patriarchal criteria, Freud's wife, beloved by her husband and pregnant with his child, is the social epitome of the *fulfilled woman.* Irma, on the other hand, as the widowed hysteric deprived of child and husband, is the social epitome of the *unfulfilled woman*. And yet, the dream is saying that *both women are unhappy*, lacking something. The dream unwittingly renders suspicious what we have come to call, today, "the feminine mystique," the conventional idea of feminine fulfilment.

Whereas apparently, the wife's position as a woman is at the antipodes of that of Irma, the dream's creative *work* seems to belie this reassuring difference, to situate the two female positions as equivalent—exchangeable and interchangeable—in an equation of complaints whose *unknown* (the very riddle of femininity) calls, precisely, for a new articulation of the question: of the question of what Freud is up against in his professional and personal, male encounter with femininity; of the question of how this encounter misses, or pragmatically subverts, all known answers, given in advance; of the question of what Freud is up against in his encounter with the enigma of these women who should by now be known, and yet are still somehow, somewhere along the line, quite crucially unknown, unreadable, misunderstood, miscured, dissatisfied; of the question of what Freud is up against when the dream is telling him that the woman in his bed is as unknown, perhaps, and as dissatisfied, as the untalkative patient in his office, hysterically and painfully choking on a speech she cannot yield. In dramatizing femininity as an equation of diametrically opposed structural complaints leveled by the paradoxical common denominator of feminine dissatisfaction, the dream seems to be asking: where does the feminine desire really lie? My wife is "bashful in my presence"—what is it that my mate, my sexual partner, and the mother of my children, truly wants? Irma resists my treatment—what is it that the patient truly wants? Is there a difference between female wish fulfilment and male wish fulfilling fantasies of female wish fulfilment? Is there a difference between what a woman wants and what a man might think a woman wants? Where, exactly, does this difference lie? *What does a woman want?*

The entire dream is up against this question, which its unconscious, searching energy endeavors to articulate, through and beyond its own male plea.

THE NAVEL OF THE DREAM

The unreadability (the resistance) of this knot of women is defined by Freud as "the navel of the dream":

> If I had pursued *my comparison between the three women*, it would have taken me far afield.—There is at least one spot in every dream at which it is unplumbable—*a navel*, as it were, that is its point of contact with the unknown. [Footnote 1, 111]

The figure of the navel is itself curiously related to the theme of pregnancy, both semantically (because of its metaphorical suggestiveness of the umbilical cord), and syntactically (because of its location in the text). Emerging, like Freud's wife, in a footnote, the navel has two important levels of connotation: it functions, on the one hand, *theoretically*, as a new concept forged by Freud in order to denominate the *dream's resistance to understanding*. But on the other hand, it functions not abstractly but *concretely* (mobilizing the singularity of an image rather than the generality of a concept), in materially evoking a part of the human body which, located in the abdomen, could suggestively refer to the (contiguous, though elliptical, suppressed) image of a pregnant belly. Could the navel of the dream and the navel of Freud's pregnant wife somehow communicate with respect to what the dream is pregnant with?

Why, indeed, does Freud choose to call "navel" the dream's relationship to the unknown? The navel marks the place where the umbilical cord which connects the infant to the mother has been cut (during delivery); it marks, in other words, at once the *disconnection* and the *connection* between a maternal body giving birth and a newborn child. The navel of the dream embodies thus, the way in which the dream is, all at once, *tied up* with the unknown and *disconnected* from its knowledge, disconnected from the knowledge of its own begetting.

And yet, the disconnection has itself the form of a *knot*. Thus, the concept of the navel is re-formulated in the final chapter of Freud's book, no longer as a passing footnote but as a central theoretical conclusion:

> There is often a passage in even the most thoroughly interpreted dream which has to be left obscure; this is because we become aware during the work of interpretation that *at that point there is a tangle* of dream-thoughts *which cannot be unravelled.* . . . This is the dream's navel, the spot where it reaches down into the unknown. The dream-thoughts to which we are led by interpretation *cannot*, from the nature of things, *have any definite endings;* they are bound to *branch out in every direction into the intricate network* of our world of thought. It is at some point where this *meshwork* is particularly close that the dream-wish grows up, like a mushroom out of its mycelium. [4, 525]

If the navel is a knot, it is not surprising that it is, precisely, *out of the very knot of female figures* that the notion of the navel for the first time springs, as a footnote to the Irma dream.

Erik Erikson suggests that the introduction of the image of "the navel of the dream" indicates that for Freud, "the Dream . . . is just another haughty woman, wrapped up in too many mystifying covers and 'putting on airs' like a Victorian lady." "In the last analysis," Erikson concludes, "the dream itself may be a mother image; she is the one, as the Bible would say, to be 'known.'"[11]

It is no doubt true that the image of the navel is connected to the image

---

11. Erik Erikson, "The Dream Specimen of Psychoanalysis," in *Journal of the American Psychoanalytic Association*, v. 2, (1954), 46.

of a mother, and that, through the dream's complex of pregnancies, the wife as mother and perhaps, the mother as a wife imbue the dream's unconscious thoughts and rhetorically affect, determine, and participate in, the riddle of the female knot. It is equally quite pertinent to point out the link interconnecting intellectual and carnal knowledge, and to suggest, along with Erikson, that "in the last analysis . . . she [the Mother] is the one, as the Bible would say, to be 'known.'"

But can the *unknown* be simply reduced to, or defined by, that "which *would be 'known'*"? In speaking of the navel as "unplumbable"— a *knot* ("a tangle of dream thoughts") which "cannot be unravelled"—, the dream interpreter is explicitly suggesting that the navel of the Irma dream, though hinging on the mystery of femininity, is by no means *a* woman (Mother, Victorian lady, Irma, etc.) but the cluster of ("comparison between") the women, that is, a *structured female knot* which cannot be untied, a knot of female differentiality with respect to any given definition; a knot, in other words, which points not to the identifiability of any given feminine identity, but to the inexhaustibility, the unaccountability of *female difference:* difference which Freud—as man, as doctor, as interpreter—stumbles on, experiences at first as purely negative resistance, but which he then insightfully associates with the inexhaustibility, the unaccountability of the very *nodal point*—the very navel—of the dream.

Now, to explain female resistance, as well as the resistance of the navel of the dream, either by the generality of the incest prohibition or by the historical idiosyncrasy of Victorian prudery, is to *explain away* female resistance, to identify female resistance with male desire and to erase the (sexual) difference between the two. But the Irma dream does not do that; or if it does that in the guise of its avowed male *wish fulfillment*, it does not do *just* that; it also writes, inscribes, the difference it erases; it also writes, inscribes, along with the discovery of wish fulfillment, the historical discovery of the *pregnancy of the difference* which its wish fulfillment narcissistically erases.

What cannot be overemphasized, it seems to me, in Freud's dream theory, is the fact, and the significance of the fact, that the theoretical emergence of the notion of wish fulfillment is *coincident* with the theoretical emergence of the notion of the navel, which is its truly revolutionary counterpart. The very birth, indeed, of the concept of the navel of the dream in the place of the oneirically wish-fulfilling male erasure of ("male solution" to) female difference, bears witness to Freud's insight that *to solve the riddle* is *to fail to account for the question of the dream.*

What is, then, the question which the dream discovers, the question which the specimen-dream is quite literally *engrossed with*? Is there a different, nonreductive way in which the unknown, the dream's navel, can be, not accounted for, explained away, subsumed by what is known, but rather, thought out as the way in which the genuine unknown of gender and of gender difference—the radical unknown of sexuality as difference—*fecundates* at once Freud's dream and the unprecedented theory to which the dream historically gives birth?

TO DREAM A QUESTION

The navel of the Irma dream is constituted, we have seen, by the unfathomability, the inexhaustibility, of the comparison between the three resistant women. But there is a paradox in the way the navel knots its own unknowability. For the dream interpreter is saying that this knot of women is, as such, "unplumbable," not because it simply is unknowable, but insofar as its very unknowability constitutes, paradoxically enough, the dream's specific *"point of contact with the unknown"* (111). The dream, in other words, through the resistance of the women, *makes contact* here with something new, something which it does not know or understand or master, but with which it nonetheless somehow communicates. Can we try to situate in the text what it is the Irma dream makes contact with at this specific moment?

At the specific textual point where the navel footnote in effect cuts off the interpretive flow of the associations, the text thus interrupted by the footnote has, in comparing the three women, just touched upon—connected with—an image: the image of a female throat.

> She [Irma's friend] would have opened her mouth properly, and would have told me more than Irma. (Footnote: I had a feeling that the interpretation of this part of the dream was not carried far enough to make it possible to follow the whole of its concealed meaning. If I had pursued my comparison between the three women, it would have taken me far afield.—There is at least one spot in every dream at which it is unplumbable, a navel, as it were, that is its point of contact with the unknown.)

Follows, in Freud's text, the quotation of the dream's text: *"What I saw in her throat: a white patch"* etc. Can this connection with the throat somehow shed light on the connection/disconnection of the navel?

The signifier of the throat may lead the reader of Freud's text in two directions: on the one hand, the ensuing vision of the female throat—the oneiric, horrifying confrontation with the unknown of an opened female cavity—leads, in the dream's narrative, to the male/medical diagnosis linked to the injection of a male solution. But on the other hand, the throat may be associated not just with the (wish fulfilling) male solution, but also with the initial feminine complaint. "If you only knew," Irma said to Freud, *"what pains I've got now in my throat* and stomach and abdomen—it's choking me." The word in the German original for the way her painful throat is strangling her is *zusammenschnüren*, which literally reads: *"it's tying me up in knots."*

THE KNOT IN IRMA'S THROAT

The *female knot* which constitutes the *nodal point* of the Irma dream—the dream's knot/navel—is thus prefigured in the initial image of the *painful knot*—the lump in *Irma's throat*—which somehow triggers, opens up the self-divided, self-analytic dialogue of Freud's dream.

In a way, it could be said that *Freud's whole dream precisely speaks out of the lump in Irma's throat*. It is out of a knot of female pain that Freud's dream issues: a dream about a knot of female pain recalcitrant to, and in excess of, Freud's discourse (Freud's interpretation); a dream about a knot of irreducibly resistant women; a dream about a knot of feminine complaints.

The dream is painful, encompassing both Freud's and Irma's pain, and measuring the irreducible discrepancy between the two. But there is an insight, a discovery in the very pain of this discrepancy.

From the singularly silent and resistant navel of Freud's pregnant wife, to the singularly painful and resistant knot in Irma's throat, through the mediating notion of the navel of the dream, Freud discovers that resistance, far from being simply negative, is a positively pregnant concept; that resistance is a textual knot, a nodal point of unknown significance, the navel of an unknown text; and that the psychoanalytic dialogue is a new way of reading, and of working with, the pregnancy of this unknown and the fecundity of this resistance. This is what the Irma dream *makes contact with*, precisely, through the navel of its female knot ("a navel, as it were, that is its point of contact with the unknown"), but what the dreamer and the dream interpreter *do not yet know*.

Freud discovers, thus, as yet unconsciously, *the very origin of self-analysis*, the very motivating force of analytic dialogue, in the oneirically unfolded navel of sexuality as difference: of sexuality as the ungraspable, intuited relation between the navel of a "bashful" pregnant belly and the choking, strangling knot of pain in Irma's throat. As the ungraspable foundation of a radical unconscious dramatized by the complex, dramatic figure of the pregnant navel/knot in Irma's throat, sexuality is, in the Irma dream, envisioned as a double reference—a connection/disconnection—on the one hand, to the body, and on the other hand, to speech. Human sexuality, in other words, is here (self-analytically) envisioned, on the one hand as a *differentiality of pain*, and on the other hand as *the unspeakability of difference:* as an irreducible *bodily gap in language*.

In much the same way as the navel of the dream, the knot of pain which ties up Irma's throat remains, indeed, ex-centric to Freud's speech, and irreducibly resistant to interpretation (although the dream itself explains this female knot of pain as the differential, symptomatic *residue* of the injection of a *male solution*).

In recapitulating the resistance of the female knot—the knot of (the comparison between the) women—the female knot of pain in Irma's throat, which symbolizes at the same time Irma's pain and Irma's choking speech, embodies, thus, the very navel of the feminine complaint, and of the feminine complaint's resistance to interpretation: a knot which is at once the *nodal point* of the female pain *and* that which makes the nodal point of the female pain *unspeakable:* unspeakable in a male dream; unspeakable in terms of a male (self-conscious, self-identical) solution.

The genius of Freud's dream is to have recognized, precisely, that; and to have situated both the psychoanalytic lesson of the feminine resistance, and this unspeakability of the feminine complaint within his own male dream, this differentiality of the female knot of pain with respect to his own theoretical solutions, as the very nodal point of his specimen-dream, and as, indeed, the very *navel* of his dream understanding.

Because Freud's dream can think beyond its conscious means, because Freud's genius gives us insight even into its own limitations, the author/writer of the Irma dream, in grappling with the female knots of his own text and in theorizing the pathbreaking notion of the navel of the dream, has nonetheless given us some *textual access into the unknown.* Freud calls precisely "navel" this textual access which he does not command and whose meaning he is not entirely in possession of.

The "navel" is, in other words, Freud's discovery—through the Irma dream—that in every theory, interpretation or conscious meaning there is a disconnection: that in every thought there is the navel of a dream; but also, that in every dream there is the navel of a thought. Whether the textual access which the navel gives us into the unknown is drifting us from dream to thought or from thought to dream is what remains to be determined at any given moment, and what is often undecidable. The visionary thinking power of the dream from which psychoanalysis proceeds resides, however, in the ground breaking way in which the dream's knot/navel knots together—for the whole future of psychoanalysis—the question of the woman and the question of the navel.[12]

V

A KNOT THAT'S CUT

[Maine] August 23, 1983

Dear Shoshana,

I am sorry for not having been able to return your essay before our departure. I had attempted to provide some modifications in order to temper an effect of insistence that had given me the fatal impression of a repetition. Looking at it more closely, however, this repetition turned out to be nonexis-

---

12. This excerpt of my text on Freud is a fragment of a much longer essay, which constitutes a chapter of my forthcoming book, *What Does A Woman Want?* (Harvard University Press).

tent, especially at the level of the paragraphs, and necessary at the level of the sentences. So that the suggested changes became all ineffectual. I therefore decided to take the text with me and to reread it at leisure, with a clear head.

The results of this reading limit themselves to some marginal notes that in most cases, you would be better off ignoring. The essay, by the way, gains a great deal in being attentively reread. It is a very powerful text, and one which will provoke interesting reactions. My only question arises, if I dare say, at the level of the navel. What should we do with the manifest bisexuality of that mark, which separates as much as it unites, and which escapes the difference between the genders? The navel is a knot that's cut, and as such, more philosophical than analytical. But it was necessary first to get to that point, and you have done it with all the force and the precision one might desire.

Rather than entrusting the (perhaps unique) copy of this text to the singularly decrepit mailman who insures postal survival in this place, I prefer to return it to you myself next week. I will put it in your mailbox Thursday or Friday.

The extraordinary beauty of the sky and of the sea does me, at moments, a lot of good, which, by contrast, renders the more difficult moments all the more painful. But on the whole the balance, I believe, is positive.

See you soon,
Paul.[13]

My only question arises, if I dare say, at the level of the navel.

In much the same way Freud's dream can be said to speak out of the lump—the knot of pain—in Irma's throat, de Man's response, in turn, answers me—with empathy, challenge and paradox—at the level of the body: of the body as the blind spot of an existential knot of pain which makes one write only to speak its own unspeakability; the gut level of a knot of pain which knots at once its gift of comprehension and its residue of incomprehensibility.

"The level of the navel" is none other, thus, than the gut level of the impossibility of reading, at which de Man reads me and at which he offers me his dialogue, his gift of reading, by offering to share with me (and to challenge me with) a question at the level of the navel.

It may well be that the question of the woman, or of sexual difference, which my essay focused on ("What does a woman want?") is indeed one of those questions that can only be posed at the level of the navel. And this is what my reading of Freud's dream attempted in effect to show: how psychoanalysis proceeds not so much from Freud's theoretical solutions as from Freud's unconsciously charged, pregnant ways of *asking questions at the level of the navel.* My own text also reads Freud, and asks questions, at the level of the navel. And de Man responds, in turn, on that level, which he for the first time points out explicitly as the very level of the question.

"In my early childhood," writes Michel Leiris,

---

13. My translation from the French. (The language in which we corresponded was French.)

... I imagined that children came not from the mother's sex but from her navel—that navel which I had been startled to learn (at an even earlier period) is, after all, a scar.[14]

To ask a question at the level of the navel is to ask a question at the level of a certain birth and of a certain scar: the question is posed out of a certain wound, a certain severance, a certain impossibility of asking. "The poem," writes de Man about Shelley's *Triumph of Life*, "is sheltered from the performance of disfiguration by the power of its negative knowledge":

> But this knowledge is powerless to prevent what now functions as the decisive textual articulation: its reduction to the status of a fragment brought about by the actual death and subsequent disfigurement of Shelley's body, burned after his boat capsized and he drowned off the coast of Lerici. This defaced body is present in the margin of the last manuscript page and has become an inseparable part of the poem. At this point, figuration and cognition are actually interrupted by an event which shapes the text but which is not present in its represented or articulated meaning. It may seem a freak of chance to have a text thus molded by an actual occurrence, yet the reading of *The Triumph of Life* establishes that this mutilated textual model exposes *the wound of a fracture* that lies hidden in all texts. [*RR*, 120]

To ask a question at the level of the navel is to ask a question at the level of "the wound of a fracture that lies hidden in all texts."

To *say* one asks a question at the level of the navel is, however, to undercut the cognitive authority of one's own question, to engage performatively, self-subversively, in an imperative to irony, to suggest one *asks*, precisely, at the very level of what one *does not know*, a level at which one cannot even be sure of one's capacity for truly asking.

> Confronted with the question of the difference between grammar and rhetoric, grammar allows us to ask the question, but the sentence by means of which we ask it may deny the very possibility of asking. For what is the use of asking, I ask, when we cannot even authoritatively decide whether a question asks or doesn't ask? [*AR*, 10]

My only question arises, if I dare say, at the level of the navel. What should we do with the manifest bisexuality of that mark which separates as much as it unites, and which escapes the difference between the genders?

My reading of Freud, in equating the figure of the navel with the female knot and through it, with the feminine stance in Freud's text, used that figure to introduce, rhetorically, a self-subversive (sexual) difference into Freud's own discourse. In displacing my rhetorical equation *navel = female (knot)*, in pointing out—imaginatively, creatively—as the blind spot of my vision of the

---

14. Michel Leiris, *L'Age d'homme* (Paris: Gallimard/Folio, 1973), 64. Translated by Richard Howard as *Manhood* (San Francisco: North Point Press, 1974), 32.

navel, the bisexuality of that same figure, de Man, at the sweep of a surprise, deconstructs the thrust of my whole discourse, in repeating my rhetorical procedure with respect to Freud but in turning that twist back upon myself—in introducing, thus, rhetorically, a self-subversive (sexual) difference into my own text, into my own reading of Freud's difference and self-difference.

Here as always, de Man's pedagogical stance, or challenge, is in saying: the rhetorical machine does not stop here (or anywhere). Keep moving. Do not stop. Go farther.

De Man's way of enjoining us, however, to keep moving, is by pointing out some residue to meaning which subverts and undercuts our illusion of co-herence, of appropriation of the text, and which actually *pulls the rug from under our feet*, reminding us, once more, that we as readers do not read the text's fall standing up, but that we, too, are *caught in the text's fall* and can keep moving only insofar as we keep falling. It is in this way, and in this way only, that de Man will open up a new and unexpected textual horizon, a new and unsuspected path of insight, by adding one more turn of the screw to the rhetorical landscape of the text, by wittily and paradoxically making apparent still another figure (blindness/insight) in the carpet.

What should we do with the manifest bisexuality of that mark which separates as much as it unites, and which escapes the difference between the genders?

If my own text reads Freud from the vantage point of a woman, with a feminist critical awareness, de Man reads me and answers me from the vantage point of a man, who understands, but challenges, my own feminine appropria-tion of the figure of the navel. If the navel, as a mark of bisexuality, "escapes the difference between the genders," then the level of the navel out of which de Man addresses me with his question is, paradoxically enough, the very level of *identity* between de Man and me: the level not of sexual difference but of the identity of a self-difference (of a difference from ourselves), out of which we can, indeed, listen to each other, hear each other, resonate with the other's work.

The navel is, however, a still more paradoxical mark "which separates as much as it unites," and in the unison, the resonance at the level of the navel between de Man's work and my work, between my text and de Man's letter, the navel (and the question of the navel) also marks what separates us, the diver-gence not just of our genders but of our chosen critical positions with respect to the very theory of bisexuality: psychoanalysis. Against the thrust of my own feminist assertion, de Man reclaims thus, paradoxically enough, his identity with me at the level of the navel only to re-assert, all the more subtly but decisively, his difference:

The navel is a knot that's cut, and as such, more philosophical than analytical.

Unlike Freud, whose image of the navel as a knot seems to convey the wish to *go inside,* to plunge *into* the unknown, de Man's vision of the knot conveys the wish—or the necessity—of *getting out* of an entrapment. For Freud, the navel is a *"point of contact* with the unknown": Freud is looking for the continuity of the paradoxical figure of discontinuity, for the connection of the disconnection. De Man, in contrast, insists on the discontinuity disrupting the continuity, on the disconnection of the connection: "the navel is a knot that's cut, and as such, more philosophical than analytical."

Analysis means, etymologically, the undoing of a knot [New Latin, from Greek *analusis,* a releasing, from *analuin,* to undo: *ana,* back + *luein,* to loosen.] However, there are some knots that cannot be undone, and have to be cut, in a Gordian manner. In some cases, survival is more pressing than analysis. In some cases, life cannot afford to wait for a knot to be undone. For birth to take place, the umbilical cord, which ties the infant to the mother, has to be cut. To cut a knot is a philosophical decision: a decision to forget, to break up with an unresolvable psychoanalytic debt, to sever what cannot be disentangled. Philosophy is founded on the violence of Gordian knots.

"To question is to forget," says de Man (*RR,* 118). To question, and thus to open up the possibility of knowing, is to forget the impossibility of asking, the analytic knot of answerlessness. Cognition is contingent on such forgetting. And it is only at this price that there can be a "triumph of life":

> The imposition of meaning occurs in *The Triumph of Life* in the form of the questions that served as point of departure for the reading. It is as a questioning entity, standing within the pathos of its own indetermination, that the human subject appears in the text, in the figures of the narrator who interrogates Rousseau and of Rousseau who interrogates the shape. But these figures do not coincide with the voice that narrates the poem in which they are represented; this voice does not question and does not share in their predicament. We can therefore not ask why it is that we, as subjects, choose to impose meaning, since we are ourselves defined by that question. From the moment the subject thus asks, it has already foreclosed any alternative and has become the figural token of meaning. "Ein Zeichen sind wir /Deutungslos. . . ." (Hölderlin). To question is to forget. . . .
>
> To forget, in this poem, is by no means a passive process. . . . Things happen because the subject Rousseau keeps forgetting. In his earlier stages, he forgets the incoherence of a world in which events occur by sheer dint of a blind force. . . . The episode describes the emergence of an articulated language of cognition by the erasure, the forgetting of the events this language in fact performed. It culminates in the appearance of the shape, which is both a figure of self-knowledge, the figure of thought, but also a figure of "thought's empire over thought," of the element in thought that destroys thought in its attempt to forget its duplicity. For the initial violence of position can only be half erased, since the erasure is accomplished by a device of language that never ceases to partake of the very violence against which it is directed. . . . The trampling

gesture enacts the necessary recurrence of the initial violence: a figure of thought, the very light of cognition, obliterates thought. . . . Each of the episodes forgets the knowledge achieved by the forgetting that precedes it. [*RR.* 118–19]

The navel is a knot that's cut, and as such, more philosophical than analytical.

Analysis is about an inescapable human bondage. Philosophy is about the price of freedom. Analysis is about resistance. Philosophy is about *self-resistance:*

Nothing can overcome the resistance to theory, since theory *is* itself that resistance. . . . The language it speaks is the language of self-resistance [*RTT,* 20]

Philosophy is, quintessentially, the allegorical and ironic rhetoric of this language of self-resistance. Philosophy, in other words, is an allegory of reading. Reading is about avoidance and about the unavoidable. Reading is an allegory of life, as a dynamic process of reading avoidance. Life is the navel of a dream. Philosophy is the "dissemination of a localized disruption"[15] at the level of the navel, a repetitive reminder of the fact that "the navel is a knot that's cut." Reading is allegorical to the extent that it is about the very navel of this cut:

Just as Keats had to break off his narrative, the reader *has to break off his understanding at the very moment when he is most directly engaged and summoned by the text.* [*RTT,* 17]

But this wound which summons and which breaks the reader at the very level of the navel, this break-up, or this breakdown, of the reading is, precisely, what demands, compulsively and endlessly, to be re-read:

. . . .The failure to exorcise the threat, even in the face of such evidence as the radical blockage that befalls this poem, becomes precisely *the challenge to understanding that always again demands to be read.* And to read is to understand, to question, to know, to forget, to erase, to deface, to repeat—that is to say, the endless prosopopeia by which the dead are made to have a face and a voice which tells the allegory of their demise and allows us to apostrophize them in our turn. No degree of knowledge can ever stop this madness, for it is the madness of words. [*RR,* 122]

The navel is a knot that's cut.

YALE UNIVERSITY

---

15. Cf. *Allegories of Reading,* 290: "The question takes us from the *Fourth Rêverie* and its implicit shift from reported guilt to the guilt of reporting, since here the lie is *no longer connected* with some former misdeed but specifically with the act of writing. . . . What can be said about the interference of the cognitive with the performative function of excuses in the *Fourth Rêverie* will *disseminate what existed as a localized disruption* in the Confessions."

BARBARA JOHNSON

Rigorous Unreliability

It may seem paradoxical to speak of an implicit evaluative system underlying the practice of deconstruction. Deconstructors, after all, are far more likely to speak of "valorization" than of "evaluation," far more likely to engage in a *critique* of value systems than to elaborate a value system of their own. Yet however "extra-moral" a critique of "truth" and "beauty" might consider itself to be, it carries with it a sense of urgency that cannot help but imply that the critiquing of value systems is itself a valuable activity. Even if the deconstructive hand is always quicker than the evaluative eye, the card trick of insight can only be appreciated by the blindness of understanding. As Paul de Man says of the word "deconstruction" itself: "No other word states so economically the impossibility to evaluate positively or negatively the inescapable evaluation it implies."[1]

The remainder of this paper can be understood as a gloss on the following sentence by de Man, in which evaluative terms flicker in and out, up and down, without reaching a stable resolution, but also without enabling one to envisage a stance beyond evaluation:

> Literature as well as criticism—the difference between them being delusive—
> is condemned (or privileged) to be forever the most rigorous and, consequently,
> the most unreliable language in terms of which man names and transforms
> himself. [19]

The present essay, originally titled "Questions of Value," was conceived as a contribution to a session of the 1983 MLA Convention. News of Paul de Man's death reached me as I was writing the final section of the essay.

This essay is reprinted from *Critical Inquiry* 11, 2, (December 1984) with the kind permission of the Chicago University Press.

1. Paul de Man, *Allegories of Reading: Figural Language in Rousseau, Nietzsche, Rilke, and Proust* (New Haven: Conn., Yale U. Press 1979), x; all further references to this work will be included in the text.

I

WRINKLES IN A WHALE'S BROW

As a critique of a certain Western conception of the nature of signification, deconstruction focuses on the functioning of claim-making and claim-subverting structures within texts. A deconstructive reading is an attempt to show how the conspicuously foregrounded statements in a text are systematically related to discordant signifying elements that the text has thrown into its shadows or margins; it is an attempt both to recover what is lost and to analyze what happens when a text is read solely in function of intentionality, meaningfulness, and representativity. Deconstruction thus confers a new kind of readability on those elements in a text that readers have traditionally been trained to disregard, overcome, explain away, or edit out—contradictions, obscurities, ambiguities, incoherences, discontinuities, ellipses, interruptions, repetitions, and plays of the signifier. In this sense it involves a reversal of values, a revaluation of the signifying function of everything that, in a signified-based theory of meaning, would constitute "noise." Jacques Derrida has chosen to speak of the values involved in this reversal in terms of "speech" and "writing," in which "speech" stands for the privilege accorded to meaning as immediacy, unity, identity, truth, and presence, while "writing" stands for the devalued functions of distance, difference, dissimulation, and deferment.

This transvaluation has a number of consequences for the appreciation of literature. By shifting the attention from intentional meaning to writing as such, deconstruction has enabled readers to become sensitive to a number of recurrent literary topoi in a new way. Texts have been seen as commentaries on their own production or reception through their pervasive thematizations of textuality—the myriad letters, books, tombstones, wills, inscriptions, road signs, maps, birthmarks, tracks, footprints, textiles, tapestries, veils, sheets, brown stockings, and self-abolishing laces that serve in one way or another as figures for the text to be deciphered or unraveled or embroidered upon. Thus, a deconstructor finds new delight in a Shakesperean character named Sir Oliver Martext or in Herman Melville's catalog of whales as books in *Moby Dick*, or she makes jokes about the opposition between speech and writing by citing the encounter between Little Red Riding Hood and the phony granny.

In addition, by seeing interpretation itself as a fiction-making activity, deconstruction has both reversed and displaced the narrative categories of "showing" and "telling," mimesis and diegesis. Instead of according moments of textual self-interpretation an authoritative metalinguistic status, deconstruction considers anything the text says about itself to be an allegory of the reading process. Hence, the privilege traditionally granted to showing over telling is reversed: "telling" becomes a more sophisticated form of "showing," in which what is "shown" is the breakdown of the show/tell distinction. Far from doing the reader's work for her, the text's self-commentary only gives the reader more to do. Indeed, it is the way in which a text subverts the possibility of any authoritative reading by inscribing the reader's strategies into its own structure that often, for de Man, ends up being constitutive of literature as such.

Deconstructors, therefore, tend to privilege texts that are self-reflexive in interestingly and rigorously unreliable ways. Since self-reflexive texts often explicitly posit themselves as belated or revolutionary with respect to a tradition on which they comment, deconstruction can both reinstate the self-consciously outmoded or overwritten (such as Melville's *Pierre*) and canonize the experimental or avant-garde. But because deconstruction has focused on the ways in which the Western, white male, philosophico-literary tradition subverts itself *from within*, it has often tended to remain within the confines of the established literary canon. If it has questioned the boundary lines of literature, it has done so not with respect to the noncanonical but with respect to the line between literature and philosophy or between literature and criticism. It is as a rethinking of those distinctions that deconstruction most radically displaces certain traditional evaluative assumptions.

II

HENDIADYS

Consider the following typical de Manian shift in the usage of the terms "philosophy" and "literature."

> The question of the relationship between philosophical and literary discourse is linked, in Nietzsche, to his critique of the main concepts underlying Western metaphysics: the concept of the one (*hen*), the good (*agathon*) and the true (*aletheia*). This critique is not conducted in the tone and by means of the arguments usually associated with classical critical philosophy. It is often carried out by means of such pragmatic and demagogical value-oppositions as weakness and strength, disease and health, herd and the "happy few," terms so arbitrarily valorized that it becomes difficult to take them seriously. But since it is commonly admitted that value-seductions are tolerated (and even admired) in so-called literary texts in a manner that would not pass muster in "philosophical" writings, the value of these values is itself linked to the possibility of distinguishing philosophical from literary texts. This is also the crudely empirical level on which one first encounters the specific difficulty of Nietzsche's works: the patent literariness of texts that keep making claims usually associated with philosophy rather than with literature. Nietzsche's work raises the perennial question of the distinction between philosophy and literature by way of a deconstruction of the value of values. [119]

Rather than asking the question of the evaluation of literary texts, de Man is here taking value itself as a characteristic *of* the literary: literature is that discourse in which arbitrarily valorized value seductions are tolerated or even admired. What this says about philosophy is more complicated: philosophy would seem to be a discourse in which values are not arbitrary, or are not seductive, or in which arbitrary seductions are not tolerated or admired. Values in a philosophical text have to be taken seriously, or they do not pass muster and the text is transformed into literature. Yet Nietzsche's deconstruction of the value of values leads precisely to the discovery that philosophy *is* always already literature. As de Man puts it: "The critical deconstruction . . . leads to the discovery of the literary, rhetorical nature of the philosophical claim to truth. . . : literature turns out to be the main topic of philosophy and the model for the kind of truth to which it aspires. . . . Philosophy turns out to be an endless reflection on its own destruction at the hands of literature. . . . What seems to be most difficult to admit is that this allegory of errors is the very model of philosophical rigor" (115, 118).

Thus the relation between literature and philosophy involves the repetitive setup and collapse of their difference: philosophy's self-definition relies on a claim to rigor that is subverted by the literariness of its rhetoric of truth, but it is precisely that literariness that turns out to be the very model for philosophical rigor. Philosophy is defined by its refusal to recognize itself as literature; literature is defined as the rhetorical self-transgression of philosophy. This positing and erasing of difference, this fluctuation between two and one, could perhaps be called hendiadys, the rhetorical figure that most aptly describes such versions of the chicken and the egg question. What is at stake in the hendiadys "philosophy and literature" is precisely the status of values: if literature resorts to philosophically inadmissible value seductions in order to "outphilosophize" philosophy, then the distinction between the "serious" and the "arbitrary" breaks down. But what has happened to the attendant functions of tolerance and admiration? And what of that most seductive de Manian hendiadys, the conjunction between rigor and unreliability? If the relation of hendiadys between literature and criticism confers the privilege or curse of being forever most rigorous *and* most unreliable, how is this conjunction enacted in de Man's own writing?

III

THE "REAL MYSTERY"

The opening essay of *Allegories of Reading*, entitled "Semiology and Rhetoric," begins with the analysis of a fact of literary studies:

> On the one hand, literature cannot merely be received as a definite unit of referential meaning that can be decoded without leaving a residue. The code is unusually conspicuous, complex, and enigmatic, it attracts an inordinate

amount of attention to itself, and this attention has to acquire the rigor of a method. The structural moment of concentration on the code for its own sake cannot be avoided, and literature necessarily breeds its own formalism. . . .

On the other hand—and this is the real mystery—no literary formalism, no matter how accurate and enriching in its analytic powers, is ever allowed to come into being without seeming reductive . . . Like the grandmother in Proust's novel ceaselessly driving the young Marcel out into the garden, away from the unhealthy inwardness of his closeted reading, critics cry out for the fresh air of referential meaning. [4]

The existence of these two stances breeds "a highly respectable moral imperative that strives to reconcile the internal, formal, private structures of literary language with their external, referential, and public effects" (3). But de Man hastens to assert that "the attraction of reconciliation is the elective breeding-ground of false models and metaphors"—here, the model of literature as a box with an inside and an outside (5). The remainder of the essay is a deconstruction of the inside/outside opposition through a speculation on the terms "grammar" and "rhetoric." The essay concludes with the sentence cited earlier: "Literature as well as criticism—the difference between them being delusive—is condemned (or privileged) to be forever the most rigorous and, consequently, the most unreliable language in terms of which man names and transforms himself."

In an effort to capture de Man's rigor and unreliability in his own enactment of the deconstruction of the opposition between literature and criticism, I shall begin by attempting to situate its "literarity." Included in de Man's list of arbitrary and therefore literary Nietzschean value seductions, you will recall, was the opposition between disease and health. That opposition appears in de Man's description of those who try to drive readers of literature out of the unhealthy inwardness of the prison house of language. But the fresh air of referentiality seems to spawn diseases of its own, which de Man, later in the essay, proposes to combat by introducing some "preventative semiological hygiene" (6). On one level, then, de Man is employing, quite ironically, the value seductions of a vocabulary of sickness and health in order, literarily, to reverse the value seductions of a certain sort of literary criticism. But the literarity of the essay does not stop there. For the literary passage on which de Man's essay primarily focuses is a passage from Marcel Proust that precisely duplicates the figures through which the essay's polemical situation is described. Marcel is in his room reading while the grandmotherly forces are trying to shoo him into the healthy outdoors. In order to overcome the guilt of inwardness, Proust's text strives to reconcile the outdoor values of light, warmth, and activity with the indoor values of darkness, coolness, and passivity. The reconciliation depends for its success on the privileging of metaphor as necessity. De Man's reading of the passage shows that the reconciliation cannot, in fact, be accomplished without recourse to metonymy, which thus subverts the ground on which the erasure of guilt was to be founded.[2] Yet if the reconciliation is not achieved, then Marcel—and, by implication, close(ted) reading—is still guilty. What, then, are the consequences for de Man's semiological hygiene?

The situation is in fact even more complex than this. In order to deconstruct the seduction of reconciliation, de Man focuses on the way in which the Proust passage privileges metaphor as necessity at the expense of metonymy as contingency. By showing that the metaphorical reconciliation occurs through a hidden metonymical accident, de Man deconstructs the rhetorical privilege accorded the notion of necessity. But necessity and contingency are precisely the terms in which the distinction between formalism and referentiality were initially described. Literature was said to "necessarily" breed its own formalism just as summer in the Proust passage "necessarily" bred flies, while the "real mystery" was the seemingly contingent fact that such an apparent necessity is never allowed to stand without seeming reductive. The moral imperative always occurs as an imperative to move "beyond formalism," beyond the questions necessarily raised by the language of the text. De Man's close reading deconstructs the very value that makes close reading unavoidable. The "real mystery" for de Man would seem to be the eternal return of the moral imperative to resist reading. Yet only by resisting reading the contradiction between necessity as the object of deconstruction and necessity as the imperative to deconstruct could we assert that de Man is simply

---

2. The logic of de Man's reading runs as follows. In order to produce the impression that " 'the total spectacle of the summer' " (the outside) has been captured within the darkened room (the inside), Marcel Proust has recourse to various figurative strategies. In one instance he explicitly states a preference for a figure formed by necessity over a figure formed by chance: " 'the chamber music' " of the flies, Proust writes, is " 'evocative not in the manner of a human tune that, heard perchance during the summer, afterwards reminds you of it but connected to summer by a more necessary link: born from beautiful days, resurrecting only when they return, containing some of their essence, it does not only awaken their image in our memory; it guarantees their return, their actual, persistent, unmediated presence' " (13). De Man glosses: "The preference is expressed by means of a distinction that corresponds to the difference between metaphor and metonymy, necessity and chance being a legitimate way to distinguish between analogy and contiguity" (14). Hence, by its own account, the Proust passage achieves its guilt-erasing totalization through metaphor (necessity). Yet later in the passage the insertion of heat into the coolness of the room (another aspect of the totalization) is accomplished by means of a linguistic accident—not by "necessity." The " 'dark coolness' " of the room, says Marcel, " 'matched my repose which (thanks to the adventures told by my book and stirring my tranquility) supported, like the quiet of a motionless hand in the middle of a running brook the shock and the motion of a torrent of activity" (13, 14). De Man here points out that the expression "torrent of activity" is able to reconcile heat and bustle with cool tranquility only through the double contingency of the fact that it is a cliché ("torrent" and "activity" do not each separately convey the property of heat, but as a cliché—through habitual contiguity—the expression works up a sweat) and that the sleeping water image in "torrent" is reawakened by mere proximity to the "running brook." The totalization of essence (metaphor) is thus dependent upon linguistic contiguity (metonymy), and the preference for metaphor preached by the passage is undercut by its own practice.

attempting to plead in favor of formalism. His text is, rather, enacting the very unreliability of the rigor any formalism might wish to posit.

But so much for the philosophical grammar of de Man's literary rhetoric.

What about the philosophical rhetoric of de Man's often bizarre grammar?

IV

DEMANDING ANACOLUTHONS

The question of guilt serves as one of de Man's favorite tropes for the resistance to reading. In two separate essays, de Man uses "guilt" as a way of reversing the relations between textuality and subjectivity.

> One should not conclude that the subjective feelings of guilt motivate the rhetorical strategies as causes determine effects. It is not more legitimate to say that the ethical interests of the subject determine the invention of figures than to say that the rhetorical potential of language engenders the choice of guilt as theme, no one can decide whether Proust invented metaphors because he felt guilty or whether he had to declare himself guilty in order to find a use for his metaphors. Since the only irreducible "intention" of a text is that of its constitution, the second hypothesis is in fact less unlikely than the first. The problem has to be left suspended in its own indecision. [64–65]

> Any guilt, including the guilty pleasure of writing the *Fourth Rêverie*, can always be dismissed as the gratuitous product of a textual grammar or a radical fiction: there can never be enough guilt around to match the text-machine's infinite power to excuse. . . . The text as body, with all its implications of substitutive tropes ultimately always retraceable to metaphor, is displaced by the text as machine and, in the process, it suffers the loss of the illusion of meaning. The deconstruction of the figural dimension is a process that takes place independently of any desire; as such it is not unconscious but mechanical, systematic in its performance but arbitrary in its principle, like a grammar. [299, 298]

By locating the text-generating agency in the text's own desire to constitute itself independently of any subject, de Man sees subjectivity itself as a rhetorical effect rather than a cause. If the one irreducible force at work is the machinelike grammar of textuality, this amounts, ultimately, to a definition of the subject's function in language as a potential for ellipsis. In Jean-Jacques Rousseau's story of the false accusation of Marion as the stealer of a ribbon, de Man describes the incompatibility between Rousseau's description of his choice of the name Marion as motivated by his desire for her, on the one hand, and his explanation that the name came to him by accident, on the other, in terms of the figure of anacoluthon—a syntactical interruption or discontinuity. What is revealed by Rousseau's anacoluthon, says de Man, is the eclipse of the subject by the textual machine. De Man goes on to conclude:

> Far from seeing language as an instrument in the service of a psychic energy, the possibility now arises that the entire construction of drives, substitutions, repressions, and representations is the aberrant, metaphorical correlative of the absolute randomness of language, prior to any figuration or meaning. [299]

What is striking about this sentence is that it is itself a grammatical anacoluthon: the participle "seeing" in the introductory subordinate clause demands a corresponding subject in the main clause, but in the main clause that subject is replaced by an abstraction: "Far from seeing x, the possibility now arises that y." The grammar of the anacoluthon thus *enacts* the eclipse of the interpreting subject that it describes. The "we" that would situate *us* as readers, who are far from seeing, drops out of the sentence that describes that very dropping out.

If the matching of textuality functions like a grammar through which subjectivity can indifferently be produced or erased, what is one to say about a grammatical error? Does de Man's dangling participle stand as the eclipse or rather as the inscription of a subject? Couldn't subjectivity be defined as a grammatical mistake? Consider another anacoluthic, de Manian sentence in which a whole intersubjective drama is caught in the discontinuities of the apparent awkwardness of the grammar:

> Thus, with the structure of the code so opaque, but the meaning so anxious to blot out the obstacle of form, no wonder that the reconciliation of form and meaning would be so attractive [4–5]

In the floating functions of anxiousness, wonder, and attraction, de Man's text inscribes signs of subjectivity in the absence of any grammatical subject. As de Man says elsewhere, "By calling the subject a text, the text calls itself, to some extent, a subject" (112). It is in the irreducible incompatibility between a code whose structure is opaque and a will-to-erase through which meaning exists as an anxiousness to blot out the obstacle of form that the "real mystery" of reading is always inscribed. But it is a mystery about which no moral imperative to leap from textuality to subjectivity or history can tell us more than de Man's stubborn labyrinths of rigor, resistance, and profoundly meaningful unreliability.

HARVARD UNIVERSITY

MINAE MIZUMURA

Renunciation

If the death of a writer makes a difference in the way we read him, one manifestation of such a difference may be the sudden urge we feel toward grasping what we read as having its own history. An end calls for a beginning—and a good story in between. It is such an impulse which directs our attention to a marginal, retrospective remark Paul de Man makes in his foreword to the second, 1983 edition of *Blindness and Insight*. After some brief comments on the collection of essays, de Man singles out "The Rhetoric of Temporality," now included in the volume, as a "slightly different case" that points to a "turn" in his career:

> With the deliberate emphasis on rhetorical terminology, ["The Rhetoric of Temporality"] augurs what seemed to me to be a change, not only in terminology and in tone but in substance. This terminology is still uncomfortably intertwined with the thematic vocabulary of consciousness and of temporality that was current at the time, but it signals a turn that, at least for me, has proven to be productive.[1]

"The Rhetoric of Temporality," one of the most renowned of de Man's works, was first published in its integral form in 1969. A turning point, then, exists in de Man's career roughly at its midpoint, dividing it into a before and an after of more or less equal lengths thus gratifying our love of symmetry. The said change, however, is not without ambivalence.

On the one hand, its gravity is brought to the fore in a phrase which claims that what has taken place is a change "not only in terminology and in tone but in substance." Yet de Man keeps qualifying his statements with such ex-

This essay was first presented at my oral examination, shortly after Professor de Man's death, in lieu of what was originally prepared for him.

I wish to thank The Japan Foundation for the grant that supported me while I was writing this essay.

1. Paul de Man, *Blindness and Insight* (Minneapolis: University of Minnesota Press, 1983), xii. Henceforth referred to as *BI*.

pressions of reservation as "what seemed to me" or "at least for me" so as to undermine the very force of his assertion. Something more than a sublime (or perverse) modesty so characteristic of de Man may be here involved. The ambivalence in the assertion indeed becomes an assertion of the ambivalence in the next paragraph: "When one imagines to have felt the exhilaration of renewal, one is certainly the last to know whether such a change actually took place or whether one is just restating, in a slightly different mode, earlier and unresolved obsessions."[2] What is the nature of such a "turn" which may be so radical that it is described in terms as exalting as "the exhilaration of renewal," yet which may just be a "restating" of "unresolved obsessions"? Since the first edition of *Blindness and Insight* was compiled after the writing of "The Rhetoric of Temporality," it is likely that the early essays collected in the book do not quite represent what preceded the "turn." We must start with the essays hitherto virtually unknown. The same impulse which directed our attention to de Man's marginal remark directs us next to the work hitherto virtually unknown but that is now being rapidly resurrected and thus posthumously becoming part of de Man's *oeuvre.*

The disadvantages of being a contemporary reader far exceed the advantages. Not to mention the obvious emotional complications resulting from awe or abhorrence—de Man was particularly gifted in inspiring both—which may bring about misreadings too personal to be text-productive, there is the unavoidable lacuna in our knowledge of the writer. This is especially true of someone like de Man whose obscurity in the early years excites our imagination as to his possibly shady past. We possess not even a vague overview of de Man's work in the way we do of other important writers whose deaths are already a part of history or of those contemporary writers whose recognitions came early in their lives.[3] It is only after gaining some familiarity with de Man's later texts which established his reputation that we turn to his earlier ones, and when we do so, we do so in a state of near ignorance. In this specific instance, however, the disadvantage we have as contemporary readers of de Man becomes an advantage. The experience of going back in the temporal axis, which has for its condition our ignorance of what will ensue (or, rather, what had preceded), is itself constitutive of our reading of de Man. This allows us to participate in de Man's feeling of "the exhilaration of renewal," though necessarily in a reversed form.

The early essays of de Man are more heterogeneous in texture than his later ones, and our sense of dislocation is by no means constant. Yet a paragraph, a sentence, or even a word that we encounter in these essays suffices for us to feel suddenly removed from familiar ground and find ourselves in a place

---

2. Ibid.
3. De Man's bibliography was not compiled until shortly before his death in 1983 and even that bibliography is not a complete one. [But see below, pp. 315–22.]

that was once familiar to us before we were initiated to the writings of de Man. From the barren land inhabited by the strangest terminologies such as metalepsis, parabasis, anacoluthon, syllepsis, catechresis, paranomasis, and prosopopeia, we find in those moments of sudden shift that we are back in the homeland of literature where even familiar faces like death, suffering, sorrow, inwarness, reflection, consciousness, and self-knowledge, are found. The shift we experience here is no doubt the reversal of the shift from the "thematic vocabulary of consciousness and of temporality" to the "rhetorical terminology" that de Man mentions in his retrospective remark about the "turn" in his life. Nostalgia is a powerful sentiment, and one may long for the days when de Man was seemingly able not only to write better but also to react a little more sensibly to literature. Nevertheless, to the extent that nostalgia implies a desire to reunite with the origin, what we also go through in those moments of sudden shift is an irretrievable sense of discontinuity that precisely obliterates any possibility of being nostalgic. The less prepared we are for the shift, the deeper our sense of radical dislocation—which, however, does not exclude our sense of a repetition of "unresolved obsessions."

Perhaps one way in which we can grasp the ambivalent movement of the "turn" may be to follow the fate, in de Man's text, of the word "renunciation" whose disappearance through the turn is suspiciously dramatic. Blatantly ethical if not religious, the word renunciation strikes a strange note when associated with the usual tone of de Man. His earlier works tell us, however, that the word is far from having always been an alien one in his text. As a "thematic vocabulary of consciousness and of temporality" par excellence, it had occupied, on the contrary, a particularly privileged place in his text before the "turn." De Man's use of the word is not of the kind that is scrupulously controlled so that its significance would be immediately perceptible. Yet as we notice that the word represents, along with its synonym (and forerunner) "sacrifice," one of the most frequent expressions in his early works, especially in the ones written during the fifties, we also notice that the word, whether "sacrifice" or "renunciation," occurs almost invariably at the high point of his articulation, often as its turning point, when what is most crucial to the entire argument is finally being revealed to us.

Paratactic quotations of several of these instances would give us some idea of how the words appear in the texts. (All translations of citations from de Man's works in English are my own.)

Without this *sacrifice*, there can be no truly objective knowledge. ["Montaigne et la transcendence," *Critique*, 9, 1953, 1011–22.]

By interiorizing the sorrow, the poet assumes it . . . and through his total *sacrifice*, which goes beyond death, gives it the value of an example and a warning. ["Heidegger's Exegeses of Hölderlin," *BI*, 246–66]

Before [the Savior's] arrival, the poet is the one who kept the minds of the people open for the perception of *sacrifice* . . . ["Keats and Hölderlin," *Comparative Literature*, 8, 1956, 28–45.]

This conflict can be resolved only by the supreme *sacrifice:* there is no stronger way of stating the impossibility of an incarnate and happy truth. ["The Dead-End of Formalist Criticism," *BI*, 229.-45.]

A novelist must *sacrifice* everything—including dialogue. ["Situation du roman," *Monde nouveau*, 11, June 1956, 57–60.]

Keats time and again emphasizes the discontinuity between the two worlds and, consequently, the total *sacrifice* involved in passing from one to the other—a *sacrifice* so absolute that it would be hubris for the poet to take it upon himself. ["A New Vitalism," *Massachusetts Review*, 3, 1962, 618–23.]

And the first step in such a reconciliation always involves the *renunciation* of the naive belief in a harmony at the beginning of things. ["The Mask of Albert Camus," *New York Review of Books*, 23 December 1965, 10–13.]

De Man's predilection for the notion of renunciation, moreover, is inextricably related to his predilection for Rousseau's epistolary novel, *Julie ou la Nouvelle Héloïse*, which represents, for de Man, a novel that thematizes the act of renunciation.[4] It is the recurrence of the word "renunciation" in the discussion of this novel which provokes a turning point of the argument in "The Rhetoric of Temporality," which, in its turn, provokes a turning point in de Man's career—marked by the sudden disappearance of the word. Since we possess two other essays de Man wrote on the *Nouvelle Héloïse*, one before and another after "The Rhetoric of Temporality," it is only logical that we try to follow the fate of the word renunciation and to grasp the movement of the "turn" through his successive readings of Rousseau's novel.

The first of the three essays de Man wrote on *Julie ou la Nouvelle Héloïse* is a short article entitled "Madame de Staël et Jean-Jacques Rousseau" that was published in *Preuve* in 1966. After a sustained discussion on the parallelism between the two authors, a turning point of the argument is reached where de Man establishes, through a comparison between *Delphine* and *Julie*, how Madame de Staël after all diverges away from Rousseau. This is the point where the word "renunciation" and its variants "renounce" and "sacrifice" suddenly recur in the text.

In *Delphine*, it is with a persistence close to an obsession that Mme de Staël places the heroine in situations where everything calls her to *renunciation*. It is with the same persistence that Delphine rejects every single one of

4. De Man, "Madame de Staël et Jean-Jacques Rousseau," *Preuves*, 190, December, 1966, 34–40. This theme is dependent on de Man's own readings of the novel. The novel may also lend itself to a (mis)reading which sees in it, for example, an indictment of social and historical injustice that victimizes and thus glorifies the passion of two lovers. (The emphases are my own).

these occasions. Neither allegiance to the words given under solemn circumstances, nor concern for the legitimate happiness of others, nothing can induce
Delphine to *renounce* the possibility of satisfying here and now her desire for
happiness. Furthermore, when, in her own comments on the novel, Mme de
Staël suggests an alternative to the behavior of her character, it is not in terms
of *sacrifice*, but in terms of decorum: the *renunciation* would not have been
desirable in itself, but necessary in the eyes of an all-powerful society. The
persistence of Delphine reflects, hence, a parallel decision of the novelist:
capable of establishing, in relation to herself, the distance of reflection (like
Rousseau), Mme de Staël is, nevertheless, not capable of not making this reflection serve the need of justifying herself in front of others. . . .

To move from self-justification to self-knowledge, the reflection must be
able to *renounce*, not only the hope of overcoming the sorrow, but also the hope
of justifying oneself by means of this sorrow, of making it subserve the
glorification of oneself. Rousseau knew it well: he placed in the heart of his
novel the *renunciation* of Julie and precisely refused to make a martyr out of
this *renunciation*. The somber happiness that dwells in the second part of the
Nouvelle Héloïse is the exact opposite of the plaintive suffering of Delphine.
The atmosphere of Clarens is that of authentic reflection. By opting for reflection instead of clinging to the equivocal pleasures of sensuality and of heroism,
the novelist chooses to prefer the success of his fiction to that of his particular
self. The world of Clarens is a world that is entirely fictive and founded on a
difficult knowledge. Everyone there knows that a failure of a particular happiness is not due to an intervention of others, but that it discloses the very
movement of being. The priority of fiction is established in the *renunciation* of
oneself.

We shall abstain ourselves from making reproaches to Mme de Staël. Her
work is of those that permit a better understanding of the nature of *chefs-
d'oeuvre*. As it is only too well indicated by the critical history of the *Nouvelle
Héloïse*, the apparent positivity of Rousseau runs the risk of concealing the
depth of negativity and of *renunciation* from which his work has come out and
at the price of which it was able to elaborate itself.[5]

It is de Man himself who later warns us against "a naive distinction between 'writing' and 'reading'."[6] An apparent focusing on the question of writing notwithstanding, the above passage ought to be understood in terms of
reading, or rather, of misreading. The main role which defines Madame de Staël
is that of a reader of Jean-Jacques Rousseau. She comes close to a full grasp of
Rousseau up until a crucial point where she fails, as a reader, to understand that
Rousseau "placed in the heart of his novel the renunciation of Julie," which is
at the basis of her failure, as a writer, to understand that "the priority of fiction
is established in the renunciation of oneself." This failure to read Rousseau,

---

5. Ibid., my emphases.
6. De Man, *Allegories of Reading* (New Haven: Yale University Press, 1979), 201. Henceforth
referred to as *AR*.

moreover, is not a personal flaw specific to Madame de Staël. Her misreading already anticipates "the critical history of the *Nouvelle Héloïse*" which turns out to be nothing but a history of misreadings.

The moment we realize that this history of misreadings to which the essay refers designates at the same time a misreading of history, then it becomes manifest that we are already in the midst of de Man's well-known critical project which had absorbed him for many years: the critique of the historical misreading of the history of Romanticism. As such, despite the tone which makes it stand out even among de Man's earlier texts as an instance of the least ironical moment, "Madame de Staël et Jean-Jacques Rousseau" shares with other essays written under the same critical intent the basic structure which, within a retrospective view now allowed us, reveals itself to be remarkably persistent.[7] Similar critiques, follow, one after another, until "The Rhetoric of Temporality" comes and places an ultimatum to the historical misreading of the history of Romanticism, naming the misreading as "an act of ontological bad faith." We shall not involve ourselves with too broad a question of what some have referred to as "de Man's existentialist backgrounds"[8] to which such an expression as "an act of ontological bad faith" immediately calls attention. What ought to be noted here in this ultimatum is the equation established between misreading and "an act of ontological bad faith." It attests to the persistence up until the very moment of the "turn," not only of the question of renunciation, but also of the necessary link between reading and renunciation in de Man's text. How is an act of reading related to an act of renunciation for de Man?

An act of renunciation presupposes the existence of a tension. Just as one does not renounce an apple for the sake of an orange, the word renunciation involves, of course, a bipolar structure in which the two poles are in everlasting conflict. The two poles hence often represent two incompatible modes of being based on mutually exclusive value systems such as, to use a familiar example, being a rich man and entering into the kingdom of God. Renunciation becomes a more intriguing notion when we realize, however, that what is to be renounced is actually not one mode of being for the sake of another but, more fundamentally, the compatibility of the two modes of being—which is even

---

7. One finds the structure persisting in the most unexpected places such as in his review of Sartre's *The Words* from the midsixties when de Man used to contribute to the *New York Review of Books*. Sartre's confessional autobiography is mercilessly dismissed as "an act of self-therapy which, as such, does not belong to literature." Sartre, we should understand, is after all another slightly incompetent reader of *chefs-d'oeuvre*, especially of the romantics: "After reading Rousseau, or Proust, or even Flaubert's letters, one may well feel that one knows more about oneself, but has, to some extent, forgotten about the author. This is because these writers have been concerned with interpreting and not with curing their own predicament. They have never left the proper domain of literature. Long before Sartre, the romantics discovered that writing was primarily a way to self-knowledge." ("Sartre's Confessions," *New York Review of Books*, 5 November 1964, 10–13.)

8. Frank Lentricchia, "Paul de Man: The Rhetoric of Authority," *After the New Criticism* (Chicago: University of Chicago Press, 1980), 285.

more difficult to bring about, let us say, than it is for a camel to go through the eye of a needle. True tension exists, therefore, between the temptation to reconcile what is forever incompatible and the renunciation of this temptation. The conflict between being a rich man and being a Christian provides a particularly illuminating example because what defines being a Christian is precisely the renunciation of the temptation to reconcile these two modes of being. Literature, for de Man, has a similarly structured ontological status.[9]

Countless polarities that we encounter in de Man's early writings, are in the end reducible to a polarity within a self. The basic polarity governing de Man's text before the "turn" can hence be located in an opposition between an empirical self and a self constituted by and in language which, in its simplest formulation, becomes a self that reflects upon the empirical self. If we borrow de Man's categories that are operative in "Madame de Staël et Jean-Jacques Rousseau," we can say that the empirical self is the self that remains on an "intersubjective" level and thus merely attains "self-justification" while the self that is constituted by and in language is the only self that attains "self-knowledge." One may come to the conclusion in associating the notion of renunciation with de Man's text that de Man must be advocating the necessity for us of renouncing the empirical self to which he often ascribes such adjectives as "contingent," "inauthentic," and "factitious." This, of course, is far from the truth—or from the possible, for that matter. The existence of a kind of exhortative moment is a necessary part of de Man's rhetorical strategy which puts into circulation value seductions often rooted in immediate, physical sensation: renunciation is valorized not only as a "difficult" act but also as a "painful" act, the one that accompanies "an infinite pain," whereas succumbing to temptation is described through unflattering images of "lethargy" and "sleep," which only evoke a vegetablelike obtuseness. The question of renunciation arises in de Man, only when literature comes into the scene. And even then, what is to be renounced in literature is not the empirical self (though de Man sometimes says so). Literature—or the self constituted by and in language, the very condition of literature, comes into being in the renunciation, not of the empirical self, but of the temptation to reconcile itself with the empirical self. The term "intersubjective" points to a state of perennial temptation because it designates a structure in which the disjunctive relationship of a reflecting self toward itself is being superseded by a nondisjunctive relationship between two selves that are, in principle, identical. In renouncing the temptation to fall into an "intersubjective" relationship, then, the self constituted by and in language simultaneously attains a knowledge which is the knowledge of the radical discontinuity between the two selves, "the gap that cleaves Being,"[10] to use de Man's own expression from one of his earliest

9. Associated with references to Heidegger. cf., "Heidegger Reconsidered," *New York Review of Books*, 2 April 1964, 14–16.
10. "The Dead-End of Formalist Criticism," *BI*, 245.

essays. When the deepest voice of de Man is heard, one sees that this radical discontinuity is located between a self that dies and a self that knows its death but cannot do anything about it. Literature is that which knows and names this cleavage: "Poetic language names this void with ever-renewed understanding and . . . it never tires of making it again. The persistent naming is what we call literature."[11] Literature hence always already speaks about the "primarily negative relationship prevailing between any kind of reflective language (including that of poetry) and the more immediate experience of reality" (de Man's own insertion in parenthesis),[12] and in so doing, its theme is always already that of renunciation, however remote the apparent subject matter may be. This is the reason why "once the author is interpreted, it can," according to de Man, "be ascertained that all authors say the same thing but through forms that are irreducibly different."[13]

Thus, in the early works of de Man, literature is the privileged place of knowledge where the negative insight on the relationship, ultimately, between man and language is revealed. Within literature, it is, for de Man, romantic literature which comes closest to directly naming this negative insight. Within romantic literature itself, the same is true of Rousseau, and within Rousseau's texts themselves, of the *Nouvelle Héloïse*. This depiction of a linear progression toward what appears as an increasingly intense source of light (de Man speaks indeed of how "by [Julie's] sole presence, all the world irradiate around her")[14] may seem too reductive to do justice to the movement of de Man's early work as a whole which treats diverse authors and texts with equal tenacity. Yet to the extent that the *Nouvelle Héloïse* represents, for de Man, a novel that thematizes the act of renunciation, it functions within his text as a privileged place of knowledge where the negative insight is most directly named. One recalls how de Man refers to the novel, not only once but thrice, in three different chapters of *Blindness and Insight*,[15] to invoke the passage about "the nothingness of human matters" ("tel est le néant des choses humaines qu'hors l'Etre existant par lui-même, il n'y a rien de beau que ce qui n'est pas"). The passage appears each time, in its given context, as an expression of the ultimate knowledge attainable in literature; the haunting words that seem to come from beyond the grave are the light emanating from the dying Julie whose "sacrificial death" is itself a reenactment of the prior act of renunciation. The light is there in *Julie* for us to see only if we are willing to face it—the light, in other words, is there for us to read only if we, as readers, are also willing not to engage "in an act of ontological bad faith." "The roman-

---

11. *BI*, 18.
12. De Man, "The Riddle of Hölderlin," *New York Review of Books*, 19 November 1970, 47–52.
13. De Man, *Les Chemins actuels de la critique* (Paris: Union Générale d'Editions, 1968), chapter 4, 86.
14. "Madame de Staël et Jean-Jacques Rousseau, 40.
15. *BI*, 17, 88, 131.

tic text we confront," writes de Man, "is indeed subtle, but it will appear illegible only to those interpreters who prefer not to see what it says."[16] Renunciation is hence the very condition, not only of writing, but also of reading itself. "The Rhetoric of Temporality," or more precisely, the first half of the essay which discusses the *Nouvelle Héloïse*, seems above all to be a systematic recapitulation through an analysis of "rhetorical terminology" of the preceding argument. Not much effort is needed for us to see that the polarity between "symbol" and "allegory" that governs de Man's reading of the novel here is a familiar one from "Madame de Staël et Jean-Jacques Rousseau." The polarity represents yet another instance of a displaced repetition of the tension between temptation and renunciation; it is hence identical, structurally, to the one between "self-justification" and "self-knowledge" that was operative in the first essay.

Contrary to the received opinion that only focuses on the notion of symbol, the crux of Romanticism, according to "The Rhetoric of Temporality," is found in "a conflict between a conception of the self seen in its authentically temporal predicament and a defensive strategy that tries to hide from this negative self-knowledge," which, "on the level of language," becomes a conflict between the allegorical and the symbolic conceptions of language. After much detour in which de Man expounds other critics' attempts at locating the romantic problem in the symbolic conception of language, the example of the *Nouvelle Héloïse* is brought into the discussion, inducing the turning point of the argument. Suddenly the word "renunciation" and its variants "renounce" and "sacrifice" inundate the text as was the case in "Madame de Staël et Jean-Jacques Rousseau." It is ascertained through the reading of the novel that the "dialectic between subject and object" which is at the basis of the symbolic conception of language "does not designate the main romantic experience," but only a negative moment in a dialectic. In the symbolic conception of language, the disjunctive relationship between subject and object, or more concretely, between man and nature has been "superseded by an intersubjective, interpersonal relationship." Hence it seeks to reconcile what is incompatible and thus "represents a temptation that has to be overcome." The subject has succumbed to the "temptation" to "borrow, so to speak, the temporal stability that it lacks from nature, and to devise strategies by means of which nature is brought down to a human level while still escaping from 'the unimaginable touch of time.'"[17] Opposed to the symbolic conception of language is the allegorical conception of language which is the language of renunciation:

> Whereas the symbol postulates the possibility of an identity or identification, allegory designates primarily a distance in relation to its own origin, and, renouncing the nostalgia and the desire to coincide, it establishes its language in the void of this temporal difference. In so doing, it prevents the self from an

---

16. De Man, "The Literature of Nihilism," *New York Review of Books*, 23 June 1966, 16–20.
17. *BI*, 208, 204, 196, 205, 197.

illusory identification with the non-self, which is now fully, though painfully, recognized as a non-self.[18]

The depiction of the Meillerie episode in the *Nouvelle Héloïse* which signals a moment of "temptation and near fatal relapse into former error" for Julie is said to be based on the use of symbolic diction whereas the depiction of Julie's Elysium, a place emblematic of her renunciation, on the use of allegorical diction. "The moral contrast" between the two scenes is "ultimately resolved in the triumph of a . . . renunciation," and it is this renunciation which de Man claims "establishes the priority of an allegorical over a symbolic diction." Since this establishment of the priority of an allegorical over a symbolic diction is held in "The Rhetoric of Temporality" to have once taken place as a fact of history, the *Nouvelle Héloïse* comes to function within this essay as a novel that directly tells the story of the history of the early romantics where the "rediscovery [of the allegorical diction], far from being spontaneous and easy, implies instead the discontinuity of a renunciation, even of a sacrifice." The misreading of the novel, that is, understanding it as if it prized the symbolic diction, is in itself the misreading, in the most immediate manner, of the romantic tradition. The rediscovery of the allegorical diction is the "painful knowledge" that is attained "when early romantic literature finds its true voice" and it is precisely this "true voice," like the voice of the dying Julie, that is "so rarely recognized for what it really is."[19]

Just as de Man later says of Nietzsche, we can say of de Man that "there hardly is a trick of the oratorical trade which he is not willing to exploit to the full"[20] in "The Rhetoric of Temporality." The high acclaim the essay has received is now legendary. Whoever reads the essay is likely to be convinced that what it presents is a final view—an ultimately correct reading—on the history of Romanticism, with an added pleasure, of course, in having been confirmed that what is ethical is in perfect accordance, as it ought to be, with what is true. If the essay had represented de Man's lay work and nothing had ever followed it, no one would have known that, within this persistent structure of the critique of the historical misreading of the history of Romanticism, the "turn" was already anticipated in the essay which transforms it into a work directed against the very critique itself, that is, against its own conclusion, and consequently, against all that had preceded the "turn."

As the introduction of "rhetorical terminology" indicates, "The Rhetoric of Temporality" is no longer solely concerned with the division within self but also with the division within language. What comes to the fore with the establishment of the priority of allegorical diction is not only the "negative self-knowledge" but, superimposed upon it, the linguistic awareness that "the

---

18. Ibid., 207.
19. Ibid., 201, 204, 205, 207.
20. *AR*, 131.

relationship between sign and meaning is discontinuous." This notion of division within language, however, is not so innocuous a repetition "on the level of language" of the notion of division within self as one may be led to believe in the essay. It already attests to an understanding of language as trope, which, when one ventures to push it to its logical conclusion, necessarily undermines the basic premise that has animated de Man's text up to this point, including the very notion of the division within self itself. For the understanding of language as trope is that which establishes, by pointing to the gap between sign and its semantic function, that language itself renders it impossible, however imperative, to attain knowledge through language. Once such an understanding is reached, reading without misreading simply becomes inconceivable. Misreading is found to be "the necessary correlative of the rhetorical nature of literary language."[21] "The Rhetoric of Temporality," in asserting the priority of allegorical diction, hence already asserts what will subsequently be termed the unreadability of a text. The tension between symbol and allegory is then already another name for the tension between a temptation of assuming the readability of a text, that is, of reconciling sign and meaning, and a renunciation of this temptation.

It is inevitable that "The Rhetoric of Temporality" becomes a work that is flagrantly contradictory. The final historical understanding reached in the essay affirms the priority of allegory over symbol. Yet it now turns out that this understanding is dependent on a prior reading of a text which is itself a reading based on a symbolic conception of language. There is nothing in the essay that, in the end, distinguishes de Man's reading of the Nouvelle Héloïse from his own definition of the symbolic conception of language. The original pairing of succumbing to temptation with the act of misreading has undergone a reversal and it is now paired with the act of assuming the readability of a text. Consequently, de Man's reading of the novel has also come to represent, along with the symbolic diction, the ultimate moment of fall. In its critique of misreading, it assumes, however implicitly, the possibility of a correct reading, whether of the novel, the author, or of the entire historical period. What must be renounced now is the possibility of reading itself, of attaining knowledge—be it a negative knowledge—through language, that is, the very possibility of renunciation itself. "The Rhetoric of Temporality," which at once establishes both the readability and the unreadability of a text, is itself unreadable and, therefore, exemplifies, in its unreadability, the necessity for the renunciation of the notion of renunciation to take place. After the first half of the "The Rhetoric of Temporality," the word abruptly disappears from his text, and in the rare instances in which it later returns, it is only used in a manner that makes it difficult to imagine that it once played a privileged role.[22] The "turn" in de

---

21. Ibid., 208, 209, 141.
22. The only exception is the chapter devoted to Rilke in *Allegories of Reading* where de Man elaborates himself on the existence of a tension between the theme of renunciation and the renunciation of thematic possibilities in Rilke's poetry.

Man's career which "augurs what seemed . . . to be a change not only in terminology and in tone but in substance" is marked by de Man's renunciation of the
notion of renunciation.

"What stands under indictment is language itself and not somebody's
philosophical error,"[23] writes de Man shortly after "The Rhetoric of Temporality" in his critique of Derrida's critique of Rousseau. This statement,
directed against Derrida within the given context, actually points to de Man's
own shift from the critique of misreading to the critique of the assumption of
the readability of a text. In thus obliquely referring to the "turn," however, the
statement also indicates how much wavering and detour were in fact needed
before such shift could finally come about. In indicting Derrida for having
indicted Rousseau when he ought to have indicted language, de Man is still
repeating here the very gesture he indicts. Much of what is written around the
"turn" (and hence the entire *Blindness and Insight*) is located within this
constant oscillation between an indictment of misreading as a human aberration and an assertion of this aberration as a permanent fact of language. The
decisive "turn" takes place only when de Man's text most rigorously works out
what is implied in his own declaration that "the cognitive function resides in
the language and not in the subject."[24] It is the moment when Julie, Rousseau,
and Romanticism no longer play a privileged role as the source of light for de
Man. The cleavage that lies between the epigraph of *Blindness and Insight* and
that of *Allegories of Reading* is a direct witness to such a move: the shift from
"'Cette perpétuelle erreur, qui est précisément la 'vie' . . . (Proust)'" to
"'Quand on lit trop vite ou trop doucement on n'entend rien.' (Pascal)" signals
the final shift from a concern with human errors to a concern with the problem
inherent in reading.
    It is as it should be, then, that the turning point in de Man's life is itself
structured as an act of renunciation. The shift from a concern with human
errors to a concern with the problem inherent in language epitomizes his
ultimate choice of language over man. In renouncing the notion of renunciation, what de Man renounces is above all the notion of renouncing and hence of
the knowing subject.
    This most immediately affects his subsequent treatment of Rousseau who
represented, along with Julie, such a subject par excellence in his text. In an
article from about the same time as "Madame de Staël et Jean-Jacques Rousseau," de Man writes: "Passages like the Socratic death of Julie attest that
Rousseau himself was able to reach the serenity of this ideal knowledge."[25] It
is this image of Rousseau as the possessor of the "ideal knowledge" that must

---

23. *BI*, 140.
24. Ibid., 137.
25. De Man, "Image of Rousseau in Hölderlin," *The Rhetoric of Romanticism* (New York:
Columbia University Press, 1984), 44. Henceforth referred to as *RR*.

undergo a total change. The detrimental effect of the "turn" is evident when we juxtapose, for example, the following two passages that treat the same text from Rousseau. In discussing Rousseau's confession of how he was guilty of having accused a young maid servant for a petty theft that he himself had committed, de Man writes in 1966:

> Romantic literature, at its highest moments, encompasses the greatest degree of generality in an experience that never loses contact with the individual self in which it originates. In the *Confessions,* Rousseau tells how an injustice committed at his expense during his youth awakened within him a universal moral sense: "I feel my pulse quicken as I write this; I shall never forget these moments if I live a hundred thousand years. . . ." It is the scope of this generalized passion which makes it possible for Rousseau to be at the same time the poet who wrote *Julie* and the moral philosopher who wrote the *Social Contract*. . . . Nowadays, we are less than ever capable of philosophical generality rooted in genuine self-insight, while our sense of selfhood hardly ever rises above self-justification. Hence that our criticism of romanticism so often misses the mark: for the great romantics, consciousness of self was the first and necessary step toward moral judgement. Keats's last poems reveal that he reached the same insight; the fact that he arrived at it by a negative road may make him all the more significant for us.[26]

The same confession which is here said to have originated from the "individual self," "genuine self-insight" or "consciousness of self" becomes, in 1977, a possible outcome of "the absolute randomness of language."

> Far from seeing language as an instrument in the service of a psychic energy, the possibility now arises that the entire construction of drives, substitutions, repressions, and representations is the aberrant, metaphorical correlative of the absolute randomness of language, prior to any figuration or meaning. It is no longer certain that language, as excuse, exists because of a prior guilt but just as possible that since language, as a machine, performs anyway, we have to produce guilt (and all its train of psychic consequences) in order to make the excuse meaningful. Excuses generate the very guilt they exonerate, though always in excess or by default.[27]

Needless to say, this initial image of Rousseau as a possessor of the "ideal knowledge" is itself a correlative of de Man's own subjectivity as it has been constituted as a reader within his text. In renouncing the notion of renunciation, then, de Man ultimately renounces his own status as a knowing subject. He is no longer the reader who can read. He thus relinquishes his power over the intelligibility of a text—a gesture which, in its final manifestation, becomes a renunciation of his power over the intelligibility of his own text. It is

---

26. De Man, "Introduction," *Selected Poetry of Keats,* ed. Paul de Man (New York: New American Library, 1966), xxxiv.

27. *AR,* 299.

no wonder that, in speaking of the "turn," he has indeed been the first to admit that he is "the last to know whether such a change actually took place or whether (he) is just restating, in a slightly different mode, earlier and unresolved obsessions."

The apparent positivity in the expression "the exhilaration of renewal" which de Man uses to describe the "turn" may be said to conceal a negativity implicit in it. The word "renewal," while pointing to a notion of rebirth, implies the presence of a negative moment which is nothing other than the negative moment of death. If any act of renunciation occurs in the mode of death, de Man's "turn" is perhaps an exemplary case since it is his own death as a knowing subject that we witness here. The story of the "turn," thus formulated, becomes, of course, yet another version of the familiar story of the death of the subject that has been circulating among us for quite a while now—another symptom, that is, of what de Man calls "the 'waning' of modernity."[28] What engages our attention nonetheless is the paradoxical nature of de Man's "turn" as it is inscribed in the paradoxical notion of the renunciation of the notion of renunciation. The story of de Man's "turn" does not close off as just another story on the death of the subject. Taking place as a renunciation of the notion of renunciation, the "turn" is reached not as a result of a disintegration but as a manifestation of the basic structure of tension that has provoked de Man's use of the notion of renunciation in the first place. This structure continues to persist in his text even after the "turn." Hence, the story of de Man's "turn" also becomes a story of an obsessive repetition. It is sometimes claimed that de Man was already engaged unawares in rhetorical analysis from the beginning of his career. Conversely, we can also claim that he continues to speak about renunciation even in his later works when the word itself has disappeared from his text. What comes to the fore this time, however, is not only the necessity of renunciation, but at same time, the impossibility of renunciation, and consequently, the all powerful presence of temptation. It is not by chance that, immediately after the sudden disappearance of the word renunciation, the word temptation saturates the second half of "The Rhetoric of Temporality" and that it keeps recurring in his text with a striking obsessiveness after the "turn."

De Man's later critical endeavor is indeed nothing but an exaltation to renunciation since all it does is to name "with ever-renewed understanding" this tension between temptation and renunciation. The persistence of the basic structure in de Man's text becomes most visible when we try to pursue the parallelism between the disjunction within self and the disjunction within language. Just as the true polarity that governs de Man's earlier text was located, not between the empirical self and the self constituted by and in lan-

---

28. De Man, "Hypogram and Inscription: Michael Riffaterre's Poetics of Reading," *Diacritics*, 11, no. 4, 1981, 17.

guage, but between the temptation to reconcile these two selves and the renunciation of this temptation, the true polarity that governs his later text is located, not between meaning and sign, but between the temptation to reconcile the two and the renunciation of this temptation. It thus becomes located in the tension between the assumption of the readability of a text and the undoing of this assumption. When a text is assumed to be readable, then, what de Man would call an "intersubjective" relationship is established. The disjunctive relationship between reader and text—between meaning and sign—is superseded by a nondisjunctive relationship. The reader has succumbed to the temptation to reduce the text into something that is identical to himself, or more precisely, to his own experience of reading. He has succumbed, in other words, to "the seductive powers of identification." In contradistinction to the assumption in the formal structure of tension, however, this moment of fall does not designate a negative and a passing moment in a dialectic that has to or can be renounced. There is no possibility of overcoming it because it represents a constitutive element in an act of reading. No reading can come to being without an attempt to identify one's experience of reading with the text, that is, without assuming the readability of a text. The moment of the fall thus becomes a necessary part of a permanent tension that inheres in any act of reading where "the pressure towards meaning and the pressure towards its undoing can never cancel each other out." What de Man calls "theory," coming into being in the renunciation of "the nostalgia and the desire to coincide" with the text, points to an aporia between the praxis of reading and the unreadability of a text. It points, in other words, to the aporia that we find in "The Rhetoric of Temporality"—the very aporia located in the void that separates the first half of de Man's work from the latter half, the very aporia, that is, of the "turn." Suspended between "the pressure towards meaning and the pressure towards its undoing," the "turn" in de Man's career is indeed structured as an aporia inscribed in the language as "trope." It is to this aporia of the "trope"/"turn" that de Man keeps pointing until the last moment of his career. And in so doing, his text continues with unrelenting perseverance to speak about the eternal tension between temptation and renunciation.

In "Allegory (Julie)," de Man's third and the last reading of the *Nouvelle Héloïse*, the scene of renunciation is conceived of as a correlative of Rousseau's admission of "the impossibility of reading his own text." The novel itself, likewise, becomes a narrative that tells "the story of the failure to read"—a story that very much resembles, in fact, the story of de Man's own life. A "turning point," marked by Julie's renunciation of her love, takes place in the middle of the *Nouvelle Héloïse* that "sharply divides the novel in two segments, a before and an after." This "reversal of the allegory (peripeteia)" occurs as a "deliberate rejection of the system of analogical exchanges that has structured the narrative of the novel's first half." The term "analogical exchanges," whose meaning extends from the "self/other substitutions" between two lovers to the "self/other substitutions" between reader and author, represents, along with such expression as "metaphorical seductions," a new name for the "intersubjective" relationship. It thus designates, in the last analysis, a reading which assumes the readability of a text, "the homology between enunciation and understanding." Julie's decision to reject this "system of analogical exchanges" "acquires its moral dimension from the fact that it moves against the 'natural' logic of the narrative." But the consequence of such decision does not lead her to a higher knowledge—nor to an actual renunciation. For, at the very moment of her renunciation when Julie is least deluded about her former errors, it turns out that she is "unable to 'read' her own text"[29] and that she is actually repeating within the same text the very errors she dispels. The *Nouvelle Héloïse* hence becomes a story of someone who, despite the necessity of renunciation, inevitably keeps falling into the same temptation. At the end of the novel, Julie is no longer the character in *Blindness and Insight* "who is about to face death with Socratic equanimity."[30] De Man mentions for the first time in this article what he has always ignored in his previous readings— Julie's last letter addressed to her former lover, Saint-Preux, written in "the language of selfhood"[31] and thus pointing to her relapse in the final moment of her life.

De Man once wrote in *Blindness and Insight:*

> Some of the difficulties of contemporary criticism can be traced back to a tendency to forsake the barren world of ontological reduction for the wealth of lived experience. Because it implies a forgetting of the personal self for a transcendental type of self that speaks in the work, the act of criticism can acquire exemplary value. Although it is an asceticism of the mind rather than a plenitude or a harmony, it is an asceticism that can lead to ontological insight.[32]

De Man himself certainly had no idea when he stated this that what he calls here "the barren world of ontological reduction" would seem incomparably filled with "the wealth of lived experience" when juxtaposed to the barren world of rhetorical reduction that we find after the "turn." The relentlessness with which de Man's text seems to have left behind "the wealth of lived experience"—including "the wealth of lived experience" of reading—gives us the impression that we are forced in reading him to become increasingly deprived of what seems most dear to us. And yet de Man actually had never left "the wealth of lived experience." For, in pointing to the necessity of renouncing it, he is in fact acknowledging the existence of temptation, and is thus already speaking about it, albeit in a negative manner. The impression of deprivation comes closer, nonetheless, to grasping the quintessence of de Man

---

29. *AR*, ix, 161, 205, 216, 213, 212, 216, 217.
30. *BI*, 17.
31. *AR*, 220.
32. *BI*, 49.

than a placid acceptance of the extreme ascesis that reigns in his work. Ascesis is the very structure of tension in de Man's text. The one who has not been tempted would not have spoken so often about the necessity (and the impossibility) of renunciation—and could not have done so with such authority. It even seems after all that de Man, from the very beginning of his career, had always been more deeply engaged in speaking about temptation than about renunciation. If we had succumbed to the temptation through the notion of renunciation to make a story out of de Man's life, that is, to make it readable, it is because we must renounce, at this very moment, "the nostalgia and the desire" to hear the living voice of such an authority.

TOKYO

JONATHAN CULLER

Reading Lyric

Several of de Man's late essays converge, in ways that have not been easy to understand, on the notion of the lyric. The difficulties are nicely exemplified in the essay "Anthropomorphism and Trope in the Lyric" in *The Rhetoric of Romanticism*, which declares of Baudelaire's "Correspondances" and "Obsession" that "the resulting couple or pair of texts indeed becomes a model for the uneasy combination of funereal monumentality with paranoid fear that characterizes the hermeneutics and the pedagogy of lyric poetry."[1] De Man concludes that we have no term to describe the sonnet "Correspondances." "All we know is that it is, emphatically, *not* a lyric. Yet it, and it alone, contains, implies, produces, generates, permits (or whatever aberrant verbal metaphor one wishes to choose) the entire possibility of the lyric" (261–62).

What, then, is the lyric? To understand these late essays one must attempt to elucidate this notion of lyric or of what is involved, according to de Man, in reading something as a lyric, or in lyrical reading. "No lyric," he writes, "can be read lyrically, nor can the object of a lyrical reading be itself a lyric" (254).

The place to start seems to me the continuity between de Man's claims here and a structuralist approach to genre—the best known is perhaps Todorov's work on the fantastic—which sees genres as sets of reading strategies or conventions for producing meaning. To treat a bit of journalistic prose as a lyric poem, for example, is to bring to bear on it a different set of expectations and strategies, including, most obviously, new assumptions about reference, but especially the assumption that something of significance is being said and a repertoire of ways to endow details with significance by establishing internal symbolic patterns and external tropological relations. One might also mention the assumption that interpretation should seek a level of abstraction at which unity can be achieved, and the convention that the text's typographic arrange-

---

1. *The Rhetoric of Romanticism* (New York: Columbia University Press, 1984), 259. Further quotations from this book will be identified by page numbers in the text.

ments can be given spatial or temporal interpretations.[2] De Man is less interested in these conventions than in the idea of the lyric as utterance—an idea fostered by the New Criticism, which in effect treated lyrics as dramatic monologues. The current formulation of this view is that the lyric is a fictional imitation of personal utterance, so that to interpret a sequence as a lyric is a matter of working out who is speaking, in what situation, with what concerns, in what tone—aiming ultimately to articulate the full complexity of the speaker's attitudes, as revealed in the tones of the overheard utterance. To interpret a sequence as a lyric is to find ways of hearing in it a speaking voice, which is taken as a manifestation of consciousness.[3]

In the *Anatomy of Criticism* Northrop Frye defines the lyric as utterance overheard: "The lyric poet normally pretends to be talking to himself or to someone else: a spirit of nature, a Muse, a personal friend, a lover, a god, a personified abstraction, or a natural object. . . . The poet, so to speak, turns his back on his listeners."[4] I have argued that apostrophe, the turning away from actual listeners to address absent or imagined interlocutors in the way Frye indicates, is the characteristic trope of lyric: apostrophe, with its "O"—O rose, thou art sick; O Wild West Wind; O chesnut tree—an O, devoid of semantic reference, is the very figure of voice.[5] Apostrophes are embarrassing, and criticism of the lyric has systematically avoided both the topic of apostrophe and actual apostrophes—translating apostrophes into description. One can argue that this embarrassment is linked to the obviousness that apostrophe is a figure, an empty O, for which one can scarcely make cognitive or transcendental claims of the sort that are routinely made for metaphor: it is embarrassing for the high callings of lyric to depend on, or even be linked closely with, this sort of figure.

Critics have characteristically translated apostrophe into description ("O rose, thou art sick," is an intensified way of describing the rose as sick), but what the lyric or a lyrical reading (to use de Man's term) does is to translate description into apostrophe and anthropomorphism. In pairing "Correspondances" and "Obsession," de Man suggests that the mysterious declaratives of "Correspondances" give way to the specular totalization of "Obsession": "La nature est un temple" through which man passes, is transformed into: "Grands bois, vous m'effrayez comme des cathédrales;" which sets speaker and natural object in an intersubjective relationship.

In these late essays, de Man takes a considerable interest in apostrophe and some interest in other critics' inclination to avoid and ignore it. In "Hypogram and Inscription: Michael Riffaterre's Poetics of Reading" he sees as

---

2. For discussion see chapter 8, "Poetics of the Lyric," in my *Structuralist Poetics* (Ithaca: Cornell University Press, 1975).

3. See my "Changes in the Study of the Lyric," in *Lyric Poetry: Beyond New Criticism*, ed. P. Parker and C. Hošek (Ithaca: Cornell University Press, 1985).

4. *Anatomy of Criticism* (Princeton: Princeton University Press, 1957), 249–50.

5. "Apostrophe," in *The Pursuit of Signs* (Ithaca: Cornell University Press, 1981).

symptomatic Riffaterre's dismissal of the apostrophe that introduces and frames the Hugo poem under discussion: "J'aime le carillon de tes cités antiques,/O vieux pays. . . ." Riffaterre calls this address "personification" and dismisses it from his commentary by stressing the banality of describing the inanimate in animate terms. "Now it is certainly beyond question," de Man writes, with that assurance with which he generally states some proposition that might seem to need demonstration, "that the figure of address is recurrent in lyric poetry, to the point of constituting the generic definition of, at the very least, the ode (which can, in its turn, be seen as paradigmatic for poetry in general). And that therefore it occurs, like all figures, in the guise of a cliché or a convention is equally certain. None of this would allow one to discard or to ignore it as the main generative force that produces the poem in its entirety."[6]

Hugo's "Ecrit sur la vitre d'une fenêtre flamande," he notes, "is a declaration of love addressed to something or someone, staged as an address of one subject to another in a je-tu situation which can hardly be called descriptive." De Man also insists in these essays on a figure linked with apostrophe: prosopopoeia, "the master trope of poetic discourse," the giving of face or voice to entities. The status of prosopopoeia and its relation to anthropomorphism is a crucial problem in de Man's conception of the lyric, and we shall return to it later. In the case of Hugo's poem, he continues, "The apostrophe, the address (O vieux pays . . .) frames the description it makes possible. It is indeed a prosopopoeia, giving a face to two entities, "l'heure" and "l'esprit," which are most certainly deprived of any literal face. Yet by the end of the poem it is possible to identify without fail the *je* and the *tu* of line 1 [J'aime le carillon de tes cités antiques] as being mind and time. The figuration occurs by way of this address."[7] The lyric characteristically depends on these figures of apostrophe and prosopopoeia, which associate lyric with voice and, by presuming and foregrounding I-you relations, generate anthropomorphism, "a conceit by which human consciousness is projected or transferred into the natural world" (p. 89). "Anthropomorphism," de Man writes,

> involves not just a trope but an identification on the level of substance. It takes one entity for another and thus implies the constitution of specific entities prior to their confusion, the *taking* of something for something else that can then be assumed to be *given*. Anthropomorphism freezes the infinite chain of tropological transformations and propositions into one single assertion or essence. . . . [241]

In reading "Obsession" as a translation of "Correspondances" into lyric intelligibility, de Man focuses on the apostrophes' I-you structure—the

---

6. "Hypogram and Inscription: Michael Riffaterre's Poetics of Reading," *Diacritics* 11:4 (Winter 1981), 32.
7. Idem. De Man writes that the *je* and *tu* can be identified "as time and mind." I have corrected this to "mind and time."

speaker addresses in turn the woods, the ocean, and the night—which con-
tributes to setting up relations of commensurability and specularity between
subject and object, and on the accompanying prosopopoeia, the attribution of
voice to the woods, for instance. The surrealistic speech of live columns in
"Correspondances" is naturalized in "Obsession" into the frightening but
natural roar of the wind among the trees:

> Grands bois, vous m'effrayez comme des cathédrales;
> Vous hurlez comme l'orgue; et dans nos coeurs maudits,
> Chambres d'éternel deuil où vibrent de vieux râles,
> Répondent les échos de vos *De profondis*.

"The final attribution of speech to the woods (*vos* De profondis) appears so
natural," writes de Man, "that it takes an effort to notice that anthropomorphism is involved" (256). While "Correspondances" asserts a series of equiv-
alences without situating them in relation to a human subject, "Obsession"
sets up a relation between inside and outside such that qualities, like echoes,
can be passed back and forth, and poses the question of whether patterns are
projected from outside to inside ("tes bonds et tes tumultes,/Mon esprit les
retrouve en lui") or from inside to outside ("Mais les ténèbres sont elles-
mêmes des toiles/Où vivent, jaillissent de mon oeil pars milliers,/Des êtres
disparus aux regards familiers"). De Man notes that the relationship between
"Correspondances" and "Obsession" can be historicized as Classical versus
Romantic (terms, he writes, that are "rather crude metaphors for figural patterns rather than historical events or acts") [254]. He sums up as follows:

> What we call the lyric, the instance of represented voice, conveniently spells
> out the rhetorical and thematic characteristics that make it the paradigm of a
> complementary relationship between grammar, trope, and theme. The set of
> characteristics includes the various structures and moments we encountered
> along the way [in the interpretation of "Obsession"]: specular symmetry
> along an axis of assertion and negation (to which correspond the generic mir-
> ror images of the ode, as celebration, and the elegy, as mourning), the gram-
> matical transformation of the declarative into the vocative modes of ques-
> tion, exclamation, address, hypothesis, etc., the tropological transformation
> of analogy into apostrophe, or the equivalent, more general transforma-
> tion . . . of trope into anthropomorphism. The lyric is not a genre, but one
> name among several to designate the defensive motion of understanding, the
> possibility of a future hermeneutics. From this point of view, there is no sig-
> nificant difference between one generic term and another: all have the same
> apparently intentional and temporal function. [261]

This last sentence is mysterious: why "*apparently* intentional"? The suggestion is that all genres are ways of convincing ourselves not only that language is meaningful, that it will give rise to an intuition or understanding,
but that this is an understanding of the world. The lyric seems to consist of

patterns of anthropomorphism and naturalization that guarantee the intelligibility of tropes. "Figural gestures—metaphor, apostrophe, prosopopoeia—are stabilized into a presentation of the naturalness of the human."[8] De Man goes on to observe that "Generic terms such as 'lyric' (or its various subspecies, 'ode,' 'idyll,' or 'elegy') as well as pseudo-historical period terms such as 'romanticism' or 'classicism' are always terms of resistance and nostalgia, at the furthest remove from the materiality of actual history" (262).

One problem that arises is this: we can understand perfectly well the notion of generic categories as modes of understanding and naturalization. Someone taking this view can argue that no text really "is" a lyric but that, as de Man puts it, these are merely nostalgic categories for classifying and mastering texts. Genres are ethical and aesthetic defenses against language. But at certain moments de Man apparently wants there to be lyrics, wants to call "Obsession" a lyric. "No lyric," he writes, "can be read lyrically, nor can the object of a lyrical reading be itself a lyric" (254). This puzzling statement at the very least assumes that there are such things as lyrics. "Correspondances" is not a lyric, for it is the object of that lyrical reading called "Obsession" (and the other translations into lyric intelligibility that make up the tradition of interpretation of this much read poem). "Obsession," a lyric, cannot be read lyrically: it cannot be translated into lyric intelligibility, both because it does not need or provoke a defensive reading-motion (it is already itself such a translation) and perhaps also because a true "reading," in another sense de Man often gives the word, would be a deconstruction or an identification of tropes—a prosaic reading rather than a lyricizing account of man and nature.[9]

The play of both "lyric" and "reading" here can be seen as instances of the "persistent dismantling or inversion of each formulation or concept" that William Ray has recently described as a source of the power of de Man's writing.[10] Terms or categories to which one gives weight prove to have been used elsewhere with a contrary valorization or in a quite different sense which nevertheless seems systematic rather than accidental. One might say that apodictic statements which prove not precisely compatible take the place, in de Man's writings, of Derrida's neologisms, his nonconcepts, and his typographical structures or devices. De Man's play consists of the slippage of terms in weighty assertions that resist reconciliation.

---

8. Cynthia Chase, *Decomposing Figures: Rhetorical Readings in the Romantic Tradition* (Baltimore: Johns Hopkins University Press, 1986), chapter 4.

9. In "Hypogram and Inscription" de Man makes glancing reference to "Correspondances" in terms which he would later call a lyrical reading but which he here identifies as pertaining "to the canonical '*idée reçue*' of the poem, not to the poem *read*" (35 n, my italics). A discussion of the term *reading* would not only have to explicate this sense of *reading* (what de Man and a few others do) and its quite different sense in *lyrical reading*, but also to decide what to call what critics have generally done to lyrics such as "Obsession" when they interpret them (since "no lyric can be read lyrically").

10. William Ray, *Literary Meaning* (Oxford: Blackwell, 1984), 191.

If "lyric" is not just a defensive reading strategy for mastering language but a particular sort of text, one wants to know which of the poems de Man alludes to are lyrics and which are not; but except for this pair, he does not tell us, and when one attempts to extrapolate by identifying as lyrics poems centrally employing apostrophe, prosopopoeia, and anthropomorphism, one encounters the difficulty I mentioned earlier: the ambiguous status of prosopopoeia. On the one hand, "prosopopoeia as positing voice or face by means of language" (81) seems the basis of anthropomorphism, and is given generic associations: "prosopopoeia, the master trope of poetic discourse." "Prosopopoeia is the trope of autobiography, by which one's name . . . is made as intelligible and memorable as a face" (76). Yet in "Wordsworth and the Victorians" de Man can be interpreted as distinguishing prosopopoeia from anthropomorphism: emphasizing that the former is "an active verbal deed, a *claim* . . . not given in the nature of things" while the latter, as he says in "Anthropomorphism and Trope," is "an identification on the level of substance, the *taking* of something for something else that can then be assumed to be *given*" (241). Rather than being a defining constituent of lyric or lyrics, then, prosopopoeia gets associated with an originary catachresis or the point at which what de Man calls in "Shelley Disfigured" "the senseless power of positional language" (117) *posits* trope—an impossible but necessary moment. Prosopopoeia would then be precisely what gets lyrically misread in a lyrical reading or a lyric.[11]

One further statement in "Anthropomorphism and Trope" suggests a line to be pursued in asking what a lyric is. De Man writes, "The lyric depends entirely for its existence on the denial of phenomenality as the surest means to recover what it denies" (259). He is discussing the fact that the sensory richness of "Correspondances" is replaced in "Obsession" by an absence of sensory representation—"je cherche le vide, le noir, et le nu," for example, or simply "les ténèbres," pure darkness—but that at this very moment the poem reasserts the possibility, even ineluctability of representation:

> Mais les ténèbres sont elles mêmes des toiles
> Oú vivent, jaillissant de mon oeil par milliers,
> Des êtres disparus aux regards familiers.

The suggestion that "the lyric depends entirely for its existence on the denial of phenomenality as the surest means to recover what it denies" is connected with the claim at the beginning of "Lyrical Voice in Contemporary Theory" that "The principle of intelligibility, in lyric poetry, depends on the phenomenalization of the poetic voice."[12] De Man goes on to argue that

---

11. For discussion, see Chase, "Giving a Face to a Name."

12. "Lyrical Voice in Contemporary Theory," in *Lyric Poetry: Beyond New Criticism*, ed. P. Parker & C. Hošek, 55. This combines sections of "Hypogram and Inscription" and the Introduction to H. R. Jauss, *Toward an Aesthetic of Reception* (Minneapolis: U. of Minnesota Press, 1982).

Riffaterre and Hans Robert Jauss, in different ways, repress figural and literal aspects of the signifier in order to make poetic voice "coincide with the phenomenality of its own discourse." The phenomenalization or actualization of voice can be shown to be challenged, however, both in the practice of their reading and in the theory that sustains it. "The consequences for a theory of the lyric," de Man writes, "and, more generally, for the relationship between genre and figure are far-reaching but too complex for summary exposition." Exposition is left to others, while he offers exemplification in two readings "in which the phenomenality of the form is critically examined in terms of figural substitutions or material inscriptions."

Phenomenality is the key term here. To gloss it one might say that the idea of perception presumes a phenomenal world—phenomena that are *given* to perception (as opposed to an imposition or positing of forms). De Man argues, by way of readings of Hegel, Hugo, and others, that phenomenality is the product of figuration; he argues for what he calls in *The Rhetoric of Romanticism* "the dependence of any perception . . . on the totalizing power of language" (91). (To take this line is to emphasize language as act over language as representation.)

However, the notion of the phenomenality of language—that there is given to perception a body of sensible signifiers which stand in a representational relation to conceptual signifieds that are given to the understanding— is crucial to the notion of reliable cognition. And one function of the aesthetic and of texts placed in the category of the aesthetic has been to link the sensuous and the conceptual in a phenomenal relation modeled on the apparent phenomenality of language and its signifying process. Of Hugo's "Ecrit sur la vitre d'une fenêtre flamande" de Man writes, "the phenomenal and sensory properties of the signifier [here the "carillon"] have to serve as guarantors for the certain existence of the signified and, ultimately, of the referent," time.[13] Cynthia Chase explains: "the process of signification, which has a material element, is made to serve as an example and a guarantee of the phenomenality of experience. But this belies the arbitrary nature of the link between signifier and signified, the sign's independence of sensory determinations; the *materiality* rather than the phenomenality of the sign. In fact, the process of signification can exemplify phenomenal experience only by means of a figuration."[14]

De Man's most accessible explanation of the supposed phenomenality of language comes in the argument that Saussure's work on anagrams, which reveals potentially endless patterns that might or might not signify, shows that to perceive the signifier at all is to confer on some patterns but not others the status of meaningful articulations. The impossibility of determining

---

13. "Hypogram and Inscription," 33.
14. Chase, *Decomposing Figures*, chap. 4.

whether such patterns signify or not, are encoded or not, amounts to "the undoing of the phenomenality of language"—that is, the undoing of the assumption that linguistic structures are given as perceivable and intelligible. He writes, "We would then have witnessed, in effect, the undoing of the phenomenality of language, which always entails (since the phenomenal and noumenal are binary poles within the same system) the undoing of cognition and its replacement by the uncontrollable power of the letter as inscription."[15]

Anagrams, a random occurrence of syllables read or misread as a key word, provide a model of language that is germane to the question of the lyric. What de Man calls the materiality of language (or of "actual history" in a passage cited earlier) is, as Chase put its, "what is prior to the figuration that give the text its phenomenal status," but which, as de Man insists, "cannot be isolated 'as such,' as a 'moment,' as an origin."[16] However, a pairing, such as "Correspondances" and "Obsession," which lets one think about figural transformations and anthropomorphisms enables one to treat certain difficulties, unintelligibilities, as what has been transformed.

But this sort of pairing poses a problem—a problem about reading lyrics. De Man's account of the lyric and lyrical reading makes "Obsession" a lyric and a lyrical reading of "Correspondances"—a translation into intelligibility, anthropomorphism, phenomenality. But that tempts one to say, reciprocally, that "Correspondances" demystifies "Obsession." De Man's analysis of the pair suggests that in reading lyrics we should seek out the infratext that exposes the lyrical translations accomplished by lyrics, but he emphatically denies that "Correspondances" can be taken as a reading of "Obsession." "No symmetrical reversal of this lyrical reading-motion is conceivable" (261).

Of course, reversal is not just conceivable but seductive, if not irresistible. Readers of "Anthropomorphism and Trope in the Lyric" will be led to seek, for every lyric, a nonlyrical infratext—whether another text or a reconstruction—that demysties it, exposes it as anthropomorphism. De Man's essay itself functions in precisely the way he denies is conceivable; by arguing that "Correspondances" is not a lyric but contains and implies all the possibilities of lyric, he makes it in effect, if not in principle, a reading of lyric: an exposition of its constitutive conditions.

Why does de Man emphatically deny this course, this possibility? In part to expose it as a recuperative strategy of understanding. To take the unintelligibility of "Correspondances" as demystification would be precisely to recuperate it: to make it no longer a materiality on which meaning is imposed by lyrical translation but a further instance of meaningfulness. Warn-

---

15. "Hypogram and Inscription," 24–25.
16. Chase, op. cit.

ing ourselves against this course, however, will not forestall it, and we seem to be left in a situation where de Man's writings will lead us to read lyrics in precisely the way he tells us not to.

However, uncomfortable or inappropriate this condition, it seems a general consequence of de Man's work. For example, though his writings focus on what resists or disrupts the hermeneutic process and repeatedly oppose an understanding which overcomes textual difficulties so as to hear in the text what it is thought to say, this is the only way to understand or interpret de Man. One can only make sense of his writings if one already has a sense of what they must be saying and can allow for the slippage of concepts, working to get over or around the puzzling valuations, the startling assertions, the apparently incompatible claims. To learn from his writings, one must read him in precisely the ways he warns us against, and the same may well prove true for reading lyrics. If we try to avoid performing lyrical readings on lyrics—and he tells us lyrics cannot be read lyrically—we will seek or reconstruct demystificatory infratexts, reversing the lyrical reading-motion in a way he says is inconceivable.

CORNELL UNIVERSITY

MICHAEL RIFFATERRE

Prosopopeia

Larvatus prodeo.

—Descartes

In his seminal discussion of Nietzsche's *On Truth and Lie*, Paul de Man analyzes the lyric in terms which match almost exactly the characteristics of the figure called prosopopeia:

> What we call the lyric, the instance of represented voice . . . includes . . . the grammatical transformation of the declarative into the vocative modes of question, exclamation, address, hypothesis, etc., the tropological transformation of analogy into apostrophe or the equivalent, more general . . . transformation of trope into anthropomorphism.[1]

The present essay addresses the problem of the relationship between prosopopeia which is suppositional in its figural essence and two declarative modes, the descriptive and the narrative. If the lyric transforms trope into anthropomorphism, does *reading* the lyric reverse the process? can there be meaning in prosopopeia without a narrative or descriptive intertext? can prosopopeia generate a narrative?

Fontanier, who wrote in 1821 what probably is the most thought out and systematic taxonomy of tropes and figures, offers this definition:

> Prosopopeia, that must not be confused with personification, apostrophe or dialogism, which however do almost always occur with it, consists in staging, as it were, absent, dead, supernatural or even inanimate beings. These are made to act, speak, answer as is our wont. At the very least these beings can be made into confidants, witnesses, accusers, avengers, judges, etc.[2]

Fontanier later specifies that apostrophe and dialogism can be removed

---

1. *The Rhetoric of Romanticism.* (New York: Columbia University Press, 1984) (hereinafter: *Rhetoric*), 261. Cf. de Man, *Allegories of Reading* (New Haven: Yale University Press, 1979) (hereinafter: *Allegories*) 110–18.

2. Pierre Fontanier, *Les Figures du discours*, Gérard Genette ed. (Paris: Flammarion, 1968), 404 ff. Fontanier's definition admirably summarizes Quintilian's 9.2.31, and the Greek and Latin rhetorical tradition; see Heinrich Lausberg, *Handbuch der literarischen Rhetorik* (Munich: Heuber 1960) on *fictio personae*, esp. paragraphs 828–29.

without altering prosopopeia (except that it might become less striking or lively as a result). These distinctions are essential, for they make it clear that no real personification need take place, that would entail a descriptive realism. At any rate, it is not necessary that the fictitious embodiment of the animated entity be physical enough to demand verisimilitude, or some rationalization that, for instance, would explain it as a supernatural vision. Thus Malherbe's "Prosopopée d'Ostende" is very typical, in which that besieged city speaks its mournful dirge without having been apostrophized,[3] and without ceasing to be a city, without being endowed with a human body.

The figure in fact only presupposes animation and this presupposition is inferred from a mock hypothesis. Far from inviting visualization, let alone sensory perception, prosopopeia in most cases merely lends a voice to a voiceless always, or now silent, entity by a mere convention: "voice" says De Man, "assumes mouth, eye, and finally face, a chain that is manifest in the etymology of the trope's name, *prosopon poiein*, to confer a mask or a face (*prosopon*)."[4]

It is indeed no more than a mask put on something that may not even have a face. The mask's simplicity gives free play to the viewer's imagination. All the mask does is put the reader in a specific interpretive mood, very much as does the donning of a comic or tragic mask in Greek and Roman plays. No mimesis, no restriction justified by referentiality may interfere with the reader's constructs on so simple and so abstract a given. If there remains any mimetic component, it must be secondary, and its normal functioning as representation must be reoriented by the given.

Figural reading derives from such abstract premises with the rigor of a logical deduction. The better to follow that logic, I now return to a poem by Victor Hugo, an allegory of Time, that I analyzed a few years ago as an instance of poetic representation. I had attempted to show that whatever mimesis was at work in it had nothing to do with referentiality. Instead of having reality for its authority, its truth or its hold on readers' interpretation resulted from a verbal overdetermination, from the fact that what the poem said was recognizable as referring to familiar stereotypes. These hermeneutic models were regulated by the combined structures of grammar, themes and descriptive systems. I rested happily on my conclusions, sure that I had covered all angles, until Paul de Man jolted me out of my complacency. He showed that I had forgotten the prosopopeia that introduces the poem and must slant uniformly all its subsequent functions. I shall therefore start all over, from my blindness through his insight.[5]

---

3. I insist on this because Jonathan Culler, commenting on de Man, especially on his treatment of the lyric, titles his argument *Apostrophe,* and rightly underscores the role of the vocative in that genre (*The Pursuit of Signs*, Ithaca: Cornell U. Press, 1981, 135–54), without, however, demonstrating that apostrophe is essential to animation. His last and best example in fact is pure animation (153–54).

4. *Rhetoric,* 77–78.

5. Paul de Man, "Hypogram and Inscription: Michael Riffaterre's Poetics of Reading." *Diacritics* 11 (Winter 1981), 17–35.

The poem refers to Hugo's memories of a tour through Flanders, during which he enjoyed a carillon preluding the chiming of the hour. These musical impressions are now translated into a vision of the personified Hour dancing to the tune. This waking dream contrasts with the lethargy of the town. Hugo opposes the latter (time wasted) to his consciousness (time well spent). He translates the sound of time into the esthetically valorized visual code of personification, thus arresting the flight of time in a moment of beauty.

Ecrit sur la vitre d'une fenêtre flamande

J'aime le carillon de tes cités antiques,
O vieux pays gardien de tes moeurs domestiques,
Noble Flandre, où le Nord se réchauffe engourdi
Au soleil de Castille et s'accouple au Midi!
Le carillon, c'est l'heure inattendue et folle,
Que l'oeil croit voir, vêtue en danseuse espagnole,
Apparaître soudain par le trou vif et clair
Que ferait en s'ouvrant une porte de l'air.
Elle vient, secouant sur les toits léthargiques
Son tablier d'argent plein de notes magiques,
Réveillant sans pitié les dormeurs ennuyeux . . .

Written on the Pane of a Flemish Window

I love the carillon of your ancient towns, o old land, keeper of your domestic customs. O noble Flanders, where the benumbed North warms itself in the sun of Castille and mates with the South! The carillon is the unexpected and mad hour that the eye thinks it sees, dressed as a Spanish dancer, appearing suddenly through the keen, bright hole made by a door of air as it opens. She comes, shaking over the lethargic rooftops her silver apron, full of magical notes, pitilessly waking the wearisome sleepers, taking little jumps, like a merry bird, quivering like a spear trembling in its target. By a fragile stairway of invisible crystal, alarmed and dancing, she descends from the heavens. And as she goes and comes and climbs up and down again, the mind, that watchman made of ears and eyes, hears her resonant foot wandering from step to step.

De Man denies that the poem should be called descriptive, or that its significance is centered on the carillon, because its description, being entirely subordinated to a prosopopeia framed by the address, only "gives face" to two faceless entities: *je,* that stands for consciousness or the mind, and the addressee, figuratively represented by the bells, the Hour, that is to say, Time.

Par un frêle escalier de cristal invisible,
Effarée et dansante, elle descend des cieux;
Et l'esprit, ce veilleur fait d'oreilles et d'yeux,
Tandis qu'elle va, vient, monte et descend encore,
Entend de marche en marche errer son pied sonore!

What is represented is not *carillon*, but *j'aime le carillon*, not an entity but "a rapport between concepts said to be structured like a sense perception," a relationship between a sensory signifier (the ringing) and a nonsensory signified (the passage of time)—nonsensory because only clocks lend phenomenality to time: the invisible crystal of the scale the melodious Hour plays confirms this transfer of a concept into sensory terms. "The senses become the signs of the mind as the sound of the bells is the sign of time, because time and mind are linked as in the embrace of a couple" (33). The convention of prosopopeia thus constitutes a new sign where mind is the signifier and time the signified: hence the allegory of cognition, the putting of a second mask on the first one, a prosopopeia of prosopopeia—*l'esprit, ce veilleur fait d'oreilles et d'yeux*, "the visual shape of something that has no sensory existence: a hallucination" (34). "The confusion and unification of the various sensory faculties" evoked in Baudelaire's 'Correspondances' "is achieved by the initial apostrophe" (35).

Finally, authority is given to the figure (that is, it can no longer be suspect of gratuitousness) by the materiality of yet another crystal, that of the window, now made visible by the inscription: "every detail as well as every general proposition in the text is fantastic except for the assertion, in the title, that it is *écrit*" (35). This materiality, this *there* and *then* of memory, or *here* and *now* of the act of reading, is the "materiality of an inscription. Description . . . was a device to conceal inscription."

In short, prosopopeia proposes a new sign for "consciousness of time." Its grammaticality (the arbitrarily established relevancy of signifier to signified) is valid only within the text's idiolect. The framing of that text is indicated by the initial apostrophe. The text itself unfolds by the semiotic transformation of the figural given into a description. *Ecrit* integrates all this back into the actual experience of a persona (a reassuring reference to a reality outside words).

Figural reading thus distinguishes three factors, or functions, in the figure. It generates a significance, represents the author, and maps out a text within the text. Let us now analyze the new "coinage," the figure as one signifying complex, the figural sign.

The first and preeeminent function of the figural sign is that it is an index of convention. As such, it testifies to its literariness, and proclaims the text that it generates to be an experiment, a conscious substitute for a recognizable equivalent in accepted usage, in the sociolect. As an index of convention, it also points to the author's intention, a first, very general way of asserting the self, of putting its mark on the external world. However, the reason that prosopopeia properly ushers in the lyric is that it is suppositive. The animation it implies in its object, overtly or not, directly or as a consequence of an initial address, is always a natural impossibility. The mimesis of a natural impossibility can be a sign of the fantastic or of the supernatural, or it can be a formal or ludic supposition, a mock hypothesis or, better, the representation of a hypothesis, a figure of figurality itself. Prosopopeia is the latter, which enables it to openly represent the truth through a fiction. Its artificiality therefore is very different from that of the apostrophe, even though these two figures are linked. The suppositional mode is final and contains its whole interpretation from the very start. The vocative, however, leaves the reader uncertain whether the animation it presupposes is a form unto itself or a mimetic one, whether it is conventional both as a generic index and as an index of content, or whether it is conventional only as genre but is justified by an actual hidden life of the addressee, for which a fantastic explanation or a supernatural reason exists, pantheism for instance (in which case the conventional form tends to be erased).[6] Clearly, apostrophe in Hugo's poem belongs to the purely conventional (from Schiller on, the voice of bells is metaphorical). It is also liminal, addressing as it does the land of carillons, rather than the carillon itself or the significance it stands for. Since prosopopeia tends to shed apostrophe in the novel, apostrophe seems to be more the marker of certain genres within the lyric, like the ode or the elegy, than a marker of the lyric itself. Apostrophe is conventional here because it is subordinated to the postulate, because it depends on the suppositive, and this will be true of every textual component derived from the figural given.

I now come to the inscription Paul de Man so perceptively digs out from under the description. Inscription, as he points out, refers to the real. Even the most unreal play of postulates presupposes a subject, and one more real than those fiction produces in novels. For fiction to exist, it must expel its author out onto the margin of origins, whereas hypothesis needs to keep its proponent within its own enunciation as the postulating subject. The persona that puts the mask on things (the grammatical subject of the verb of perception introducing the animated object, or the implied viewpoint from which the object appears animated), this persona cannot therefore be distinguished from the author (this being the one instance in literature where the intentional fallacy does not apply); consequently, any metonymic or synecdochic periphrasis substituted for the subject (like the title in Hugo's poem) is the inscription of the self in the text—the very definition of the lyric.

If, however, the writing self is thus objectified, writing is but the means of expressing this objectification, and the text is but the recording of that significance. Somehow, the end to which these means are used must be found inscribed as well. It cannot be just the animating convention, since that too is still a means. The answer must be in the nature of the lyric, which *is* the end here pursued, in the I-Thou relationship to the universe. This relationship is indeed expressed by *j'aime le carillon*, but if this were its only expression, there would be nothing in such an empirical assertion that the reader would not be free to find gratuitous, an idiosyncrasy lacking in general human interest. He would only assent if there were a sociolectic consensus putting carillons in the class of the picturesque (which of course is a fact, but hardly a stable literary factor). In order for the prosopopeia to be indeed one sign of which mind and time are the two facets, mind must conquer time or be suffused with the feeling of it. They must have something in common, and some-

---

6. See Culler, *Pursuit*, 140.

thing that language has recorded and that will therefore be the true authority of figural significance. Paul de Man thought it might be an intertextual reference to a literary commonplace—the writing of poems, maxims, or epigrams on windowpanes exemplified by various poems of Swift. This intertext is unlikely because it belongs in another language, and it does not involve subject and object.

A better answer is provided by stricter obedience to de Man's own model, for there is another intertext, a French one, that illustrates a more general principle, de Man's second major theoretical contribution to our understanding of prosopopeia as *the* lyric figure. De Man posits a corollary to prosopopeia: the address calls for a reply of the addressee, the gaze that perceives animation invites gazing back from the animated object to the subject daydreaming a Narcissistic reflection of itself in things. This corollary is chiasmus, the transfer or crisscrossing exchange between subject and object, a most striking example of which de Man finds in Milton's epitaph of Shakespeare: the living, overwhelmed by the voice from the grave, by Shakespeare's ever living verse, his true monument, are literally petrified (". . . thou our fancy of itself bereaving/Dost make us Marble with too much conceiving"). Chiasmus, the symmetrical structure of prosopopeia, entails that, by making the dead speak, the living are struck dumb—they too become the monument.[7] Prosopopeia thus stakes out a figural space for the chiasmic interpretation: either the subject will take over the object, or it will be penetrated by the object.

This fusion is the lyric, and the stereotype that makes its inscription possible here refers to the one windowpane famous in the French sociolect for having been engraved with a poem. "Ecrit sur une fenêtre flamande" is a variant of the celebrated inscribed window of the royal chateau at Chambord. Among the many to exploit the motif and infer a moral from it, Chateaubriand put it best: "Francis I, well aware of the vanity of his pleasures, had written with a diamond these two lines on a windowpane: Woman often changes. Foolish he who trusts her." That Hugo's allusion was intentional goes without saying: we know that, while touring Chambord, he took away a splinter from the supposed window. And later, out of the royal dictum he composed a cynical song about women's fickleness in *Le Roi s'amuse* (1832), which Verdi was to immortalize in *Rigoletto* as "La donna è mobile."

The burgeoning mythology about the Chambord window is the linguistic authority for the meaning of the Flemish window, and for the chiasmus effect. The myth itself and its significance stem from an older cliché: a windowpane is an appropriate place to inscribe a thought about fickleness, for glass's fragility has symbolized the whims of fate ever since Horace. A Corneille quotation schoolchildren have had to recite for centuries says that happiness is unstable: "Just as it has the brilliancy of glass, it also has its fragility." Quoth Chateaubriand: "where is the windowpane now?"[8]

---

7. *Rhetoric*, 67–81, esp. 77–78; cf. 89, 257, 260–61; *Allegories*, 44 ff, 61, 77, 107–13, etc.
8. Chateaubriand, *Vie de Rancé* (1844), ed., F. Letessier (Paris: Didier, 1955), book 2, 107.

Hence the applicability to our prosopopeia: the theme actualizes the *je-tu* exchange pattern. Time translated into the female persona of the Hour, the spectator under her spell and writing about it on glass, make woman's fickleness into a metaphor of mutability. The writer inscribing himself on a medium specialized for fate's vagaries incarnates mutability as well, projecting his own fleetingness onto fleet-footed Time.

Clearly, figural meaning does not depend on sensory perception, referentiality or a descriptive grammar. If anything, these raise a momentary obstacle and make the reader's decoding arduous. But in doing so, they make his final assent to the poem's lesson all the more compelling. Fontanier's cautionary remark that prosopopeia must not be confused with personification is well-taken. For there is no way we can relate the dancer's portrayal, scanty as it is, and Time. While we may find a term for term relationship between time described as decay, impending death, itself running out, and the traditional personification of Time as a winged graybeard carrying a scythe and an hourglass, no such translation is conceivable here because the poem's significance is not based on the mutual substitutability of two descriptive systems or fragments of such systems, as would be the case with metaphor and metonymy. It is based on the grammar that translates the chiasmus structure into language. It is based on the predication linking the representations of the subject (the title) and of the object (the female personifying the Hour). This predication does not involve the two pictures and their separate meanings directly (the first one being left to our own deductions anyway), but rather the significance (mutability) whereby the identical predication had displaced these meanings into another story—the intertext in which the two pictures are one (the Chambord story) and symbolic in their oneness. Predication and the interchange it permits, the absorption of the object by the subject or vice versa, is therefore the interpretant (in the triadic relationship that founds semiosis) if the sign generating that interpretant is a figure instead of being a word or a phrase.[9] In such cases where the interpretant is intertextual in nature, the figure owes its authority either to the sociolect (as in Hugo's poem), or to another text.

Maximal inscription, coming as close as it will ever be to the totalization towards which all literature tends, takes place when the interpretant authorizing the predication is already a text of the object, when the object to be absorbed or dominated by the subject is not an external world of things, but an external world of words. This is precisely the case when the object inscribes a writer. Such is the case, as I will try to show, for Proust, with whom both subject and object are the same textual entity. And such is the case with Mallarmé's "Tombeau de Verlaine" that I single out for no other reason than that de Man especially focussed on two aspects of the lyric, and that the sonnet is relevant to both. It is related to the epitaph, a genre identifiable with prosopopeia, and, on

---

9. On the integration of figurality and semiotics, de Man's "Semiology and Rhetoric," *Allegories*, 3–19, esp. 8–9; cf. my paper on "The Interpretant in Literary Semiotics," *American Journal of Semiotics* 3 (1985).

the other hand, to Mallarmean obscurity, which so destroyed representation that it tempted Hugo Friedrich's followers and the "Konstanz School" to define modernity in the lyric as a loss of the object.[10]

Paul de Man has no trouble demonstrating that mimetic absurdity does not remove the presupposition of reality: as the interpretation of each successive phrase deconstructs the previous one, the text gives rise to mutually incompatible metaphors, all of them, however, contributing their disparate stones to the Verlaine monument. Together they form a uniquely Mallarmean idiolect. They therefore *in*scribe the writer's self in the text and *de*scribe the object, Verlaine's work, in conformity with the rule of the genre. An epitaph, or as here, a memorial poem erected as a verbal cenotaph, must be built on the interpretation and the praise of the works that make the dead poet immortal. Consider the first line: "Le noir roc courroucé que la bise le roule" [The black rock angered at being rolled about by the north wind.]

The rock (a typically Mallarmean word) of course is Verlaine's tombstone. While it is hard to believe that it could be driven about by the wind, there are passages in Mallarmé's where a rock is equated with a black cloud (a not unfamiliar oxymoron, or even adynaton, for which Magritte's boulders levitating above earth provide visual analogs). There follows in the second stanza a bodily ascension of the dead Verlaine, as befits a Christian poet (since Mallarmé thought *Sagesse* Verlaine's most important work, he could legitimately suggest that Verlaine meant his life to be an *Imitatio Christi*). Moreover, the rock can also evoke the hulking shape of the forlorn drunkard that Verlaine had been in his life of the flesh. In all the preceding, de Man concludes, "the poem uses a representational poetics that remains fundamentally mimetic throughout."

My first point is that while de Man may be entirely correct in this linear reading of successive interpretations of *roc*, his insistence on an ontological priority of reality prevents him from explaining why each symbol has to take the circuitous path of absurdity. My second point is that a figural reading strictly in accordance with his own principles solves the problem. All it takes is to recognize that, rather than metaphor, prosopopeia is at work here, as de Man himself has shown should be the case in an epitaph.

And so it is: the inanimate rock is angry in the first line. In the second tercet, a passer-by (the stereotyped silent role in epitaphs) is looking for Verlaine, and the familiar voice from the grave replies he is hidden in the grass, where, as a stone, he ended his rolling. This of course implies that the object of the I-Thou predication must be somehow embedded in the discourse of the subject, in Mallarmé's praise of his object, and this praise, like pattern poems of the metaphysical poets, must assume the shape of Verlaine's monument.

It does: Mallarmé's first line is a variation on a hypogram, the proverb

10. *Rhetoric*, 67–81; and "Lyric and Modernity," *Blindness and Insight*, 2nd revised ed. (Minneapolis: University of Minnesota Press, 1983), 166–86, esp. 174 ff.

Pierre qui roule n'amasse pas mousse [a rolling stone gathers no moss], popular wisdom's indictment of rootless, aimless people, of whom the artist as a fallen angel is one. The popular image of Verlaine is just that, and the first tercet indeed calls him a tramp (*vagabond*)—a word of which the adage is evidently the periphrastic equivalent. The proverb would not be specific enough to match *courroucé que la bise le roule*. This, however, is accounted for by a second hypogram, this time a quotation from the errant poet's "Chanson d'automne", a verse regarded to this day as quintessential Verlaine:

> Et je m'en vais
> Au vent mauvais
>   Qui m'emporte
> Deçà, delà

and there I go pushed around by the mean wind that rolls me now here now there

Every mimetic aberration that made the avatars of the *rock* at once so obscure and so Mallarmean is thus repeating the signal that a Verlaine discourse is now embedded in the subject's. Within the figural frame of suppositive animation, a subtext develops where chiasmus keeps passing the stone from subject to predicate and back—the uniform marking of all pertinent words by the same "stoniness" enacts a sensory presupposition that in fact is no more than an index of the mutual substitutability of these words. While the headstone in *Le Tombeau d'Edgar Poe* is granite, and marble in *Le Tombeau de Charles Baudelaire*, where the absorption of the object by the subject is achieved by other means, the mineral here is a novel one called "wandering" or "Verlaine." However appropriate it may be, this genre-induced petrifaction forces us to give up "stoniness," a seme, which would have been for Mallarmé and Verlaine the same kind of interpretant that "mutability," also a seme shared by the subject and object sememes, is for Hugo and Time. The interpretant here is directly the whole stone, the whole thing, or rather the representation of the thing, a mimesis to which diverse symbolisms are attached. These have nothing to do with "stoniness," but language does habitually associate them with a stone. And the stone is presupposed real, so that a figurative sense can be anchored onto it by catachresis. The praising, mourning subject, the writer of a text halfway between ode and elegy, Mallarmé is the rock because it is his word, one of his clichés. The praised, mourned object is rocky twice over, a rolling stone in the abjection of this life, a stone monument in the glory of eternal life. The predication, therefore (I write a Verlaine monument), has for its interpretant a descriptive and narrative intertext. And the predication is indeed an inscription, the double inscription of two writing entities, but that inscription is realized diegetically.

One constant remains unchanged in these shifts from the suppositive (the significance-carrying predication) to the declarative (the interpretant, and the physical, linguistic actualization of the sonnet's convoluted sign system): the conventional, artificial nature of the figure.

This aspect of it, so obvious in the Mallarmean ungrammaticalities but equally present in Hugo, through the veil of the preexistent convention of the deified Hour, is in the final analysis the carrier of meaning and the reader's hermeneutic guideline. It is the means whereby the figure signifies.

This, I believe, becomes self-evident if we turn to prosopopeia in the novel, to the suppositive obtruding onto the narrative. Proust's *Recherche* will be my text. In it prosopopeias evidence the same double inscription I just outlined in Mallarmé's sonnet, which is only natural: in a novel built as a mimesis of autobiography, the subject and the object are one and the same, or rather one is the writer as self, one the writer as projected or cathected on an external world—but external by convention only.

There are indeed many prosopopeias in Proust, lending a spurious life to inanimate objects, and complete with addresses and apostrophes. In accordance with *La Recherche*'s leitmotif, chiasmus is rationalized in terms of memory. External objects requite the narrator for the desire he long ago invested in them. The inscribed subject is the writer; the object, the inscription of the subject in mnemonic surroundings, the not so silent witnesses of remembered pleasure; and the interpretant is in each instance the description of the locale where the first I-Thou exchange took place.

Two traits characterize prosopopeia in the narrative: it tends to be comical, and it generates subtexts within the text. Comicality is the avatar of the figure's fundamental artifice. Instead of being abstractly suppositive, convention emphasizes mock hypothesis as if the self changed its mask for the Cheshire Cat's smile.

Subtexts develop because prosopopeias repeatedly re-play an initial experience, the story of the self projecting itself onto its environment. Long stretches of narrative may separate these revivals of the lyric, but comical animation each time insures that we remember the preceding instance.

One of the most developed such subtexts grows out of the memory of the *cabinet*, a term I leave untranslated, the better to account for the variety of unrelated meanings this one word calls forth. The triggering incident, the diegetic matrix for the subtext, is the well-known story of the narrator's first masturbation when he was twelve. Through the window of the bathroom where he locked himself up, he can see an expanse of open country that his arousal fills with phantasms, an exemplary expression of the subject invading the object, of the inner taking over the outer. He senses in this climax that he has stopped the flight of time:

> ma pensée exaltée par le plaisir sentait bien qu'elle était *plus vaste, plus puissante que cet univers* que j'apercevais au loin par la fenêtre, dans l'immensité et l'éternité duquel je pensais *en temps habituel avec tristesse* que je n'étais qu'une *parcelle éphémère.*

my mind uplifted by pleasure perceived keenly that it now was vaster, more powerful than this universe which I could see in the distance through the window; whereas normally I would think sadly that I was but an ephemeral particle of its immensity and eternity.

Every reminiscence of this moment will make him enjoy anew this coincidence of pleasure and sensory triumph over the universe. He guesses the identity between the solitary orgasm in which he is his own master, and the writer's inspiration. And every reminiscence will depend on his finding again the same setting, combining overt sexual sublimation, covert scatological association, the same commanding view, and synecdoches that anchor memory (like the detail of orris-root scent used as deodorizer). One could not hope for more decisive inscriptions of the creative artist in a diegetic context.[11]

The night at the Doncières hotel is one such instance. The piece develops, almost metalinguistically, everything that was implicit in its *Contre Sainte-Beuve* hypogram, that is, the writing (even some of its themes) ushered in by the masturbating release, while keeping implicit the act itself. Because the surroundings make sense only as mediators between now and the past, their depiction shifts from objective descriptive to subjectivizing prosopopeia. *Accueillante* [welcoming] would be the descriptive cliché to render the coziness of the bedroom where the narrator's childhood awaits anamnesis.

Prosopopeia derives from that cliché the parody of the royal entrance of a sovereign into his kingdom, with the furniture and appurtenances playing the part of the loyal servants:

J'ouvris une chambre, la double porte se referma derrière moi, la draperie fit entrer un silence sur lequel je me sentis comme une sorte d'enivrante royauté; une cheminée de marbre ornée de cuivres ciselés, dont on aurait eu tort de croire qu'elle ne savait que représenter l'art du Directoire, me faisait du feu, et un petit fauteuil bas sur pieds m'aida à me chauffer aussi confortablement que si j'eusse été assis sur le tapis. Les murs étreignaient la chambre, la séparant du reste du monde. [Pléiade, v. 2, 83.]

I looked into a room; the double doors closed themselves behind me, the hangings let in a silence in which I felt myself invested with a sort of exhilarating royalty; a marble mantelpiece with ornaments of wrought brass—of which one would have been wrong to think that its sole idea was to represent the art of the Directory—offered me a fire, and a little easy chair on short legs helped me to warm myself as comfortably as if I had been sitting on the hearthrug. The

11. *Contre Sainte-Beuve* (Paris: Gallimard, 1954) 63–67. (My emphases). The *Recherche* version that generates the subtext represses the more explicit details (Pléiade ed., vol. 1, 158). Albert Sonnenfeld was the first to spot the connection between onanism and writing, cf. *Kentucky Romance Quarterly* 19, 461–69; see also Philippe Lejeune's penetrating "Ecriture et sexualité," *Europe* 502–03 (1971) 113–43; Serge Doubrovsky, *La Place de la Madeleine* (Paris: Mercure de France 1974), and Joan T. Rosasco's indispensable guidebook through the *Voies de l'imagination proustienne* (Paris: A. G. Nizet 1980).

walls held the room in a close embrace, separating it from the rest of the world.[12]

The hall acts likewise ("I walked down a long gallery which paid me homage successively with all that it had to offer me if I could not sleep") and finally addresses him: "it said to me simply: 'Now you must turn and go back, but, you see, you are at home here' (*tu es chez toi*)." All these cute details actually are but mimetic stepping stones to the climactic appearance of the *cabinet* reborn complete from the forgotten past. It has kept the dried plants whose function, now semiotic, is to embody memory in smell. It still combines safe seclusion and vast visual perspectives, safety in pleasure and the lofty viewpoint that makes sensory perception an exercise in domination: the privy "had hanging from its wall, to scent the occasion on which one had recourse to it, a voluptuous rosary of orris-roots; the doors, if I left them open when I withdrew into this innermost retreat . . . not only allowed my eyes to enjoy the delights of extension after those of concentration, but added further to the pleasure of my solitude, which, while still inviolable, was no longer shut in, the sense of liberty."

The periphrasis around bad smell and its fragrant cover-up, later to become a text-intertext link, unveils the repressed—in this literature beats analysis. The fact that a landscape is made visible from the *cabinet* only to cathect sexual desire is just as apparent here as in *Contre Sainte-Beuve*. But while in the original version this sexuality was expressed by the cliché simile comparing the hills to female breasts, prosopopeia here resists the lure of automatism: the courtyard, a feminine word in French, is amusingly called a *captive*. The noun is like shorthand for a full-fledged personification—perhaps a woman in a Sadian castle, or a harem odalisk, or Albertine herself.

Sensory details are not significant per se, but only as recognizable, visible actualizations of a structure. This structure is descriptive inasmuch as it organizes a locale, but the locale itself is no more than an outline for a possible functional equivalency. Prosopopeia translates it into the actual exchange of functions. Its mediating role is independent of whether it is positively or negatively valorized. The hotel room at Balbec seems the very antithesis of the Doncières room, for it is spatially the point by point negation of the protective womb of Marcel's bedroom at home. But otherwise, the Balbec room is, like the Doncières suite, patterned on the original bower of bliss: it encloses the self and yet provides it with a lofty perch from which it can dominate the world; it has the same props for the play of fantasy; it is but an anteroom to the significant *cabinet*. Dysphoria and euphoria are therefore intertextually related. A revealing sentence says so as clearly as a critic's metalanguage could: "the anxiety and alarm which I felt as I lay outstretched beneath that strange and too

---

12. All translations are from C. K. Scott Moncrieff, *Remembrance of Things Past*, New York: Random House, 1934).

lofty ceiling were but the protest of an affection that survived in me for a ceiling that was familar and low" (vol. 1, 672). The clock's ticking sounds as if it were saying nasty things about Marcel in a language unknown to him. The mirror stops him as if its reflection were a barrier. The orris-root's seduction is replaced with vetiver to which he is allergic, but the reverse version plumbs the depths of repressed motivation just as well: "in that region more intimate than those in which we see and hear, that region in which we test the quality of odours, in the very heart of my inmost self, the smell of vetiver launched its offensive against my last feeble line of trenches, where I stood up with the futile defence of an anxious sniffing" (vol. 1, 667). Chiasmus is equally at work in the negative and in the positive variant. Negative: "the unfamiliar objects which encircled my body, forcing it to set its perceptions on the permanent footing of a vigilant defensive guard, would have kept my sight, my hearing, all my senses in a position as cramped" as that of a prisoner in a dungeon (vol. 1, 666). Positive (a perfect equation of *sight* as perception and *sight* as spectacle): "I raised my gaze which the things in my own room in Paris disturbed no more than did my eyeballs themselves, for they were merely extensions of my organs, an enlargement of myself" (667).

This identification of desire and of perception, and the resulting valorization of the universe perceived, is best exemplified in what might be called the supreme prosopopeia. The figure reaches its climactic significance when the locus of sublimation (from anal gratification to genital, from masturbation to writing), shifts roles with the former little boy who once sat there. The setting becomes the character it once enclosed, and is simultaneously reduced to its pertinent part, to the means for the pertinent function: the window. Formerly a mediator between the enclosed refuge and a world to conquer, between the inner and the outer self, the window now becomes the eye, an eye engaged in the act of viewing—not just passive perception, taking it all in innocently. It is the act of viewing when it is basically, primitively almost, desire. This metamorphosis occurs at the end of the Doncières variant. By now the subtext has run out of material, having accumulated all possible ways of transference from subject to object. The animation paradigm has now gathered enough momentum to produce the most decisive exchange of functions. The *cabinet* itself becomes the watcher of the spectacle, as well as the instrument of the libido. It incarnates at one and the same time the subject as sight and the subject as desire. It thus becomes evident that literary description, cathecting each synecdoche with the same libido, serves to express the self through the portrayal of what it is not:

> Et derrière une tenture je surpris seulement un petit cabinet qui, arrêté par la muraille et ne pouvant se sauver, s'était caché là, tout penaud, et me regardait avec effroi de son oeil-de-boeuf rendu bleu par le clair de lune. [Vol. 2, 84]

> And behind a hanging curtain I surprised only a little closet which, stopped by the wall and unable to escape any farther, had hidden itself there with a guilty

conscience and gave me a frightened stare from its little round window, glowing blue in the moonlight.

Obviously, the *cabinet* here stands for the child (*petit*, but above all, *tout penaud*, an adjective reserved for embarrassment in the presence of a parent, nurse or teacher) caught in the act of voyeurism. It is not by chance that this new avatar of the privy representing the child's new awareness of sex should be lit by a round window, the name for which, *oeil-de-boeuf* [bull's eye], makes it the ideal locus for transferring the indiscreet gaze from subject to object. The significance is all the less in doubt when one realizes that *oeil-de-boeuf* opens again and again in *La Recherche*, each time for yet another revelation (e.g. Charlus in a sadomasochist scene), that is, for taking one more step towards reality, for lifting one more illusory veil. To be sure, there is another spy-hole in *La Recherche*, and it is used in vain by the narrator to surprise the homosexual encounter of Charlus and Jupien. He does not get to the bottom of the mystery, can see nothing, but only hears bizarre sounds (vol. 2, 609). In other words, that symbol of the ultimate realization of the self as artist, as exposer of life's secrets, voyeurism, seems to fail. The *eye* constant seems unaccountably to suffer a major exception. But this spectacle, half-understood, only overheard, this apparent defeat of the eye, is in fact the closest one gets to reality—it is a replay of the primal scene. And prosopopeia instantly perks up again, if through a variant: the *cabinet*'s window, a square one this time, is a *vasistas*, and whether the etymology of the word is true or, better still, a phantasm, every French reader knows it: *was ist das?*

Thus, at intervals, synonymous prosopopeias form in the fabric of narrative a loose string of fragments of lyric. These repeat again and again the libido-loaded story from which they all derive, and whose affect they perpetuate. But if such a sequence does constitute a subtext (and indeed the generating model, and the iterative variants prove its existence), there must be a clausula—no closure, no textuality. Indeed, the subtext ends together with the affect, when the plot in obedience to narrative structures brings about the release of the self's initial frustration, a satisfaction to its yearning for the other. The effacement of desire erases the prosopopeias. If my hypothesis is correct that artifice is the key to figural meaning, and if comicality is the form this artifice takes in a narrative, the clausula of the subtext will be signalled by the disappearance of the figure's grammar, of the chiasmus predication. Comicality will vanish. But on the other hand, the objects that the self had invested—the lexicon of the figure—will remain, bereft of predication, scattered about by the resumption of the narrative, but still close enough to suggest the ghostly presence of their erstwhile symbolism.

Narrative is then generated as if it were compensating for the repression or suppression of prosopopeia. When finally fulfillment or nonfulfillment of desire renders anamnesis pointless, the setting recedes into the background, objects lose their capacity to exteriorize, underscore, and comment upon traits of the characters. But while these fragments of the vanished figure now seem only justified as realistic details, anchoring the scene in the sensory world, each of them remains focussed upon by formal peculiarities. The outline of the *cabinet* can still be traced from one emphasis to the other, sometimes to be deciphered only by a specialized reader, sometimes to lead the ordinary reader to an interpretation that parallels symbolically, in the discourse of things, the erotic story that is unfolding in the narrative.

When the narrator finally gains entrance to the long forbidden kingdom of his love, that is, when he receives an invitation to tea at the Swanns', in Gilberte's private world, every step he takes towards bliss can be translated into *cabinet* code, so that every word from the *cabinet*'s descriptive system stands for an erotic word. Not only prosopopeias disappear, but revealingly, as if to make the point, one is left behind, as a witness to the pretransformation stage: the windows of the Swanns used to look at the narrator with a distant and indifferent gaze, "interposed" between him and "treasures that were not for him." At the posttransformation stage, the windows are no longer hostile eyes. They are back to their normal function as passive, inert casements, back to verisimilitude, back to the narrative, where our hero now opens them from inside and looks out, next to Gilberte, while her hair brushes against his cheek (vol. 1, 503). The cabinet meanwhile multiplies hypostases to remind us of its former dominion. Repressed as privy, and as the stage setting for masturbation, it reappears under various homonyms. First, innocently enough, the narrator is admitted by Gilberte's father to his library: Swann's *cabinet*, the homonymy equating the two shelters, the temple of reading and the temple of anal gratification.

Then our hero loses his head (he says so in italics), and this preliminary to orgasm precedes his being led deeper into the recess where femininity lurks:

> Mme Swann me recevait un moment dans sa chambre où trois belles et imposantes créatures, sa première, sa deuxième et sa troisième femme de chambre préparaient en souriant des toilettes merveilleuses, et vers laquelle, sur l'ordre proféré par le valet en culotte courte que Madame désirait me dire un mot, je me dirigeais par le sentier sinueux d'un couloir tout embaumé à distance des essences précieuses qui exhalaient sans cesse du cabinet de toilette des effluves odoriférants. [Vol. 1, 510.]

> Mme Swann received me for a moment in her own room, in which three beautiful and impressive creatures, her principal and second and third maids, smilingly prepared for her the most marvellous toilets, and towards which, on the order conveyed to me by the footman in knee-breeches that Madame wished to say a few words to me, I would make my way along the tortuous path of a corridor all embalmed by the precious essences which exhaled without ceasing from her dressing-room fragrant effluvia.

Here everything comes together: the bedroom truly seems to be the pronaos to the inner sanctum. The one, two, three chambermaids are but three ritual steps towards sexual admission to the *toilettes merveilleuses* [marvelous dresses] they are preparing. In its literal sense the plural would make Gilberte's mother an unlikely quick-change artist, but at the parallel, imagistic level of repressed significance it also directs us to *toilettes*, "toilet," "bathroom." The inner sanctum itself is named, another opportunity to repeat *cabinet* and *toilette*, and indeed it is a boudoir, but it cannot be by chance that the initiate should be taken there by two intercessors: one is *le valet de pied en culotte courte*, a flunky in knee breeches, but also the ghost of the little boy who was pulling down his short pants in our archetypal intertext. The second, even more to the point, is the scent that guides him through the strangely sinuous, live, organlike corridor. These tautological *effluves odoriférants* pack into one compound word the scent of sex (*odoriférant*, but the word is also a euphemism) and *effluves* that in French is, again, suggestive of an overpowering, almost magical, olfactory sensation, and a euphemism for scatological smells. The text plays on both pleasure motivations, with the emphasis on a more tolerable eroticism. Swift, in another boudoir, a parodic one ("The Lady's Dressing Room") chose to emphasize the scatological side of the double entendre.

Then, as a third insistent signal of what counts, *cabinet* reappears: Gilberte naughtily affects to believe that a guest of her mother's is the wife of a minor civil servant, and her father angrily corrects her: "you speak as if you were a two-year-old. . . . He is quite simply chef de cabinet" (vol. 1, 511), that is, the chief of staff of a member of the government, but that is not enough for Swann. He now corrects himself: "il n'est pas chef de cabinet, il est *directeur du cabinet*." Here the subtext comes to a close, moving on, as it does, to an apparently gratuitous portrait of that functionary as a "joli garçon" (pretty boy). Does it really, or rather should we not take the italics emphasizing *directeur* quite seriously? They bring us back to other italics, at the beginning of the episode, to the Latin phrase that ushers the narrator into the Garden: Gilberte's motto on her letter of invitation reads *Per viam rectam*, surely a laughably pretentious affectation, especially for a girl who is not without deviousness (vol. 1, 499, 504), but also, in the vicinity of our shadow *cabinet*, a rather unavoidable allusion to *par voie rectale*, a medical cliché (as Boileau did say: *le Latin dans les mots brave l'honnêteté*). Even the periphrasis is stereotyped and significantly harks back to one more statement of what should not be said except through a mask.

The vanishing act of prosopopeia has something else to reveal: with the return to the narrative, comicality also vanishes. It was not therefore caused by psychological repression. The utter seriousness of the other mnemonic mechanisms (like the *madeleine*) corroborates this conclusion, for the repressed contents these disclose are much the same as with our figure, and they are just as rhetorical as it is. Comicality therefore must be linked to the suppositional convention, to the blatant fictitiousness of the figure which is the condition preliminary to our reading it. Prosopopeia says the truth, as always in the lyric, through means that themselves do not have to suggest a reality or be credible. It says it by obeying rules that are purely tropological, that is, as abstract as those of grammar, not a matter of the lexicon, and in no need therefore of any referentiality. The lyric, to be sure, is not comical. But it must be so in a context where all statements, however "false," however fictional, have to be credible. Our figure, a figure of figurality, as Paul de Man called it, is comical in the narrative because the basic rule of fiction is verisimilitude. Under this rule, truth is unacceptable if its representation is not only arbitrary but a plain impossibility. Putting Thalia's laughing mask on top of Erato's false face, prosopopeia finally becomes a figure of truth.

COLUMBIA UNIVERSITY

HANS-JOST FREY

Undecidability

No degree of knowledge can ever stop this madness, for it is the madness of words.[1]

How to read? If one applies what de Man's texts say about the rhetoricity of the text to those texts themselves, then one takes them literally precisely by not taking them literally. For to read them in accordance with their own conception of reading is to take from them a fixed doctrine which they themselves have always already undermined. To read them literally, on the other hand, is to be told that to do so is to miss them entirely. These are texts that, although they can be misread, cannot be read correctly, since they render what they say insecure by saying that all statement is unreliable and perhaps sheer madness. That the undecidability of the referentiality of the statement is stated does not establish control over it, but rather confers on undecidability, in its turn, the uncertain status of all statement, thereby preventing it from being turned into a truth. And that the status of the statement may not be determinable—not even as undecidable—speaks neither for nor against the fact that it occurs constantly, without our ever knowing whether it succeeds.

In "Autobiography as De-facement," prosopopeia appears as the figure of autobiography. *Prosopon* is the face or the mask, and prosopopeia as *fictio personae* is the lending of a face to that which has none. One tells one's life, not because one has a face, but in order to give one to oneself, and to preserve rather than to lose it. In autobiography the self is not given in advance, but only emerges as what the biography outlines. But the face that permits the faceless to appear is therefore, from the beginning, saddled with the error of not corresponding to what it shows. What the face makes visible is only accessible through it, but the form in which it appears is not its own. Form is always already the <u>defiguration of the formless</u>, whose place it takes. The self-reflexive "autobiographical moment,"[2] in which the "I" presents itself to itself, always already involves two subjects, each of which substitutes itself for the other, so that both have always already been replaced by what they are not.

---

1. Paul de Man, "Shelley Disfigured," in *Deconstruction and Criticism* (New York: Seabury Press, 1979), 68.
2. De Man, "Autobiography as De-facement," *MLN* 94 (1979), 921.

From here on, the concept of defacement becomes available, to be used in a twofold manner. First, the act of face-lending as such is already a defacement in the sense just described. But this is easily forgotten, because the constructive urge, seeking to create coherence, does not like to recall the disaccord from which it springs. A systematizing drive is at work in prosopopeia. The face fixes itself into a rigid order and is taken seriously. In order to reestablish itself as the hypothetical figure it is, the face must decompose itself again. This removal of the face is the second form of defacement, and serves the disillusioning function of recalling the substitutive character of the face and the forgotten fictivity of the system.

Using the example of Wordsworth's "Essay on Epitaphs," de Man shows how the system constitutes itself, and demonstrates that, despite the closure of the system, the text contains elements that unsettle the principle of its own production and cannot be integrated into it. The most important point here is Wordsworth's attack on the language of tropes, upon which the system he constructs still rests. By denouncing its own language, the text de-faces the face it constructs for itself. This complicated relation makes up the difficulty of the final sentence of de Man's essay: "Autobiography veils a defacement of the mind of which it is itself the cause."[3] As prosopopeia, autobiography *like* makes the unknown accessible. This means, however, not only that the self- *un concealment* representing subject becomes legible and intelligible, but also that, precisely because it is now understood, it still remains withheld in the essential unintelligibility that it is, eluded in the de-facement. As the attempt to give a face to the faceless, autobiography is the very source of de-facement; but insofar as it becomes visible as face, it veils the latter's character as de-facement. In this connection, meanwhile, the metaphor of the veil needs to be read in yet another way. The veil is the clothing of that which it veils and makes visible as being veiled, just as language as clothing makes the thought it clothes available as being covered. Autobiography as veiling, then, is what brings de-facement itself to light, as long as it retains, as de Man claims Wordsworth's text does, the memory of itself as veil by tearing it.

The metaphorics of clothing does not creep into de Man's text unreflectively; it is taken over from the very passage of Wordsworth under discussion. Wordsworth turns against the mis-use of language that consists of regarding language as the clothing of thought rather than as thought's incarnation. Since clothes are external to what they contain, they can be changed. The word that is clothing lacks an essential connection with what it says. This exteriority of language makes up the danger that Wordsworth ascribes to it, a danger that de Man interprets as the mutilation of the speaker, who, never reaching that which is to be said, becomes the deaf-mute prophet of a world that dissolves behind the veil of tropes that replace it. Now, for de Man's argument, it would have been enough to demonstrate that the language that Wordsworth de-

---

3. Ibid., 930.

nounces is the language of tropes, on which the system that the text itself constructs is based. This would have made it obvious enough that the text endangers its own foundation. But de Man goes farther. Wordsworth opposes clothing to incarnation: "If words be not (recurring to a metaphor before used) an incarnation of the thought but only a clothing for it, then surely they will prove an ill gift."[4] The previous use occurs in a passage that reproaches the followers of Pope and Dryden for giving up those feelings that are "the pure emanations of nature," and with them "those expressions which are not what the garb is to the body but what the body is to the soul, themselves a constituent part and power or function in the thought. . . ."[5] Language as incarnation could not be detached from things in the same way as clothes from the body; that which it spoke about would, rather, be present within it. De Man is not satisfied to show that Wordworth's language is not the language of incarnation; instead, he negates the difference between incarnation and clothing that Wordsworth insists upon. De Man takes the relation clothes-body-soul as a metaphorical chain, in which clothes are to the body as the body is to the soul. This identification, which Wordsworth expressly challenges, is not defended by any argumentation; it is simply asserted. If the body is the clothing of the soul, rather than its incarnation, then the distinction that Wordsworth postulates is irrelevant and all language is clothing. Or: all language is figural. Or: the face is always already a mask. And in fact, in de Man's explanation of *prosopon poein* as "to confer a mask or a face,"[6] the distinction remains meaningless for him.

How does this violent suppression of incarnating language come about? De Man's text makes it seem certain that the language that Wordsworth denounces as clothing is the language that Wordsworth himself speaks. "The language so violently denounced is in fact the language of metaphor, of prosopopeia and of tropes, the solar language of cognition that makes the unknown accessible to the mind and to the senses."[7] That incarnating language, too, is mere clothing must be demonstrated inasmuch as the danger exists that it might be the language of Wordsworth's text; if this were the case, it would threaten the argument de Man uses to prove the inconsistency of the text. The apparently superfluous attempt to dismantle the concept of incarnating language entirely can therefore be read as an indication that the clothing character of language, its figurality, is less indubitable than de Man's text assumes. It might be that the distinction between clothing and incarnation is suppressed because it poses a potential threat to the system that de Man's own text constructs, a system that would rest (if anything could rest upon it) on the irreducible figurality of language, which can never be anything other than substitution.

---

4. William Wordsworth, "Essays on Epitaphs," in *The Prose Works of William Wordsworth*, ed. Owen/Smyser (Oxford: Oxford University Press, 1974), v. 2, essay 3, ll. 180–82, 84.
5. Ibid., ll. 162–65, 84.
6. "Autobiography as De-facement." 926.
7. Ibid., 929.

De Man discusses the question of the figurality of language, in connection with Derrida's interpretation of Rousseau, in "The Rhetoric of Blindness." Against Derrida, de Man attempts to show that Rousseau does not understand language as the representation of presence, but rather denies its connection to an extralinguistic given. This argument is developed, first, on Rousseau's theory of music, and then on the text that argues for the original metaphoricity of language. If a man, encountering other men for the first time, describes them as *giants* because he is frightened by them, this is, for Derrida, a metaphor, one that replaces the literal meaning *I am frightened*. De Man admits this, but adds that the passions that, according to Rousseau, underlie language are, for their part, constituted as nonreferential. In Rousseau's words: "L'amour n'est qu'illusion; il se fait, pour ainsi dire, un autre Univers; il s'entoure d'objets qui ne sont point, ou auxquels lui seul a donné l'être; et comme il rend tous ses sentiments en images, son language est toujours figuré."[8] ["Love is but an illusion; it creates for itself, so to speak, another world; it surrounds itself with nonexistent objects, or whose life stems uniquely from it. Since it expresses all its feelings in images, its language is always figurative."] So the metaphor, in pointing to its literal meaning, points to a state of mind that is, for its part, a fiction without reference. Rousseau's text entails the following: "The metaphorical language . . . has no literal referent. Its only referent is 'le néant des choses humaines.'"[9] The metaphoricity of language is outlined here as doctrine. All language is figural; there is no possibility of ever reaching through to a literal meaning. This means that anything that is not language is inaccessible; and the assurance that everything is language provides little comfort, because *everything* here can only refer to the linguistic, and not to whatever remains external to language. The inaccessibility of the extralinguistic belongs to the metaphoricity of language. The absence of the literal is "le néant des choses humaines" as the groundlessness of the figural, and signifies the fictivity of all orderings, which are always linguistic and cannot be secured anywhere. Each ordering can be understood only if it is not taken literally, but is seen through in its rhetoricity, which includes insight into the inevitability of taking it seriously. It seems that the literary text is, for de Man, the one that achieves this insight for itself.

What can be regarded, on the basis of the passages already considered, as de Man's system, has as its principle the figurality and the nonreferentiality of language. "Autobiography as De-facement" speaks in the name of this doctrine. The inaccessibility of the extralinguistic is explicitly established here: ". . . what we are deprived of is . . . the shape and the sense of a world accessible only in the privative way of understanding."[10] The nonreferentiality of

---

8. J.-J. Rousseau, "Deuxième préface à *La Nouvelle Héloïse*," *Oeuvres complètes* (Paris: Gallimard, Bibliothèque de la Pléiade, 1964), vol. 2, 15.

9. *Blindness and Insight*, Second Edition (Minneapolis: University of Minnesota Press, 1983), 135.

10. "Autobiography as De-facement," 930.

language also explains de Man's preference for a figure like prosopopeia, which excludes, at the outset, any thought of representation. What receives a voice and a face is the voiceless and faceless. Prosopopeia is the fiction of the face. But at the same time it becomes clear why de Man could not permit something like Wordsworth's incarnating language to stand. Even its mere possibility would endanger the validity of the principle on which the system is based. Insofar as Wordsworth's text postulates this possibility, it unsettles the conclusiveness of de Man's argument and undermines its basis. That de Man does not disable the hypothesis of an incarnating language by means of argument, but simply eliminates it by ignoring Wordsworth's distinction, intensifies suspicion of the indubitable principle of the figurality of language.

Can the figurality of language be fixed as doctrine at all? Is it not, rather, the impossibility of every doctrine, insofar as doctrine claims to make literal statements about something? The clearest formulation of the principle of the figurality of language can be found in the paradoxical sentence: "The only literal statement that says what it means to say is the assertion that there can be no literal statement."[11] The sentence that says there can be no literal statements can only become a principle by exempting itself from what it says. Taken literally, however, the statement is false, because what it says is contradicted by its being able to be said. If the statement is not taken literally, then what it says applies to itself, and the statement cannot serve as a principle, since it continues, for its part, to refer back to a literal meaning that is always missing. If it were the case that all discourse is figural, this would make it impossible to announce the fact, since any discourse would itself be implicated in the rhetoricity it asserts. De Man's theory of the rhetoricity of literature necessarily moves in the wake of its own pronouncements, and his texts are therefore constantly exposed to the temptation which they themselves point out: "The rhetorical character of literary language opens up the possibility of the archetypal error: the recurrent confusion of sign and substance."[12] De Man succumbs to this temptation when he takes the impossibility of literality literally, but also when, in "The Rhetoric of Blindness" in connection with Rousseau, and in "Autobiography as De-facement" in connection with Wordsworth, he asserts the nonreferentiality of language. Such referential determination always brings with it fixed world views such as "le néant des choses humaines" or the inaccessibility of the world, which are no longer seen through as fictions. The suppression of Wordsworth's incarnating language is possible precisely to the extent that discourse about the rhetoricity of language takes itself so seriously as to posit itself as the very incarnation it challenges. It belongs to the rhetoricity of language that literality cannot be denied, since this would have to occur in an utterance that took itself literally.

In at least one case, de Man himself returns to the petrification of his own thought into doctrine. The "Metaphor" chapter in *Allegories of Reading* con-

---

11. *Blindness and Insight*, 133.
12. Ibid., 136.

tains a second reading of the text in which Rousseau derives the metaphorical character of language. In "The Rhetoric of Blindness," Rousseau's explanation of the metaphor *giant* as stemming from fear is treated as an error, fear of the other not being, in Rousseau's sense, a passion, but rather belonging to the sphere of needs. An underlying passion, however, is necessary in order to demonstrate the nonreferentiality of language. The new departure of the "Metaphor" chapter, apparently, consists above all in that Rousseau's choice of example is no longer taken as an oversight; instead, the text is interpreted as it stands. In fact, however, the chapter contains a reinterpretation of passion in Rousseau, together with an altered assessment of the question of the referentiality of language. At first, the argument, agreeing with Derrida, runs just as before. The metaphor *giant* has the literal meaning *I am frightened*. But whereas previously the nonreferentiality of passion, and fear as a bad example of passion, appeared at this point, now fear itself is analyzed. Since, in Rousseau's text, there is no indication of the other's aggressivity, fear can only be based on distrust. It is uncertain whether the peaceful exterior does not conceal a malicious interior. It could be that appearances are deceiving, and that the face is a mask. According to de Man, this suspicion of a possible dissonance between exterior and interior founds, for Rousseau, not only fear, but all passion: "It can be shown that, for Rousseau, all passions—whether they be love, pity, anger, or even a borderline case between passion and need such as fear—are characterized by such a discrepancy; they are based, not on the knowledge that such a difference exists, but on the hypothesis that it might exist, a possibility that can never be proven or disproven by empirical or analytical means. A statement of distrust is neither true nor false: it is rather in the nature of a permanent hypothesis."[13] This differs from the earlier understanding of passion in that it is no longer an issue of the nonreferentiality of passion, but rather of the <u>undecidability of its referentiality</u>. And yet, as undecidable as the suspension of passion may be, it is as rapidly dismantled in favor of an arbitrarily posited literality. In Rousseau's example, this occurs through the formation of the metaphor *giant*, in which the mere suspicion of the other's dangerousness is expressed as a certainty by fitting the external appearance to the imputed maliciousness. It is, however, important that fear, as the literal meaning of the metaphor, is now no longer without reference, but rather remains suspended in an irreducible doubt about its own justification: "The metaphor 'giant,' used to connote man, has indeed a proper meaning (fear), but this meaning is not really proper: it refers to a condition of permanent suspense between a literal world in which appearance and nature coincide and a figural world in which this correspondence is no longer *a priori* posited."[14] With this insight into the hypothetical character of fear, and the associated undecidability of referentiality, de Man confronts the paradox that underlay "The Rhetoric of Blindness" without being thought through in its ramifications. If the sentence that

13. *Allegories of Reading* (New Haven and London: Yale University Press, 1979), 150.
14. Ibid., 151.

proclaims the impossibility of literal statements cannot be taken literally, then the possibility of literality must still persist. That is to say, it remains undecidable whether discourse about the rhetoricity of all discourse can be read referentially or not.

It seems that this undecidability cannot be sustained, and that all discourse is a decision. In "The Rhetoric of Blindness" and in "Autobiography as De-facement," the uncertainty is decided in favor of the nonreferentiality of language. *Allegories of Reading* sees through this process of decision and describes it. It becomes clear that decision is defacement. By resolving the uncertainty as to the inner disposition of the other in favor of his hostility, the metaphor *giant* (in which, moreover, defacement is physically evident) may express the fear of danger; but the representation defaces this fear as much as it does the other man it designates. For the metaphor decides that danger actually exists, whereas the state of fear imagined the possibility of danger, but without being able to decide whether the image corresponded to any reality. From this perspective, the metaphor appears as an attempt to master fear. It allays the intolerable suspense by determining a danger. De-facing decision is an exit from fear. The fear is undecidability. The refusal of fear in "The Rhetoric of Blindness," and the assertion of the nonreferentiality of language, is the repetition of the procedure described in *Allegories of Reading*. It is the attempt, coming from a fear of fear, to eradicate undecidability through an abrupt decision. De Man's disfiguring reading of Rousseau proceeds according to the movement of metaphor-formation that the text describes. De Man's text is the metaphor of the fear of the undecidability of fear. The analysis of fear in *Allegories of Reading* dissolves the systematizing rigor of the earlier text, albeit so that now any other passion could take the place of fear. But fear, precisely because it is a borderline case between passion and need, may not be arbitrarily chosen. For it disables the distinction between *besoin* and *passion* on which Rousseau's text is constructed, and makes it recognizable as a fixation that, in its turn, is already attempting to avoid undecidability.

If there is no discourse that can sustain undecidability without disavowing it, one can at least ask what the implications of this undecidability are. The explicitness with which it is stated in *Allegories of Reading* invites the question. Where no decision can be made, the metaphor decides. It cannot be traced back to a literal meaning, but only to the uncertainty whether such a meaning exists at all. The metaphor *giant* may refer to fear, but the referentiality of fear remains suspended. The metaphor itself thereby becomes undecidable, and it can no longer be determined whether it actually is one. The system in which the difference between the figural (giant) and the literal (fear) functions, rests on certain norms that are themselves linguistically posited, and posited on the basis of decisions that cannot be justified. The metaphor can only be indubitably a metaphor if the undecidability of the (possibly groundless) fear that underlies it is disregarded. Insight into this condition not only exposes the metaphor as the disfiguring mask of what it stands for, but also disables the separation between figurality and literality that depends on it. When the referentiality of language is suspended, the criterion for the assignment of an expression to the literal or the figural domain is no longer applicable. Such a criterion is possible only intratextually, that is, where an extralinguistic world has already been simulated linguistically and what should count as literal has thereby been decided. When this decision is exposed, as in de Man's analysis of fear, as being as unavoidable as it is unjustifiable, the system collapses. It becomes evident that the best understanding of metaphor has been reached when it has become uncertain whether it is one. No longer can it be established whether any expression reaches an extralinguistic reality or whether it is a groundless fiction. Discourse that does not suppress the undecidability of the extralinguistic anchoring of its own utterance cannot but suggest that what it takes as its Other, in order to speak about it, might, perhaps, not exist. But what is taken as given without being the case is hallucination. All discourse is possibly hallucinatory. In an essay on Michael Riffaterre, hallucination appears as the occasion of a poem by Victor Hugo. The verse "Et l'esprit, ce veilleur fait d'oreilles et d'yeux" is treated as hallucination by Riffaterre as well. For him, hallucination comes to function in the text inasmuch as he understands the poem as discursive speech, not visionary in itself but representing the vision as imaginary. The poem, therefore, is not hallucinatory, but employs hallucination as an effect. This presupposes that a guaranteed realm of perception exists, in relation to which hallucination can be determined as such. Hallucination can be employed as a means only if there is no doubt about what one sees and what one merely believes one sees. Hallucination, however, to the extent it appears as a possibility, is the unsettling of precisely this distinction. In hallucination, one believes that what one is seeing exists. But exactly this is also the case for perception (*Wahrnehmung*). In hallucination, as in perception, the impossibility of deciding between the two is disavowed by deciding each time in favor of *I see* and against *I believe I see.* But precisely because hallucination takes itself for perception, perception itself should come under suspicion of being hallucination. "The hypothesis, or the figure, of hallucination, undoes sense certainty."[15] Riffaterre's distinction between hallucination and hallucinatory effect collapses along with the certainty of the referentiality of perception, which alone would make it possible to keep the hallucinatory under control.

If the referentiality or the nonreferentiality of language can only ever be asserted, this damages the credibility of any construction that rests on such an assertion. Now, one could try (as happens every day) simply to brush this aside, and to live with these constructions as best one can. Indeed, there may be nothing else to do. But a construction that hopes to dispense with the extralinguistic is just as illusionary as one that is convinced of having attained it.

15. "Hypogram and Inscription: Michael Riffaterre's Poetics of Reading," in *Diacritics* 11 (1981), 34.

Both are undermined in that the extralinguistic announces itself as that of which one can never know whether discourse has attained it or not; so that although no construction can reach and integrate its own relation to whatever is outside it, neither can it avoid contact with it. Every construction, every system—that is, every text—has within itself the ignorance of its own exterior as the rupture of its coherence which it cannot account for. No text can remove itself from a relation to the extralinguistic, and none can determine that relation. This undecidable relation to what it is constantly related to, prevents the text from closing into a totality. The undecidability of its referentiality means that the text is open, and so fragmentary, at every point. But the inaccessibiliity of the relation to the extralinguistic is most accessible at the point where the two come together: in beginning and ending.

Where discourse begins, it can—before diverting attention from itself to what it says—be known as an act of linguistic positing. This act cannot be derived. It is unconnected and abrupt. This means: it does not signify. Discourse as act is the presupposition for everything that can be said, but this act itself remains outside the range of language. It has no communicable meaning. That language is, is not comprehensible. That discourse takes place is, from the beginning, what it cannot be done with; it is, so to speak, the extralinguisticality of discourse that, as its meaningless facticity, disturbs the meaning as whose vehicle it occurs.

Where discourse ends, there is something else. Ending, discourse comes up against that which has neither entered, nor can it enter, discourse, yet which still helps to form what it borders on. In "Shelley Disfigured," Shelley's last poem, interrupted by his death, is understood in this way as a fragment. "At this point, figuration and cognition are actually interrupted by an event which shapes the text but which is not present in its represented or articulated meaning."[16] The text does not recuperate the death that ends it. But that the abruptness of the fragment is thereby understood makes this understanding itself questionable. No one knows if death stands in the causal relation to the breaking-off of the poem, as de Man asserts (an assertion that is his own abrupt position [*Setzung*]). This explanation simply integrates the fragmentary text into a text-for-the-reader which is of a higher order and which avoids the undecidability of the fragment by assigning the abrupt ending a meaning. But the breaking point of the fragment has no meaning. To the extent that meaning is assigned to it, it is disavowed. It is the border of meaning. The fragment ends without being at an end. It is discourse that does not come to an end, that does not reach the point towards which it is underway. It ends before the end, not because it does not reach the end, but because there is no knowing whether it reaches the end or not. Insofar as a discourse that runs into the undecidability of its own referentiality can never say whether it has reached it, every discourse

---

16. "Shelley Disfigured," op. cit., 67. Here, as well as in the essay on Riffaterre (n. 15), there is discussion of the act of linguistic positing.

is fragmentary. In breaking-in and breaking-off, the discontinuity between language and the extralinguistic becomes visible. Between the text and that to which it claims to refer is the gap of not-knowing whether such a relation exists. The text stands there as a ruin, without our knowing where it fits.

The suppression of the fragmentary is the price of order, an order that understanding, writing and reading achieve. But the text that constitutes itself each time as the overcoming of the abrupt is itself abrupt, and preserves, like the metaphor *giant*, in which fear disfigures both itself and the world, the deposing of its own position (*das Entsetzen seiner Setzung*) within it. No text detaches itself from what it never controls. Whatever the text may say determines, in one way or another, a relation to the extralinguistic that cannot be determined. The abruptness of this determination makes it unverifiable and thereby always leaves open the possibility of hallucination. So it remains questionable whether speaking has any meaning. Discourse does not have a meaning as it takes place; it could, at most, receive one retrospectively from that which it says. Insofar as it may actually grasp what it treats, discourse cannot finish so long as any uncertainty remains about it; yet insofar as it may miss its mark and end up with all the ghostliness of a spectre, all its statements, and thus discourse itself, are suspended in doubts about their possible unsoundness. How to read?

UNIVERSITY OF ZURICH

Translated by Robert Livingston

SHULI BARZILAI

A Review of Paul de Man's "Review of Harold Bloom's *Anxiety of Influence*"

Paul de Man's review of *The Anxiety of Influence* (1973) opens as follows: ". . . Harold Bloom's latest essay is by no means what it pretends to be."[1] This can be read in two ways: either the avowed intention of the author and the apparent meaning of his work do not coincide with the actual results, and the author doesn't know it; or the discrepancy in the text is deliberate, and the author is aware of what he's doing. The first reading assumes a claim which, coming from Paul de Man, raises expectations of a rigorous disclosure of the "blinded vision"[2] which both blocks and enables the critic's insight. The latter, however, would seem to be the case, for the opening sentence of the review begins with these words: "Like most good books. . . ." In full it reads: "Like most good books, Harold Bloom's latest essay is by no means what it pretends to be." The first paragraph concludes, moreover, that Harold Bloom "can be called, in his own terms, a 'strong' critic and it does not come as a surprise to hear him assert his intention to change rather than just to expand the course of literary studies."

The reader may thus presume that this strong critic, and author of a good book, is not blind to his own statement but rather knows what his latest essay is about. But the ambiguity of de Man's opening statement has only briefly been suspended. The conclusion of the first paragraph is immediately qualified by the sentence with which the second paragraph opens: "Yet, if read in the light of this intention, one will fail to do justice to this book." Is that to be continued: ". . . which is better than its author's own intention?" This uncertainty holds sway for several pages. De Man, in the manner of *The Anxiety of Influence* according to de Man, does not rush to reveal his meaning. The ques-

---

1. Paul de Man's review essay first appeared in *Comparative Literature*, 26 (1974), 269–75. The essay is reprinted as "Review of Harold Bloom's *Anxiety of Influence*," in *Blindness and Insight: Essays in the Rhetoric of Contemporary Criticism*, 2nd ed. (New York, 1971; London: Methuen, 1983), 267–76. Hereafter cited as BI. All further references in the text will be to this revised edition.
2. Paul de Man, "The Rhetoric of Blindness: Jacques Derrida's Reading of Rousseau," BI, 106.

tion now becomes not only: is the gap between the explicit and implicit content of *The Anxiety of Influence* a deliberate and controlled one? But also: in what direction is the seesaw movement of de Man's own argument tending? And even more so: if the avowed subject, the question of influence announced by the title, is not the real subject of Bloom's book, then what is?

These questions may be of some interest from a theoretical perspective. Beyond our immediate concern with Paul de Man's views of an influential theory of poetry, his essay on Bloom gradually discloses certain basic premises which inform his critical procedures. I would like, therefore, to follow closely de Man's reading of *The Anxiety of Influence* as it is worked out in the pages of his review.

In keeping with the promise of his opening statement, de Man proceeds to show what *The Anxiety of Influence* seems to be and, then, what it is actually about. This two-step demonstration is not, however, purely descriptive; for with each stage, there also goes an evaluation stated in no uncertain terms. Thus de Man begins by mapping Bloom's progress as a highly innovative and acute theoretician of the romantic imagination. What sets Bloom "apart and above other interpreters of English romanticism," writes de Man, is the insight already shown in his early work on Shelley that the "romantic imagination is *not* to be understood in dialectical interplay with the presumably antithetical category of 'nature' " (271 and 269, respectively). Bloom goes beyond the mind-nature, subject-object dichotomies of his fellow critics and gropes for a new definition of "an autonomous power that develops according to its own laws into areas where the category of nature no longer operates. . ." (270). Bloom thus calls into question the polar structures of a widely accepted and powerful tradition of interpretation by suspending, by almost eliminating the category and cult of nature. A bold move indeed, and one which de Man (for reasons he has already given in "The Rhetoric of Temporality"),[3] fully appreciates: ". . . in his understanding of the catchall term 'imagination' he was philosophically shrewder and, in some respects, better informed than all the other historians and theoreticians of English romanticism, including Frye, Abrams, Wasserman, and others" (269). Note, however, the switch to the past tense.

In *The Ringers in the Tower*, a collection of essays published two years before *The Anxiety of Influence*, de Man already detects the signs of a falling off, a process which is completed in Bloom's latest essay—if we accept at face value what *The Anxiety of Influence* pretends to be. This is unequivocally described as a "regression" (272) and a "relapse": "Just when we were about to free poetic language from the constraints of natural reference, we return to a

---

3. De Man's views on romanticism are developed at length in "The Rhetoric of Temporality," in *Interpretation: Theory and Practice*, ed. Charles S. Singleton (Baltimore: Johns Hopkins University Press, 1969), 173–209; rpt. in BI, 187–228. See also his earlier essay on "Intentional Structure of the Romantic Image," in *Romanticism and Consciousness*, ed. Harold Bloom (New York: Norton, 1970). The accuracy of de Man's interpretation of Bloom's interpretation of romanticism is a subject for another study.

scheme which . . . is still clearly a relapse into a psychological naturalism" (271). Now for reasons which are not within the scope of this discussion, the word "psychological" is for Paul de Man a strongly pejorative term. "Naturalism" alone would be bad enough, but "psychological naturalism" is just too bad. And there is a tone of regret here as de Man watches the "step backward" which constitutes for him the movement of *The Anxiety of Influence:* "we return to a relationship between subjects"; to a "story of influence told in the naturalistic language of desire"; to the "solipsism of an alienated self" (272).

The first stage of de Man's description and evaluation of Bloom's project is complete. It would not be far wrong, I think, to characterize its tone as elegiac: a lament for an early Bloom. This explains in part the motive for the next step: "one feels that the book deals with something else" (273). That verb "feels," within the context of de Man's generally cool and distancing style, alerts us that the stakes have just been raised, the ante upped. As a precondition of the second stage, de Man waives the possibility of taking Bloom at his word, of accepting the plain sense of what he says and treating his theory of influence "as the central statement it appears to be." Therefore, he tells us, "We can forget about the temporal scheme and about the pathos of the oedipal son;" all these "intentional schemes . . . can be ignored" (273 and 274, respectively). Instead of the distortions brought about by desire and rivalry, by the struggle for power and priority—an argument which Bloom states in complex oedipal terms—de Man would have "patterns of error that are . . . rooted in language rather than in the self" (272). This is the first mention of a major premise which has, however, already determined de Man's point of departure in this essay: the epistemological unreliability of texts. The real subject of *The Anxiety of Influence,* that which the "book deals with" (and exemplifies, it should be noted, with its either naive or ironic double modes of meaning), is "the impossibility of reading" and, again, "the indeterminacy of literary meaning" (273).

What is at stake here for de Man, and closely linked to the presupposition of the duplicity of language, is an ontological conception of being as nonbeing. This is only hinted at in his review. But if the agents and events of life are "themselves treated as texts" as is suggested here, in the paragraph which immediately and significantly follows the assertion of the impossibility of reading, then the question of indeterminacy clearly encompasses not only the specific epistemic state of literature but also an ontological negativity or, as de Man develops the thought in his essay on impersonality in Mallarmé and Blanchot, a "persistent negative movement that resides in being."[4] Thus de Man situates the subject, even within Bloom's humanistic discourse, as a grammatical function, as a cog within a linguistic system—which is inherently unreliable. It is in order to protect ourselves against knowledge of the darkness at the heart of being that we surround ourselves with what de Man

---

4. Paul de Man, "Impersonality in the Criticism of Maurice Blanchot," *BI*, 73. Hereafter cited as "IMB."

describes as "stratagems, ruses of language and of thought that hide an irrevocable fall." Such as, we may presume, all firmly held religious beliefs. De Man overtly rejects these opiates: "The existence of these strategies reveals the supremacy of the negative power they are trying to circumvent."[5] But to speak of the revelation of negation is to entertain a paradox that is itself not devoid of belief. De Man obliquely reinforces this paradoxical affirmation, using Mallarmé to mediate his thought, when he suggests that "the self could, to some degree, maintain its power; enriched by the repeated experience of defeat. . . ."[6]

This complex "negative movement," central though it may be to de Man's thinking about literature, criticism and the agents of life, is not the immediate subject or strategy of his review. Rather the metaphors he used disclose a recurrent pattern of reading: de Man insistently directs our attention away from the "exterior" psychological scheme to the inside story being told. Let us look, he instructs us, "behind the arbitrariness of the psychological plot," and "underneath . . . the book," and "underneath all the drama" (273–74). Prepositions lose their innocence as de Man deploys them here; "behind" and "underneath" are turned into figural propositions. They prepare us for the thrust of his argument: "If we are willing to set aside the trappings of psychology" and peer behind the arras, as it were, we will finally encounter truth. De Man, of course, does not actually say the word "truth." For truth is nothing, nothing truth, to the poststructuralist imagination. But he does say: "It begins to shine through" (273). The Heideggerian metaphor is a giveaway. It points to an entity de Man cannot properly name;[7] therefore he must call it indirectly, metaphorically, following Heidegger's language of veiled revelation which speaks of the being of beings that "comes into the steadiness of its shining" and the "unconcealedness" of a painter's color or a poet's word that "now comes to shine forth."[8]

What exactly is It that "begins to shine through" the surface question of influence? Behind the scenes and underneath the gloomy boards of Bloom's "psychologism," de Man finds what he is looking for. It is a "pretty tight linguistic model" (274). In a word, substitution. Substitution, it is specified, is a linguistic construct not to be confused, in any way, with natural or psychological models of substitution. Rhetorical substitution is described as "paradigmatic," as a "key concept," as the denominator that "all the revisionary ratios have in common" (274–75). It is, in de Man's view, the "underlying

5. De Man, "IMB," 73.

6. De Man, "IMB," 72.

7. On the problematics of "proper" see the translator's note in Jacques Derrida, "White Mythology: Metaphor in the Text of Philosophy," *New Literary History*, 6 (Autumn 1974), 5–6.

8. Martin Heidegger, "The Origin of the Work of Art" (1935), in *Poetry, Language, Thought*, trans. Albert Hofstadter (New York: Harper and Row, 1971), 36 and 47, respectively. See also Heidegger's definition of truth as "uncoveredness" in *Being and Time*, trans. John Macquarrie and Edward Robinson (1927 in German; Oxford: Basil Blackwell, 1962), sections. 219–21.

structure" of the book. It is also a "fact" that must not be ignored: substitutions or tropes are "epistemologically unreliable," "always, by necessity, a falsification" (274). For proof de Man briefly goes to each of the six ratios and finds, in spite of their apparent differences, what he calls the "universality of the substitutive pattern" (275). At this stage of the presentation, it can no longer be determined whether "universal" still refers and is restricted to Bloom's ratios or points way beyond these six specific tropes.

That there is a "pretty tight" hermeneutic circularity to de Man's argument becomes evident here: the interpreter finds that which is in a sense already found. It's just a question of time, of the tortoise of interpretation catching up with its implicit purpose. But since, as interpreters, we all move in the same circle, the structure of de Man's interpretative statement cannot be dismissed with equanimity on the grounds of its circularity. Because it is unavoidable, Heidegger advises us not to deny the hermeneutic circle or to make a secret of it: "we must rather endeavour to leap into the 'circle', primordially and wholly. . . ."[9] De Man, in his own way, also recommends the circle as "a path that we have to construct ourselves and on which we must try to remain." "At most," he adds with unusual directness, "the circularity proves the authenticity of our intent."[10]

More problematic, however, in terms of de Man's critical procedures is the rhetorical strategy he adopts in his review: the recourse to the inside-outside dichotomy. The dichotomy is implicit from the very first sentence of the review, and its visibility increases as de Man reaches the conclusion of the second stage of his exposition of the meaning of *The Anxiety of Influence*. It is disturbing because, as de Man himself has often demonstrated with admirable and vertiginous tenacity, these polar structures are notoriously reversible. The rule of reversibility is basic and frequently applied by deconstructionist critics. In his reading of *A la recherche du temps perdu*, for example, de Man illustrates the complexity of Proust's "language of consciousness," a language which constantly gets outside itself and becomes its own cover, by means of the comparison with a rolled-up sock: "which is its own outside and which, when unrolled, like the Möbius strip, is also its own inside."[11] It is impossible, de Man argues, to decide between container and contained, between what is outside and what is inside.

Given this frame of relative reference, we may well ask: what enables the positioning of substitutive rhetorical systems "behind" *The Anxiety of Influence* rather than "up front"? On the contrary, it may be argued that there is nothing hidden or implicit about the linguistic substitutions Bloom employs

---

9. Heidegger, *Being and Time*, sec. 316.

10. De Man, "IMB," 77. It is an irony (though whether calculated or not remains an open question) that the essay on impersonality is one of de Man's most personal and self-revealing meditations on criticism.

11. Paul de Man, "Reading (Proust)," *Allegories of Reading: Figural Language in Rousseau, Nietzsche, Rilke, and Proust* (New Haven: Yale University Press, 1979), 70–71.

in his book. In the explanatory introduction Bloom openly declares, foregrounds, as it were, the metaphoricity of his six revisionary ratios: clinamen, tessera, kenosis, daemonization, askesis, and apophrades. The term "clinamen" is introduced, as are all the other terms, by a figural definition: "*Clinamen*, which is poetic misreading or misprision proper; I take the word from Lucretius where it means a 'swerve' of the atoms so as to make change possible in the universe. A poet swerves away from his precursor. . . ."[12] The extravagant rhetoric of *The Anxiety of Influence* may be considered a kind of cover, a carapace which envelops the core vision of a desperate and ongoing struggle between the poet and his precursors. The superordinate term "ratio" is itself an open metaphor, a substitution for interpersonal relationships. This is what really shines through the trappings of Bloom's terminology.

But bearing in mind the shifting grounds on which we stand, the undecidable oscillations we experience, as when we view a drawing by Escher and are caught up by the instability of our perceptions, perhaps the very distinction between the drama and the rhetoric of *The Anxiety of Influence* is untenable? It may be no longer possible to say what is foreground and what is background. Or perhaps, and this would be a very different way of looking at it, it is a case of our not being able to know the dancer from the dance? of a text written with such a strong and single-minded impulse that we cannot reconcile, because we cannot distinguish, a division between its form of discourse and its content? And when I ask a rhetorical question, am I not dramatizing as well as verbalizing a problem to which I think I already have the answer?

In these Derridian days of de-centering and free play, it is difficult to appeal to authority, presence or origin for support. The author has no say in his saying. Nevertheless for the record, in *A Map of Misreading*, published the year after de Man's review, Harold Bloom addresses the turn his book has taken. He unequivocally rejects de Man's reading and insists that "influence remains subject-centered, a person-to-person relationship, not to be reduced to the problematic of language."[13] With a willful turn of his own, Bloom adds this "insight" into de Man's "inside" view of his book: ". . . a trope is just as much a concealed mechanism of defense, as a defense is a concealed trope."[14] This last is a reversal which, if stared at too long, may cause us to begin to blink. Seemingly and typically a deconstructive statement, it is called into the service of an assertion of authenticity and commitment. The rhetoric of presence and persuasion returns—via the rule of reversal.

And so the self remains. What de Man reveals by his reversal or unveiling of *The Anxiety of Influence* is not, so to speak, the real Bloom but the real de Man. It is not surprising, therefore, that instead of the "heavily emotional"

---

12. Harold Bloom, *The Anxiety of Influence: A Theory of Poetry* (New York: Oxford University Press, 1973), 14.

13. Harold Bloom, *A Map of Misreading* (New York: Oxford University Press, 1975), 77.

14. Bloom, *A Map of Misreading*, 77.

tone of the book, de Man hears a "very different tone and terminology" (274). The voice which he hears is his own. To quote de Man quoting Bloom: "We can redirect our needs by substitution or sublimation." De Man cites this statement as a proof and summary of the substitutive systems which govern the theory of influence. It also serves to describe what de Man does, as he tropes *The Anxiety of Influence* and transforms its author, by means of sympathetic magic, into a deconstructor of rhetoric.[15]

Ironically enough, it would seem that de Man's review of *The Anxiety of Influence* proves the accuracy of Bloom's central thesis—that all reading (or, inevitably, misreading) is a power play in which the later text attempts to displace and usurp the text which preceded it. But this, in turn, proves de Man's point—that all intratextual relationships are rooted in rhetoric, that we are governed by the play of substitutions or tropes. Viewed in a certain light, it might seem that Bloom and de Man are speaking of the same thing. However, for Bloom, misreading is a function of intentional being, of will striving against will; for de Man, it results from the mechanism of the sign, from its duplicitous or, rather, "multi-plicitous" nature. De Man offers us a negation which is at the same time an affirmation, or what he might call a metaphor of metaphors: Nothing is what it is. To which Bloom might well shake his head and say: it is unalterably sad, but things are just the way they are.

In conclusion, I feel uneasy: the authoritative tone of de Man's review, its value-laden lexis, and its privileging of linguistic models of interpretation over and above all others seem to clash too obviously with the reiterated claim made for the "impossibility of reading." This feeling of unease is not improved by Geoffrey Hartman's finely apt description of Paul de Man, in the preface to *Deconstruction and Criticism*, as a boa deconstructor, "merciless and consequent." Thus it seems to me that de Man's misreading of *The Anxiety of Influence* can be read in two ways: either de Man is actually mystified by the text and has repressed its content; or he deliberately misreads it. If the latter, then one would want to ask further: did De Man mean to deconstruct Bloom, or did he mean this to happen? That is, was it a part of his intentional scheme to have an eager reader review his review and repeat the lesson she has learned from a master, thereby assisting him to exemplify and confirm his own critical theory of blindness and insight? For while most texts are unable to account for, are blind to their own duplicitous directions, some texts possess mechanisms of demystification, "possess, from the start," as de Man phrases it, "all the elements of distance and negation that prevent written language from ever achieving a condition of unmediated presence."[16] Is de Man's review of Harold

---

15. The precedents or models for this practice of "speaking through"—or "shining through"—another critic are provided by de Man himself, for example, in his discussion of Baudelaire's essay on Constantin Guys in "Literary History and Literary Modernity" and, especially, in "Heidegger's Exegeses of Hölderlin." See *BI*, 156–61 and 246–66, respectively.

16. De Man, "The Rhetoric of Blindness," 115.

Bloom's *Anxiety of Influence* one of those unmystified, self-deconstructing texts? His essay seems designed to prevent the formation of any definitive solution. All that I can venture to say is: it is once more a case of either . . . or. . . .

HEBREW UNIVERSITY, JERUSALEM

Reading with de Man

GEOFFREY H. HARTMAN

Meaning, Error, Text

Meaning, despite the effort of *maîtres-penseurs*, does not remain stable. The meaning, for example, of this French phrase is shifted when Foucault applies it, ironically, to German thinkers like Hegel and Nietzsche, who reappear in Nazi doctrines about the *master* race. Unforeseen historical events and their interpretation keep meaning nomadic, though the instability does tempt us toward projects of codification or canon making.

Let me take a simple case and then go to a much more complicated one—complicated because it involves a tradition spanning twenty centuries. The simple case is the trial of Hitler, Ludendorff, and their associates in March, 1924. The *Boston Transcript*, under a dateline of March 14, entitles its column "Trial Farce" and begins as follows:

> Alice in Wonderland's classic courtroom remark, "Nonsense, you are nothing but a pack of cards," is a perfect comment on this year's most important political process—the trial of Ludendorff, Hitler and their associates for high treason—which continues in comic fashion in Munich.
>
> As the trial proceeds it becomes apparent that the protagonists, including the military hero Ludendorff; the would Mussolini, [sic.] Hitler; ex-Dictator Von Kahr, once described as the "strong and silent," like Alice's Queen, are collapsible when not taken seriously.

Obviously, the unpredictable career of one of the defendants, Hitler, puts these judicial proceedings in a new light. Whether or not the trial was a farce deserving, as the paper says in closing, "international volleys of laughter," one cannot but wonder how long it took for the world to take Hitler seriously. Not to take him seriously was a tactic that might have worked, but did not; and it raises questions concerning our failure to interpret political events. We seem to be unable to measure them, to guess at their future resonance. We underestimate or overestimate, dismiss or slander, shrug or fly into opinionated fits of rage. Hitler is not an inept example, since the height of overestimation always produces a Messiah figure and the extreme of underestimation the deceiving image of a buffoon or trickster.

145

The more complicated case spans a tract of time named after its founder. I refer to the Christian era, which has its first trial transcripts in the Gospels. The Gospels, as a New Testament, look back to the so-called Old Testament. That a carpenter's son should be the Messiah is a scandalous event not predictable by any soothsaying text. Yet the text about that event, the "new" testament, turns previous scripture into a pre-diction, degrading it as blind while investing it with a missed (or dismissed) capacity for illumination. The new text at once confirms and disconfirms the older one, which remains extant.

Two questions arise from this pattern. The question of error: if the Synagogue is blind to a truth it reveals, how is this state of affairs to be explained? The question of originality: are there texts which affirm themselves without that twofold structure of "new" (enlightened) and "old" (blind)? Do we know a type of writing that appropriates traditions so effectively that we cannot recover what was there, what is radically, permanently displaced?

Let me start with the second question. It is the Hebrew Bible, the "Old" Testament, that evokes the possibility of an original appropriation. Modern scholarship has been trying to reassemble the appropriated traditions for well over a hundred years by positing an alphabet soup of sources and redactors. The importance of transmission in a more than technical sense—of *traditio*—is crucial here and can lead to diametrically opposite evaluations. The Hebrew Bible, it has been shown, tries to receive, censor or reconcile various traditions. But it also replaces them so that the originals disappear into an authoritative scripture that has become their only source. So the Hebrew Bible can be praised or blamed, depending on one's point of view toward tradition. We may admire the fact that it incorporated so much, or regret that it displaced so much, and by becoming the original made us forget other origins. The same kind of reflection could be applied to the New Testament. We can admire it for struggling with the incumbency of what it calls "old"; we can also blame it for trying to liquidate a precursor text by degrading it as the shadowy prefiguration of its own truth.

The impossibility of making truth and text coincide is what threatens all writing as it strives to transmit definitively a "body" of knowledge. We try to prevent that body from becoming a corpse, or losing its coherence and being scattered, dismembered, disremembered. The study of meaning, therefore, is coextensive with studies of textual embodiment and verbal incorporation. We learn how the commentary process is related to works that want commentary to cease, or to revolve around them like satellites.

My main concern, however, is with error. Can we talk of meaning and error together, as if error were part of the structure of meaning? Why is it so difficult for truth and text to coincide? Or, what is equally surprising, why should anyone think they could come together?

It is not clear that there was ever a belief in an absolute Scripture. So the Hebrew Bible, though divinely inspired, is held to speak in "the language of man." There is accommodation or condescension (to use the Christian term that alludes to God taking on human form). The Hebrew Bible, moreover, is really two books: the written law, and the oral law (commentary), both given to Moses on Sinai. A beautiful Rabbinic story has Moses attending a seminar of Rabbi Akiva's and not understanding what is being said. In a related story, God intervenes in a debate about His law by means of the *bat kol* (echo-offspring of the founder's voice). But the Rabbis dismiss its authority in a postprophetic age, and God accepts their argument. "My children have defeated me." It is the equivalent of a voice coming from heaven to declare that there is no longer such a voice. Or a voice that says, in effect: "The results of your exegetical labors is my Law, in which I am pleased." Even the Protestant return to the plain text of Scripture and the rejection of Catholic safeguards express not an idolatry of the letter, but a precarious and spiritually burdened view of the relation between letter (text) and reader. Faith comes through hearing: through the internal echo, through the responsiveness of auditors to Scripture. The authority of belief resides in that transactive relation. The truth of the text is the text, but only as it inspires such a relation.

The Synagogue, nevertheless, was depicted as blind, and judged culpable. It failed to see what it transmitted: it could not read its own message of deliverance. The Church considered this failure as an act of God, similar to when He hardened Pharaoh's heart. The Exodus, the liberation from Egypt, becomes in Christian interpretation a "type" or "figure" of the very release from spiritual bondage effected by Christ and not fully understood by the Hebrews.

This concept of error, which combines an idea of inevitability with a judgment of blame, is indeed a scandal. However, it proved effective in fashioning a triumphant mode of interpretation, masterful toward the Hebrew text and consoling toward historical time, which remained, even after Christ's advent, a "waiting in patience." Figural typology, the instrument of the Church, enriched that time and sustained the believer. But just as there are two testaments, there are two modes of interpretation: Patristic, chiefly typological, and Rabbinic, which stands in a "negative" relation toward the Messianic event as a fulfillment of time and of the Word. The second mode has reemerged in recent thought but has not generally been recognized as having an affinity with a major Jewish tradition of exegesis (*midrash*).[1]

What we learn from and against typology is the temporal complexity of the text-reality nexus, even the temporal complexity of signification generally. The meaning of signs is always being displaced or revised by the mythical and seductive image of a *grand temps* (Eliade) or the latest realism. While realism is demystifying and myth is restorative, they are functionally similar in positing a realm of error made visible by haunting ideas of reference. (I find the psychoanalytic term useful in this context.) The drive toward reference is a kind of terminal illness, with us from the beginning, or from "In the Beginning."

---

1. See, however, Susan Handelman's *The Slayers of Moses: The Emergence of Rabbinic Interpretation in Modern Literary Theory* (Albany: State University of N.Y. Press, 1982).

Reality itself, rather than its signs, is the desideratum, even when reality may turn out to be the dark side. Error is identified with unfulfillment; and there is an assumption that with fulfillment, the language of signs, including the Great Code itself, will change utterly or disappear.

What the Church holds against the Synagogue is not so much its blindness as its stubbornness: its continuance in blindness. The chosen people might have seen the truth. It is not God who limits their role: they limit themselves until their vision becomes opaque. Israel, then as now, refuses to be mature, to emerge from its self-imposed minority. Its position in providential history is a judgment it has passed on itself.

Such self-humiliation is hard to explain, since the basis for group consciousness is rather the opposite: self-glorification, the sort of motive furnished, for example, by the idea of being a chosen people. The "error" attributed by Christian typology to the Old Testament is just not believable, except from the perspective of Church propaganda. A more likely view is that interpretation, when problematic rather than doctrinaire, is always involved in such "error." Its main feature is an imbalance, an oscillation, between self-humiliation and self-glorification, between an underestimation and an overestimation of private capacities or public actions, as our first example, that of Hitler, demonstrated.

In typology, exaltation—and exultation—are based on the humbleness of the subject being transfigured. This structure reminds us that on the level of individual psychology, delusional ideas of reference may clothe every detail with an aura of ultimate significance. The simplest happening becomes a sign, a clue, and the indifferent or unconscious person, the "bystander," is drawn into a plot of divine or demonic dimensions. Similarly, on the level of political or group psychology, almost anything (a "straw") can precipitate conflict.[2] Indeed, the expressed reason for violent action, including war, is generally that of avenging a "humiliation," of restoring national or class pride.

In the Hebrew Bible this reversal from low to high, as well as the opposite movement of dejection, is less marked than in Christian story. One need only compare Hanna's "psalm" (Samuel 2:1–10, perhaps interpolated) with Mary's *Magnificat* (Luke 1:46–55). The words are not unlike, and both women rejoice, having been freed from childlessness. The verbal and domestic contexts are very similar. Yet Christian story emphasizes the humility and the humiliation—the humility of Mary herself, as a woman, and the pastoral and realistic world of the manger; while the humiliation, linked to this circumstantial frame, is that of religious persecution.

In the Hebrew Bible, too, there are famous reversals of fortune, as in Joseph's career, or that of Moses. Yet neither man enters the vision or the Holy Land. Fulfillment is withheld. Joseph's bones are returned to his country, and

---

2. So the *Boston Transcript* reports that Hitler grew "purple with rage in an interchange with Kahr regarding the meaning of 'Word of honor.'"

Moses is vouchsafed only a Pisgah-peek. This reserve, especially toward the leader, whose humanity is not associated with humility but with fallible pride, is what teases typological interpretation and allows it to "complete the figure." Typology, as an instrument of interpretation, is forcefully anagogical, expunging the reserve of Hebrew Scripture as if it were blindness rather than insight. This blindness is the "wilderness error" that alienates God from Israel, though it also draws Him closer to mankind through the visible condescension of the Incarnation.

A more temporal or temporizing view marks both normative Rabbinic exegesis and "deconstructive" literary criticism. The impossibility of speaking the truth once and for all, of stabilizing meaning or memory through canonized textual closure is the issue. Not to acknowledge the validity of commentary, or of interpretation generally as it reenters the primary, even the sacred text, and discloses that the latter too is layered, stratified, mediated—a "temporal labyrinth"—is to neglect the secularity of literature. Our only excuse for this neglect is a new and abrupt fundamentalism. This fundamentalism in a postprophetic age is, however, too much like messianism in its furor and intransigence.

YALE UNIVERSITY

J. HILLIS MILLER

Impossible Metaphor:
Stevens's "The Red Fern" as Example

Two ways of honoring Paul de Man may be distinguished. I mean honoring him in the sense that one speaks of honoring a check, paying it back or paying it off, keeping its value in circulation, making it pass current.

One way to honor de Man is to read him. That this has happened, is happening, or will ever happen does not go without saying. The argumentation of his essays is so intricate and goes so much against the grain of common sense assumptions about language and its relation to empirical reality, including the "self," that it is exceedingly easy, perhaps inevitable, that we should misread him, forget what he says, in one way or another suppress his teaching, even in the act of paying him homage. This happens perhaps most effectively when something he explicitly denies is affirmed as his position. As readers of de Man will know, a recurrent theme in his work is the question of why expert readers, not to speak of ordinary ones, tend to misread the plain sense of texts they discuss. "Hölderlin," affirms de Man, "says exactly the opposite of what Heidegger makes him say."[1] Speaking of Jean Starobinski's interpretation of Rousseau, de Man observes, "How curious that, when a text offers us an opportunity to link a nonlinguistic historical concept such as perfectibility to language, we should refuse to follow the hint. Yet a critic of Starobinski's intelligence and subtlety goes out of his way to avoid the signs that Rousseau has put up and prefers the bland to the suggestive reading, although it requires an interpretative effort to do so. . . . There must be an unsuspected threat hidden in a sentence that one is so anxious to defuse."[2] "Interpretation" is here opposed to reading and may even be implicitly identified with "misreading."

What de Man applies to Heidegger and Starobinski must no doubt apply to us as readers of de Man. Moreover, the reader of de Man may uneasily re-

---

1. Paul de Man, *Blindness and Insight*, 2nd ed. (Minneapolis: University of Minnesota Press, 1983), 254–55, henceforth *BI* 2.
2. Paul de Man, *Allegories of Reading* (New Haven and London: Yale University Press, 1979), 144, henceforth *AR*.

member that one of de Man's conclusions about reading is that it is "impossible" if one means by reading the reaching of a single logically consistent interpretation of a given text, an interpretation clearly and exclusively supported by evidence from that text. Any text, for example, can be shown to be "rhetorical," including de Man's own essays, and, as de Man says, "considered as persuasion, rhetoric is performative but when considered as a system of tropes, it deconstructs its own performance. Rhetoric is a *text* in that it allows for two incompatible, mutually self-destructive points of view, and therefore puts an insurmountable obstacle in the way of any reading or understanding" (*AR*, 131). This seems clear enough, but insofar as *Allegories of Reading* or this citation from it is itself a *text*, which it evidently is, what de Man says about the impossibility of reading must also apply to his apparently so lucid statements about the impossibility of reading.

In the light of this double difficulty (a general tendency of even distinguished readers to misread, to suppress even the apparently straightforward sense of declarative sentences, and in addition an intrinsic impossibility of the enterprise of reading in any case), it would be naive to assume that there is a broad understanding of de Man's work, that that work has been "assimilated" by the community of critics and theoreticians, and that we can go on from there. As de Man himself says, in anoher context, "one sees from this that the impossibility of reading should not be taken too lightly" (*AR*, 245). One way to honor Paul de Man, then, is to renew the attempt to read him, even in the teeth of the possibility that this may be impossible, since the encounter with that impossibility may be what distinguishes reading from nonreading or from the interpretative imposition of some presupposed pattern of assumptions about the meaning of a given text.

A second way to honor Paul de Man and to help keep his work current, passing from hand to hand, is to attempt to read this or that poem or novel or philosophical text on one's own, or, to return to my initial metaphor, to write one's own checks rather than cashing those of de Man. This assumes of course that one has money of one's own in the bank. To say that one might do one's own readings in the light of Paul de Man's work or with help from his thought is mere foolishness, since each critic in the work of reading is on his or her own, face to face with the text, alone with it, never so alone as at that moment. One thinks, to vary the metaphor quite a bit, or perhaps not all that much, of the narrator of Henry James's "The Aspern Papers" appealing for help in a crisis to the portrait of Jeffrey Aspern: "He seemed to smile at me with friendly mockery, as if he were amused at my case. . . . What an odd expression was in his face! 'Get out of it as you can my dear fellow!' "[3]

One way to understand the isolation of each act of reading, and in addition one further reason for the inevitability of falsifying de Man's work in any report

---

3. Henry James, *The Aspern Papers and Other Stories* (Harmondsworth, Middlesex, England: Penguin Books, 1979), 97, 99.

of it or borrowing from it, however scrupulous and careful, is to recognize a curious ironic doubleness in all those general "theoretical" statements about language and reading he makes, for example those about the impossibility of reading I have just cited above. On the one hand, these statements are affirmed with universal apodictic generality, as for example when he says, "The paradigm for all texts consists of a figure (or a system of figures) and its deconstruction" (*AR*, 205). There is no reason to doubt that de Man means what he says here, that "all texts" means all texts whatsoever, in all times and places. On the other hand, all such statements in de Man are made in the course of a specific reading of one text or another. They draw their validity from this context, also whatever comprehensibility they may have, in defiance of de Man's own theory of unreadability. In spite of their apparent universality they mean something else or are even emptied of meaning when they are detached from their original context within the intricate manoeuvers of a particular act of reading and appropriated either in any account of "Paul de Man's theory of reading" or as the justification by another critic of a reading of his or her own. There is no help for it. Each of us is alone as a reader and must "get out of it" as he or she can, no doubt by repeating one or another of the inevitable "aberrancies" de Man so indefatigably analyzed.

Take, for example, Wallace Stevens's "The Red Fern," a little poem from *Transport to Summer* not even included by Holly Stevens in *The Palm at the End of the Mind*, nor commented on by Harold Bloom in his comprehensive book on Stevens's poetry. No doubt the extraction of a single poem from the vast shifting panoramic linguistic theater of Stevens's work is another version of that falsification by citation out of context which I have already mentioned apropos of de Man's work. It is an example, that is, of citation as such, since citation is the extraction of a fragment from its home and its insertion in unfamiliar surroundings, where it means something different, if it has meaning at all. All citation is therefore tropological and ironic. No claim of synecdochic similarity, part like whole and bringing that whole virtually along with it, will stand scrutiny. "The Red Fern" is not a valid sample of Stevens's work "as a whole." The part, in this case the extracted citation, is unlike the whole and it becomes even unlike itself when it enters as a far fetched stranger within another house, the discourse of its reader or critic. The question of the entry of the "unfamiliar" into the "familiar" is in fact thematic and named as such in "The Red Fern."

In spite of these preliminary and persistent difficulties "The Red Fern" appears to open itself relatively easily to exegesis. Not only is it bound by many ties of conceptual and figurative terminology to Stevens's other poems, for example, "The Man with the Blue Guitar," "A Primitive Like an Orb," and "The Rock," poems I have elsewhere discussed.[4] The poem is also, in itself,

---

4. In *The Linguistic Moment* (Princeton: Princeton University Press, 1985).

detached from *The Collected Poems* and inserted here, woven of manifold conceptual and figurative interchanges, substitutions, displacements. It gives the reader all sorts of interpretative lines to follow. Here is the poem:

The Red Fern

The large-leaved day grows rapidly
And opens in this familiar spot
Its unfamiliar, difficult fern
Pushing and pushing red after red.

There are doubles of this fern in clouds
Less firm than the paternal flame,
Yet drenched with its identity,
Reflections and off-shoots, mimic-motes

And mist-mites, dangling seconds, grown
Beyond relation to the parent trunk:
The dazzling, bulging, brightest core,
The furiously burning father-fire . . .

Infant, it is enough in life
To speak of what you see. But wait
Until sight wakens the sleepy eye
And pierces the physical fix of things.[5]

This poem itself opens like a red fern, unfolding its leaves from stanza to stanza of proliferating phrases, like mist-mites and dangling seconds. The first stanza is a single sentence stopped at the end. The second sentence unfurls more generously in a string of appositives and ends in the open with the three dots of elipsis. These are followed by the abrupt new start in the fourth stanza of direct address to the "infant" reader or perhaps to some infant within the poet himself. The title says this is a poem about a red fern, but the reader soon sees that the fern is a figure. Like "A Primitive Like an Orb" and like many other poems by this solar poet "The Red Fern" is a poem about the sun. Or perhaps it would be better to say that is about the day as governed, centered, and powered by the sun: "The large-leaved day grows rapidly." Unlike some of Stevens's solar poems "The Red Fern" is explicitly about sunrise, the "appearance" of the sun out of its nighttime occultation at dawn. "The Red Fern" joins a long tradition of sunrise poems, for example the great opening lines of Part Two of Goethe's *Faust,* where deafening sound substitutes for blinding sight: *Ungeheures Getöse verkündet das Herannahen der Sonne.* In Stevens's case the substitution is not of sound for sight, but of one "sight" for another, fern for sun. In "The Red Fern," as in "A Primitive Like an Orb," the unspoken law of the poem is that though the poem has as its goal to name the sun the

5. Wallace Stevens, *The Collected Poems* (New York: Alfred A. Knopf, 1954), 365, henceforth *CP.*

word *sun* may not be used. It is banished from the dictionary. This convention indicates the impossibility or at least the impropriety of naming the sun in so many words, looking it in the eye, so to speak.

Why is this? Though the sun is the source of all seeing and of all procreative energy, vitality, and growth, for example those of red ferns or of human fathers and mothers, it cannot itself be looked at directly. To look the sun straight in the eye is to be blinded, to see nothing. The sun does not therefore, strictly speaking, "appear" at all when it rises. Though it is the condition of seeing, there is nothing to see where sight arises. One sees nothing there. Since by definition literal naming is possible only of things which are open to the senses, phenomenologically perceptible, especially available to eyesight, and since the "sun" does not ever appear in this way, it is, paradoxically, improper or indeed impossible to name the "sun" in the way the things made visible by the sun may be named. The sun is not one of those things we encounter, see, and know "under the sun." The "sun" can therefore only be named in figure, veiled or misted in metaphor, covered by a word or words which serve as a protection against the danger of blinding. Even the word *sun*, or its equivalents in other languages, is, as Aristotle long ago saw, already a metaphor, not a literal name, since the conditions for literal naming are not fulfilled in this case. These conditions are, for example, made incomplete by the invisibility of the risen sun or by our inability to track the sun even out of the corner of our eye when it has set and is out of sight, beneath the horizon. Any name for the "sun," even the most apparently literal one, *sun*, is a kind of blank place in the syntax of a sentence, a coverup of the fact that there is nothing there for perception to know and then to name. The word *sun* is not even a catachresis, since it is not transferred from some other realm where it has a straightforward literal meaning, as in the case of *face* or *leg* in "leg of a table," "face of a mountain." The word *sun* is, strictly speaking, nonsense, a kind of surd within language, however easily we all, even a great poet like Goethe, use it every day. Stevens's avoidance of the word may therefore be seen as a kind of linguistic scrupulosity or fastidiousness, an unwillingness to use a word which names nothing though it appears to be an ordinary name.

There are, however, two ways to respond to this avoidance in "The Red Fern," two ways to read the poem. Or rather, following a useful distinction proposed by Andrzej Warminski, the poem may be either *interpreted*, that is, misinterpreted, or it may be *read*.[6] The first way, hermeneutic interpretation, assumes that the sun, origin of seeing and knowing, symbol of the transcendent one, the *logos*, is in fact itself visible. Do we not see it rise each day? The problem is to name its unfamiliarity, its diurnal novelty, adequately. Metaphor is the means of doing this, but not by imposing the known on the unknown, rather by the mechanism of the classic Aristotelean proportional met-

6. In "Prefatory Postscript: Interpretation and Reading," *Readings in Interpretation: Hölderlin, Hegel, Heidegger* (Minneapolis: University of Minnesota Press, 1985).

aphor in which all the elements of the metaphorical displacement are seen, therefore open to being known and literally named. Literal naming depends on seeing and on the knowing which follows seeing: "it is enough in life/To speak of what you see." Naming or speaking in fact depends on seeing, since literal language, the base and origin of all metaphorical transfer, is defined as the match of the word with the perception of the thing. We see the sun and we call it "sun." Or rather, seen from this perspective of interpretation, the poem apparently depends on the exchanges among the elements in a chain of such metaphors. As the sun rises with each new day and sheds light everywhere, illuminating the clouds, so tropical red ferns grow rapidly from their genetic nodes and then reproduce themselves on runners or stolons, and so the male organ of generation becomes erect and ejaculates semen. "The Red Fern," on this interpretation, is generated by the play of substitutions among these three realms, each open to perception, knowledge, and naming. Terms from one realm are dispersed, disseminated, carried over, transported, according to the etymological meaning of *metaphor*, to another region in a crisscross of substitutions which can go both ways. If, according to that familiar romantic assertion that poetry "lifts the veil of familiarity from the world," the unfamiliarity of the new sun on the new day is named and kept in the open by calling it a red fern and an erect male member, words from the realm of the sun are borrowed to call that erect penis a "furiously burning father fire." The resemblances and consequent verbal displacements in both directions are objective. They are in the nature of things as they are, things as they are seen and known. This seeing and knowing precedes the names for things and the subsequent shifting of names involved in making metaphors. Such shifting fulfills Aristotle's affirmation that a "command of metaphor" is "the greatest thing by far" in a poet: "it is the mark of genius, for to make good metaphors implies an eye for resemblances."[7] The resemblances are there. The poet of genius has an eye for them. For this reason it is enough in life for the infant poet to speak of what he sees. The word *sun* is a legitimate part of the lexicon, but it has through much use become too familiar, its effigy effaced, like a worn out coin. To call the sun a fern or a phallus corresponds to our sight and knowledge of the sun by affirming what the sun resembles. The basis of the poet's speaking is mimetic. The infant poet is a child of the sun, one of its reflections, mimic motes, and exterior resemblances. The poet is himself a mimetic doubling. The poet's speaking, in turn, say in the form of a poem, is not autonomous creation, nor even in itself the revelation of something invisible, but another form of mimesis. The poem, for example "The Red Fern," is another of the offshoots of the sun. The poem is a resemblance of the sun. It is governed entirely by the prior ontological authority of the sun as substance: visible, knowable, namable.

7. S. H. Butcher, *Aristotle's Theory of Poetry and Fine Art, With a Critical Text and Translation of The Poetics* ([New York]: Dover Publications, Inc.: 1951), 87.

If, however, we now take a close second look at the poem and *read* it rather than *interpret* it, problems with the clear schematizing of its meaning I have just proposed begin to appear. Three anamalous features of the language of the poem may be identified which forbid reading it according to the logical scheme of a chain of Aristotelean metaphors, forbid reading it, that is, as logocentric, as governed by the *logos*, here apparently represented, in the most traditional of images, by the sun. These anomalous, unlawful, or alogical features of the language of the poem mean that it is in fact a series of impossible metaphors. "Impossible" is here meant as a discrepancy between the language and any possible physical fact. Rather than being grounded in nature, in things as they are, in perception leading to knowledge leading to naming and then to that interchange among such firmly grounded names called *metaphor*, such alogical language indicates the unsettling freedom of language from perception and its ability to pour into the mold of its syntactical and grammatical patterns forms of locution which, in relation to the empirical world, are strictly speaking, nonsense, for example that something should be simultaneously all male and all female. Such impossible metaphors are in fact a regular law of words describing the sun. "The Red Fern" is one of the latest in a long line of resemblances of the sun which includes Plato's parable of the cave as well as those passages in Aristotle to which I have alluded, comes down through Shelley's "The Triumph of Life" to a passage in Nietzsche's *The Birth of Tragedy* to a passage in Proust to Derrida's "La Mythologie blanche," and passes along the way almost innumerable other examples of man's wrestling in words with the sun.[8]

Stevens in a well-known formulation in the *Adagia* asserts that "poetry should resist the intelligence almost successfully."[9] It is perhaps too easy to assume that because it is poetry it is all right for it to be nonsense from a logical or empirical point of view. The reader would err in underestimating the importance in Stevens's poetry of that resistance to the intelligence, that presentation of alogical or impossible locutions, locutions that do not make sense when tested against empirical reality, though he would also no doubt err in underestimating the force of that "almost." Poetry should resist the intelligence *almost* successfully. It may be that the moment when the intelligence resumes mastery over poetry is the moment of a shift from interpretation to reading, that is, the moment of a shift to the intelligence of those linguistic features in a poem which do make sense either tropologically or empirically. Or it may be the other way around. The moment when the intelligence resumes mastery over a poem may be no more than an illusory clarity of the mind gained by suppressing elements which can never be mastered by logic. It depends on

---

8. The passage in Proust is discussed in a remarkable footnote in Paul de Man's "Reading (Proust)," AR, 60–61, and the passage in Nietzsche is read by Andrzej Warminski in the essay cited above.

9. Wallace Stevens, *Opus Posthumous* (New York: Alfred A. Knopf, 1957), 171.

whether you consider the experience of the impossibility of reading as a victory or a defeat for the intelligence. As Paul de Man says, in another context, the implications of such an intelligence of the limits of intelligence in relation to language are "far-reaching" (AR, 61). Let me try to identify three moments of such alogic in "The Red Fern" and attempt to figure out their implications, working against the strong resistance of the poem, as of Stevens's poetry in general, to the reader's intelligence.

The first alogic is the absence of the word *sun* in the opening sentence of the poem. I have already said something about the conspicuous absence of the word *sun* in this poem about the sun, and of the way this corresponds to the absence of the sun from direct empirical perception. You cannot look the sun in the eye without being blinded and therefore, though it is the source of seeing and speaking, it cannot itself be spoken of in literal language based on direct perception. The sun must be spoken of indirectly, in the shifting into the place where the sun might be, but where there is in fact nothing for perception, nothing to see and nothing to name, of a word borrowed from some realm where seeing and naming are possible. In the first stanza of "The Red Fern" the absence of the sun is signalled by the fact that Stevens says not "The sun rises," but "The large-leaved *day* grows rapidly" (my italics). It can be day or daylight in the absence of the sun, for example on a cloudy day. The word *day*, in its encompassing abstraction, as a name for the whole temporal period we oppose to night, names not the sun but what the sun brings. *Day* is a name for everything under the sun but the sun. The day might be expressed by a vast empty sky stretching from horizon to horizon, a place of light but a place of the absence of any source of light. The fact that there is nothing there where the sun might be is indicated by the alogical shift in Stevens's lines between figuring the day itself, in its totality, as a large-leaved plant of some kind ("The large-leaved day grows rapidly . . ."), and then going on to speak of the day as the locus, milieu, or "spot" within which the invisible and unnamable sun grows as a red fern: "And opens in this familiar spot/Its unfamiliar, difficult fern,/Pushing and pushing red after red." The sentence does not make sense as the description of any empirical phenomenon. It is like Proust's description of the sun on a cloudless day turning its eye elsewhere. It is impossible for the day to be simultaneously a large-leaved plant and at the same time the place within which a red fern opens and grows. As a literal representation of an empirical phenomenon the sentence is impossible, but as the mainfestation of a linguistic necessity it is scrupulously accurate. It exposes or expresses the necessity of presupposing a center or *logos* for the exchanges of metaphor, while that center is always absent, a vacancy, not even a negation, since it cannot be said whether or not there is anything there, only that there is nothing there to be perceived and named. Into that vacant place in the syntax is introduced one or another figure, for example the figure of the red fern, but this figure must name simultaneously the presupposed center and something which is derivative from that center. Into the emptiness of a sky vacant of any sun, in the syntactical place of that originating motivation for speech is put the name of something else, for example a red fern, which is one of the children of the sun and owes its life and growth to the sun's warmth and light. The empirical impossibility or absurdity of the sentence brings into the open the necessity of presupposing an originating *logos* in any act of speaking, while at the same time, never by even the most extravagant contorsions of language, being able to speak of that source of language except in words which presuppose the very thing the sentence is supposed to interrogate, to try to face clearly, and to name. The sentence uses the invisibility of the sun to reveal a linguistic necessity. Such sentences can never do more than name once more something derived and secondary and put that name in the place of what can never be named because it is the presumed base of language, for example by putting a red fern simultaneously in the place of the sun and in the place of the whole region of day within which the sun rises.

A second alogic in the poem is the impossibility of deciding for certain whether the sun is personified as male or as female. It seems certain that the sun must be male, especially if the reader knows the Pennsylvania Dutch slang meaning of *fern*, links this with "trunk," "furiously burning father fire," and sees the imagery of tumescence and ejaculation in "bulging" and "mimic motes/And mist-mites." On the other hand a shadowy underthought suggests a female rather than a male gender for the sun. The sun "pushing red after red" may be giving birth to all those infants of the sun, including the poet. There is an incompatibility between that phallic image of the sun as trunk and the image of a "dazzling" "brightest core," the sun as a fire which cannot be looked at without blinding the beholder and which therefore is experienced as an absence, as a hole in the sky. It will not be advisable to take too lightly the double gender of the sun, to speak of it as if it were a simple oscillation within perception between *Gestalts:* "Now you see it, now you don't." It is impossible for something to be male and female at once with the full powers of each gender. It does not make sense. Though the androgyne may be possible it has always been a scandal to reasonable habits of classification. If the reader takes that second look at the text, the male gender of the sun can be "seen" to correspond to *interpretation* governed by the presumed referentiality of the words, while the female gender of the sun corresponds to *reading,* that is, to a shift of attention to the language of the poem as such. Rather than being a free oscillation, the movement from male to female gender is a one-way road in which there is no return from reading to interpretation, only a further movement deeper into the intelligence of what resists the intelligence almost successfully.

To see the sun as male, as a father, corresponds to the male child's reassuring (or perhaps not so reassuring) sight of his father's member, in the obscure (not all that obscure) sexual drama of the poem. As might be expected, Stevens imagines this drama in the traditional androcentric way, that is, from the point of view of the male child. As soon as something intrinsically linguistic is expressed in terms of sexual difference, even the gender of nouns or the sex of the reader or protagonist, either one, is no longer indifferent. What it would be like to see and speak of what "The Red Fern" names from the point of view of a female child is being explored by some feminist critics, though not, so far as I know, in terms of this poem as example. In "The Red Fern" the implied perspective is definitely male. It should be remembered that the father's "fern" is not the penis as such but the phallus as head signifier, what the male child may appropriate and control by putting himself in the place of the father, what guarantees the validity of the metaphorical exchanges of naming, speaking of what you see.

A possible female gender for the sun, on the other hand, still thinking of it from the point of the male child, corresponds to reading, not interpretation. In the place where the phallus, head signifier, might be there is nothing, an absence, or nothing perceptible, or something that dazzles and blinds. The Greeks embodied their fear of the sight of female genitals in the story of Baubo, who used self-exposure, lifting her skirt, as a power. In the case of "The Red Fern" if there is nothing or nothing but a dazzling brightness when we try to look the sun in the eye, this means that the metaphorical exchanges involved in speaking are governed and validated by no empirically known chief signifier, though speaking necessarily presupposes such a first signifier at the head of the chain of substitutions. It is then impossible to speak of what you see because the ground or presupposition of all speaking can never be seen. The place where that signifier should be but is not is a syntactical requirement. The place is filled, groundlessly, illegitimately, without authority of seeing, by one or another name brought over from somewhere else, the word *fern*, for example, though the word *sun* would be no more legitimate, since what is in question here is a linguistic necessity, not an empirical fact. The sign that it is a question of signs rather than of extralinguistic reality is, once more, the absurdity of the language when the reader tries to take it as having a literal, referential meaning. The poet has not spoken of anything one could see.

After what has been said so far, the final area of alogic is Stevens's language here, that in the last stanza, is easy to "see." If it is enough in life to speak of what you see, on the one hand that would mean never speaking at all, since speech presupposes always some original and originating governor or leading signifier whose referent, it turns out, can never be seen. The infant poet, child of the sun, always remains *infans*, deprived of language by his inability to look the fathering or mothering fire in the eye, so to speak, though that confrontation is necessary to any authoritative speaking. On the other hand, this means that it is enough in life, must be enough, since there is nothing else, to speak of what can be seen in place of what cannot. This means speaking of other children of the sun that rise up in the sun's heat and light and make themselves visible, tropical red ferns, for example, or the father's erect member, though, as we have "seen," when the fern as plant turns into the fern as phallus, it becomes invisible. There is nothing there to see but a dazzling core, core as absence rather than core as central presence, father turned to mother or to Baubo.

This double meaning, nonsense according to referential logic, of the sentence telling the infant poet it is enough in life to speak of what you see is doubled again by the final alogic of the last sentence of all: "But wait/Until sight wakens the sleepy eye/And pierces the physical fix of things." *Sight* here, like *day* in the opening line, is a curiously nonlocatable abstraction, everywhere at once, inside and outside at once. A "sleepy eye," like that childhood partial blindness in one eye called "lazy eye," is an eye which is not using a power of seeing which it has. Sight wakens the sleepy eye as a body becomes conscious, by a wholly internal change. On the other hand, *sight* may be a figure for the illumination of the external world when the sun rises. The eye is sleepy because there is nothing to see, but when light floods the world and is disseminated everywhere, then the fact that there is now something to see wakens the sleepy eye, as light penetrates under the eyelids of a sleeping infant and wakes him. *Sight* is a metonymy for "something there to see," the name of one part of the process substituted for another part which is next to it, or for the general condition of illumination. *Sight* is in this reading a synonym of *day* in line one, that is, it names what the sun brings without ever being visible itself. *Sight* in this sense is a name for the absence of the sun. If it is enough to speak of what you see, this speaking has to wait on seeing, and what can be seen are things under the sun, red ferns, for example, not the sun itself. The ultimate cause of sight can never be seen, just as the chief signifier, generator, guarantee, and legitimizer of all speech, can never be seen and named as such, only seen and named in displaced representatives of it, for example the sun.

Something exceedingly odd happens, however, in the completion of the last sentence in the last line when sight is taken not as an intrinsic property or power of the eye, which may be awake or asleep, but as something done to the eye from the outside, waking its latent power of sight. This oddness is the final alogic of the poem: "But wait/Until sight wakens the sleepy eye/And pierces the physical fix of things." When *sight* is read the first way, this sentence says the awakened eye has a power of penetration, as when one says someone has "piercing eyesight," a power to penetrate nature, lift her veil of familiarity, go beyond the stillness, "the physical fix of things," behind which movement and life are hidden. The fix nature is in forces it to repeat the familiar, the same, as in the stuttering alliteration of "phys" in "fix." The piercing eye of the infant poet is here, as I have said, a male power of penetrating and possessing a female nature which includes even that feminized mothering sun present shadowily behind the furiously burning father fire. On the other hand, if *sight* is taken in the second way, as something done to the sleepy eye of the infant poet by the light, then that "physical fix of things" is also internalized. It is a condition caused by the infant's sleepy way of seeing things as fixed and dead. He is one of those who seeing, see not. For a moment, before the intelligence protests and says the lines cannot be saying that, the words "Until sight wakens the sleepy

eye/And pierces . . ." are read as saying "sight," a power coming in from outside, wakens the sleepy eye by piercing it, blinding it, as Oedipus blinded
himself as punishment for seeing what he should not have seen, as looking on
the goddess naked is punished, and as the sun is a dazzling core, blinding the
one who looks it in the eye. The sentence cannot logically say both these things
at once, since they cannot both make sense referentially at once, and yet if the
sentence is read to the end as opposed to being interpreted according to some
hermeneutical principle of assumed coherence and unity, it does, impossibly,
say these two things at once, two things which can in no way be reconciled or
dialectically sublated. If it is enough in life for the infant poet to speak of what
he sees and if he waits until sight pierces his eye, he will be blinded and will
have nothing to speak of. Speaking can only be of what cannot be seen. This
includes in the end red ferns and ferns in the phallic sense as much as the
blinding sun. The poem demonstrates this, though not as something that can
be "seen," in the noncorrespondence of its speaking with any conceivable form
of seeing.

   What happens to the infant poet, finally, happens also to the infant critic
when he or she tries to speak of what he or she "sees" in the poem. Far from
inviting a shift from *sight* as seeing, that is, an interpretation of the poem
according to its referential logic, to *sight* as insight, some presumed mastery of
the language of the poem gained through a shift to reading, the act of reading
leads to a double experience of that blinding by the text which Paul de Man
calls its unreadability. An interpretation of the poem based on its presumed
referential sense leads to irreducible alogical absurdities. This experience of
the impossibility of reading leads to a doubling demonstration of this unreadability in the way the reader's insight into this first unreadability, the one at
the level I have called interpretation, is powerless to prevent in the act of
deconstruction it performs the repetition of the errors it denounces. The example of that here is my illicit use of the metaphor of blindness and insight, in
spite of myself, to name a mastery and failure of mastery over what can in
neither sense of the word be "seen" and therefore clearly "spoken of." The
second unreadability, then, is the inability of the critic to read and draw lessons
from his own act of reading. To put this in another way, in my reading I have of
necessity used as the instrument of deconstruction a version of the very thing I
have deconstructed, or shown to deconstruct itself in the text, namely acceptance of the myth of the necessity of a head signifier beyond and outside the
play of language in order for there to be logical language, for example the
language of the critic even in "reading" (as opposed to "interpreting") a poem. I
have made use of this myth in one of its most powerful forms, that is, the one
depending on sexual differentiation for its figures (the presence of the paternal
phallus and the absence of the maternal one). In order to read the poem on this
basis I have yielded to the literalization of the figurative, in this case the
confusion of the symbolic phallus with the literal penis, as when I have said of

the sun, "There is nothing there." Whether it is possible ever to escape from this androcentric or phallogocentric myth through any conceivable act of contesting it is another question. It is a question that for the moment, and perhaps indefinitely, must remain open. Certainly my own procedures here would rather confirm once more that "impossibility of reading" which Paul de Man says should not be taken too lightly.

YALE UNIVERSITY

CAROL JACOBS

On Looking at Shelley's Medusa

"On the Medusa of Leonardo da Vinci in the Florentine Gallery"[1] has been disregarded by Shelley's most prominent readers. Thus such canonical critical works as Wasserman's *Shelley: A Critical Reading*, Bloom's *Shelley's Mythmaking*, or Baker's *Shelley's Major Poetry*, to list only a few, do not discuss the poem. One volume borrows its title from the text in question, Kroese's *The Beauty and the Terror*,[2] but never analyzes the poem. In *The Romantic Agony*[3] Mario Praz entitles his first chapter "The Beauty of the Medusa"; it opens dramatically with a full citation of Shelley's poem for, we are told, "it amounts almost to a manifesto of the conception of Beauty peculiar to the Romantics."[4] Yet, despite the privileged place given to the piece, Praz seems all too eager to leave it behind rather than contemplate its intricacies in detail. To what can we attribute this critical oversight? Such reticence makes good sense from several points of view. Significant problems abound with respect to establishing the correct text. There is the unresolved question of the final stanza, whether or not Shelley intended it to be attached to the main body of the poem[5] as well as the lacunae Shelley left in several lines that necessarily challenge the comprehension of his reader. Moreover, despite its unusual literary grace, what kind of light can one hope to shed on a poem that seems simply to reproduce the lineaments of the well-known painting it describes?

Nevertheless, two contemporary critics have written with exceptional insight on the problematics of this text, although, strangely enough, in order to

1. The poem is cited in full from Percy Bysshe Shelley, *Selected Poetry*, ed. Neville Rogers (London: Oxford University Press, 1968), 357–58.

2. Irvin Kroese, *The Beauty and the Terror* (Salzburg: University of Salzburg, 1976).

3. Mario Praz, *The Romantic Agony* (New York: Meridian, 1956).

4. Praz, 25. For a rebuttal of Praz's argument, see Jerome McGann, "The Beauty of the Medusa" in Studies in Romanticism, 11 (1972), 3–25.

5. Neville Rogers, "Shelley and the Visual Arts," *Keats-Shelley Memorial Bulletin*, 12 (1961), 16–17. Rogers was the first to publish the sixth stanza and also the first to give the text well-warranted critical attention.

Head of Medusa, Uffizi Gallery, Florence.

ON THE MEDUSA OF LEONARDO
DA VINCI
IN THE FLORENTINE GALLERY

I

It lieth, gazing on the midnight sky,
   Upon the cloudy mountain-peak
     supine;
Below, far lands are seen tremblingly;
   Its horror and its beauty are divine.
5 Upon its lips and eyelids seems to lie
   Loveliness like a shadow, from which
     shine,
Fiery and lurid, struggling underneath,
The agonies of anguish and of death.

II

Yet it is less the horror than the grace
10   Which turns the gazer's spirit into
     stone,
Whereon the lineaments of that dead
   face
   Are graven, till the characters be
     grown
Into itself, and thought no more can
   trace;
   'Tis the melodious hue of beauty
     thrown
Athwart the darkness and the glare of
   pain,
16 Which humanize and harmonize the
   strain.

III

And from its head as from one body
   grow,
   As   grass out of a watery
     rock,
Hairs which are vipers, and they curl and
   flow
20   And their long tangles in each other
     lock,
And with unending involutions show
   Their mailèd radiance, as it were to
     mock
The torture and the death within, and
   saw
The solid air with many a ragged jaw.

IV

25 And, from a stone beside, a poisonous
   eft
   Peeps idly into those Gorgonian eyes;
Whilst in the air a ghastly bat, bereft
   Of sense, has flitted with a mad
     surprise
Out of the cave this hideous light had
   cleft,
30   And he comes hastening like moth
     that hies
After a taper; and the midnight sky
Flares, a light more dread than obscurity.

V

'Tis the tempestuous loveliness of
   terror;
   For from the serpents gleams a brazen
     glare
35 Kindled by that inextricable error,
   Which makes a thrilling vapour of the
     air
Become a   and ever-shifting
   mirror
   Of all the beauty and the terror
     there—
A woman's countenance, with serpent-
   locks,
40 Gazing in death on Heaven from those
   wet rocks.

Additional Stanza

It is a woman's countenance divine
   With everlasting beauty breathing
     there
Which from a stormy mountain's peak,
   supine
   Gazes into the   night's
     trembling air.
45 It is a trunkless head, and on its feature
   Death has met life, but there is life in
     death,
The blood is frozen—but unconquered
   Nature
   Seems struggling to the last, without a
     breath—
The fragment of an uncreated creature.

do so, they fix their critical glances on quite another object. It is a question, to begin with, of the figure under whose aegis this volume is published. To publish under the aegis of Paul de Man, however, perhaps this goes without saying, is not to write under his protection or patronage. Nor will an erasure of the dictionary definition in favor of the mythical origin of the term set things straight. The aegis was the singularly adorned shield borne by Pallas Athene. To be sure, she was also the provider of that very different shield whose brazen glare allowed Perseus to contemplate the Medusa while escaping the powers of its gaze. Nowhere in de Man's work does he make such a gesture. He may offer us a mirror of sorts, but his writings, more like that other shield borne by the Goddess herself, are an aegis to which the head of the Medusa is affixed and which we contemplate at our own risk. One aspect of those writings, especially in de Man's later criticism, is a rhetoric of temporality in which a complex temporal strategy drives the critical enterprise. It is the metaphor of time that opens a reflective space, enables a semblance of knowledge and, coincidentally, elaborates a theory of figural language while ironizing all sense of theoretical progress.[6] What takes place in Shelley's poem might be called a 'rhetoric of spatialization' for "On the Medusa of Leonardo da Vinci" does with space what de Man performs with time. If that places this essay under de Man's critical aegis, it places it under the aegis of his irony. Also of considerable critical significance is Louis Marin's *Détruire la peinture*[7] in which he offers a remarkable analysis of what it means to observe Caravaggio's painting of "The Head of the Medusa" and at the same time, of necessity, comments on that other Medusa at the Uffizi.

In the case of Shelley, of course, we are confronted not with a painting, but rather with a text that cites a painting as its subject matter. At least the title of the poem, "On the Medusa of Leonardo da Vinci in the Florentine Gallery," does this with the insistent and unpoetic precision of a catalogue entry. The title functions then as a double frame placing the reader at several levels of remove from the object of artistic representation, the dangerous head of the Medusa. Yet nowhere in the forty-nine lines that follow are we reminded that the poet describes a painting rather than the real thing. This poses unending problems in situating ourselves, in fixing the object of our scrutiny as text, painting, or Medusa to the exclusion of the other two. It raises a tangle of questions that are as predictable as they are maddening. Does Shelley gaze directly at the Gorgon as suggested by the poem or at the painting attributed to Leonardo, as suggested by the title? What does it mean to look at the Medusa? What does it mean to look at a work of art, to look at a painting or for that matter to read a poem? Does the text expose *us* directly to the gaze of the Medusa or does it function like the shield of Perseus, mirroring the Gorgon's head and protecting us from its effects?[8] How does a literary text operate whose

6. I develop this in an essay forthcoming in *Reading de Man Reading* (Minneapolis: University of Minnesota Press, 1985).

7. Louis Marin, *Détruire la peinture* (Paris: Galilée, 1977), 117–80.

8. If so, we could, in Shelley's terms, then attribute to the literary text a fundamental

fundamental gesture is to describe the objective world or another work of art, and what would it mean to describe? Who is the gazer—Perseus, his predecessors, the painter, the poet, the reader?

There are no clear-cut answers to these questions although all six stanzas are bent on nothing if not on describing the scene at hand and on situating the observer with respect to it. The poem immediately dispels any simple concept of mimetic description that the title might seem to have proposed, for neither the scene nor the perspective of the gazer are identical to those of the painting.[9]

> It lieth, gazing on the midnight sky,
>   Upon the cloudy mountain-peak supine;
> Below, far lands are seen tremblingly;

The Medusa gazes on the midnight sky, yet there is another line of vision, that of the viewer: "Below, far lands are seen tremblingly." This line of vision shifts the head to a level much lower with respect to the observer than that suggested by the canvas: he stands above the slain Gorgon as he views the lands beyond, tremblingly. This is not to say that either the gazer or the scene itself trembles, rather that, despite his shift to the position once occupied by the triumphant Perseus, there is something precarious in his manner of seeing.

This is intensified if not explained by a sense of struggle in the contradictory attributes of his object of contemplation, both here and in the other stanzas that concentrate on the face of the Medusa where its horror and its beauty, its loveliness and its agonies, are uttered in the same poetic breath.[10]

> Its horror and its beauty are divine.
> Upon its lips and eyelids seems to lie
>   Loveliness like a shadow, from which shine,
> Fiery and lurid, struggling underneath,
> The agonies of anguish and of death.

If we are to believe these lines (in a stanza perhaps all too suggestive of a pun on lies) loveliness veils "the agonies of anguish and of death." In a text that openly announces a work of art as its subject matter, it would seem legitimate to read this as a nonironical version of Baudelaire's statement: "The intoxication of art is more apt than any other to veil the terrors of the eternal abyss."[11] Shelley himself was soon to write (although the passage is somewhat out of context):

> Poetry turns all things to loveliness; it exalts the beauty of that which is
> most beautiful, and it adds beauty to that which is most deformed: it marries

---

"wisdom" for in "Adonais" Shelley speaks of "wisdom the mirrored shield" (l. 240). To be sure, he speaks of Keats, and perhaps all exemplary poets, failing to wield it.

9. See Rogers, 13.

10. Also in lines 9, 33, 38, and 46.

11. Charles Baudelaire, "Une Mort héroïque," in *Oeuvres complètes* (Paris: Pléiade, 1964), 269–73.

exultation and horror, grief and pleasure, eternity and change; it subdues to union under its light yoke all irreconcilable things.[12]

Is it then the loveliness of art, of Leonardo's painting and of Shelley's poetry, that masks the horror of its object and protects the onlooker and reader? Is the representation of art such that it distances us from the effects of the Medusa?

At the end of stanza 2 it is once again a question of the relationship between the beauty and the agony. The beauty at issue is now unmistakably that of the work of art, for the elements of painting and song (hue and melody) enter explicitly into play.

> 'Tis the melodious hue of beauty thrown
> Athwart the darkness and the glare of pain,
> Which humanize and harmonize the strain.

If art is here as before that which is cast athwart the pain, it is hardly that which conceals the terrors of death. For, according to the unexpected plural forms of the verbs in line 16, it is not "the melodious hue of beauty" that mitigates the strain, but rather, with an unexpected shift, "the darkness and the glare of pain." The loveliness of art, then, does not lessen the strain of the Medusa's agony: rather the darkness and glare of pain humanize art and harmonize a strain that here, as elsewhere in Shelley, suggests the strain of poetry.[13]

The "melodious hue of beauty" is not like the mirror held by Perseus that reflects its monstrous object while shielding him from its powers. For, if the first stanza offers a conventional description of its supposed, external object, if it also takes pains to separate the Medusa's gaze from that of the observer, if at the same time (for these are necessarily bound to a unified concept of representation) it speaks of art as mask and balm, in the second stanza it is precisely this loveliness of art, its "grace," that menaces the gazer.

> Yet it is less the horror than the grace
> Which turns the gazer's spirit into stone,

What kind of art is this that is more threatening to the gazer than the horror of looking directly at the Medusa? How does the mirror of art function? What is its mode of reflection? Suddenly, it is no longer the Medusa who is to be portrayed but the spectator, for the Medusa was, of course, something of an artist in stone. Yet whereas the myth would seem to speak of a reification of the

---

12. "A Defence of Poetry" in Percy Bysshe Shelley, *Shelley's Poetry and Prose*, (New York: Norton, 1977), 505.

13. The word appears quite often in Shelley's poetry, most often with the sense of a strain of poetry or music. For a reading counter to this one, see Jerome McGann (op. cit. 7) who reads the poem rather as "an allegory about the prophetic office of the poet and the humanizing power of poetry." Daniel Hughes also sees the hope of the poet here that the "'melodious hue of beauty' might 'humanize and harmonize the strain.'" It makes sense, then, that he goes on to read Shelley's position as that of a "reverse Perseus" who could escape the threat of transformation to stone, mastering the Medusa as he brings "under his own submission this now 'identified' monster of thought." ("Shelley, Leonardo, and the Monsters of Thought," *Criticism* 12 (1970), 204–05).

physical attributes of the observer, what concerns Shelley is no longer physical reality,[14] neither that of the poem's object, the painting of the Medusa, not that of its onlooker: it is the gazer's *spirit* that is transformed into stone.

> Yet it is less the horror than the grace
>   Which turns the gazer's spirit into stone,
> Whereon the lineaments of that dead face
>   Are graven, till the characters be grown
> Into itself, and thought no more can trace;

To trace what transpires here is indeed impossible. Despite his positioning with respect to the Medusa in stanza 1, the fate of the gazer is more akin to that of Perseus's predecessors than to the hero. And if his spirit is turned to stone, this takes place not as a reifying process that preserves form but as a radical transformation. It is neither the features of the onlooker nor his spirit but rather the lineaments of the dead Gorgon's face that are graven at the point of articulation between the Medusa and the would-be Perseus. The gazer loses his identity, but this is not to say that the Medusa retains hers, for in Shelley's text it is no longer a question of who dominates whom. The contours of the Medusa's face are graven, but the monster as the single, fixed locus of petrifying powers is dead.

Nor are the "characters" in this performance of artistic production simply the features, the cast of countenance, delineated in stone. They include all those creatures we have seen the poem to conceive—the Medusa as object imitated, the gazer as poet, artist, reader, or beholder, and the graven work of art, poem or painting. What takes place is an inexorable process to the point that each of these progressively and irreversibly grows into a single, if unfixable "itself," an "itself" that might plausibly be designated as any and none of these.

Were it possible to extricate our gaze from this scene, we might be able to contemplate its critical implications. For Shelley's poem is about nothing if not about our own interpretative predicament as readers. The "characters" of line 12 are drawn into a process of unending involution in a notion of art that can no longer be regarded as preserving what happens to serve as the cornerstones of so much of our contemporary critical endeavor. In this scene of unthinkable creation, each of these characters is dislocated as a possible point of valorization. Yet it is such valorization of the artist that determines much psychoanalytic and all biographical interpretation, such valorization of the object imitated that underlies, for example, historical criticism, and such privileging of the spectator on which the various forms of reader response commentary are based.[15] Nor are we witness to a pseudo-Mallarméan sacrifice of

---

14. The poem imitates or describes the painting, but within the poem the image of another mode of reflection also takes place.

15. See Paul de Man, *Blindness and Insight* (Minneapolis: University of Minnesota Press, 1983), 285–86.

the object, artist, and beholder in favor of a work of art that can then be contemplated in isolation, aesthetically or semiotically, with no such points of reference. One begins to understand the reluctance of Shelley's interpreters with regard to this text.

The process of involution is such that "thought no more can trace." Can no longer trace what? one is tempted to ask, for Shelley breaks off his thought by leaving the usually transitive verb "trace" without an object. Thought is no longer the trace of something else, which is certainly not to say that the bizarre mirroring that takes place in this text would be one of simple and triumphant self-reflection. Perhaps we might make sense of the phrase by reading thought as the object of trace. But what is it then that can no longer trace thought? Either the thinking subject or the object of thought remains absent. What the text insists on is a lack in thought and this lack is coincident with a grammatical failure, with the inability of language to complete its meaning.

If the relationship between thinking subject and object, between gazer and Medusa is seen to tremble, if "thought no more can trace" takes place in the name of the grace of art rather than the horror of art's monstrous object, if the "darkness and the glare of pain" promises, as we have seen, to humanize and harmonize the strain of poetry (lines 14–16), one might nevertheless regard stanza 2 as a moment of error and aberration in a poetry that now seems to return to a more harmonized and humanized concept of itself. Beginning with stanza 3, the text seems intent upon describing the painting attributed to Lenardo in a manner that no longer menaces or even problematizes the human beholder. Nowhere else in the poem does its voice seem more matter of fact, more true to the simple task of description posed by the title of the text. Or could it be that the beholder has already grown into "itself"? For if it is true that he no longer figures as the subject matter of the poem's statement, he is implicitly involved, here as elsewhere, as the narrative voice. And the entire point of his narration in stanza 3 is that one cannot make heads or tails of it.

> And from its head as from one body grow,
>   As   grass out of a watery rock,
> Hairs which are vipers, and they curl and flow
>   And their long tangles in each other lock,
>   And with unending involutions. . .

The unending involutions, the inextricable tangles that would make the matching of head and body impossible are in no way problematic for the narrative voice. For, while insisting on their inextricability, an inextricability that it will later even speak of as "error," the intent does not lie in rectifying this error. Contrary to appearance, though, this is not to say that the text simply reproduces their tortuous visual form in words. It is quite the other way around. At the same time that the stanza speaks of involutions with evident detachment, it performs far more radical gestures through the intricacies of its figural language. The hairs of the Medusa grow "from its head as from one body." What has happened to our head? What the last stanza of the poem will call a "trunkless head" here becomes a headless trunk, a body without a head of its own. It becomes the very inverse of what it was before the thrust of simile transformed it. Simile, here as elsewhere in Shelley,[16] is certainly no sign of similarity, nor is it, however, a limited operation of inversion or negation. One is not witness to a Persean decapitation, for figural language is no hero, severing the head of the monster and mastering her powers. The simile maintains the trunkless head in proximity to the headless trunk: each both completes the meaning of the other and makes it unreadable, for the two merge into that which thought no more can trace.

One is especially hard put as to the nature of such figures when Shelley compounds his first adverbial simile with a second.

> And from its head as from one body grow,
> As   grass out of a watery rock,

The medusa head, first transformed into a headless trunk now seems smitten by its own mythical force—turned to stone with a turn of phrase that compares it to a rock. At the very moment that the text apparently carries out the task of description, just when poetry would seem to devote itself to the most straightforward concept of representational art, a mimetic recreation of the canvas attributed to Leonardo, something utterly unspeakable takes place as well. The simile of line 17 divests the object of its identity, and that of line 18 leaves it as unlike itself as possible, for it becomes totally other, victim to its own power to transform into stone, a self-reflection gone awry. The force of the Medusa is allied with poetic figuration and, as we saw in stanza 2, this is hardly a force of mimetic reification. The Medusa is described as object, it is depicted as in the painting, but, in the same breath, the force of its figuration is such as to (in the language of the closing stanza) un-create the same creature.[17] The Medusa, then, is both the object of these lines and the poetic strain that mocks

---

16. The first stanza of the "Hymn to Intellectual Beauty," for example, is an attempt to define that elusive poetic force through a long series of similes whose terms of comparison seem peculiarly at odds with one another. Thus the "awful shadow" is compared to "moonbeams," floating to creeping, "hues of evening" to the colorless "clouds in starlight," "harmonies" to "memory of music fled." Like the figures in the "Medusa," those of the hymn mark the refusal of language to define by affirming an identity. Intellectual beauty, its inconstancy, is nothing if not this refusal, a denial then of those conventional concepts of language as naming or invocation, the "frail spells" and "poisonous names" of the later lines. On related questions in the "Hymn to Intellectual Beauty" see Jonathan Baldo, "A Semiotic Approach to Prospection in Shelley," forthcoming in *Semiotica*. An extended study of such gestures in Shelley would have to confront the figure of Demogorgon in "Prometheus Unbound."

17. This critical moment of figural language as un-creation pivots, ironically enough, around the verb "grow." Ironically enough, because it upsets, of course, all that the concept of growth would seem to guarantee, a linear progression with a sense of origin. As the involutions of stanza 5 will show, figural language upsets as well that particular temporal and spatial ordering implicit in the title of the poem—Medusa: painter: painting: poet: poem: reader.

and undoes the concept of object.[18] It is these two modes that are endlessly entangled in one another throughout the text.[19]

There are at least two ways, then, of looking at the Medusa. The one allows the spectator to regard it from a safe distance, as object; the other draws the beholder into a conception of the Medusa as the performance of a radical figural transformation, of itself, of the beholder, of the language that attempts to represent it. In stanza 4 these two roles are played by an eft that looks with neither interest nor sense of danger into the Gorgon's eyes and a "ghastly bat" that is driven mad by what it perceives.

> And, from a stone beside, a poisonous eft
>   Peeps idly into those Gorgonian eyes;
> Whilst in the air a ghastly bat, bereft
>   Of sense, has flitted with a mad surprise
> Out of the cave this hideous light had cleft,
>   And he comes hastening like a moth that hies
> After a taper; and the midnight sky
> Flares, a light more dread than obscurity.

The passage reads like a parody of Plato's "Allegory of the Cave,"[20] for the bat is drawn into the light of midnight rather than dragged into the light of the sun. The journey upwards also dazzles Plato's cave dweller, but there, he who was previously doomed to seeing mere shadows of images seems promised, once outside the cave, a progression in enlightenment that will allow him to pass from shadows, to reflections, to real objects, and finally to the contemplation of "the immediate source of reason and truth."[21] Plato's philosopher learns then to disentangle image from reality in the light of the intellectual world. But the bat in Shelley's text encounters a light that is "more dread than obscurity," for it reveals a situation in which one is "bereft of sense" and "thought no more can trace."

The Medusa herself is yet another version of those creatures in the cave, restrained from turning their heads, a fire lit above and behind them, for above and behind the Medusa, as the fifth stanza shows, is a light of dubious nature. "This hideous light" is not a heavenly body as in Plato, but rather the "mailèd radiance" of the serpentine involutions, the source of illumination for a remarkable scene played out before gazing eyes. The bat, then, leaves the cave of shadows, not for the sun of dazzling enlightenment, but only to confront the

---

18. In these same lines the rock becomes watery while, shortly thereafter, the air becomes solid. The poem is riddled with such unpredictable reifications and unshapings.

19. On the question of an implicit double reading throughout Shelley's work, see J. Hillis Miller's fine essay "The Critic as Host" in *Deconstruction and Criticism* (New York: The Seabury Press, 1979), 217–53.

20. Book 7 of *The Republic*.

21. Plato, *The Republic*, trans. Benjamin Jowett (New York: Vintage) 257.

illusion of false figuration repeated in another form.[22] Indeed, this creature, suspended in that strangely "solid air" has every reason to be driven mad, witness as he is to the "tempestuous loveliness of terror" described in the lines that follow and, once again, in the final passage. As in stanza 2, where the grace of art rather than the horror of its subject matter turned the gazer's spirit into stone, so here the loveliness of terror involves a spectacular if bizarre mirroring.

> 'Tis the tempestuous loveliness of terror;
>   For from the serpents gleams a brazen glare
> Kindled by that inextricable error,
>   Which makes a thrilling vapour of the air
> Become a   and ever-shifting mirror
>   Of all the beauty and the terror there—
> A woman's countenance, with serpent-locks,
> Gazing in death on Heaven from those wet rocks.

Stanza 5 is where, as the saying goes, everything comes together, or fails to. A glare kindled by the "mailèd radiance" of "long tangles" makes the air into a mirror of sorts that sets up a disconcerting model of reflective activity. If it makes good sense along with Neville Rogers to read "error" as the physical windings of the serpents,[23] one cannot entirely repress the more literal insistence on an "inextricable error," a mistake from which there is no recourse. It is this ineluctable error in both senses of the word that brings about the production of a mirror from the trembling vapors of the air, a looking glass that finds no fixed position but rather shifts its locus perpetually. What it reflects is "all the beauty and the terror there." Like a limited view of the painting or poetic text, it might seem to portray the Medusa, caught in a temporality that line 42 calls "everlasting," as a fixed object of description: "A woman's countenance, with serpent locks." Strange that such a questionable reflecting device should, for the first time in the text, give us a clear and decisive breakdown of the elements of beauty and terror, the loveliness of the countenance, on the one hand, the horror of the serpent-locks on the other. Strange also that it is only at this point in the poem that we are reassured of the human quality of the Gorgon, for until now she had always been referred to as "it." Striking that the endless involutions of serpents and "watery rock" that in stanza 3 marked the threat of figurative language as displacement, radical self-reflection, and transforma-

---

22. The poem is a parody only of a literal reading of that text since Shelley's "Medusa" might well be viewed as an enlightened allegory of all that takes place in Plato's passage. Just as Shelley's Medusa repeats the scene within the cave, so Plato echoes that scene in the voice of Socrates. For the philosopher, in narrating his parable, as one cannot fail to note, repeats the structure he denounces. He stands, as it were, behind Glaucon and asks him to "Behold" "in a figure how far our nature is enlightened or unenlightened" (253). One might argue that Glaucon and Socrates are, nevertheless, at least one level of reflection beyond that of those they observe: the same might be said for the Medusa as we shall see.

23. Rogers, 16.

tion should here be present as the most matter of fact objects, "serpent-locks" and "wet rocks." Of course, this all takes place just when the basis of such mirroring is clearly announced as error, its instrument as ever-shifting, its reflections, therefore, inevitably an illusion, the illusion, among others, of set distinctions between beauty and terror, the human and the monstrous, the literal and the figurative.

And yet, we have not even begun (and how could we begin among these unending involutions) to trace the intricacies of speculation implicit at the close of the text. The mirror, we have seen, resembles both the painting and poem that take the head of the Medusa as their model; but that reflection is also the image of a work of art produced from within the work of art. It becomes easier to visualize this passage if one looks to the painting where there is indeed a very distinct vapour. It arises from the slightly parted lips of the Medusa. The "thrilling vapour of the air" that forms the psyche comes from the mouth of the Medusa, not only as her breath, but also, since the mirror appears as an image of poetry, as the spoken word. The last lines of the poem speak somewhat indirectly of this.

> It is a trunkless head, and on its feature
>   Death has met life, but there is life in death,
> The blood is frozen—but unconquered Nature
>   Seems struggling to the last, without a breath—
> The fragment of an uncreated creature.

The Medusa's death is a birth of sorts out of which a certain creature arises. According to myth, Pegasus sprang from the blood of the Gorgon at the moment she was slain. In Shelley's text the figure for poetic inspiration results from a struggle between life and death, breath and its loss. It appears as a questionable source of poetry, a vaporous mirror that both reflects and withdraws the locus of reflection. This is why, in the closing verse of that "additional stanza" that has one line too many perhaps (and not only because it has nine lines instead of eight), the result of poetic reproduction is called "the fragment of an uncreated creature." For nothing in Shelley's work of art bears witness to completeness and we have seen the manner in which the concept of creation is uncreated time and again.

We might think of the close of the text as itself uncreating what came before, rewriting the earlier lines as it draws them into itself in a final gesture of involution. If the opening verses focus descriptively upon the lips and eyelids of the Medusa's countenance, these features become the crucial points of a bizarre self-reflection in stanza 5. But it is not only a question here of uncreating the simplistic mimetic thrust that seems intermittently to govern the poem.[24]

---

24. Intermittently, because the entire poem functions like the vaporous mirror, ever shifting between a mimetic concept of reproduction (stanzas 1, 4, 6) and another that has yet to be traced. Those seemingly simple descriptive moments, therefore, are, from the very beginning, *images* of the mimetic.

The position of the spectator, and therefore the reader, is even more radically at stake than one could have realized. For the gazer's "spirit," transformed into an engraving in which death meets life (stanza 2) is mirrored later in the "thrilling vapour" (l. 36) exhaled by the Gorgon. Spirit in both its etymological and conventional significance is breath, "the breath of life" as well as "the soul of a person passing out of the body in the moment of death" (OED), that struggle of which we have read, between breath and its surrender. In stanza 5 the figure of the external beholder is taken into the countenance of the Medusa where she is once again seen "gazing."

She gazes "in death on Heaven" (l. 40) or, as the opening words of the poem would have it, "It lieth, gazing on the midnight sky." But what does it see? That "Heaven" or "midnight sky" is the same sky that earlier flared with "a light more dread than obscurity," a light that threatens thought and sight far more than the darkness of obscurity. This is no blank stare into the heavens above, for the last stanza has the Medusa gazing "into the   night's trembling air."

> It is a woman's countenance divine
>   With everlasting beauty breathing there
> Which from a stormy mountain's peak, supine
>   Gazes into the   night's trembling air.

The "trembling air" is that same "thrilling vapour of the air" that becomes an "evershifting mirror." What the Medusa contemplates, then, and it is indeed enough to rob one of one's senses, is the evershifting image of herself gazing into a mirror formed of a vapor that arises from her own mouth. The Medusa becomes, then, in a sense, if one can follow the windings of the points of articulation in this scene, the artist poet from whose mouth the reflective work of art arises, the object depicted by that work of art, and the beholder of the work of art. All at once, one is tempted to say, and yet they cannot logically be conceived simultaneously.

The "characters" have "grown into itself," but this does not mean that we are witness to a perfect union. Quite the contrary. If our reading of the phrase "thought no more can trace" showed language necessarily lacking either object or subject, this is the object lesson taught, if never quite comprehended in those closing lines. The Medusa views herself in a mirror that trembles between the "everlasting" and the "ever-shifting." Everlasting since what she sees might be represented as fixed in the manner of the painting at the Uffizi. But what she gazes on is an image of herself as the beholder of herself as the origin of an image that reflects herself as the beholder. . . . It is impossible for thought to hold the reflecting subject, the producing subject, and the object produced (that in turn reflects) all in the same time frame.[25] The refusal of

25. On the question of fragmentation in relation to self-knowledge and mirroring, see Paul de Man, "Shelley Disfigured," in *Deconstruction and Criticism*, Bloom et al. (New York: The Seabury Press, 1979), particularly 40, 45, and 55.

closure, then, offers to view the production of the perpetually fragmented "uncreated creature." In ways that would be too vertiginous to outline, one can imagine the endless involutions added to this by remembering those other beholders, painter and poet, spectator and reader, who may be envisioned not only within but also without the text.

All this is kindled[26] by the light of the unending tangles we saw in stanza 3. For, from the moment that the subject or object in question is thought, that is to say language,[27] the lack of which we have spoken is bound to take place. This becomes clear if we reflect once again on the turns of phrase in Shelley's similies, since the simile is to some extent emblematic of what happens in all figural language.

> And from its head as from one body grow,
>   As   grass out of a watery rock,

If these lines are the phrase "from its head . . . grow" in search of an analogon, what is their thrust and that of all similes if not the attempt of language to name itself—language in search of its own image. Such a moment not only mocks the pretention to denominate an objective realm located elsewhere, but, as we have seen, more crucially mocks the concept of a subject identical to itself. In verses that are framed as a narrative subject naming the other (Medusa), verses that nevertheless show a linguistic "subject" naming itself, the force of the simile transforms the other into a self and that self into yet another, everlastingly, evershiftingly. Figurative language, which for Shelley is the same as literary language, mocks itself, like the Medusa gazing on her trembling vapor of the air: such is the inextricable error of the text.

Errors of this sort cannot be confined to the particularities of the poem at hand, to the Medusa and the particular kind of art she inspires, as though we might mark the limits of the monstrousness and protect ourselves from its theoretical implications. Such a gesture would deny the inextricability of beauty and horror on which Shelley insists; it would repeat the historical repression of the final stanza where the text openly gives life to an "uncreated creature" that, metaphorically, can be none other than poetic inspiration in general. In Shelley's most definitive statement on the nature of the literary text, written less than two years after the poem, we encounter precisely the same complex of elements, except, tellingly, that man rather than the Medusa is the locus of reflection.

"Poetry," Shelley writes in "A Defence of Poetry," "in a general sense, may be defined to be 'the expression of the Imagination': and poetry is connate with the origin of man."[28] This is no banal historical assertion of poetry's role

---

26. Daniel Hughes makes the link between "kindling" and the poetic act in Shelley's poetry in "Kindling and Dwindling: The Poetic Process in Shelley," *Keats-Shelley Journal*, 13 (1964), 13–28.

27. See "Prometheus Unbound": II.4.72: "He gave man speech, and speech created thought."

28. Defence, 480. All future references to this text will simply be noted as page numbers within the essay proper.

in the youth of the world. Poetry is connate with the origin of man because man is, only in so far as there is poetry. Of poets, Shelley will go on to say: "Their language is vitally metaphorical; that is, it marks the before unapprehended relations of things. . . ." (482). What can it mean that the language of poets is vitally figural?[29] On the one hand poetry "strips the veil of familiarity from the world, and lays bare the naked and sleeping beauty which is the spirit of its forms" (505). Yet this stripping of the veil hardly gives us a privileged proximity to that which lies beneath. "Poetry lifts the veil from the hidden beauty of the world, and makes familiar objects be as if they were not familiar. . ." (487). This is because, although poetry may lay bare the naked beauty which is the spirit of the world's forms, that beauty is never present to us as meaning. "Veil after veil may be undrawn, and the inmost naked beauty *of the meaning* never exposed" (500, emphasis mine). This strange lifting of a veil that refuses meaning and that renders the once familiar a chaos is equivalent to spreading the curtain of figural language, that is to say, of poetry. "And whether it spreads its own figured curtain or withdraws life's dark veil from before the scene of things, it equally creates for us a being within our being. It makes us the inhabitants of a world to which the familiar world is a chaos" (505).

Poetry, then, which renders the familiar unfamiliar and denies us access to any core of meaning, poetry as the expression of the imagination in figural language, is connate with man. Shelley goes on now to speak of man in this context through a series of metaphors and similes.

> Poetry, in a general sense, may be defined to be "the expression of the Imagination": and poetry is connate with the origin of man. Man is an instrument over which a series of external and internal impressions are driven, like the alternations of an ever-changing wind over an AEolian lyre, which move it by their motion to ever-changing melody. But there is a principle within the human being, and perhaps within all sentient beings, which acts otherwise than in the lyre, and produces not melody, alone, but harmony, by an internal adjustment of the sounds or motions thus excited to the impressions which excite them. [480]

Were man merely an instrument, he would simply produce "reflected image[s]" (480) of the impressions driven over him. But there is a principle within him that makes him other than the lyre to which he is first compared, that alters these reflections, "the sounds or motions thus excited," so that they respond to the impressions that excited them to begin with. What is at stake here in the contrast between the passive and the active lyre is the relation between Reason and Imagination, for just before calling man an instrument, we read, "Reason is to the Imagination as the instrument to the agent. . ." (480).

---

29. On the more general question of the relationship of metaphor and power in Shelley (and for a thorough review of the secondary literature), see the superb essay of Jerrold Hogle in "Shelley's Poetics: The Power as Metaphor," *Keats-Shelley Journal* 31 (1982), 159–97.

> [Reason] may be considered as mind contemplating the relations borne by one
> thought to another, however produced; and . . . [Imagination], as mind acting
> upon those thoughts so as to colour them with its own light, and composing
> from them, as from elements, other thoughts, each containing within itself the
> principle of its own integrity. [480]

Imagination is that which acts so as to alter; it acts upon thoughts to produce
other thoughts and each of these contains "the principle of its own integrity."

What is the principle of the integrity of the thoughts produced by Imagination, poetry, figural language? Shelley does not tell us, but he performs it. For,
to clarify his distinction between man as an Aeolian lyre and man who acts
other than the lyre, he goes on to write:

> It is as if the lyre could accommodate its chords to the motions of that which
> strikes them . . . even as the musician can accomodate his voice to the sound
> of the lyre. [480]

The first part of the sentence is clear enough for it simply reiterates the gesture
that came before, a call for "the internal adjustment of the sounds . . . to the
impressions which excite them" (480). But Shelley then offers us a simile. The
lyre that does more than being passively driven, that *adjusts* its chords to the
everchanging wind, is like a musician who accomodates his voice to the lyre.
The second "lyre," it would seem, can no longer be understood as part of the
extended metaphor. In order to make common sense of what we read, the term
should be read literally, the metaphorical frame forgotten. The reader, nevertheless, cannot help but hear the vibrations from the recent metaphorical use
of lyre at the beginning of the sentence, and this, of course, is the point.

What the musician does in adapting his voice is to respond to and comment on the lyre, a lyre which can also be read metaphorically, as the figure of
Reason. This means, first of all, that Reason and Imagination are not to be
imagined as two separate faculties, for Imagination contains Reason within it
as a moment of its fictional history. But, in a harmony whose reverberations
get quite out of hand, the lyre in question could just as well be that in the first
clause of the sentence—no passive lyre of Reason, but one that, in turn, has
already "accomodate[d] its chords to the motions of that which strikes them."
The precise phrasing of the second clause would speak for this, for it is not
simply a singer who accomodates his voice but a musician, he who plays the
lyre of Imagination to begin with. The "principle of its own integrity" (480)
that each thought contains within itself is one that ruptures all attempts to
circumscribe its limits, for there is no way to fix the frame of its figurality.

> Poetry enlarges the circumference of the imagination by replenishing it with
> thoughts of ever new delight, which have the power of attracting and assimilat-
> ing to their own nature all other thoughts, and which form new intervals and
> interstices whose void for ever craves fresh food. [488]

[Poetry] is a strain which distends, and then bursts the circumference of the hearer's mind. . . . [485][30]

As in the "Medusa" where the beholding subject, the producing subject, and the object produced can never coincide, where all takes place under the aegis of an endless mirroring in which thought no more can trace, Poetry or Imagination can never close definitively on that to which it makes its internal adjustment. "Lift[ing] the veil from the hidden beauty of the world" as it spreads the curtain of figural language, it must always refuse to expose meaning, creating rather intervals of noncoincidence with that upon which it reflects. It is in this sense that criticism, too, another attempt to behold, might well be regarded as an act of the Imagination.

STATE UNIVERSITY OF NEW YORK AT BUFFALO

---

30. The passage refers to the works of Francis Bacon.

ROBERTO GONZÁLEZ ECHEVARRÍA

Threats in Calderón: *Life Is a Dream* 1, 303–08

The history of modern poetry in Spanish can be told as a series of episodes concerning the acceptance or rejection of baroque poetry. The Neo-Classics rejected Góngora and Calderón, who they thought were embarrassing examples of Spain's backwardness, of her failure to be a part of Modernity. The Romantics accepted these poets partially, but only because they had been anointed by the Germans, who found them (especially Calderón) to be worthy precisely because they seemed to be untouched by modern poetics. Critics of the late nineteenth century, particularly that most influential of Spanish critics, don Marcelino Menéndez y Pelayo, again rejected the baroques, both because he considered them barbarous and at the same time too unrealistic. In this period, the realist novel dominated Spanish literature, and there was almost a total absence of significant poets (save for that minor and belated romantic, Gustavo Adolfo Bécquer), not the best climate for the rare flowers of baroque poetry. Ramón Menéndez Pidal, the great philologist, was too preoccupied with the origins of popular poetry and the epic to bother with poets as rabidly cultured as the baroques. It was left to the Generation of '27, the avant-garde poets concerned with the foundations of poetry in a way similar to the European romantics, to rediscover Góngora and Calderón, to be aware that they represented the most powerful poetic tradition in Spanish. Federico García Lorca, Jorge Guillén, Pedro Salinas and above all Dámaso Alonso, launched a thorough reappraisal of these poets, which was accompanied, and sometimes preceded by, that of Latin American poets and essayists like José Martí, Rubén Darío and Alfonso Reyes, all of whom, searching for the roots of their own poetic language, also reached back to the great baroque poets of the Golden Age. This reappraisal was also carried out by a splendid group of English critics and scholars, the best among them being Edward M. Wilson, Bruce W. Wardropper and Alexander A. Parker, the first having performed the herculean task of translating Góngora's *Soledades* into English.[1]

---

1. Bruce W. Wardropper, "Preface," *Critical Essays on the Theatre of Calderón* (New York: New York University Press, 1965), vii–xiii; Manuel Durán and Roberto González Echevarría,

180

Only after reading Octavio Paz's *Children of the Mire* can we fully understand the historical reasons for the importance of the baroque poets in modern Spanish poetry.[2] Paz underscores an unpleasant, yet unavoidable fact: that there are no first-rate romantic poets in Spanish. Scholars with an investment in Spanish or Latin American Romanticism may quibble, but next to Goethe or Blake, Spanish and Spanish-American nineteenth-century poets pale. With minor exceptions, Spanish- language romantics derived their inspiration from the French, who were themselves derivative of the English and German. With the exception of Leopardi and some Hugo, Romanticism was essentially a Nordic phenomenon, including the United States and particularly Whitman. Without a recent tradition on which to base their search for a poetic language, Hispanic poets had to look back to the Baroque, when the most radical revamping of poetry had been carried out, and when a truly original tradition had emerged from the ruins of Petrarchism. In Baltasar Gracián *culteranismo* had even had a theoretician who saw in the Baroque conceit the workings of a creative force, the likes of which would not be found until the German romantics. Contradictory as it may appear—and this will be the main argument in this paper—the most genuine and authentic poetry in Spanish is the one that is most contrived and artificial. Poetry shows this consistently, regardless of what critics and even the poets themselves often say, due to the influence of a postromantic ideology that obscures the issue.

While Góngora gained a high degree of acceptance as the result of this reevaluation, Calderón lagged somewhat behind. This was due in part to the religious themes of a good deal of his theater, which did not find an echo in modern sensibility. While Dante's Catholicism could be seen with a certain detachment as the unifying cultural system of the Middle Ages, Calderón's Spanish Catholicism, with its more militant ring, and its association to the relatively recent and highly polemical history of Spain, was more difficult to accept. In addition, Góngora's poetry was read and savored by poets and scholars in the quiet of their studies; it did not have to be performed. Góngora's more audacious syntactical and metaphorical figures do not easily lend themselves to oral performance. In fact, his most persistent trope, the hyperbaton, makes his poetry hard to *breathe*; its syncopated periods are difficult to read out loud, let alone recite. Calderón, on the other hand, had to test his poetry on the stage, and had to endure having generations of schoolchildren all over the Spanish-speaking world recite it. Everyone knows by heart some of the most bombastic lines from *La vida es sueño*. As a result, parodies abound, and with them the feeling that Calderón's poetry is excessively contrived and artificial, as far, in short, from modern poetry and drama as can be imagined.

No other lines from Calderón's masterpiece have been more consistently

---

Calderón y la crítica: historia y antología (Madrid: Gredos, 1976), vol. 1; Henry W. Sullivan, *Calderón in the German Lands and the Low Countries: His Reception and Influence, 1654–1980* (Cambridge: Cambridge University Press, 1983).

    2. *Children of the Mire* (Cambridge, Mass.: Harvard University Press, 1974).

read according to these prejudices than those uttered by Clotaldo in the first act, when he finds that Rosaura and Clarín have discovered the secret place where the King has concealed his son Segismundo. Clotaldo says, in what the great Spanish poet Antonio Machado called a "stick'em up in slow motion":[3]

> rendid las armas y vidas,
> o aquesta pistola, aspid
> de metal, escupirá
> el veneno penetrante
> de dos balas, cuyo fuego
> será escándalo del aire.
> [Act 1, ll. 303–08][4]

It seems to me that we have much to learn from these lines in spite and perhaps because of their rejection by modern critics and translators. They contain in my view the essence of baroque poetry and play a very important role in *La vida es sueño*.

The lines have fared reasonably well in Edwin Honig's fine modern translation:

> put down your arms and lives, or else
> this pistol like a metal snake
> will tear the air apart with fire,
> and spit out two penetrating
> shots of venom.[5]

Honig, has managed nevertheless to tone the lines down by translating the very charged "aspid" merely as "snake," by rendering "escándalo del aire" as to "tear the air apart," and by turning the metaphor pistol-metal asp into a simile. To tear apart the air relies on an English idiom so that the expression sounds familiar enough to the ear. To scandalize the air, in contrast, does not sound familiar to the Spanish ear at all. It is a catachresis that the listener immediately perceives as a breakdown in speech. In other translations and annotated editions, these lines suffer an even more bizarre fate, making up a striking list of beguiling and instructive misreadings.

In some they are simply left out. This is the case in Alexandre Arnoux's prose adaptation, where Clotaldo merely says: "rendez vos armes et vos vies" ["Surrender your arms and lives."][6] In his 1871 prose version, de Latour translates the lines almost completely, and then some: "rendez vos armes, ou ce

---

3. Quoted by José María Valverde, in the note to the lines under discussion in his edition of the play: (Barcelona: Planeta, 1981), 15.
4. I am using Albert E. Sloman's edition of *La vida es sueño* (Manchester: Manchester University Press, 1961).
5. *Life is a Dream* (New York: Hill & Wang, 1970), 12–13.
6. *Trois comédies: La vie est un songe, Le Médecin de son honneur, L'Alcalde de Zalamea*, adaptation et introduction de Alexandre Arnoux (Paris: Grasset, 1955), 36.

pistolet, serpent de métal, vous crachera au visage le venin pénétrant de deux balles, dont le feu et le bruit vont étonner l'air" ["Surrender your arms, or this pistol, a metal snake, will spit at your faces the penetrating poison of two bullets, whose fire and noise will astonish the air."][7] Having, like Honig, turned the asp into a snake, de Latour feels the need to add that the pistol will spit at the faces of Rosaura and Clarín, remembering perhaps that the basilisk was reputed to strike at the eyes. He also has Coltaldo ask Rosaura and Clarín to surrender only their weapons, not as in the original, their lives, which is, as we shall see, a substantial omission. Frank Birch and J. B. Trend, in their 1925 translation to be "spoken not read," feel compelled to make explicit the tropes: "Surrender, or this iron snake, my pistol will spit the poison of its bullet-sting, and rend the air with fire."[8] Like Latour, Birch and Trend leave out "scandal," and collapse the snake's two forms of attack, stinging and spitting, into one. As if this were not enough, Birch and Trend put the lines in brackets, a device they use to point out passages "too characteristic of the style and dramatic convention of the country and period to be sacrificed altogether, and yet, perhaps, too 'Gongoristic' for modern taste, or for other reasons likely to prove ineffective." In other words, in a stage presentation, the lines could be left out.

F. D. Cries, in the translation included in the handsome *Ausgewählte Werke*, provides an elegant and fairly accurate version of Clotaldo's threat, though also with significant additions and suppressions:

> Übergebet Wehr und Leben;
> Oder dies Pistol hier, Natter
> Von Metall, wird sich alsbald
> Seines scharfen Gifts entladen
> In zwei Kugeln, deren Donner
> Wird die Luft in Aufrhur jagen.[9]

Surrender weapons and life, or this pistol, a metal asp, will soon discharge its burning poison in two bullets, whose thunder will disrupt the air.

Cries explains away the trope "to scandalize the air," and turns fire into thunder, perhaps under the influence of nineteenth-century nature poetry. C. V. West's *Das Leben ein Traum* takes more liberties, changing the weapon from pistol to spear, and multiplying death by ten:

> übergebet
> schnell Wehr' und Leben; oder Augenblicks
> Soll zehnfacher Tod von unsern Spiessen
> Auf ewig Aug und Lippen euch verschliessen.[10]

---

7. *Oeuvres dramatiques de Calderón*, tr. Antoine de Latour (Paris: Didier, 1871), 149.

8. *Life's a Dream*, translated for the English Stage by Frank Birch and J. B. Trend (Cambridge: W. Heffer & Sons, 1925), 7.

9. (Leipzig: Hesse und Becker Verlag, 1910), 1, 33.

10. *Das Leben ein Traum* (Leipzig: Verlag von Philipp Reclam, n.d.), 10.

immediately surrender your weapons and lives, or within the flicker of an eye, death ten times over from our spears will forever seal your eyes and lips.

Clotaldo's threat has not fared much better at the hands of commentators and annotators of *La vida es sueño*. As sober a *calderonista* as Albert E. Sloman, in his splendid and widely used edition of the play, singles out Clotaldo's speech as one of those lines that are "primarily decorative," and calls them "absurdly pompous."[11] Everett W. Hesse writes, in a note to his also fine edition, that these verses are "an example of a favorite conceit of Calderón's. The eighteenth-century critics considered this type of extended metaphor 'mal gusto,' but modern critics take an entirely different view."[12] Obviously, the "entirely different view" does not apply to these lines, which the great Cuban neobaroque poet, José Lezama Lima remembers as he compares Calderón unfavorably to Góngora, giving, in passing, the most likely source of one of the figures: "Hablábamos de ese escándalo de la luz, en recuerdo de una de las cetreras, el jerifalte, llamado por don Luis 'escándalo del aire,' y que más tarde en Calderón, y lo hacemos para diferenciar el barroco concentrado e incandescente de Góngora, del barroco curvo, suelto y lánguidamente sucesivo de Calderón, produce el disparo de la pistola también 'gran escándalo del aire'" (sic). ["We were talking about a scandal of light, remembering one of the hawking birds, the *jerifalte*, called by don Luis, 'a great scandal of the air', which later in Calderón gives us the shot of the pistol, 'a great scandal of the air', to distinguish Góngora's concentrated and incandescent baroque, from Calderón's more sinuous, loose and languidly repetitive."][13]

It is significant how often translators of *La vida es sueño* have left out or altered these lines, either by suppressing elements (life, pistol, scandal), or by adding explanations or new tropes (thunder). I believe that this reaction obeys the logic of the tropes that make up Clotaldo's threat and indicate to what extent his lines constiute the most resilient part of his poetics, as well as that which unveils most effectively the ideology of modern poetics.

Despite the combination of astonishment and revulsion that modern critics and translators of *La vida es sueño* experience before these lines of Clotaldo's, threats of this nature are common among Calderón's most illustrious predecessors. In Lope de Vega's version of *El médico de su honra*, for instance, Don Jacinto says:

> Pues, ¿hay quién pueda
> darme a mí celos, o yo,
> si en mi pensamiento apenas
> sospechas acreditara,

---

11. Op. cit., xxxiv.
12. (New York: Charles Scribner's Sons, 1961), 126.
13. "Sierpe de don Luis de Góngora," in *Orbita de Lezama Lima* (Havana: Colección Orbita-UNEAC, 1966), 267–68. The line is from the second *Soledad*: "el Gerifalte, escándalo bizarro/del aire" (lines 753–54).

más pedazos no os hiciera
que átomos el sol deslumbra,
que peces el mar navegan.[14]

Could there be anyone who would dare make me jealous, or could I in my own mind give credence to any suspicion, before I smashed you into more bits than atoms are illuminated by the sun, that fishes sail the sea?

In Tirso's *El condenado por desconfiado*, Enrico thunders:

que a poder, ¡ah cielo airado!
entre mis brazos soberbios
te hiciera dos mil pedazos;
y despedazado el cuerpo
me lo comiera a bocados,
y que no quedara, pienso,
satisfecho de mi agravio.[15]

For if I could, oh vengeful heaven! Between my proud arms I would crush you into two thousand bits, and once your body was dismembered, I would feast upon it and even then I would not feel that the insult has been satisfied.

There are a number of similar threats in Shakespeare. In *Romeo and Juliet*, for instance, the desperate lover warns Balthasar not to meddle in what he is about to do in the crypt,

But if thou, jealous, dost return to pry
In what I further shall intend to do,
By heaven, I will tear thee joint by joint
And strew this hungry churchyard with thy limbs.
[Act V, Scene 3, 33–36]

The presence of such threats in Lope, Tirso and Shakespeare (to mention only three predecessors) clearly indicates a common European source: the *miles gloriosus* of classical comedy, and his various reincarnations in Renaissance theater.[16] The *fanfarrón* in *Celestina* and the Spanish theater, the boastful soldier in Molière, all owe their existence to this tradition. Another source, common to both Shakespeare and the Spanish theater is, of course, the *commedia dell'arte*, where, although the violence is not verbal, it is equally excessive and many scenes hinge on the threat of violence more than on violence itself. One may add to this that in the *commedia* the boastful captain was traditionally a Spaniard—the *capitano spagnuolo*—with an exaggerated mar-

---

14. Quoted by Albert E. Sloman in his *The Dramatic Craftsmanship of Calderón* (Oxford: The Dolphin Book Co. Ltd., 1958), 30.

15. Tirso de Molina, *El condenado por desconfiado*, in *Teatro español del Siglo de Oro*, annotated and edited by Bruce W. Wardropper (New York: Charles Scribner's Sons, 1970), 456–57.

16. María Rosa Lida de Malkiel, "El fanfarrón en el teatro español," *Romance Philology*, 11(1958), 268–91.

tial air and a penchant for empty threats, obviously a mockery of Spain's military exploits in the sixteenth century and her imperialistic adventures in Italy. Yet another source may very well be purely linguistic. It is a well-known fact that elaborate blessings, curses, harangues and other such performative kinds of language made their way into Spanish from the Arabic during the eight centuries of wars against the Moors.[17] Could the sort of threat discussed here not have the same origin? Even today, it seems to me, Spanish retains this quality. A friend of mine in Madrid last year, when told that someone had done something evil, roared that if it were done to him, he would seize the culprit and: "le pego una hostia que se le acaba el cielo para dar vueltas" ["I will give him such a blow that the heavens won't be large enough for him to spin around."] All of these sources serve to show that Clotaldo's lines belong to a very theatrical tradition, and that their being rooted in the language is further evidence of their appropriateness as part of the Spanish *comedia*. One can certainly imagine the delight of the *mosqueteros* at hearing such elaborate threats, which no doubt competed in complexity and verbal bravado with their own. The language of *germanía*, of thugs, is by nature highly figurative and baroque, as the literature of the Golden Age shows insistently in the picaresque and Cervantes. It is as much a language for initiates as Góngora's.[18]

Calderón must have understood this to be so, for the threat that Clotaldo uses to intimidate Rosaura and Clarín is commonplace in his theater. There are many others that compare favorably with Clotaldo's in ornateness and the promise of mayhem, though the one in *La vida es sueño* contains all of the important elements of what is no doubt a common conceit in Calderóns theater, almost a topic. It is such a common one, in fact, that the public may very well have expected it and looked for it in every play, to judge by the contrivance of each, which seems to put it in competition with others. For instance, in *La hija del aire*, after listening to a long speech by Lidoro, an ambassador from her son and bitter enemy, Semíramis rages:

> no sé cómo mi valor
> ha tenido sufrimiento
> hoy para haberte escuchado
> tan locos delirios necios,
> sin que su cólera ardiente
> haya abortado el incendio
> que en derramadas cenizas
> te esparciese por el viento.

---

17. Américo Castro, *La realidad histórica de España*, 3rd ed. (Mexico: Porrúa, 1966), 219; Rafael Lapesa, *Historia de la lengua española*, 5th ed. (Madrid: Escelicer, 1959), 110.

18. John M. Hill, *Poesías germanescas*. Indiana University Publications. Humanities Series No. 15 (1945); *Voces germanescas*. Indiana University Publications. Humanities Series No. 21(1949).

I don't know how my courage has been able to suffer all your foolish and insane stories, before my burning ire erupted and sent you flying like cinders through the air.

Dismissing the messenger, she thunders again:

> temo
> que la ley de embajador
> su inmunidad pierda, haciendo
> que vuelvas por ese muro
> tan breves pedazos hecho,
> que seas materia ociosa
> de los átomos del viento.[19]

I fear that if you don't leave quickly the law protecting ambassadors at time of war will lose its effects, and you will return over that wall in pieces so small that you will be like playful matter for the atoms that make up the air.

In *La fiera, el rayo y la piedra*, Irífile tells Anjarte that she will give her such a blow with her staff that

> de la tierra el centro
> tan gran sepulcro te abra,
> que muerta aquí, las exequias
> los antípodas te hagan
> de esa otra parte del mundo.

the very center of the earth will open up like such an immense tomb that although you will die here, the antipodes will celebrate your wake in that other part of the world.

To which Anjarte replies with lines that by now begin to have a familiar ring, that her rage is such that it will blast her into such small pieces that

> esparcidos por el viento,
> suban a esfera tan alta
> que en pavesas encendidas,
> o caigan tarde o no caigan.[20]

scattered in the wind, they will raise to so high a sphere that, like glowing cinders, they may be late in dropping, or may never drop at all.

We have so far shown that Clotaldo's lines belong to a long-standing the-atrical tradition, and such threats appear with a certain degree of frequency in Calderón's theater. While demonstrating that these lines are not as unusual as the reaction of critics would make them out to be, we have yet to see them in

---

19. *Obras completas*, ed. Angel Valbuena Briones (Madrid: Aguilar, 1966), 1, 755 and 757.
20. *Obras completas*, 2, 1602–03.

the context of the play. What is their meaning and function, and are these in any way related to the fate of these lines in modern scholarship and poetry?

I would venture to say that Clotaldo's threat has been the object of such scorn because it is an extreme example of a relationship between meaning and language in poetry that is the opposite of the one proclaimed by the modern tradition. Modern poetics would make the following equation: the more intense the feeling, the less ornate the poetry. Or, put in positive terms, the more intense the feeling the more direct and natural the expression. In baroque poetry the equation can be reversed: the more intense the feeling, the more ornate and artificial the poetry. Rhetoric increases in direct proportion to feeling in baroque poetry. Feeling is completely external, contained in the language, which unlike modern literature, does not appear as an inadequate medium that reveals only partially the character's inner world. There is no inner world that cannot be externalized in language. All emotion is represented, without leaving a residue in some inaccessible chamber of the soul. This is true when the feeling is love; it is also the case when it is anger or aggression, but then the relationship is more visible and the results are stranger to the modern ear. The swelling up of language is such in these cases, that rhetoric, more obviously than in the case on love, replaces action. Language itself becomes action.

In all of the threats quoted here, the promise of physical violence is never fulfilled. No one is ever scattered in the winds. It is the act of vowing to do so that takes place on the stage. The character's feelings are not expressed so much as they are enacted in language; the violence takes place in the tropes themselves. This is evident if we take into account the fact that the action of scattering, of disseminating, threatened in the utterance, is the very same taking place in the trope. To scandalize the air is to shock it, to send waves, to disseminate signs. Hesse is right in referring to this trope as an "extended metaphor." The "extended metaphor" is like the particles of the body rising to fall late (i.e., when least expected), or never fall again. The explosion is an explosion of language. The actors must be almost motionless as the laborious, slow motion threat is recited and the echoes of the verbal blast resonate through the theater.

By replacing action, however, Clotaldo's lines do not appear as something disconnected from the rest of the play. On the contrary, they not only signify through the very act of being uttered, but also signify in relation to the rest of the play, and enact the way in which signification functions in Calderón's dramatic poetry.

But let us return to the scene of the threat. Clotaldo's warning is directed against two characters he does not yet know, Rosaura and Clarín, but whose presence will bring more misfortune to him and the kingdom than he can imagine at the time. His lines prefigure their own threat to him and Basilio. Rosaura is Clotaldo's long abandoned daughter, of whose existence he does not even know. Clarín, as his name suggests, is about to publicly proclaim, at great risk, everything that should remain a secret in Poland. In *El mayor encanto, amor*, a trumpet is described in the same words used to describe Clotaldo's pistol, an "aspid de metal."[21] Clarín, a trumpet, can also "scandalize the air" (In *En la vida todo es verdad y todo mentira*, discordant music is also an "escándalo del aire.")[22] It is clear, then, that together, these two characters will cause a scandal in the same way that the report from Clotaldo's pistol will "scandalize the air." Clotaldo's elaborate threat, unbeknownst to him, will be realized not on Rosaura and Clarín, but on himself. By airing all the secrets of the state, these two characters will bring about shocking changes: Basilio will be deposed, his hidden son will replace him on the throne, Clotaldo will have to recognize Rosaura as his daughter, Astolfo will have to marry Rosaura, and Estrella, Segismundo. The blast will scatter the figures and reassemble them in pairs that are as surprising as the sound of the tropes. In short, Clotaldo's threat, with its promise of mayhem, dismemberment and dispersal, prefigures the fragmentation of the social order, the revolution that will come about in Poland.

This prefiguration, of course, is independent of the one who utters the threat. Clotaldo has no idea that his verbal violence will boomerang back to him, in the same way that his relationship with the aptly named Violante many years ago produced Rosaura as a tangible aftereffect. Like the noise of the pistol, the voice scatters sound to the wind, whose significance is not immediately apparent. The air is always an uncertain medium in Claderón, more a prism than a neutral filter. In *El médico de su honra*, both light and sound are distorted in the air, and the wind blows out candles at critical moments, causing confusion and violence.[23] This is also what happens with Clotaldo's verbal shots. Once the significant particles of sound, of poetic language, are scattered, they have a way of gathering together in unusual, shocking formations. These formations are the tropes of poetic language itself. Poetic language is like the shots that "scandalize the air," for through persistent catachresis it tears apart and fragments the space in which language exchange takes place. Clotaldo's threatened shots stand for the very act of uttering sound, for the moment at which poetic language is created, and for the troubled reception of that sound; delayed, deformed, fragmented. Could the displacement of the source of language from mouth to hand signal also the writerly nature of baroque poetry?

Such proliferation of meaning becomes evident if we look more closely at the most astonishing trope in Clotaldo's threat, the one that seems to have troubled most modern translators and commentators of *La vida es sueño*. I refer, of course, to the description of the pistol as a "metal asp." Like the shots that the pistol might discharge, this trope is full of implications. By describing the pistol as something that will "spit the penetrating venom of two bullets,"

---

21. *Ibid*, 1, 1543.
22. *Ibid*, 1, 1115.
23. See above all lines 973–980 of act two, *Obras completas*, 1, 338.

Calderón invests it with the qualities of a mouth, which made it possible for us to equate its function with that of uttering poetic language. But, of course, the act of poetic utterance as spitting through a metal asp is itself full of suggestions. We do not have to go too far to search for the traditional meaning of "metal asp," for Calderón wrote an *auto sacramental* entitled *La serpiente de metal* (1676) that gives us many clues, and also reveals how important this trope was for him.

La serpiente de metal is based on the Old Testament story of Moses leading the Israelites through the desert, and its basic theme is that of idolatry.[24] In the *auto*, after Moses destroys the golden calf, Idolatry scatters snakes in revenge, and also as a reminder of the sin committed in the Garden. The Israelites beg Moses to save them from this plague. He complies by appearing with a metal snake wrapped on a magic wand. Those who have been stung by real snakes are cured by looking at Moses' metal one. When asked why he cures with a metal snake, and not with a real one (since it is known that poison is cured by another poison), Moses answers allegorically: the snake on the wand prefigures Christ on the cross, therefore He can only assume the shape of sin (the snake), but not its real, natural form, for He can have no sin. The source for these last scenes of the *auto*, whence the title is taken, is Numbers 21, where the metal snake is at one point described as fiery, and bronze is the substance of which it is made.

The sense of "metal asp" in Clotaldo's threat should be clear now. Clotaldo has given life to Rosaura, though he is not aware of it, but he is now threatening her with death. The threat, however, is ambiguous, for its object is one that can both cure and harm. The first line of Clotaldo's threat suddenly acquires meaning. Whether it is an idiom or not, in asking Rosaura to surrender her life Clotaldo is asking her to return to him what he has given her. Of course, Clotaldo gave Rosaura life through his sin with Violante, and Rosaura herself has sinned in her relationship with Astolfo. The "metal snake" in the threat is a reminder of these original sins. Clotaldo gave Rosaura life, but also took it away by leaving her mother. The phallic nature of the metal snake adds a darker significance to the threat. Clotaldo is threatening his own daughter with the same sort of act that he perpetrated on her mother. There are often "flickers of incest" in Calderón, which Honig has already studied.[25] Rosaura is a part of Clotaldo himself, though he does not know it. Perhaps this implicit incest prefigures the rebounding quality of the threat, which will strike Clotaldo more than Rosaura, as we have already seen. More significant, of course, is the dual nature of the metal asp, which both kills and cures, an ambiguity that has been observed in relation to Clotaldo and Rosaura.[26] It is in

24. *La serpiente de metal, Obras completas*, 3, 1527–51.
25. Honig, "Flickers of Incest in the Face of Honor: *The Phantom Lady*," in *Calderón and the Seizures of Honor* (Cambridge, Mass.: Harvard University Press, 1972), 110–57.
26. Jacques Derrida, "La Pharmacie de Platon," in his *La Dissémination* (Paris: Seuil, 1972).

this duality that baroque poetic language will forever be stalled. The disseminating shots of language scatter meaning in a performance of its own annihilating force, yet the rebound invests the tropes with an order and meaning that, while unexpected and certainly delayed, is still there. The aporia is suggested in one of the threats in *La fiera, el rayo y la piedra,* when, as we saw, the burning cinders created by the explosion may fall late or not at all.

Clotaldo's threat is one of the most characteristic passages of Calderón's dramatic poetry. It is language as action, staging its own performance, and performing its own meaning. It is also a language of spectacular indirection, which means much more than the characters or even the audience suspects at a given moment. Meaning in Calderón's theater is always subject to this dispersion, which must be brought together by the spectator as he remembers words and figures that suddenly become significant when other words and figures are spoken. But most of all, it is a language whose elaborate performance stands in an inverse relation to that established by the modern tradition. The stronger the feeling, the more intense its artificiality. Baroque poetry performs its meaning and the way in which meaning is produced. This simultaneity is its own peculiar form of authenticity, one that does not melt together intention and form, but instead sets into motion their violent ritual of approximation and separation. Modern poetry in Spanish, particularly that of neobaroque poets in Latin America, has come to accept this kind of poetic language as its origin.

YALE UNIVERSITY

E. S. BURT

Developments in Character: Reading and Interpretation in "The Children's Punishment" and "The Broken Comb"

Reading is a term that, through overuse, easily becomes confused with interpretation. But in fact there is a crucial difference: reading involves the undoing of interpretative figures, for it questions whether any synthesis, any single meaning, can close off a text and satisfactorily account for its constitution. Unlike interpretation, which implies a development over the course of a narrative toward a single figure reconciling all its diverse moments, reading states the logic of figures and the logic of narratives to be constantly divergent. Such a divergence implies that an autobiographical text, for example, does not simply serve to bring meaning to the disorderly events of a subject's experience, and self-recognition to author and reader, but serves the further function of making those events available to a reader allegorically, as exemplary of the manner in which all narratives are constructed.[1] We could even define as autobiographical any textual pattern of interference, interruption, or crossing produced by the confrontation of a narrative of consciousness with effects of order produced in excess of the capacity of totalizing figures to regulate them. Rousseau's *Confessions*, which provide a particularly rich source for the study of narrative figures and strategies, will allow us to pursue the distinction between interpretation and reading and to determine some of the stakes involved. The issue is whether the synechdochal relation that reading and interpretation bear to one another is a metaphorical relation, which would make reading simply a

---

1. Paul de Man's description of autobiography by way of figures has made possible its analysis in other terms than the psychological and moral issues raised by a given individual's capacity for self-knowledge and self-deception. De Man legitimates the study of autobiography by showing that its logical tensions do not spring from an individual subject's inadequacies, but are the objective expression of a linguistic predicament. Because he has been able not only to describe and explain those tensions with incomparable acuteness and theoretical precision, but also to point out the regular paths along which the understanding moves as it confronts its figurality, he can be said to have made it possible to study autobiography with the rigor of a critical method [cf. especially "Autobiography as De-Facement," in *The Rhetoric of Romanticism*. (New York: Columbia University Press, 1984); "Reading (Proust)" and "Excuses (Confessions)" in *Allegories of Reading* (New Haven: Yale University Press), 1979].

special case of understanding, or a metonymical relation, in which case understanding would prove one mode of reading. Some rehearsing of familiar narratives schemes will be necessary in order to clarify the stakes.[2]

The divergence can be seen dramatized in two episodes emblematic of an autobiographical sequence: "the children's punishment," and "the broken comb."[3] Let me recall the events for you briefly. In the pastoral paradise of Bossey where the protagonist and his cousin are studying Latin and the catechism with M. Lambercier, the hero discovers he enjoys being spanked. The first spanking recalls another, less pleasant punishment to the narrator, which he recounts to us from the perspective of an apparently disinterested observer: Mlle. Lambercier's comb is broken; the child undergoes a cross-examination but insists that he did not break it; all the evidence points to his guilt, and he is severely beaten—for willful mischief, for lying and for stubbornness. The narrator then declares that he did not break the comb.[4]

A DEVELOPING CHARACTER: BILDUNGSROMAN

The chronological narrative naturally imposes the form of a *bildungsroman* on the *Confessions*. We follow the hero as he passes through various learning experiences that appear as exemplary stages in his moral and psychological development. In interpreting the educational progress made by the protagonist, we could understand the two episodes in question as representing two formative experiences linked together in a chain by a developing consciousness, the first of which leads naturally to the second, and the second of which implies the first.

A first spanking, administered by Mlle. Lambercier, irrevocably determines the shape of the child's desire: "this child's punishment . . . disposed of my tastes, my desires, my passions, myself for the rest of my life" (15).[5] Henceforth, the hero will seek his pleasure in the re-creation of a masochistic relation: "to be at the knee of an imperious mistress, to obey her orders, to have forgiveness to ask of her, were very sweet pleasures to me, and the more my imagination inflamed my blood, the more I had the air of a transfixed lover" (17).

Simultaneously with the education into pleasure, occurs the child's introduction into the hitherto-uncharted territory of fault and merit, a preethical

---

2. It will be obvious how much what follows owes to Starobinski's analyses of Rousseau: particularly, for the first narrative scheme, to *La Transparence et l'obstacle* (Paris: Gallimard, 1971), and for the second, to "Le progrès de l'interprète" in *La Relation critique* (Paris: Gallimard, 1970).

3. Rousseau himself seems to have accorded the two scenes emblematic value: the draft of the *Confessions* recounts only those two anecdotes from early childhood. Cf. Marcel Raymond and Bernard Gagnebin, ed. *Oeuvres complètes* (Paris: Gallimard, 1959), v. 1, 1155–58.

4. Ibid., 12–22. All page numbers referring to the *Confessions* will henceforth appear in the text.

5. The translations are my own.

world where the morality of good intention reigns, "the sway of benevolence" as Rousseau will call it. The transition is marked by the introduction of a moral vocabulary of merit, fault, will, conscience, etc., conspicuously absent from the first pages of the *Confessions*. The appearance of intention in conjunction with the awakening of the senses can be explained by the fact that, according to the description of the scene, a single interpretative error is responsible for the awakening of both sense and the senses. The scene is worth quoting because the error is a direct result of the child's first positive encounter with written signs—a spanking is an impression made on a *tabula rasa* of sorts—and shows both the effects on the hero of his attempt to explain the excesses and deficiencies of written signs in terms of his old value system and the effects on the old value system itself:

> As Mlle. Lambercier bore the affection of a mother for us, so she also had a mother's authority, and carried it sometimes so far as to inflict on us the children's punishment when we had deserved it (*quand nous l'avions méritée*). For quite a long time she held herself to threats, and that threat of a punishment entirely new to me seemed very dreadful; but after it was carried out, I found it less terrible in fact than its expectation had been (*assez longtemps elle s'en tint à la menace, et cette menace d'un châtiment tout nouveau pour moi me sembloit très effrayante; mais après l'execution, je la trouvai moins terrible à l'épreuve que l'attente ne l'avoit été*), and what is even more bizarre was that this punishment made me more affectionate toward the one who had imposed it on me. Indeed, all the truth of that affection and all my natural sweetness were needed to keep me from seeking the return of the same treatment by deserving it (*pour m'empêcher de chercher le retour du même traitement en le méritant*): for I had found in the ache, in the shame itself, a mingling of sensuality that had left me with more desire than fear of undergoing it (*de l'éprouver*) again at the same hand. It is true that, since there was no doubt mingled in with it all some precocious sexual instinct, the same punishment received from her brother would not have seemed pleasant at all to me. But with a man of his humor, that substitution was scarcely to be feared, and if I abstained from deserving correction (*si je m'abstenois de mériter la correction*), it was solely for fear of angering Mlle. Lambercier; for such is the sway of benevolence in me, even of that one born of the senses, that it has always ruled over them in my heart. [15]

Mlle. Lambercier has promised the child a punishment, which the child anticipates will be as great as he imagines he deserves, that is, very fearful. But upon execution, the punishment turns out to be smaller than the one expected, the pain less terrible than the anticipation. It is the difference between the punishment promised and the impression actually received that is accorded significance by the child. The change is marked in two ways. In the first place, his sensual being is awakened by it: he experiences as a positive pleasure the release of anticipatory tension. In the second place, and more importantly for the development of a system of moral values, the difference between a promise and its execution provkes a full-scale reinterpretaion of Mlle. Lambercier by the child. Hitherto the *moi* has read her feelings of content or discontent with him from her expression ("I knew nothing so charming as to see everybody content with me and with every thing . . . "; "nothing troubled me more . . . than to see on Mlle. Lambercier's face marks of disquiet and pain" 14), and her love and severity have been undifferentiated from her brother's ("When it was necessary however, she was no more lacking in severity than her brother . . . "(14). But after the punishment, Mlle. Lambercier wields a specifically female authority and is a figure on whom the child concentrates his affection ("this punishment made me more affectionate toward the one who had imposed it on me," "a person whom I loved like a mother, and perhaps even more" 22), in contrast to the brutal, legalistic forms of masculine authority he will encounter in the next scene.

Now the hero's revision of his interpretation of Mlle. Lambercier seems to occur by means of a simple inversion of cause and effect, bringing about a consequent reassessment of values: if he didn't receive the punishment (pain) he deserved, did he perhaps deserve the punishment (pleasure) he received? A slippage occurs in the value attributed the action to which the spanking (the deserved punishment) refers. The different meanings of the word *mériter* in the passage indicate a path the child might have followed as he revised his ideas of Mlle. Lambercier's severity and love: in the first instance, it refers to "retribution for a fault" ("when we had deserved it"). In the second, it appears to have been emptied of all value, and to be, like the pleasure of seeking pleasure, its own reward: ("seek the return of the same treatment by deserving it"). By the third appearance, however, the deserved punishment has been ascribed a positive value, and appears in the context to mean a recompense accorded a deserving subject, or, even more specifically, a recompense for the virtue of deferring the pleasurable reward by deferring the action that will bring it about ("if I abstained from deserving it."[6]

What has happened is that the child has come up with two hypotheses to cover the failure of the sign to mean what it promised, one of which addresses the issue of a fault in the transmission of meaning, and the other of which assumes an insufficient understanding of the promise on the part of the self. Mlle. Lambercier's hand may have slipped in the act of making her meaning clear: the mistake in intention frees the written sign from its conventional meaning, and makes it available to the child for private interpretation. Desire awakens when the overruling interpretative structure is shown to be inadequate to include the written sign, and becomes determined as the desire for a repetition of that demonstration. At the same time, the protagonist posits that his own understanding of the code might have been insufficient: he learns not

---

6. The *Ebauches* use the term only once, but also give it the meaning of reward for delaying the reception of rewards: "although it never happened that I did anything with the plan of deserving it" (*à dessein de le mériter*" 1158).

to read people's faces for signs of their intentions and comes to suspect that Mlle. Lambercier, a watchful and benevolent teacher, might have wished all along to teach him that meaning involves a temporal unfolding.

The imaginative freedom the child enjoys and his paradoxical good conduct—he prefers to imagine passively a masochistic relation rather than to pursue actively any other kind of relation with the opposite sex—as well as his bizarre concatenation of female affection and authority in the figure of the loving dominatrix or teacher, is owed to an interpretative gesture that lands him in an impasse. The hero discovers a sign (the spanking) in excess of the intent to punish, which makes it undecideable whether his voluntaristic view of signs is actually faulty, or whether a more far-reaching teleological system than he has hitherto suspected reigns at Bossey under the benevolent eye of Mlle. Lambercier. The child cannot determine whether written impressions are arbitrary signs, appropriable by the stealthy imagination, or whether they are motivated signs whose meaning has not yet been revealed.

The substitution of an imaginary relation for a real one accrues a positive benefit to the child's conduct, but arrests the development of his conscience at a preethical stage, and actively interferes with the development of his reason. Indeed, his reason is so impaired that, as Rousseau suggests, the very subject of his greatest curiosity, the differences between the sexes, is the one he will have the least knowledge and the fewest ideas about. Because his only interest in the opposite sex is to transpose women into imaginary scenes as imperious school-mistresses, he will have little objective curiosity about them, and will consequently learn the facts of life very late: "until adolesence I had no distinct idea of the union of the sexes" (16). In a word, the substitution of teleological fictions of desire for the literal world empowers the imagination, blocks the moral faculty at the level of the morality of good intention, and, temporarily at least, paralyses judgment.

In the second episode, the child experiences "[the] first sentiment of injustice and violence" (20). He is spanked, after a trial and a conviction, by an executioner officially appointed, for a crime he claims he did not commit. He discovers that, however unfairly, persons are sometimes attributed responsibility for actions. Too young to know that "appearances condemned [him]" (19), he himself blames an unjust human agency. "Butcher, butcher, butcher" (*"Carnifex, carnifex, carnifex"*) (20), he cries, mistaking the impersonal hand of the executioner for the hand of a sadistic butcher. The experience of injustice provokes and justifies unjust indignation, mistrustful vigilance, secrecy, stubbornness, cunning—all the evils the punishment was calculated to correct. It makes the child an expert in using appearances, whose capacity to veil intentions he now appreciates; he learns to hide behind them, to harbor secrets, to conceal his projects. He loses his fear of acting reprehensibly and directs his energies at hiding the traces of his actions, for now he only fears getting caught. "We were less ashamed of doing bad things, and more fearful of being accused" (21).

In the account just given the hero's character undergoes a distinct evolution over the course of the two episodes. In the first, he discovers desire and the private, interior world of the imagination. In the second, he learns to know the world of appearances and how to manipulate them. The second stage comes to correct the child's early substitution of subjective categories for objective ones, without ever entirely eradicating that original desire, which will continue to dominate his relations with the opposite sex and will explain his persistent preference for fictions over objective accounts of human history. We recognize in the sequence the beginning of a genetic account of human development, similar in its linearity to the one Condillac's statue follows as it gets progressively more complex ideas, and that could lead toward a dialectical resolution in the fully formed psychological and moral being of an adult once the protagonist learns to renounce completely the errors of his imagination for the rewards of reason.

DEVELOPING A CHARACTER: DISCURSIVE UNITY

But of course, an illusion quickly dispelled by autobiography is the illusion that the chronological narrative, the story of the events, *l'histoire*, is a true representation of a natural progression toward a single, recapitulative figure.[7] For, while we follow the development of the protagonist's character over the narrative in our naive first reading, in fact the end toward which the development leads is in sight from the very beginning, in the figure of the narrator the hero has become.[8] It is he who tells the story, whose modelling presence shapes the narrative from the beginning. The work remembers and restores already played-out scenes. The *Confessions* can be understood according to a hermeneutical model then. They take as their horizon the final revelation of an original fold in the narrative: the end, the self developed, has become the beginning, the self being exposed. That fold had to occur for the narrative to be possible, and the narrative itself is the unfolding of the fold as an interpretation. The discrepancy between a literal understanding, arrived at in proximity to events, and their figurative significance which is only revealed later on, is the note on which autobiography always opens. Its pedagogical claims are based on its ability to show that progress in the understanding involves the gaining of access to the figural dimension. Hence the reference in Rousseau's preamble to a teleological being, to a future moment of Divine Justice, when the end of all events will be revealed and justified: "Let the trumpet of the Last Judgment sound when it will; I will come this book in hand to present myself

---

7. Cf. Gérard Genette, "Discours du récit" in *Figures III* (Paris: Seuil, 1972) for a definition.

8. Georges Gusdorf, "Conditions et limites de l'autobiographie" in *Formen der Selbstdarstellung* (Berlin: Dunker & Humblot, 1956); trans. as "Conditions and Limits of Autobiography" in *Autobiography: Essays Theoretical and Critical* ed. James Olney (Princeton: Princeton University Press, 1980). Cf. also Starobinski, op. cit., *La Relation*, for more explicit formulations of this position as they pertain to Rousseau.

before the sovereign judge" (5). Present at the very least in the choice of events told, the narrator naturally predetermines the meaning of the events that appear to determine him: from the outset every episode in the narrative represents either a normal moment in the development of the model, or a temporary deviation away from that main path. The autobiographical narrative, in this simplified hermeneutical account, is a teleological fiction. Each episode of the *récit* is understood to be a signifier pointing toward the omnipresence of a shaping self-referential intent.

Since the narrative implies a reformed narrator, one who is no longer doing but is only recounting, the events appearing nearer the end of the narrative will explain why the story is told and determine its mode of exposition. The episode of the broken comb, claims Starobinski,[9] is an emblematic scene containing the explanation of Rousseau's driving need to confess, and thus the motivation for the autobiographical narrative in its entirety. In that episode, the narrator learns to feel the accusing eye of Protestant Geneva upon him. From an early accusation and the fear of being accused to which it gives birth—"more fearful of being accused"—comes Rousseau's need to disculpate himself in advance, to write the *Confessions*. Lejeune,[10] who agrees with Starobinski, finds evidence in the scene to suggest that the trauma of being falsely accused and unjustly punished has not been resolved for the narrator. For no apparent reason, and to a rather ridiculous effect, the narrator of the episode, from his present vantage point, categorically denies having broken the comb: "This adventure happened almost fifty years ago, and I am not afraid today of being punished again for the same act. Well, then, I declare in the face of Heaven that I was innocent of it, that I neither broke nor touched the comb, that I didn't even approach the ledge [on which the comb lay], and that I didn't even dream of doing it" (19). The passage gives a clear instance, according to Lejeune, of *dénégation*.

In such a view then, the *Confessions* develop as an exposition of the storyteller, in his character as fiction maker. The narrative is teleological rather than causal and emerges, under the impetus of an obscure accusation and an unnamed guilt, from a sack of memories that is being emptied out.

The compulsion to confess comes from the second episode, but what Rousseau wishes to achieve, in emptying out the sack and exposing what is at its bottom, is a return to the innocent state represented in the first episode, as it would pertain to the narrator and his *récit*. Just as the general impression the child gives is of good behavior, despite all the delirious erotic scenes he is imagining, so the general impression the narrator wants to give is of having a good intention in revealing all the actions of his earlier, deluded self.

The narrator's aim is to convince, after telling his story that he stands fully revealed as a transparent intention to communicate the truth. The model of

---

9. Op. cit. *La Transparence*, 18–21.
10. Philippe Lejeune, "Le Peigne cassé," *Poétique*, 25 (1976).

the *bildungsroman* has been put into place by the first episode. The second episode, the episode of the broken comb, does not merely provide the necessary corrective to the hero's fiction-making tendencies within the narrative of developing consciousness. For, as the second episode shifts the focus of interest from hero to storyteller, from *récit* to *discours*, it extends over the whole narrative precisely the same hypotheses concerning the relation of written sign to intention that the protagonist had discovered in the isolated case of the deserved punishment. Narrative continuity is the stake in the second episode; whether the anecdotes reveal a single far-reaching design, or whether Rousseau's hand, like Mlle. Lambercier's, has occasionally slipped in delivering its message is the issue. The entire thrust of Lejeune's proof in "Le Peigne cassé" is to show that the episode exemplifies the self even in its inadequacies: occasional memory lapses or miscalculations in the effects of self-presentation are exceptions proving the general rule of the autobiographical pact.

The complication Lejeune brings to the hermeneutical model is possible because the act of confessing, what Genette would call *narration*, also figures within the *Confessions*. In the act of confessing, Rousseau repeats the fault he wants to expiate, and thereby renews the possibility of misunderstanding, since the story he tells in order to reveal himself is a performative, in excess of the content—his simple good faith—it reveals. Each confession is therefore potentially damaging to the promise of total self-revelation because, as pure performance, it is capable of engendering further misinterpretations. We may, for example, wonder whether Rousseau does not get more pleasure out of the shameful act of confessing than we get truth from the revelations of the salacious secrets of his erotic life. Once Rousseau begins excusing himself for confessing, each confession will potentially branch off into a supplementary series of confessions.

At best, Rousseau can manage to convince his readers by the confessing of confessions that the performative excesses of each confession are involuntary faults, that he, Rousseau has been caught up in the machinery of a communicating process that he is attempting to explicate. At worst, the excesses will simply generate further misunderstanding. In either case, Rousseau will feel disculpated, since he will have done his best to explain the problem at its source.

The hermeneutical model, the most totalizing account of the confessional narrative possible, has to grapple constantly with misfires in the performances of confessions, but it recuperates those misfires by revealing that they are localized misunderstandings which do not put into question the teleological structure and discursive unity of the whole. Thus Lejeune will show how the potential for misunderstanding confessions can be made into the object of the confession, how, "failing the possibility of ever telling the truth of desire, one tells to the end what keeps it from being told."[11] That Rousseau finally under-

---

11. Lejeune, *Le Pacte autobiographique* (Paris: Seuil, 1975), 85.

stood social concepts like justice to be predicated on a mere morality of good intentions would follow from such a model, as would the establishment of his persuasive aim in his autobiographical texts to be the unfolding, by way of the narrative, of figures of the self.

DEVELOPING PRINTS: THE NEGATIVE CHARACTERS

But questions arise. Is Rousseau's autobiography as seamless as this model makes it? Is his undoubted ability to make pathos and strategy converge the effect he is seeking? Is the discrepancy between the order of persuasion and the order of conviction dramatized in the episode of the broken comb actually overcome in the figure of the strategic narrator, who explains the misunderstanding in order better to persuade of his good heart, or does it persist as an active threat to narrative coherence, a persistence that Rousseau wants to explain? If it is thinkable, as Lejeune would have it, that an objective stance might be only a pose, are there any circumstances in which the subjectivism and pathos of the *Confessions* might also prove a ruse? Critics have long divided over whether to privilege the view that Rousseau's systematic works are actually self-justifications in disguise (the view of Starobinski),[12] or whether, for an unsystematic spirit like Rousseau, the autobiographical works are part of a gigantic strategy for revealing the truths of the system (the view of Cassirer).[13] The decision to privilege the autobiographical works over the systematic works may depend on the axe one has to grind; a more interesting question is: what explains the fact, that both of these views appear legitimate, authorized by Rousseau?[14] If Rousseau provides the answer to that question, we would have to conclude that explanation, rather than self-disculpation, has determined the order and manner of presenting the episodes. He may have wanted to show how totalizing figures, like the *amant transi* of the first episode, who collects and expresses opposing narrative forces in his ecstatic state of suspended animation, are inevitably followed by a fall into a narrative of literal events, uncollectable by recapitulative figures. The second episode, which gains its meaning from reference to literal events—the breaking of a comb, the beating of a child, the declaration of innocence—would follow the first because it expresses the inevitability of such literalizations. The representation within the confessional narrative of Rousseau's life as a process of degeneration, in which fragmentary effects of order are increasingly found in

12. Cf. esp. the introduction to *La Transparence et l'obstacle* in which Starobinski asserts that Rousseau confused existence and idea.

13. Cf. esp. "Dans Problem J. J. Rousseau," *Archiv fur Geschichte der Philosophie*, 41 (1932), 177–213; 479–513; trans. Peter Gay, as *The Question of Jean Jacques Rousseau* (New York: Columbia University Press, 1954).

14. Cf. Blanchot's review of Starobinski, printed as "Rousseau" in *Le Livre à venir* (Paris: Gallimard, 1959).

events (plots) resisting the subsumption by the imagination into its categories, would lend credence to such an allegorical reading.

Is there such a narrative as the one we've been describing in the *Confessions?* How does it differ from the genetic development of the hero's understanding, or the unfolding of an interpretation of the self? Are there traces in the broken comb that its uncertainties are not merely local? We will need to examine more closely what the scene leaves suspended, to print, as it were certain significant negatives, in order to determine whether the divergence between persuasive strategy and convincing order of exposition does not outlive persuasive recuperative strategies in general.

> J'étudiois un jour seul ma leçon dans la chambre contigue à la cuisine. La servante avoit mis sécher à la plaque les peignes de Mlle. Lambercier. Quand elle revint les prendre, il s'en trouva un dont tout un côté de dents étoit brisé. A qui s'en prendre de ce dégat? personne autre que moi n'étoit entré dans la chambre. On m'interroge; je nie d'avoir touché le peigne. M. et Mlle. Lambercier se réunissent; m'exhortent, me pressent, me menacent; je persiste avec opiniâtreté; mais la conviction étoit trop forte, elle l'emporta sur toutes mes protestations, quoique ce fut la prémiére fois qu'on m'eut trouvé tant d'audace à mentir. La chose fut prise au serieux; elle méritoit de l'être. La méchanceté, le mensonge, l'obstination parurent également dignes de punition: mais pour le coup ce ne fut pas par Mlle. Lambercier qu'elle me fut infligée. On écrivit à mon oncle Bernard; il vint. Mon pauvre Cousin étoit chargé d'un autre délit non moins grave: nous fumes enveloppés dans la même execution. Elle fut terrible. Quand, cherchant le reméde dans le mal même, on eut voulu pour jamais amortir mes sens dépravés, on n'auroit pu mieux s'y prendre. Aussi me laisserent-ils en repos pour longtems.
>
> On ne put m'arracher l'aveu qu'on exigeoit. Repris à plusieurs fois, et mis dans l'état le plus affreux, je fus inébranlable. J'aurois souffert la mort et j'y étois résolu. Il fallut que la force même cédat au diabolique entêtement d'un enfant; car on n'appella pas autrement ma constance. Enfin, je sortis de cette cruelle épreuve en piéces, mais triomphant)

I was studying my lesson alone one day in the room next to the kitchen. The servant had put Mlle. Lambercier's combs out to dry on the ledge at the back of the fireplace.[15] When she returned to take them, one was found to have a whole row of broken teeth. On whom to cast blame for the damage? No one other than myself had entered the room. I am interrogated; I deny having touched the comb. M. and Mlle. Lambercier join forces; exhort me, press me, threaten me; I obstinately persist; but conviction was too strong, and prevailed over all my protestations, although it was the first time that they had found me so audacious in lying. The thing was taken seriously; it deserved to be. The ill-nature, the deceit, the obstinacy all seemed equally worthy of punishment: but

---

15. A *plaque,* according to the *Pléiade* footnotes (1243), is a kind of niche made in the wall of a chimney and opening out into the contiguous room. I know of no English word to translate it.

for once it was not by Mlle. Lambercier that it was inflicted. My Uncle Bernard was written to; he came. My poor Cousin was charged with another offence no less grave: we were envelopped in the same execution. It was terrible. If, seeking the remedy in the evil itself, they had wanted to deaden my senses for ever, they could not have gone about it any better. For a long time they left me quiet.

The exacted confession could not be pulled out of me. Taken up several times and put into an awful condition, I was inflexible. I would have suffered death itself, and was resolved to do so. Force itself had to give in to the diabolical pig-headedness of a child, for that was what my constancy was called. At last I emerged from that cruel trial, in pieces, but triumphant.

In keeping with the two ways we have been organizing the narrative, the episode of the broken comb can be read as a dramatic representation of two very different kinds. In the first place, it confronts an autonomous subject, a *moi*, and an agent or representative of another subject, the servant, over the issue of responsibility for an event, the breaking of a comb. The servant, unlike the *moi*, is not an independent entity, but merely acts to carry out the commands of another. The alibi of the child appears to be that he has been lost in study, his mind on his books, and his senses asleep. But the Lamberciers find it infinitely more convincing, more logical,—"conviction was too strong"—that an independent subject should have caused the damage than that a mere servant, a hand animated only in the service of Mlle. Lambercier, should have done so. Similarly, the Vicar will state in the *Profession de foi* that his mind refuses to assent[16] to the idea that any movement could begin without cause; " . . . seeing a body in motion, I immediately judge either that it is an animated body, or that motion has been communicated to it. My mind refuses all assent to the idea of unorganised matter moving by itself, or producing any action."[17] No suspicion is attached to the servant because she plays the role here of unorganised matter, moved under Mlle. Lambercier's communicated orders, incapable of inventing or destroying things on her own. In shortsightedly overlooking the servant, the Lamberciers assert as a fact that there can be such a thing as a deliberate destruction and determine the breaking of the comb to be one such planned event.

On the other hand, because every episode in the *Confessions* can alternately be understood as a fiction into which the narrator has projected himself, the scene can be read as representing, within the autonomous subject who

---

16. In the *Profession*, inner assent is neither belief nor conviction, but designates an earlier stage in the formation of ideas when persuasion and logic have not yet been differentiated: the stage of examining opinions to decide which to reject as "invraisemblable" and which to investigate as the simplest and most reasonable. Cf. p. 569, *Oeuvres complètes*, ed. Raymond et Gagnebin, v. 4 (Paris: Gallimard, 1969) and Paul de Man, "Allegories of Reading (Profession de foi)" in op. cit. *Allegories*, 227–28: "The only claim made for the 'inner light' that the mind is able to throw upon its powers is a dubious, unfounded hope for a lesser evil, entirely unable to resolve the condition of uncertainty that engendered the mental activity in the first place."

17. *Oeuvres complètes*, v. 4, 575.

provides the decor of the scene "I was studying," the dramatic moment when a new idea is formed, abstracted, like the teeth from the comb, from several perceptions. Does the child get that new idea from an unaccustomed perception, or does judgment create it by moving things around? The scene is highly Cartesian[18] and the drama is centered on the possibility of distinguishing the role of perception from that of judgment in the passage to a new idea (like the passage from the idea of combs, based on a simple resemblance, to the idea of a broken comb, in which difference between teeth and comb plays within resemblance between comb and comb, and resemblance between teeth plays within difference between broken and unbroken comb): in one room, a *moi*, a reason abstracted from its senses is studying; in the other room, the kitchen, the senses go about their business of providing fragmentary and isolated perceptions for consciousness to appraise; between the two an opening, a ledge, on which the combs are placed. Without the senses, judgment can have no perceptions to compare for resemblances and differences. But without judgment, it seems impossible to get anything like the organized perception of a comb, in which teeth are differentiated from the connecting back of the comb and compared to one another. For the combs to be presented to consciousness as perceptions analyzable into parts, they need to have been "moved" around by consciousness: the senses, however capable of preventing two separate perceptions they might be, cannot find resemblances between teeth, or differentiate between teeth and comb. Just so, the Vicar states that judgment, while it appears inactive, actually plays an active role in comparing perceptions which sensation would be incapable of distinguishing or combining:

> By sensation, objects offer themselves to me separately, in isolation, as they are in nature; by comparison, I move them, I transport them, so to speak, I set them one on top of the other to pronounce on their difference or their resemblance, and generally on all their relationships . . . . I seek in vain in a purely sensitive being that intelligent force that superposes and then pronounces, I do not know how to find it in its nature. That passive being will feel every object separately, or will even feel the object formed of the two, but

---

18. It seems likely that the lesson the child is studying is a lesson from the *Méditations*. The rooms represent quite literally the Cartesian distinction between man's soul and body; the interpretative dilemma inherited from the scene of the children's punishment resembles Descartes's reasons for suspending judgment. The main problem of the narrator—the establishing of the certainty of memory—also alludes to the *Méditations*. The fiction of the *Malin Génie*, which allows Descartes to suspend his judgment, may here be serving the narrator as proof that the child has an alibi, since until the *cogito* has been founded and memory made certain, it ought to be impossible to state whether the senses or reason is responsible for our ideas, whether the will or a simple nervous mechanism is responsible for our actions. That fiction is carried further by Rousseau than by Descartes, however. For it will allow the narrator to extend doubt to include the source of the memory, and finally the source of the narrative of the *Confessions* in their entirety. Cf. esp. Henri Gouhier, "Ce que le Vicaire doit à Descartes" in *Les Méditations métaphysiques de Jean-Jacques Rousseau* (Paris: Vrin, 1970) for a discussion of themes borrowed. That for Rousseau judgment is always practical will naturally imply differences from the Cartesian situation.

having no force to fold them back onto one another, it will never compare them, it will not judge.[19]

As far as the representation of the subject is concerned, then, the active role of judgment in the formation of perceptions is being foregrounded. The *moi*'s denial of having literally touched the comb, in the representation of the events, is the equivalent, in the representation of the subject's judgment, of an admission that he has been figuratively moving the combs about in order to abstract ideas from them. The narrator assents to the organizing power of judgment over an orderly presentation by the senses. The senses can lay perceptions on the ledge between the rooms, but judgment denies them any force to compare or differentiate between them.

The two representations—of events and of the subject—bear a synechdochal relation to one another. The animated being capable of independent action in the representation of events, is shown in a close-up view, to be ruled by an active force of judgment which gets its ideas by forcefully transporting and comparing perceptions. The two representations, despite the contradictions they present as far as the comb is concerned (in one case, a comb is actually broken, and there is an event for which the subject is called to account; in the other case the broken comb is a metaphor for the invention of ideas of resemblance and difference by abstracting from perception) and despite the differences in the kinds of evidence provided (opinion, as yet undifferentiated into persuasion and conviction, provides the basis for thinking the damage deliberate, whereas a lack of evidence to the contrary, the impossibility of discovering whether the senses actually are organised or not, explains the *moi*'s conviction that judgment is as figuratively active as the senses are literally active) both support a consistent reasoning: the child could have broken the comb if he had wanted to, but he didn't because he was studying, judging things instead. The notion that autobiography aims at the presentation of the self-willed subject, for whom interpretation has come to take the place of action is supported by the dramatic scene. It is significant as well that the synechdoche linking the two ways of understanding the scene is consistent with reason. The possibility of finding a metaphor for the self in each representation of an action is not only not inconsistent with logical presentation, but can even provide an idealist philosophy like that of Descartes with some of its finest insights.

But there is another synechdoche in the episode that substitutes wholes and parts by way of metonymy rather than by metaphor, and that involves the status of the memory, rather than that of the subject or his actions. For the question of the passage is: what connects the two passages in which the episode is remembered? More specifically, what explains the return to the punishment scene after the story has reached a first closure in the death of the senses?

---

19. *Oeuvres complètes*, v. 4, 571–72.

The first paragraph provides a formally perfect mystery story, complete with beginning (suspect deeds), middle (review of evidence and conviction) and end (execution). It reviews the substantial evidence, names names and cites a proliferation of circumstances. The second paragraph, on the other hand, blows up a single scene from the narrative, and repeats the same information over and over: "a child is being brutally punished." Not only does the second paragraph provide no new evidence concerning the events, but it is even possible to wonder whether it is indeed a memory of the same event: no names, no material circumstances, no times or places are cited.

Now, the proximity of the two passages makes it seem likely that they refer to the same painful spanking. It would be possible to make the part, the punishment scene, stand in for the whole—the circumstances leading up to and including the punishment—because it can supply what is missing from the narrative, namely, evidence of the child's inner feelings, and of his moral integrity, in the shape of a brave refusal under torture to admit guilt for a crime he did not commit. It serves as well to show the disproportion of the punishment to the crime, and to lay the Lamberciers under suspicion. For, however reasonable it might be for the misunderstanding between the Lamberciers and the child to have arisen—the Lamberciers have evidence for their conviction, whereas the child has only his repeated and uncomprehending denial to speak for him—the misunderstanding becomes an injustice when the Lamberciers presume to punish him for the moral faults of lying and stubbornness without consulting him for inner evidence of moral corruption. Lejeune, for example, chooses to privilege the view that Rousseau has set the two paragraphs side by side and made the fragment stand in for the whole by synechdoche first because it provides the pathos missing from the *récit*, persuading that the boy was a feeling subject, not the sort to go around wantonly breaking combs and lying about it afterwards.[20] The synechdoche is then an ornament used by the narrating consciousness to persuade that, while the Lamberciers's conviction that only autonomous subjects commit crimes is correct, they are wrong in thinking the stick figure represented in the actions of the scene to be such an autonomous subject; without inner evidence, the subjective perspective, the *moi* is no more an autonomous figure than the servant. In such a view, the synechdoche restores the whole inside from a partial reminder of it. For Lejeune, proof of Rousseau's innocence as to the breaking of the comb (and his guilt as to his desire to break it)[21] comes from two sources: on the one hand, he has no memory of having touched the comb; on the other hand, he is a well-inten-

---

20. Cf. for example, op. cit., "Le Peigne," 14: "The narrator has abandoned his position of adult observer situated next to the Lamberciers and pretending to look at the child. He lets the attitude of the narrator become expressed more and more as it can only be known from the inside, although he still does not provide all the information."

21. Ibid., 29.: "If external appearances condemned him, we have also to believe that internal appearances were at the very least ambiguous. It must indeed be a nightmarish situation to be wrongly accused of having done what one had avoided doing precisely because one wanted to do it.

tioned youth, incapable of deliberate acts of violence and of untruths. By showing the inadequacies of the formal evidence in the case at hand, the narrator
would justify the confessional enterprise as supplementing for such lacks.

But the narrator does not appear interested in revealing what the protagonist thought or felt, nor does his conviction of his innocence come from
that source. Indeed, he states quite categorically that the hero's ideas and
feelings are impenetrable mysteries to him, that even imagination does not
allow him to establish a continuity between the past self and the present:

> Imagine a child (*un caractère*) timid and easily led . . . who has not even
> the idea of injustice, and who for the first time undergoes (*éprouve*) one so
> terrible at the hands of precisely those people he loves and respects the most.
> What an upset in the ideas! What disorder in the feelings! What a revolution in
> his heart, in his brain, in the whole of his little moral and intellectual being! I
> say, imagine all this if possible; but as for me, I don't feel myself able to
> disentangle, to follow out, the slightest trace of what was going on inside me
> then [19].

Not only does the narrator seem reluctant to accord belief to inner evidence, but he also leads us to think that belief and persuasion are not really the
main issue in proving the boy's innocence. He states without any equivocation
that he *knows* he did not break the comb: "Let no one ask me how the damage
was done (*comment ce dégat se fit*);[22] I do not know nor can I understand it;
what I know very certainly is that I was innocent of it" (19). What is the source
of that knowledge and of that certainty?

Perhaps the two parts of the passage do not provide the objective and the
subjective view of the same event. We can as easily understand the whole for
which the part substitutes to be the second paragraph as the first. In other
words, we can understand the narrative as the frame provided by invention to
set off a memory fragment that returns unaccompanied by any other circumstances. What that would mean, first of all, is that the compositional techniques of memory as it presents memories to consciousness would be at stake,
rather than two perspectives on the same event. We could easily understand
why the narrator is so certain that the child is not guilty of touching the comb,
or even of wanting to touch it, if he were raising the possibility that he might
have made up the crime to fit the punishment.

There is evidence that our ordinary notion of storytelling in autobiography—in which events precede the memory of events, and invention works to
put the memories together into a persuasive narrative—has been stood on its
head in this passage. Events do not determine the punishment and thus provide
the memory its objective and subjective tales (the review of the evidence, the
hero's feeling of injustice), and a convincing synechdoche to persuade that the

---

22. Note that the narrator appears to be concluding, against the Vicar, that matter can sometimes destroy itself.

latter is more valuable. Rather, a repressed sensation (pain) appears to have determined the second passage (the nonconfession of pain), itself the source of the first passage, the so-called remembered events, the convincing frame. The evidence that such a reversal may have occurred lies first in the way the second passage loudly insists that no substantive confession is going on, at the same time that it silently indicates the referent to be a sensation, pain. Indeed, the second paragraph fills in some holes in the representation of the subject, for it answers the question of how the *moi* can get new ideas by reminding that consciousness depends on forgetting. The judgment that judgment is just as active when it abstracts, as sensation is when it proffers perceptions, must forget all literal sensations like touching or being touched in order to understand the comparison. Just so the child studying denied the evidence of his senses: "I deny having touched" (*je nie avoir touché*). The model that allows the conception of such a repression is the model of reading. For just so reflective consciousness remembers he must have "touched," perceived the letters of the lesson he was studying in order to abstract meaning from them. The proliferation of signs indicating pain as their referent in the second passage serve as reminders of what had to be destroyed in order for meaning to be discovered. The sequence would thus give evidence that remembering repressed sensations, fragmentary and uncollected parts, can be the cause of ideas.

Evidence that the narrative is elaborated to explain the holes of the punishment scene would be provided by a series of compositional features. The circumstances of the crime appear to literalize figures and resemanticize the missing signifiers of the second passage. For example, the attempt to yank a meaningful confession out of a mute sensation—"The exacted confession couldn't be pulled out of me"—could serve as the origin for the yanked-out teeth of the comb. The fragmentariness of sensation, against the underlying unity of the subject—"I came out of that cruel trial, in pieces, but triumphant"—can be read as the source for the comb with its broken off teeth. The sensation of having been a white page on which impressions are made, a proof or *une épreuve* as it were, could have been translated into the letter sent off to Uncle Bernard, the offense itself (the *délit*), the punishment in which the children were "enveloped," the piece of inscribed metal (*la plaque*, in its other sense), the book the child is studying, and finally, into the whole series of *mise à l'épreuve*, that is, tests, trials, or study—all various ways of finecombing the evidence. The lack of a convincing content to confess—no *dans*, but plenty of exiguity ("exacted"; "pulled out," "came out," etc.)—and the sensation of the kind of *peine* one experiences when extraction is going on would explain the *peigne* and its missing *dents*. Rather than the fragmentary scene of punishment being supplied to disculpate the hero or justify the narrator after the fact, the narrative has been invented to explain the persistence of a memory fragment of uncertain provenance; in other words, the holes in the evidence have been invented to convince that the fault was in the memory not in the boy: the narrative of the broken comb would be only one of those indifferent ornaments that Rousseau explains he will use from time to time "to fill in an empty space occasioned by my faulty memory" (*pour remplir un vide occasionné par mon défaut de mémoire*, 5).[23] The evidence for this reading is fundamentally negative: the two passages are connected by proximity and by the signifying code. Rousseau's famous "charlatanistic transitions"[24] here reveal their law: resemanticized signifiers, fragments placed side by side *persuade* that there is continuity of development in the narrative at the very moment that they *prove* that in fact there is none.

The synechdoche that lets the part of the memory stand in for the whole does not lead to the convergence of the codes of belief and conviction then. On the one hand, it restores what is lacking from the review of the evidence— persuasion, feeling—by means of a mechanical trick, placing two memories side by side, so that the order in which the memories are presented comes to be taken for a causal order. On the other hand, it reminds that what is lacking from the story is the sensation of pain, and suggests as a reason for the synechdoche the need to represent that lack. The scene provides two contradictory arguments: either, the child, a subject with lots of high moral feelings, wouldn't have broken the comb; or, he couldn't have broken it, because, in writing down his memories the narrator becomes convinced that the narrative was made up. The aporia which pits the synechdoche as the subject's strategic weapon for reminding of inner feeling, against the synechdoche as gaining its persuasion from order alone, cannot be resolved. The persuasion that there is a moral being like the self arises in the face of convincing proof that there is no guarantee of continuity with the past, and that consequently the continuous development of protagonist or narrator is a mirage. But that conviction itself is based on a masked persuasion: namely, that some very diabolical author has made up the whole story about missing authors in order to explain why there are so many parts.

Textual reflexivity as well as self-reflexivity is at work throughout the narrative, then, and indeed the former prepares the crucial recognition that perception can provide new ideas by way of memory. The model suggesting

---

23. Rousseau tells us in the preamble that he may occasionally find himself using such fictions. What better ornament to represent both the cause (faulty memory) and effect (empty space) than an ornamental comb with half its teeth missing? For the teeth of the comb are a catachresis, and as such both substitute a figure for the missing proper term and are the proper term. The catachresis expresses very well the uncertainty in Rousseau's phrasing as to whether his faulty memory shows up in the substitution of fictions, like the fiction of the children's punishment, for the actual events, or as literal holes (ranging from windows, missing teeth, to narrative sequences of uncertain origin). It is clear from the preamble that Rousseau does not himself claim to know when he has substituted fictions for the holes in his memory, and when he has, in all ignorance, simply represented them: "I *may* have supposed to be true what I knew could have been so, never what I knew to be false" (5. My emphasis.)

24. Letter to Dom Deschamps, September 12, 1761. *Correspondance générale*, ed. T. Dufour (Paris: Armand Colin, 1926).

that part of the episode of the broken comb has been entirely invented can be extended to both the episodes of the Bossey sequence, and indeed will even threaten the *Confessions* as a whole. For what better origin could there be for the sentiment of injustice and violence[25] than the feeling of pain without a cause, a punishment received for which no memory of a reason remains? That would be the case if the pain of a single spanking had been repressed, in order that it might be remembered first as the cause of pleasure and delight in imaginative pursuits in the episode of the children's punishment, and then as the causeless pain around which the enigmatic narrative of the broken comb is built. Indeed, the crime without an author, the breaking of the comb, could easily have been invented to suit such a half-forgotten pain: *une peine sans cause* is not hard to transform into its near homonym *un peigne cassé*. We post-Freudians should not be surprised that the repressed pain of the spanking should take the odd form of an inconclusive narrative about an uncertain crime, for the inconclusiveness, the resemanticizing of signifiers, would be clues that the feeling, the sensation repressed so that Bossey can be sentimentalized in the first episode, is being recalled through a process recognizable as dreamwork. While the whole Bossey sequence would be misleading in its details—the sentimental paradise did not really exist and the events of the broken comb episode are as likely to have occurred as what you dreamed last night—still it would tend to demonstrate that a subject on whom a sense impression was once made has persisted over time. The memory fragment would restore the whole, the endurance of the subject, as the meaning of the episode. In remembering the same spanking twice Rousseau would still be vindicating the confessional project.

But nothing insures that there ever was such an impression as a spanking made on the hero, and consequently that the episode provides a certain link to the past. Rousseau will suggest toward the end of the spankings sequence that restoring sequentiality to the past involves destruction as well as construction:

Almost thirty years have passed since I left Bossey without my having recalled my stay there in any agreeable fashion by memories somewhat connected (*par des souvenirs un peu liés*): but now that I have passed maturity and am declining into old age, I feel that those same memories are being born again while the others are being erased (*tandis que les autres s'effacent*), and are engraving themselves in my memory with traits whose charm and force augment from day to day; as if, feeling life already escaping, I were seeking to seize it again at its beginnings. [21]

---

25. The phrase "sentiment of injustice and violence" has excited no comment. But the odd pairing of a differential moral concept like injustice (understandable in comparison to justice) and of a differential concept of force like violence (understandable in comparison to the "tender, affectionate, peaceful" [14] manifestations of the passions in the earlier episode) under the term "sentiment" is worthy of note. It would be difficult to say whether sentiment is an inner feeling, or a sensation here.

The entire passage on spankings may have been made up to illustrate the two-part process of creating connections—called remembering—explained here: memory restores connections that had been destroyed, then recalls what it had to efface (a disagreeable lack of connection) in order to do its work of restoring. That would be the sense of the passage if we understood the last part of the sentence, an extension whose antecedent is uncertain, ("and are engraving . . . ") to refer not to the reconnected memories, but to the other, unconnected ones that are being wiped out. But in that case, no subject would underlie the confessing of confessions. What that would mean is that the story of the first *fessée*, the *fessée* that gives the *moi* access to meaningful sexual difference, is told with, *con*, another *fessée* so that the law of the production of confessions can be revealed. The *confesser confessé*, one a meaningful confession of a self disculpating and knowing itself, and legitimating confessions, and the other a confession that the sequence has been made up to illustrate the pieces of the word *confesser* would be at the origin of the autobiographical sequence. Textual reflexivity—for a word that represents itself in its two aspects as a text not a subject—would be at the origin of the *Confessions* in their entirety.

But if the Bossey sequence can be read either as two ways of remembering a single impression, in support of Rousseau's recuperative self, or as having as sole cause the illustration of the two aspects of words on a page, in support of the text's reflexivity, it cannot be read as both. For in one version, the version of the understanding, the memory of a repression is the cause of a small interruption of the narrative thread, leading to the constitution of the self as a readable book, by way of a persuasive substitution of part for totality. But in the other version, restoration of meaningful order is merely a pretense for the retrieving of literality. No subject could understand what all those letters spell, since they spell the end of understanding. The part can stand in for the whole by synechdoche because the whole is: part after part after part. The passage asserts a disjunction, a mutual miscomprehension, between the two ways of organising the episodes of an autobiography. The gap constituting that miscomprehension, the divergence between reading and interpretation cannot be closed, since the effort to throw a bridge across it by an act of understanding is itself the reenactment of the persuasion into the agreeable illusion of narrative, and has as its effect the obliteration of the literality signified.

YALE UNIVERSITY

BARBARA JONES GUETTI

"Travesty" and "Usurpation" in Mme de Lafayette's Historical Fiction

The title page of Mme de Lafayette's first historical novel, *La Princesse de Montpensier* (1662), bore the following notice:

> *The Publisher to the Reader:* The respect owing to the illustrious name on the title of this book, and the consideration due to the eminent descendents of those who bore it, obliges me to say, in order not to offend either of these parties in presenting this book to the public, that it is not derived from any manuscript that comes down to us from the times of the characters of whom it speaks. The Author having wished, for his own diversion, to write adventures invented for the sheer pleasure of it, felt it would be more fitting to take names that are known to us from history than to use the names we find in novels, being certain that the reputation of Mme de Montpensier could not be harmed by a story so clearly incredible. If he should not share these scruples, I nevertheless must express them in this notice, which would be to the author's advantage, and at the same time shows my respect toward the Dead who are interested parties, as well as toward the Living who might also be concerned.[1]

Unlike many notorious title pages and prefaces by such novelists as Cervantes, Richardson, Rousseau, or Laclos, this one does not presuppose the reader's awareness that the real author is masking his fiction under the guise of historical fact, or ironically bowing out of the picture in deference to the "authenticity" of the work. If such manifestly fictional forgeries, the stock-in-trade of the novel from its very origins, tend to involve their readers in a vertiginous series of counterstrategies,[2] the document we are considering can, it seems, be read much more straightforwardly for what it says it is—an open admission of literal forgery, a legal announcement, made on behalf of the author by her

---

1. Mme de Lafayette, *Romans et Nouvelles*, ed. Emile Magne (Paris: Gallimard, 1961), 3. All subsequent citations from Mme de Lafayette are to this edition; page references will be given in the body of the text. All translations from the French in this article are mine.

2. See Paul de Man's discussion of the second preface to *La Nouvelle Héloïse in Allegories of Reading* (New Haven and London; Yale U. Press, 1979), 191–205.

publishers, in order to notify the public that historical facts have been tampered with, the real names misappropriated.

The scrupulous concern expressed here for the rights of the dead as well as of the living finds an emphatic echo in a text published seven years later by Mme de Lafayette's friend, collaborator and literary mentor, Pierre-Daniel Huet. Huet's *Treatise on the Origin of Novels* (1669) was a pioneering effort to mark off the territory of the novel from that of more traditional literary genres; it offers a resourceful and flexible treatment of the psychology of reading, leading to an eloquent defense of the novel's capacity to present "figures of truth" or "significant fictions" with as much appeal to wise as to foolish readers.[3] Huet's generally permissive treatment of the novel does not, however, prevent him from expressing very strict reservations on one point. In the following passage he emphatically excludes one kind of novel—as it turns out, the kind of novel Mme de Lafayette actually wrote—from the precincts of acceptable fictional practice:

> . . . the plausibility (*vraisemblance*) that is often absent from History is essential to the Novel. So that as one might apply to historians what the Muses said of themselves in Hesiod, when they boasted of knowing how to speak the truth, one might apply to novelists what they add: that they also know how to tell lies which resemble the truth. But I exclude from the category of novels certain stories (*histoires*) that are entirely false, as a whole and in their parts, but must be invented in cases where the truth cannot be known—such as the imaginary accounts that are given of the origins of most nations, whether civilized or barbaric; or such as those stories so crassly invented by the Monk Annius Viterbus, which so justly arouse the indignation and outrage of scholars. I make the same distinction between novels and such works as I would between those people who, by an innocent artifice, disguise themselves (*se travestissent*) and put on masks in order to divert themselves by diverting others, and those who, assuming the name and the clothing of dead or absent people, use this resemblance to swindle them of what is rightly theirs (*usurpent leur bien*).[4]

Annius Viterbus was a notorious forger, in the fifteenth century, of historical documents; the crime Huet denounces so emphatically here is the same one committed in *La Princesse de Montpensier*, and openly announced on its title page. It appears, after all, that the questions of authorship and authorisation this document raises go well beyond the immediate issue of whether, in fact, we can attribute it directly to Mme de Lafayette, to her publishers, or even, for that matter, to Huet himself, who might well have resorted to such interven-

3. Pierre-Daniel Huet, *Lettre-Traité sur l'Origine des Romans*, ed. F. Gégou (Paris: Nizet, 1971). The phrases cited come from a central statement about the psychology of reading, 103–33. The treatise was originally published as a preface to Mme de Lafayette's only full-length *roman*, *Zaïde*.

4. Ibid., 49–50. My translation.

tions in an effort to patch up the discrepancies between his theories of literary decorum and Mm de Lafayette's actual practice as a novelist. If we are brought up short before this inscription—"stymied," to repeat the word Paul de Man used to initiate a discussion of autobiography which swiftly conducts its readers to the *Sta, Viator* engraved on tombstones,[5] readers of Mme de Lafayette have tended to express their response to her work in much the same terms of stunned astonishment—*surpris*[e], in the vocabulary of the seventeenth century.[6] The title page of *La Princesse de Montpensier* may be read, in the context of Huet's discussion of fiction, as an abbreviated version of a gesture Mme de Lafayette performed again and again in her writing, a gesture by which she perpetually committed the very type of forgery which seeks to usurp historical truth, replacing it with an alternative, rival truth. Certainly, whatever intricate maneuverings may lie behind the production of this text—or be reproduced in us as we attempt to read it—it resembles Mme de Lafayette's novels in being a hyperbolically anonymous document, characteristic of a mode of writing which has made the identification of a distinct authorial "tone" or "point of view" a perpetual embarrassment to commentators on her work. And like this document, it is also characteristic of Mme de Lafayette's novels to advertise a scandal, openly giving notice of their profound disregard of laws that ought to govern the conduct of lovers, authors, or mourners of the dead.

The most notorious of these scandals is, of course, the confession which the heroine of *La Princesse de Clèves* makes to her husband of her passion for another man. Among those, within and without the novel, most scandalized by this gesture, we should not fail to count the lover himself, M. de Nemours. Deeply frustrated, after overhearing the interview between Mme de Clèves and her husband, over her refusal to name the other man he rightly suspects to be

---

5. Paul de Man, "Autobiography as De-facement," in *The Rhetoric of Romanticism* (New York: Columbia U. Press, 1984), 67–81.

6. Valincour's *Lettres à Mme la Marquise * * * sur le sujet de la Princesse de Clèves* (1679), ed. A. Cazes (Paris: Bossard 1925) presents imaginary dialogues among three readers (two men and one woman) who frequently express such *surpris[e]* in attempting to describe their complex reactions to the novel. For instance: "You don't understand the pride of the human intellect. It can't permit anyone to startle it (*le surprendre*) by presenting it with something that passes for the truth, but is in fact false. And even if someone does want to be fooled, that is, if he goes to plays or reads novels, at least he expects to be cheated with respect" (*il veut qu'on le trompe avec respect*). [140–41] This masculine reader takes offense at a breach in the decorum of *vraisemblance* in much the same terms that M. de Clèves, in the novel, takes offense at his wife's confession; in both cases, it is preferable to be "trompé avec respect" than to be *surpris* by a discrepancy between the real and the plausible. A less critical, but equally wary, reaction is expressed by the woman reader: "In reading books like these it becomes difficult to remain on one's guard against passion, and not to be taken unawares (*surpris[e]*) by an enemy who sets such agreeable traps" (227). Within the novel, *surpris* covers a range of emotional crises and impasses, from the first impression created by the heroine when she arrives at court (248) to the bitter erotic humiliation expressed in a letter which passes from hand to hand in the second volume (308–10).

himself, Nemours is overcome by incompatible emotions; quite beside himself, he has recourse to an interesting remedy:

> This prince was so overcome by passion and so astounded (*surpris*) at what he
> had heard, that he fell into a rather ordinary indiscretion, which is to speak in
> general terms of one's particular feelings, and to recount one's own adventures
> under borrowed names. [337–38]

The indiscretion Nemours commits is, as Mme de Lafayette tells us with some contempt, *assez ordinaire:* it is, in fact, the sort of indiscretion normally committed by writers of fiction as well as by frustrated lovers in real life—essentially, the kind of fictional "travesty" of which Huet approves in his treatise. Nemours's best defense against the *surpris*[e] he has undergone is to translate it immediately into general terms which divert its impact into the sort of common gossip that might apply to anyone. He does not, like the villainous impostors in Huet's text, appropriate real names for imaginary stories; instead he uses borrowed names, permitting what might have been his private property to circulate as public currency.

Nemours receives the assurance which might have prevented this indiscretion in a scene which Mme de Lafayette's most devoted readers—among them, Michel Butor—have been able to recognize as the scene for which the novel was written.[7] Once again, a series of coincidences brings Nemours to the window of Mme de Clèves's country estate: he finds her engaged in a ritual involving a set of objects referring to him, notably an especially distinctive (*fort extraordinaire*) Indian cane he used to carry. As she weaves ribbons of the colors Nemours wore in a recent tourney around this cane, Mme de Clèves gazes raptly at a painting of the siege of Metz, which also contains Nemours's portrait (366–67). In accounting for the *surpris*[e] even a modern reader may experience at this point in the novel, Butor dwells, quite appropriately, on the sexual significance of the cane, which Mme de Clèves has taken from her lover without asking his permission. But the cane is not the only thing Mme de Clèves has covertly appropriated for her own purposes. The painting of the siege of Metz, we learn a few pages earlier, was copied at her orders from the original, which belongs to Diane de Poitiers, the recently bereaved mistress of the king, Henri II. This artifact celebrates an important victory, the kind of battle that accounted for the king's real power. Now, removed from its proper context in Diane de Poitiers's estate, it represents Mme de Clèves's love for Nemours.[8] If we see the theft of the cane, in the Freudian terms suggested by

---

7. Michel Butor, *Repertoires*, 2 (Paris: éditions de Minuit, 1960), 74–78.

8. When Mme de Clèves retires to her estate, she takes with her what amounts to a complete replica of Diane de Poitiers's most significant furnishings: "She departed for Coulommiers; and, when she went, she took care to take with her some large paintings she had had copied from the originals commissioned by Mme de Valentinois for her beautiful house, Anet. All the outstanding events that had occurred during the king's reign were depicted in these paintings. Among them was the siege of Metz, and those who had distinguished themselves were portrayed very accurately" (363–64).

Butor, as theft of the phallus, we can also see the theft of the painting, in Huet's terms, as an equally drastic act of usurpation, carried out by Mme de Lafayette on behalf of her heroine in an effort to appropriate the literal force of actual historical events.

The major historical event around which the action of *La Princesse de Clèves* revolves is one of those spectacular accidents which, as Huet says in his treatise, often lack the plausibility (*vraisemblance*) of fiction. The coincidences in the novel, which continually bring the hero and heroine together in scenes such as the ones we have been discussing, are rivalled by the actual death of Henri II, which occured at a tourney in which he received a lance wound in the eye. Mme de Lafayette's treatment of the court, from the beginning to the end of the novel, exploits the peculiar *éclat* of such an event, in which a symbolic public ceremony turns out to have fatally real consequences. The novel's opening sentence, "Opulence and gallantry have never appeared in France with such splendor as in the last years of the reign of Henri II" (241), is echoed in the description of the fatal tourney as "the most magnificent spectacle ever seen in France," and in the epitaph pronounced at the moment of the king's death: "He died in the prime of his life, adored by his people, and loved by a mistress with whom he was madly in love" (357). It is this combination of glamorous display and effective historical actuality which Mme de Lafayette transfers to her heroine in allowing her to abscond with the painting owned by Diane de Poitiers.

Up to a point, we can regard Mme de Lafayette's historical fictions as mere travesties, in Huet's terms: acceptable manipulations of documentary sources in the interest of *vraisemblance* [plausibility] and *bienséance* [propriety].[9] It has commonly been acknowledged that she transformed actual Renaissance history, as recorded by its chroniclers, into stories that suited the style and manners of the period in which she lived.[10] We could also say that she performs a similar kind of travesty in feminizing history, making women and their concerns a central focus in her stories, as they were not either in recorded history or in actual political fact. Even the possible satiric—or at any rate admonitory—intention of such strategies might be allowed to remain within the bounds of acceptable travesty, as set down by Huet. For if "telling lies which resemble the truth" involves assuming the mask of the terms of discourse which obtain in a given society, such a critique still presents itself as nothing more than a complaint against society for failing to live up to the promises inscribed in its maxims: it does not constitute a challenge to the validity of the maxims themselves. Just such a complaint is lodged by the heroine's mother, Mme de Chartres, in a maxim which many commentators

9. See Gérard Genette's discussion of the link between aesthetic decorum and social propriety in "Vraisemblance et Motivation," *Figures 2* (Paris: Seuil, 1966), 71–99.

10. See M. Chamard and G. Rudler, "La documentation sur le XVIe siècle chez un romancier du XVIIe," *Revue du XVIIe siècle* (Paris, 1914), v. 2, 92–289; 1917–18, 1–231.

have taken to be the key statement of the book: "Ce qui paraît n'est presque jamais la vérité" (265) ["Appearances hardly ever correspond to reality."] The heroine's final *askesis,* her refusal, as René Girard puts it, "to take part in the infernal game at court,"[11] would thus make her very much her mother's daughter, standing lucidly apart from a world finally denounced as being, itself, the emptiest of travesties, a meaningless and potentially endless exchange of identical masks.

But such interpretations fail to account for the *surpris*[e], or scandal, most profoundly characteristic of Mme de Lafayette's practice as a writer. Indeed, far from opposing "appearance" to "truth" as Mme de Chartres would have it when she speaks contemptuously of Diane de Poitiers, Mme de Lafayette's narrative never allows the real deficiences of the king's mistress (her advanced age, her infidelities, or the other sordid details recounted with disapproving relish by Mme de Chartres)[12] to interfere with the prestige accorded her from the opening pages of the novel to the moment of the king's all-too-literal, but splendid, death. If the legitimate queen, Catherine de Medicis, must, for practical purposes, become a mistress of dissimulation, Diane de Poitiers, legitimately or not, successfully imposes her distinctive mode of appearing on the court: "les couleurs et les chiffres de Mme de Valentinois paraissaient partout" (241–42). And while Catherine de Médicis eventually takes over the power of the throne, Mme de Clèves, the imaginary heroine of the book, inherits (or usurps) the status of her fictional predecessor, Diane de Poitiers—the very figure who, for her mother, epitomized the scandalous discrepancy between "appearance" and "truth" characteristic of the court in general. Mme de Clèves becomes, like Diane de Poitiers, a woman with no peer, no rival—just as she had asserted herself to be during her quarrel with her husband over the disconcerting circulation of her story as "travestied" by Nemours: "But there could not be another story like mine, no other woman would be capable of such a thing. It could not have been invented by chance or imagined, and such a thought has never entered another mind but my own" (349).

Such claims are not acceptable travesties—innocent diversions which offer plausible substitutes for literal reality. Indeed, they call into question the legitimacy of what Huet sees as genuine History. For such stories (*histoires*) as these radically de-legitimize history—either by giving it a false beginning to which it is not entitled ("such as the imaginary accounts that are given of the origins of most nations, whether civilized or barbaric"), or by stealing the rightful property to which it *is* entitled, "assuming the name and the clothing of dead or absent people" to produce a rival reality, not merely an equivalent truth. The vehemence of Huet's protest against fictions which present them-

---

11. *Deceit, Desire and the Novel,* trans. Yvonne Freccero (Baltimore: The Johns Hopkins Press, 1965), 175.

12. Mme de Chartres's maxim refers specifically to Diane de Poitiers, whom she portrays as a bad example in the cautionary tale delivered to her daughter, 264–69.

selves under such false credentials seems to arise from a half-acknowledged awareness that they threaten to reveal the hybrid quality of his concept of "History"—not so much to make history appear just another form of fiction as to expose the literal, arbitrary force which must always underlie (or underwrite) its documents. If history lends itself to the apparently innocuous substitutions of fiction, thereby acquiring a generalized, transferable "meaning," it becomes that much more evident that the documents professing merely to record or to certify "what happened" must, after all, impose an authority whose legitimacy is always open to question. To assert the priority of "real facts" for which there can be no substitutes is also, implicitly, to give up the pretension that such facts inherently possess the kind of meaning that can be "certified" or lawfully "transferred," as property and titles and proper names might be transferred from one generation to another. Such claims to orderly progression evaporate when history is placed next to fiction: either all substitution is equally "legitimate," or no substitution is ever exclusively so. If history must, at all costs, be distinguished from fiction, the price of this distinction is indeed high: without in any sense denying the reality of history, we can, nonetheless, regard it as a chain of successful impostures and forgeries.[13]

Paul de Man's remarks, in his essay "Autobiography as Defacement," about the difficulty of classifying autobiography as a literary *genre* may be extended to Huet's efforts to classify the novel. What is at stake in both cases is, in de Man's words, "the possible convergence of aesthetics and history."[14] In fact, as our examination of Huet's strictures against documentary forgery have shown, the novel can constitute a serious threat to history, taking away with one hand what it gives with the other. For if novels in a sense come to the aid of history, supplying the plausibility real history often lacks, they also threaten to undermine its authority entirely, robbing it of everything it might properly call its own.

Huet's way of imagining this danger as a calamitous interference with the laws governing legitimate inheritance, in which actual, living people are swindled out of their rightful property, bears an uncanny resemblance to the issues which, literally, haunt autobiographical discourse in the "exemplary"

---

13. See Nietzche, *On the Genealogy of Morals*, trans. Walter Kaufman and R. J. Hollingdale (New York; Vintage books, 1967), Second essay, section 12, 77; " . . . whatever exists, having somehow come into being, is again and again reinterpreted to new ends, taken over, transformed, and redirected by some power superior to it; all events in the organic world are a subduing, a *becoming master*, and all subduing and becoming master involves a fresh interpretation, an adaptation through which any previous "meaning" and "purpose" are necessarily obscured or even obliterated." See also Paul de Man, "Shelley Disfigured," in *The Rhetoric of Romanticism*, op. cit., 122: "*The Triumph of Life* warns us that nothing, whether deed, thought or text, ever happens in relation, positive or negative, to anything that precedes, follows or exists elsewhere, but only as a random event whose power, like the power of death, is due to the randomness of its occurrence. It also warns us why and how these events then have to be reintegrated in a historical and aesthetic system of recuperation that repeats itself regardless of the exposure of the fallacy."

14. Op. cit., 67.

instance of Wordsworth's "Essay upon Epitaphs," which de Man goes on to discuss in the rest of his article. De Man calls our attention to Wordsworth's hesitant treatment of the trope of prosopopeia, "the fiction of an apostrophe to an absent, deceased, or voiceless entity, which posits the possibility of the latter's reply and confers upon it the powers of speech."[15] The latent threat of novelistic forgery for Huet is essentially the same one that Wordsworth, according to de Man, senses in prosopopeia: "by making the dead speak, the symmetrical structure of the trope implies . . . that the living are struck dumb, frozen in their own death."[16] In both cases, whether we are speaking of the loss of individual identity which, for de Man, constantly undermines autobiography, or the "usurpation" of legitimate property (*biens*) which, for Huet, happens when fictions "represent" history too effectively, the same dangerous border-crossing threatens to occur, cancelling out intelligible distinctions between authors and their readers, history and fiction, the living and the dead.

Such displacements are quite evident in the title page of *La Princesse de Montpensier.* Whoever is responsible for this document (and this is the very question the text poses, and fails to resolve), it may be the closest thing to a literary manifesto we might expect from a writer who never assumed the role of an author entitled to speak, publicly, in her own voice—perhaps because she knew as well as Paul de Man did that such voices are difficult to locate with any confidence.[17] "Any book," says de Man, "with a readable title page is to some extent autobiographical." Yet he adds, "just as we seem to assert that all texts are autobiographical, we should say that, by the same token, none of them is or can be."[18] The reason why no title page is any more readable than the one we have been discussing is that no such document can, in fact, clearly mark the barrier between the author as subject of a story "inside" the text and the writer who, in inscribing and signing the text, authorizes its passage into the public domain, thus performing a contractual guarantee of the literal force of the

---

15. Ibid., 75–76.

16. Ibid., 78.

17. See, for instance, her private letter in regard to the authorship of *La Princesse de Clèves:* "For myself, I'm flattered to be suspected of writing this book, and I believe I would gladly confess having done so, if I were sure the author would never come to reclaim it. I find it most agreeable, well written without being overdone, full of things that are admirably subtle and that need to be read more than once. But most especially I find it a perfect imitation of the court and of the manner in which people live there. Nothing about it is too much like a novel, too contrived; in fact it is not a novel at all: it is really a set of *mémoires,* and from what I hear, that was originally the title, but they changed it." *Correspondance de Mme de Lafayette,* ed. André Beaunier, (Paris: 1942), volume 2, 62–63 (my translation). This private disavowal of authorship is similar to the gesture later novelists (see above, note 2) performed in public, on title pages and in prefaces. Mme de Lafayette, however, only allows her books to be publicly advertised in even more impersonal terms than these. Accounts of her complex relation to the issue of authorship, and her collaboration with Segrais, Huet, Ménage and La Rochefoucauld are given in Charles Dédéyan, *Mme de Lafayette* (Paris: The University Press, 1955) and Harry Ashton, *Mme de Lafayette: sa vie et ses oeuvres* (Cambridge: The University Press, 1922).

18. Op. cit., 70.

work, asserting its validity as a historical event, if not its constative validity as a statement of truth. According to de Man, it is never possible to locate the source of the authority which would allow this exchange to occur successfully, since the reader of such a text must now assume the problematic status of judging subject which the author attempted to cast off and pass on to the public in writing and signing (his) work.[19] Self-representation is impossible, not because authors lie about themselves, but because it is never certain just who is entitled to "represent" or "speak for" the historical subject. Nor is it clear to whom such an utterance might be addressed, if not to other equally untrustworthy subjects—the alternative being a kind of monolithic collective authority, "the public," whose impassive and implacable face haunted Rousseau, for instance, in his more paranoid moments.

The title page of *La Princesse de Montpensier* deftly traces the process by which authorial assertion (perhaps inevitably) gives way to prosopopeia. The voice of the publisher claims, at first, to represent just such an author as Huet might have condoned: "the Author having wished, for his own diversion, to write adventures invented for the sheer pleasure of it." Such an author readily disavows any connection between his fictional inventions and the real historical figures whose names he thought it would be "more fitting" (*plus à propos*) to use than "the ones we find in novels." That offhand expression *à propos*, is not however, the least bie *à propos* in the context of Huet's discussion of literary forgery, since it begs the very question that demands an answer: the question of *whose* "propos" are being ap-propriated. Who speaks, with what authority, about the dead, or for them? Who, under what title, takes over the "names we know from history"? The last sentence of the document, in ostensibly rectifying these problems, constitutes a retraction of the publisher's claim to represent the author: "If he [the author] should not share these scruples, I [the publisher] nevertheless must express them in this notice, which would be as much to the Author's advantage as respectful, on my part, toward the Dead who are interested parties and toward the Living who might also be concerned." Instead of speaking "for" the author, the perpetrator of this document must *replace* that missing voice, (*j'y supplée*), must supplement its silence. The concern expressed, literally, about the possible hostile reactions of Mme de Montpensier's living relatives is phrased, far more generally and far more radically, as an inquiry into the nature of the transactions that may be carried out between the Living and the Dead. If all title pages are unreadable, this one is both prosopopaic—since it attributes to the dead "les Morts qui y sont intéressés," a (lively) interest in these proceedings, and strongly apotropaic, an *avertissement* which seeks to turn away the wrath of the dead from the living who have taken their places, names and voices.

Such a manner of expressing "respect" for the dead does not in fact respect

---

19. I attempt here to summarize de Man's argument (71–72), made in response to Phillipe Lejeune.

the specific identity of actual historical individuals. Instead, this inscription quite blatantly disfigures its literal historical subject, as de Man says all epitaphs and autobiographies must, whatever the avowed intentions of their authors. We might, indeed, describe the act Mme de Lafayette repeatedly performs in writing her novels by saying that she smuggles the bodies of impostors into the tombs of their real historical namesakes, and then proceeds to write appropriate epitaphs for these impostors.[20] Mme de Lafayette continued to commit such forgeries, and contined to advertise them. In her last work, *La Comtesse de Tende,* she committed another "posthumous affront" to an actual historical woman, Clarisse Strozzi, who was, according to the most reliable documentary evidence, virtuous and childless.[21] In the novel she is portrayed as an adulteress who gives birth to an illegitimate child and who makes a point of informing her husband about her pregnancy in a letter which leaves him as stunned (*surpris*) as if he had seen a ghost.[22] Such overt impostures as these, recurrent themes within the fiction and recurrent gestures by which it is offered to the public, persistently challenge the notion that history is the legitimate property of those who profess to certify, authorize or authenticate its documents, or even of those who are lawfully entitled to pass on its proper names. And such fictions are not proposed as harmless "figural" extensions of "literal" history. If the women in Mme de Lafayette's novels must usurp the place of actual women who lived and died, this may be her way of saying that women cannot be "represented" in the "universal" codes which render the harsh facts of actual power decorous and plausible. Her heroines are not figures for some "general truth," and she makes every effort to distinguish the stories she wants to tell from the essentially interchangeable fictions ordinarily recounted by such as Nemours, and approved by her mentor, Huet.[23] In main-

---

20. *La Princesse de Montpensier* concludes with such an epitaph, which reads like a summary of the central dilemma that subsequently recurred in *La Princesse de Clèves:* "She could not withstand the sadness she felt at having lost the esteem of her husband, the heart of her lover, and the most perfect friendship that ever existed. She died a few days later, in the prime of her life, one of the most beautiful princesses in the world, and who might no doubt have been happier, if virtue and prudence had conducted all her actions" (33).

21. Ibid., 432–33; cf. notes 1 and 8.

22. The letter serves the same function in this novel as the notorious confession (*aveu*) in *La Princesse de Clèves.* Although the content of the message, a blunt "Je suis grosse," is markedly different, Mme de Lafayette speaks of the impact of this gesture on its recipient in strikingly elevated terms: "Jealousy and well-grounded suspicions ordinarily prepare husbands for their misfortunes; they are always in some doubt, but nothing compares with the certitude conveyed by a confession, which is higher than anything our intellects can reach" (*cette certitude que donne l'aveu, qui est au-dessus de nos lumières*). The question of whether to take the semireligious diction used in such a context "seriously" or "ironically" typifies the way in which Mme de Lafayette's writing perpetually stumps or "stymies" her readers.

23. The last word of the final sentence of *La Princesse de Clèves,* "inimitables," (395), again asserts that the heroine's distinctive qualities cannot be translated into the general principles of mimetic decorum upon which Huet's entire argument rests.

taining an authorial silence that is not so much ironic as it is ruthless, Mme de Lafayette supplements the silence of real women with fictions designed to usurp the priority (and the propriety) of all modes of discourse—legal, fictional, or historical—that have, so effectively, imposed that silence upon them.

HAMPSHIRE COLLEGE

MOSHE RON

The Art of the Portrait
According to James

The earliest date claimed with any currency for the appearance of a portrait likeness is about 5000 B.C. In the prepottery strata of the excavations at Jericho, seven skulls were found buried under the floor of a single room; each of these skulls had been modeled over with clay and fitted with "eyes" of shell . . . , to simulate the appearance of a fully formed human head. . . .

Skulls preserved in such societies can be derived, broadly speaking, from two sources which would seem to the outsider psychologically antithetical: honored members of the community itself and enemies. In the latter case, the skulls were obtained in battle or by head-hunting.[1] Such ideas, however, have sprung from the soil of unbounded self-love, from the primary narcissism which dominated the mind of the child and of primitive man. But when this stage has been surmounted, the "double" reverses its aspect. From having been an assurance of immortality, it becomes an uncanny harbinger of death.[2]

The real subject of this essay is more pretentious than that announced in the title, since in treating the theme of the portrait what I'm after in the final analysis is James's most personal involvement in the problem of representation in general. I will be using the portrait as a convenient—and, I hope convincing—illustration of that more general theme. What may be in need of more justification is my conferring so much authority on one single tale, "The Liar," which is, after all, merely fiction and but one of over a hundred tales, not to mention the twenty-odd novels written by James over half a century of literary activity, during which he also made public his opinions on the subject in a great many critical essays and reviews.

One major aim I have is to pit James's official views on representation (so

<hr />

1. Breckenridge, *Likeness: A Conceptual History of Ancient Portraiture* (Evanston: Northwestern University Press, 1968), 15, 18. In this work, Freud is mentioned only once, to be attacked as an enemy of individualism.

2. Sigmund Freud, "The Uncanny," in *The Standard Edition*, v. 17 (London: Hogarth Press and the Institute of Psychoanalysis, 1955), 235.

widely known, commented and accepted by a whole tradition of novel criticism) against the picture emerging from a generalized reading of his fictional
narratives where the portrait occurs as a theme. An important side issue is
whether the portrait thematized in "The Liar" is merely a theme, or whether
one may take it as an emblem of the work itself. My contention is that it must
be taken as placed *en abyme*, although it is by no means clear in what sense
James can be said to be responsible for placing it there.

It is quite possible that this contention, as well as the claim that "The
Liar" has an emblematic authority for James's work as a whole, may be found
lacking in credibility or utterly misguided. Yet the ultimate success of this
essay does not strictly depend on the truth of either argument. If it is granted
that the portrait in "The Liar" is a *mise en abyme* of that work as a whole, and
that that work is emblematic of what representation is for James in general,
then I will have made my point. But if in what follows I fail to impose these
views, my essay will at least have displayed the reflexive structure of these
arguments by in fact turning out to have done that which it purports merely to
thematize, and in being so it would be mirroring the text itself.

OF BEING ILLUSTRATIVE

As a critic of art and literature and a theorist of representation—all for him
indeed one and the same thing—James would appear to have professed se-
renely optimistic views. Let me recall some of his most celebrated statements
on the subject culled not at random, but without strenuous research, from the
famous essay on "The Art of Fiction" (1884):

> The only reason for the existence of the novel is that it does attempt to repre-
> sent life. When it relinquishes this attempt that we see on the canvas of the
> painter, it will have arrived at a very strange pass.
> A novel is in its broadest definition a personal, a direct impression of life: that,
> to begin with, constitutes its value, which is greater or less according to the
> intensity of the impression.
> I cannot imagine a composition existing in a series of blocks, nor conceive, in
> any novel worth discussion at all, of a passage of description that is not in its
> intention narrative, a passage of dialogue that is not in its intention descriptive,
> a touch of truth of any sort that does not partake of the nature of incident, or an
> incident that derives its interest from any other source than the general and
> only source of the success of a work of art—that of being illustrative.
> Art is essentially a selection, but it is a selection, whose main care is to be
> typical, to be inclusive.[3]

The broad outline emerging from these fragments is of a theory of the kind
which the late W. K. Wimsatt proposed to call "the concrete universal," and

---

3. Henry James, *The Future of the Novel* (New York: Vintage Books, 1956), 5–20.

which, he argued, constitutes the major tradition of poetics from Aristotle to the New Critics.[4] According to this kind of theory there is nothing essentially problematic about the possibility of representation. There *is* an apparent paradox in the requirement that artistic representation be both concrete and universal, but this, as James might say, is but a challenge cheerfully to be met.

The prominence of words like "free" and "personal" in "The Art of Fiction" might create the impression that James embraced one horn of the apparent dilemma. In fact, however, he occupies an exemplary central position within the tradition of the concrete universal. According to him, the impressions which make their way into art must be personal, but this is not to say that art is concerned with representing the particular, much less the factual, for its own sake. The artist must exercise an intelligent selection ("see") and construct his work so as to exhibit all and only the essential relations of a given case. And the given case, so one must assume, is not to be a contingent matter of some particular fact, but the necessary illustration of a more general truth. Furthermore, art has no ulterior aim beyond the concrete representation of universals—*that* is purpose enough. Some such statement may be said to represent James's version of Kantian disinterestedness and purposeful purposelessness. In this he clearly dissociates himself from the purposeless purposelessness of Art for Art's sake and much of subsequent modernity.[5]

This then would seem to be the picture: here is consciousness, there the world: if only the eye be knowing enough to *see* and the hand skilled enough to *do*—and they are, sometimes—the outcome must be no less than a true representation of some truth. This idyllic picture also accounts for James's nearly unreserved adherence to the classical principle of *Ut pictura poesis*. If the essentials in a representation are the eye, the hand and the subject, then it can only be a matter of secondary significance whether the hand holds a brush or a pen.

MORE THAN A PORTRAIT

For any theory of art or fiction which seeks to justify its claim to truth by appealing to some notion of the universal, the portrait, as an art form concerned—at least ostensibly—with representing the individual for its own sake, might seem to pose a problem. Where an extreme neoclassicist might see an ineluctable dilemma mandating the rejection of the portrait from the realm of art,[6] James envisions the possibility of a powerful synthesis. This, for him, is

4. W. K. Wimsatt, "The Concrete Universal," in *The Verbal Icon* (Lexington: University of Kentucky Press, 1954).

5. Cf. René Wellek, *A History of Literary Criticism*, v. 4, *The Later Nineteenth Century* (London: Yale University Press, 1966), 218 ff.

6. In Rousseau's "Préface dialoguée" to *La Nouvelle Héloïse, Oeuvres complètes* (Paris: Gallimard, Pléiade, 1964), v. 2. 11, N. says: " . . . Un portrait a toujours son prix, pourvu qu'il ressemble, quelqu'étrange que soit l'Original. Mais dans un Tableau d'Imagination toute figure humaine doit avoir les traits communs à l'homme, ou le tableau ne vaut rien."

not merely a theoretical possibility. Such, for instance, is the success of the portrait of Miss Burckhardt (1882) by Sargent, as described in James's essay on this painter:

> The picture has this sign of productions of the first order, that its style clearly would save it if everything else should change—our measure of its value of resemblance, its expression of character, the fashion of dress, the particular associations it evokes. It is not only a portrait, but a picture, and it arouses even in the profane spectator something of the painter's sense, the joy of engaging also, by sympathy, in the solution of the artistic problem.[7]

The article ends with words of advice to the painter, a sort of Horatian Art of Portraiture, which is one of James's most explicit pronouncements on the subject:

> There is no greater work of art than a great portrait—a truth to be constantly taken to heart by a painter holding in his hands the weapon that Mr. Sargent wields. The gift that he possesses he possesses completely—the immediate perception of the end and the means. Putting aside the question of the subject (and to a great portrait a common subject will doubtless not always contribute), the highest result is achieved when to this element of quick perception a certain faculty of brooding reflection is added. I use this name for want of another, and I mean the quality in light of which the artist sees deep into his subject, undergoes it, absorbs it, becomes patient with it, and almost reverent, and, in short, enlarges and humanizes the technical problem.[8]

This prose has a seamy figurative underside which I cannot stop to expose (some pivotal words being "weapon," "deep," "absorbs," "reverent"). I am quoting it here only—if possible—for its most innocuous face value. At this level of reading one might wonder how to reconcile James's praise of the portrait as the greatest kind of art with his praise of Sargent's "Miss Burckhardt" as not only a portrait, but presumably something more, a picture.[9]

This paradox is readily resolved by the concrete universalist. A portrait would be a portrait if it represented no more than some concrete individual. A properly universal picture might perhaps fall short in concreteness, be too

---

7. "John S. Sargent," in *The Painter's Eye* (London: R. Hart-Davis, 1956), 219. This is an 1893 revision of an essay first published in 1887.

8. Ibid., 227–28.

9. In volume 3 of his biography of James, *Henry James, v. 3, The Middle Years* (Philadelphia: Lippincott, 1962), 108–09, Leon Edel has this to say about the two men (his subject, the writer, and *his* subject, the painter [Sargent]): "They had so much in common that they must have seemed to each other, in certain respects, mirror images. . . . It was no accident that the author of *The Portrait of a Lady* and this painter of portraits of great ladies should have found common bonds between them. Both were facinated by the human face and what it expressed." The last sentence echoes with some omission of emphasis the following sentence from "The Liar," whose subject is the portrait painter Lyon: "He often thought it a mercy the human mask did interest him and that it had such a need, frequently even *in spite of itself*, to testify, since he was to make a living by reproducing it." *The Novels and Tales of Henry James* (New York: C. Scribner's Sons, 1907–09), v. 12, 316–17 (my emphasis; henceforth, numbers in parentheses refer to this text).

schematic, seem unreal. The greatness of the conjunction of both portrait and picture in one representational object resides in the simultaneous satisfaction of the two requirements, both concreteness and universality.

A CONCRETE, FICTIONAL CASE

In James's fiction there are numerous cases involving portraits and the making of portraits in a literal sense. There are also cases where other art forms are discussed or attempted and the representation of particular individuals comes into play. In the overwhelming majority of these cases there is nothing peaceful or serene about the making or disposing of a portrait (or some equivalent of one). It invariably becomes the focal point of bitter, violent, sometimes tragic (and more rarely, grotesque) conflict between the parties concerned. The richness of the material is enormous, and here I can merely scratch the surface of one such text, "The Liar" (first published in 1888, the dead center of James's career).

Here is a summary of the story: Having been invited to the Ashmore country house to paint the aged Sir David, Oliver Lyon, a successful portrait painter, observes among the guests at dinner the striking figure of one Colonel Capadose and later also the unique beauty of Mrs. Capadose, née Everina Brant, to whom Lyon had years before proposed only to be rejected. In the conversation struck up between the two men, the Colonel reveals a propensity for telling anecdotes which strain his listener's credulity. On two occasions at least it is proven to Lyon that statements he has made do not accord with the truth. Later, Sir David entertains the painter by describing the Colonel's addiction to lying, characterizing it, however, as disinterested and no more than a social foible. Lyon, who considers lying the worst vice, wonders what the ever-veracious Everina makes of her prevaricating partner for life, and whether she might not regret her choice. He toys with the conjecture that she might not as yet realize her husband's depravity. He offers to paint Amy, the Capadoses' little girl, and before the portrait is completed, proposes to do the Colonel himself. His plan is to encourage the Colonel's mythomania, and thus to bring out the inner essence of his character by representing him as "The Liar." He hopes thereby to create a great work of art as well as to put to the test Everina's attitude towards his untruthfulness. During one of the sittings, a tipsy woman enters the studio unannounced in search of work as a model. The painter sends her off, and the sitter spins out an incredible story about her past. When the painting is nearly finished, everyone goes away for the summer, Everina having been particularly enjoined not to see it until it is declared completed. One day Lyon comes back to his studio on a sudden whim to find there the Capadoses who, they too on a whim, came to see the portrait. The Colonel seems uncomprehending, but his wife explodes in a scandalized wail. From behind a tapestry the painter watches, without interfering and with a sense of triumph, as the Colonel slashes at his portrait savagely, destroying it beyond repair. The couple then retreat through a side door. Lyon now waits for Everina's reaction, which fails to come. At a later meeting the couple present a united front, pretending ignorance of the violent act. The true wife professes to have loved what she saw, and the Colonel tries to shift the blame onto the disgruntled model. Left *tête à tête* with Lyon, Everina continues to lie in support of her husband and even seems to join in the false accusation against the innocent model, thus crushing Lyon's last hope for her.

The temptation is great to give this text a full dress close reading, evidently impossible here. The most obvious interpretive question (for any post-Jamesian, post-Boothean reader at least) concerns the reference of the title: who is "The Liar"? Is it the Colonel who is called a liar in the text, or, perhaps, the artist, who is not? Like other Jamesian texts, which have recently once more attracted critical attention, "The Liar" is rigorously ambiguous both thematically and through a trick of perspective.[10] The trick of perspective in this case is not the hierarchic embedding of several narrative instances with all the explicit marks of direct discourse (first person etc.) at each level, but the more unobtrusive stylistic device of free indirect discourse,[11] in which authorial discourse and character perspective are mingled together in uncertain doses (there are very few sentences in the text whose propositional content must be assigned to the author and cannot be assigned to Lyon). The mode is not ostensibly that of the fantastic, and the thematic presence of pathetic or uncanny elements, while not in doubt, is far less evident and not quite so startling as in "The Turn of the Screw" (e.g. the possibility of involving a child in the fatal search for truth and purity is indicated, but not pursued).

One might expect the Governess's supporters to have taken arms in favor of the self-professed (and here entirely self-appointed) champion of truth and virtue, Lyon, against the brazen pair, in this fiction proven guilty without recourse to supernatural vaguenesses. But first, this tale has provoked less commentary; and second, it could not be easy even for James's most credulous readers to discount the evidently loving and in this case also legitimate matrimonial attachment between the two sinners. Here legality and morality do not always seem to be on the same side, and this can pose a problem for legalists and moralists.

Consequently, few commentators seem to have adopted Lyon's perspective to the point of applying the title of the text to the Colonel alone.[12] In-

---

10. The two possible answers in this case do not logically exclude each other (both can be called "liars"); so this is not the classic type of narrative ambiguity as defined by Shlomith Rimmon, *The Concept of Ambiguity: The Example of James* (Chicago: University of Chicago Press, 1977). Wayne Booth has usefully tabulated and contrasted Lyon's view of the story with the implied author's. He opts for Lyon as the chief referent of the title. *The Rhetoric of Fiction* (Chicago: University of Chicago Press, 1961), 347–54.

11. On free indirect discourse see Brian McHale, "Free Indirect Discourse: A Survey of Recent Accounts," *PTL* 3 (1978), 249–87, and my more eccentric "Free Indirect Discourse, Mimetic Language Games and the Subject of Fiction," Poetics Today 2 (1981), 18–39.

12. Booth discusses some of them, op. cit., 349–50.

terestingly, some comments made by James himself are among the very few which imply such a reading (of these later). Clifton Fadiman, for example, in a note appended to this tale, hails it for being "more complex than it first appears," and goes on to say: "Then, as we re-read, or reflect, the character of Colonel Capadose emerges as 'The Liar's' center of gravity." One may well wonder what could be the simpler reading that suggested itself before reflection. Yet even this reader, into whose field of vision Lyon's share in the lying does not seem to have entered at all, cannot endorse the latter's severity *vis à vis* the poor Colonel: "Here is Munchausen analyzed by a psychologist skillfully, almost professionally, yet with a continuous play of sympathetic humor. We perceive that this is not in the least so banal a thing as a story about lying as a vice but rather so imaginative a thing as a story about lying as a passion."[13]

A reading which places Lyon's *perspective* in the thematic center stage is to be found in Manfred Mackenzie's fine book *Communities of Honor and Love in Henry James*.[14] The starting point for Mackenzie's reading is the precarious symmetry between the two men in the story, or rather, Lyon's perception of the Colonel as his "gallingly superior-inferior double," "at once his successful sexual rival and a 'liar Platonic' who 'doesn't operate with the hope of gain or with a desire to injure. It is art for art and he is prompted by the love of beauty . . .. He paints, as it were, and so do I!'"[15] Mackenzie then outlines Lyon's predicament *vis à vis* his mirror image as a crisis of self confidence resulting in an obsessive need to give his rival the lie in order to gain or regain for himself the position of truth, which happens to coincide with the approval and, more ambivalently, with the possible possession, of the woman involved. His commentary is worth quoting in its entirety, but I am forced to mutilate it, limiting myself to his reading of the crucial scene:

> It is a situation that, like any transaction between doubles, must end in a rupture or a wound. In one of James's characteristic voyeurist scenes, Lyon comes upon Colonel Capadose and his wife just as they discover "The Liar." So grave an insult is this picture that its victim reacts by mutilating it "exactly as if he were stabbing a human victim: it had the oddest effect—that of a sort of figurative suicide." The effect of this paroxysm of self-rejection (as well as rejection of Lyon) is that Lyon seems wholly to displace his rival from his identity and to insinuate himself as a superior would-have-been. Indeed, when questioned by a servant about the vandalism, he becomes "The Liar" in the letter as well as the spirit: "Lyon imitated the Colonel. 'Yes, I cut it up—in a fit

---

13. *The Short Stories of Henry James* (New York: Random House, 1945), 185.

14. (Cambridge, Mass.: Harvard University Press, 1976). Mackenzie is a critic from Australia. The index to his work lists no mention of Freud, and neither Lacan nor Girard merits an allusion.

15. Mackenzie, 96. In the text there are more instances of the Colonel's verbal activities being reflected through Lyon's consciousness in painterly metaphors. The two share, furthermore, what Peter Brooks has described "the melodramatic imagination" (the Colonel, for example, in his far-fetched story about Miss Geraldine, Lyon in his interpretation of the Colonel's character and corruption of his wife).

of disgust.' " By telling this lie he consummates his own figurative suicide. He has only painted his own dishonor.[16]

To any reader not averse to the language of psychoanalysis, the entire episode must reek of the "primal scene" (he sees them in the act, a crime committed with a sharp instrument, etc.). It is the melodramatic equivalent of Isabel coming upon Osmond unceremoniously seated while Mme. Merle is on her feet, or Strether spotting Chad and Mme. de Vionnet in their boat. Lyon's having engineered this test clearly validates Leo Bersani's suggestion that in James's fiction "there is a tortured identity and contrast between masochistic and sadistic 'moments' in the act of seeing, between seeing as punishment submitted to and seeing as punishment inflicted."[17] More particularly, this scene seems almost a rearrangement of the bedroom scene in *Hamlet*, where the protagonist wishes to bring home to his mother her complicity in her husband's guilt by speaking daggers to her. Only here, it is Hamlet behind the arras (and the canvas) rather than Polonius (the usurper's foolish representative), the dagger is wielded by his intended victim, and indeed it is he who in the end will have suffered the blow directed by himself. As in Jones's classic reading, in beholding the other's criminal desire, Lyon has only seen his own. And even the possibility of his regarding Capadose as the usurper of Everina's love may be glimpsed, if we recall that by his own admission the Colonel fell in love with her after seeing her portrait by Lyon. Significantly, in that portrait she was represented as a "regular Bacchante" and not, as Lyon chastely supposed, as Werther's Charlotte dispensing bread and butter to children. Everina herself is praised by Lyon for the motherly care she took of her younger siblings following her mother's death while living in Germany. The presence of Goethe's novel *en filigrame* is thus strong enough to enhance the reading which sees "The Liar" as Lyon's own symbolic suicide.

THE ART OF THE PORTRAIT

What is the specific role of the portrait in this drama? Lyon himself refers to his enterprise as a "masterpiece . . . of legitimate treachery," "a painted betrayal." If Mackenzie's reading is right, as I believe it is, then the portrait is an ultimate aggressive challenge which *boomerangs*.

Giving James the credit of having duly aimed at some general truth, we may be warranted in disengaging three general propositions about portraits:

1. The use of the portrait is to annihilate its subject.

---

16. Ibid., 97. I take only one exception to this account: in James's story the Colonel fails to read the message encoded in the portrait and is only reacting to his wife's anguish. In fact, he sees in it nothing but a flattering image of himself: "Why ain't I a good-looking fellow? I'll be bound to say he has made me handsome" (374). The refusal to know, as Shoshana Felman has shown, can be a distinctive feature of mastery. "Turning the Screw of Interpretation," *YFS* 55/56 (1980).

17. Leo Bersani, *A Future for Astyanax* (Boston: Little, Brown, 1976), 135.

2. The portrait robs the subject of his secret essence.
3. Every portrait is also a self-portrait.

The second may be subsumed under the first as a means to an end. The confluence of the first and the third points beyond the pleasure principle. All three seem a far cry from, in fact a vicious caricature of, any views likely to have been voiced by James as a critic or simply as a grown-up in his right mind. And, indeed, each of these malignant propositions may be rewritten to form a benign counterpart:

1. The use of the portrait is to immortalize its subject.
2. The portrait reveals the subject's inner essence.
3. Every portrait is evidence of the artist's talent.

Furthermore, all three of the daemonic propositions are raised at some point in the text only to be ironically dismissed or discredited by the immediate narrative context. The first to appear is the self-reflexive principle (my no. 3). At the dinner table, Lyon seeks information concerning the man who will turn out to be Colonel Capadose from a gossipy young lady (a ravenous talker who turns to him "from her other interlocutor with the promptness of a good cook who lifts the cover of the next saucepan"). She recognizes in him the successful painter:

> "I know your pictures; I admire them. But I don't think you look like them."
> "They're mostly portraits," Lyon said; "and what I usually try for is not my own resemblance." [319]

Far from it. So much for superior common sense and verbal irony. But the text nevertheless gives the shallow young thing the last word, when in a sentence added for the New York Edition, she is made to ask: "Don't you think Vandyke's things tell a lot about him?" (319).

A portrait, then, if one may theorize from so trivial a remark, *can*—but as some modern theorists have argued, need not—be an *iconic* representation of the *portrayed* subject; what it cannot escape is being an *indexical* representation of the *portraying* subject. The strict iconicity of a representation is at least once presented in James's fiction as unsuccessful art and a despotic claim to primacy by the model: this is the case of the drawings made after Major and Mrs. Monarch in "The Real Thing" (1891).[18] On the other hand the ego of *any person* connected with the making, the display or the possession of a portrait may be thought to be represented by it indexically (or metonymically): this may be the painter (e.g. the narrator in "Glasses," Mary Tredwich in "The Tone of Time"); the sitter, whether merely a model (the Monarchs) or the actual subject (Flora Saunt in "Glasses," the unnamed man in "The Tone of Time," Sir David in "The Liar"), or the patron (Mr. Dawling, Mrs. Bridgenorth

---

18. Cf. my "A Reading of the Real Thing," *YFS* 58 (1979).

and the young Ashmores respectively). The raison d'être of the portrait, then, is to be somebody's vicarious self-image. As such it is used to establish an imaginary social position by invidious comparison (Veblen's expression). It is simply a matter of reading it or having it read in the desired sense.

As the comparison with Vandyke does not ruffle Lyon's feelings, the dinner table conversation continues. The same unreliable source of information then refers to the prospective sitter as "an old mummy" and in answer to the painter's inquiry explains why Sir David has not been painted yet:

> "Ah, that's because he was afraid, you know; it was his pet superstition. He was sure that if anything were done he would die directly afterwards. He has only consented today."
> "He's ready to die then?"
> "Oh now he's so old he doesn't care."
> "Well, I hope I shan't kill him," said Lyon. "It was rather unnatural of his son to send for me."
> "Oh they've nothing to gain—everything is theirs already!" his companion rejoined, as if she took this speech quite literally. . . . [319]

When told that he didn't "look like" his pictures Lyon insisted on perfect literality. Throughout the text there is oscillation between strict adherence to the letter and undeterminedly broader latitudes. That a portrait might be a harbinger of death is of course just an old man's pet superstition (this too will later be denied). That a son might wish "unnaturally" to have his father done in in order to inherit his place, his property, his title, is no more than a harmless joke not meant to be taken literally at all. Later in the story, Sir David is described

> submitting to the brush as bravely as he might have to the salutary surgical knife. He sat there with firm eyes and set smile of "Well, do your worst!" He demolished the legend of his having feared the operation would be fatal, giving an explanation which pleased our friend much better. He held that a gentleman should be painted but once in his life—that it was eager and fatuous to be hung up all over the place. That was good for women, who made a pretty wall-pattern—but the male face didn't lend itself to decorative repetition. . . . He spoke of his portrait as a plain map of the country, to be consulted by his children in a case of uncertainty. [341–42]

In denying the unfounded report of his alleged superstition, the old man—I believe he is the oldest character in all of James's fiction—only reaffirms its validity. His explanation merely eliminates any *causal* relation between the portrait and death. If portraits are fit for women and for posterity, he has nothing left to fear, being already emasculated and dead to the world.

The second principle of the art of the portrait enters the story at a later scene, when Lyon proposes to Mrs. Capadose to do her husband's portrait. She objects to the idea of receiving yet another *gift* from the painter, reminding him of her old portrait sold for cash and her daughter's unfinished portrait which he has given them already. Lyon now has to explain the interest *he* has in the project, and he must do so without betraying his true intent (of which he may not be fully aware himself):

> "How will it do you a lot of good?" Mrs. Capadose asked.
>
> "Why he's such a rare model—such an interesting subject. He has such an expressive face. It will teach me no end of things."
>
> "Expressive of what?" said Mrs. Capadose.
>
> "Why of his inner man [*early version:* his nature]."
>
> "And you want to paint his inner man?"
>
> "Of course I do. That's what a great portrait gives you, and with a splendid comment thrown in for the money. I shall make the Colonel's a great one. It will put me up high. So you see my request is eminently interested."
>
> "How can you be higher than you are?"
>
> "Oh I'm an insatiable climber. So don't stand in my way," said Lyon.
>
> "Well, everything in him is very noble," Mrs. Capadose gravely contended.
>
> "Ah, trust me to bring everything out!" Lyon returned, feeling a little ashamed of himself. Mrs. Capadose, before she went humored him to the point of saying that her husband would probably comply with his invitation; but she added: "Nothing would induce me to let you pry into *me* that way!"
>
> "Oh you," her friend laughed—"I could do you in the dark!" [360]

Behind the banter there is a maxim concerning the source of greatness in a portrait, and behind that—a sinister intent. Everything in this bit of dialogue is to be read not with one ironic twist—as presumably intended by Lyon and possibly by the author—but with two or more. Lyon *is* a dangerous, insatiable climber, he *will* draw the Colonel out (by egging him on to new feats of mendacity), Mrs. Capadose *won't* let him invade the privacy of her person, he *would* like to do her in the dark.

This, then, is how the three tenets of the pernicious art of the portrait are inserted into the text without becoming a part of its explicitly sanctioned meaning. The introduction of dubious or outrageous propositions into texts designed to test them—usually inconclusively—is a recurring device in James's fiction. The problem of doing so without violating decorum and common sense verisimilitude is solved by modalization: such propositions are fictionalized as jokes, lies, conjectures, superstitions, fantasies, allegations, obesssions and the like. There does not seem to be any safe way of getting at the truth propounded by the author.

THE CONCRETE UNIVERSAL

Every portrait is also a self-portrait because it is not only a representational object which stands for the other. It is, or is also, an outward act of the self which inevitably expresses his inner character (at least to the perceptive viewer or reader). It is by laying bare and serving up, as it were,[19] the other's secret

---

19. Cf. the story "The Real Right Thing" (1899) in *Novels and Tales*, v. 27, especially 493. In this story a young man commissioned by a widow to do a late master's life seems to get himself caught in the predicament of *Totem and Taboo*.

self that the likeness figuratively assumes magic powers and becomes a lethal weapon.

But what is the other's innermost shameful secret self? In "The Liar" it is his unavowed desire—one which to the painter at least seems unavowed and not to be avowed—to please, to shine in society, to win friends and charm people, to impose on all (and most of all his wife) his own infatuation with himself. That unfounded, blind, mendacious self-infatuation which one sees in the other is a general truth. Lyon exposes it in, or attributes it to the Colonel by concretizing it in his particular features:

> It was in the eyes and it was in the mouth, it was in every line of the face and every fact of the attitude, in the indentation of the chin, in the way the hair was parted, the moustache was twisted, the smile came and went, the breath rose and fell. It was in the way he looked out at a bamboozled world in short—the way he would look out forever. [361]

But in his attempt to force out the secret of the other's self-infatuation the artist ends up betraying his own unavowed self-infatuation. And this is founded precisely on his claim to being an artist, i.e. the claim to be capable of truly representing the universal in the concrete. The Colonel is a liar and perhaps a sort of artist; he certainly is not The Liar. And Lyon is a liar and an artist; can he be The Artist? The Portrait Painter according to James?

The most general truth a penetrating reader can come away with from this particular fable about a portrait is that the portrait is not a likeness of the other but a reflection of one's desire in the likeness of the other. The truth revealed in "The Liar" is then the dangerous truth of mimetic rivalry (Girard's phrase): the absolutely identical claim to the object of desire—the truth, the self, honor—that one unwittingly knows in the other; an absolute sameness to which one reacts by violently attempting to establish an absolute difference between oneself and the other. In this text this is negotiated mainly in terms of truth and falsehood, and the difference which seems to be established is not an absolute one. It is at best a relative difference between the socialized narcissism of the English country house society (and perhaps all of nineteenth-century bourgeois civilization) on the one hand and savage primary narcissism on the other, here embodied in the figure of the portrait painter whose ostensible function is to serve that socialized narcissism.[20]

THE SKELETON IN THE MIRROR

This discussion takes us very near the imaginative core of James's whole fictional enterprise. His characteristic hero is someone—most often an American or an artist, in any case, an outsider—out to obtain, by honorable or other means, something which is in the possession or under the guardianship of

---

20. Gogol, in his "Portrait," presents this function as a pact with the devil.

another person. This may be a thing or a person or both, the possession of which would crown his sense of self-achievement, while at the same time, as a possible unfortunate consequence, depriving the other of his essential identity. Upon meeting with resistance from the other, which is most often the case, the hero—sometimes aided and abetted by James's fictional facts—may resort to attacking the other's title to the coveted essence. His motto could be: if I want it and he's got it, there must be a skeleton in his closet. He will then set out to portray the skeleton in the other's closet, thereby betraying his own.

A variation, and a tactic less frequently used in James, is to cheapen the object by promoting unflattering representations thereof (rather than of its master or guardian). This is one possible way of reading one of James's earliest efforts, a story published twenty years before "The Liar," of which the latter is clearly a reworking. In "A Story of a Masterpiece" (1868) the portrait is that of a pretty Miss Everett, who is perhaps what James at that period liked to call (after Browning) a bit "light." It is executed by a young artist whom she had previously unfairly rejected (and who claims to have overcome his disappointment, which has remained conveniently secret). And it is ordered by and paid for by the girl's elder fiancé. In the resultant painting she is represented as heartless, i.e. narcissistic, desiring no one but herself, which is as much as the nervous fiancé suspected. But in this story by the twenty-five year old Henry James Jr., it is the older man who destroys the telltale masterpiece and marries the original.[21]

Another variation, characteristic of James's later ingenuity with negative values, is to be found in "The Tree of Knowledge" (1900). There the outsider imagines his triumph in life to consist in his refraining from the portrayal of the skeleton in the master's closet, in this case, by an ingenious reversal, the other's ineptitude as an artist (the poor man is unable to produce sculptures that resemble). He imagines that if the truth were out the master's wife would desert him, and his son disavow him. The son ultimately does rebel against his father, for reasons of his own, but the discovery that the wife had known all along only reaffirms her unconditional commitment to her husband. The story thus ends with the utter discomfiture of the man, who not only abstained from advertizing the true nature of his rival-friend, but also renounced his own writing ambitions—it may be conjectured—so as not to appear to outshine him by invidious comparison! The art of the portrait according to James may then masquerade even as a self-imposed preventive iconoclasm: a "portrait" may be destroyed by its maker on the other's behalf before its exposure to public view—which of course does not preclude its being on permanent display in the solitary *salon* of one's soul. The possibility of such melodramatic renunciation, although not its ironic debunking, has been present in James at least since *The American* (1878).

---

21. Like Everina, Miss Everett has formerly been the object of a portrait. The subject: "My Last Duchess."

THE MASTER EN *ABYME*

The final question to be determined—and it is an outmoded critical question, of this I am sorely aware—is: where is the Master himself in all this? Is James, to use Girard's old opposition, in the position of *mensonge romantique,* or does he show evidence of having acceded to the position of *vérité romanesque?* Is the truth of mimetic rivalry (which I interpreted here as the irruption of "primary narcissism" into the domain of its latter-day socialized derivative) a truth which James presents or represents, or is it merely a truth unwittingly reflected in his fictions and extricated from them only by the interpreter's will to power? Is Lyon's lying practice of the portrait in "The Liar" also the Art of the Portrait according to James?

The answer hinges on two formal literary questions broached in the introduction to this paper. First, is there *mise en abyme* in "The Liar" and if so by whom? Only two predicates are stipulated by Lucien Dällenbach for a minimal determination of this concept: "1) le caractère réflexif d'un énoncé; 2) la qualité intra- ou métadiégétique de celui-ci." [1)The reflexive character of an enunciation; 2) its intra- or metadiagetic nature.][22] He adds that strictly speaking, no diegetic shift is required. These nonoptional conditions are met by "The Liar" with flying colors, provided we do not insist on equating self-reflexiveness in the text with self-consciousness in the author. Secondly, in support of the idea that "The Liar" is emblematic of the art of James's fiction I can cite his professed prinicples to the effect that 1) a work of art, this being one, must be illustrative, and 2) verbal and pictorial representations are essentially interchangeable. I admit that this is a somewhat obtuse legalistic approach on my part. It does however land him in the dilemma of having represented the typical portrait as submitting the concrete to the universal in violation of the requirement of disinterestedness. More astutely, perhaps, one might point to the *insistence* with which representations of persons in his fictional worlds, even when they profess to be artistic, commit such violations.[23]

Finally we are fortunate to be in possession of some external evidence of James's attitude not only with regard to the liar in "The Liar," but also concerning the consequences of knowledge in "The Tree of Knowledge." First, it is remarkable that both stories start out in his surviving *Notebooks* as anecdotes whose burden is just the reverse of what we find in the published versions. The germ of "The Liar" concludes with "she lies—but then she hates him" (i.e. the liar, her husband). The climax of "The Tree of Knowledge" was to have de-

---

22. Lucien Dällenbach, *Le Récit spéculaire* (Paris: Seuil, 1977), 74.

23. "It is impossible to reconcile this picture of the artist's task with any view James ever espoused; it is, in fact, James's portrait of what happens to art when it is made to serve 'interested' or practical ends," Booth, op. cit., 351. This is letting James off the hook by demoting the picture into a mere portrait. The text itself gives no indication that "The Liar" was not a masterpiece.

prived the master of his wife's esteem, "the son *in fact* NOT consoling her pride for the ridiculousness of the father."[24]

Even more remarkable is the reading implied by the comments of the editors of the *Notebooks*. Noting the different ending of the finished text of "The Liar," they praise it for increasing "the effectiveness of the story by making it almost a case of the 'possession' of a pure spirit by an impure one . . ." (i.e. the wife's by the husband's)—a reading to match the ghostliest readings of "The Turn of the Screw." As to the final "Tree of Knowledge," Matthiessen and Murdock see a progressive series of shocks experienced by the young son as he discovers, first, that his papa is not what he was supposed to be, and then, that the friend-of-the-family as well as the mother-and-wife had known this all along. But in the actual text is is plain to see that all the emphasis is laid on the equanimity with which the actual son receives these news, as opposed to the dismay and surprise by which the self-denying "friend" is taken. In both cases these seasoned Jamesians have failed to "see" the "reflector" or "vessel of consciousness" as forming part of the picture. They simply see "through" him! As Christine Brooke-Rose commented, "the state of the governess is contagious."[25] This method of reading "The Liar" goes back at least as far as Joseph Warren Beach's pioneering study where it is mentioned as one of three tales where "the third person is used even of this objective observer of the scene.[26] Is the problem strictly a perceptual one, or does it have to do with the nature of the material which goes unperceived?

Curiouser and curiouser, James's subsequent prefatory remarks, written some ten and twenty years respectively after the event, imply just this sort of reading. "The Tree of Knowledge" he traced back to an anecdote relayed by someone who had "personal knowledge" of the protagonist. The protagonist was a son who "had found his father out, artistically," only to succumb to an early death.[27] Again the crucial event is the son's discovery, and there is no trace of the prurient third party nor of the melodramatic renunciation of denunciation falling flat at the end.

As the germ for "The Liar" he "recalls" a certain dinner party in company of an "unbridled colloquial romancer" as well as "this magnificent master's wife, who, veracious, serene and charming, yet not once meeting straight the eyes of one of us, did her duty by each and by her husband most of all, without

24. The Notebooks of Henry James, ed. F. O. Matthiessen and K. B. Murdoch (New York: Oxford University Press, 1961), 62, 289.

25. "The Squirm of the True," *PTL* 1 (1976), 268.

26. James Warren Beach, *The Method of Henry James* (New York: 1954, 1918), 69. Beach goes on to insist on distinguishing this type of observer from another one: "Often, as in 'The Figure in the Carpet,' he has some little axe of his own to grind; sometimes, as in 'The Beldonald Holbein,' a little grudge of his own to gratify. And so by insensible degrees, this character passes over into that of the interested observer, the actor himself. But we are at present considering the observer whose concern in the action remains slight and secondary."

27. *The Art of the Novel* (New York: C. Scribner's Sons, 1934), 235.

as much as, in the vulgar phrase, turning a hair."28 Here the observer's interest and an incipient mirror-image relation to the other are glimpsed in the language of the Preface ("master," "romancer"; the Colonel in the story is a *raconteur* in the verbal medium: if he can serve as a double for the painter, he can do so *a fortiori* for the author). A faint trace of *ressentiment* at being excluded may perhaps be read into the otherwise arbitrarily noted detail that "I made but a fifth person, the other couple being our host and hostess."29 The arithmetic of the scene becomes slightly puzzling when after the pause of a semi-colon the sentence continues: "between whom and one of the company, while we listened to the woven wonder of a summer holiday, the exploits of a salamander, among Mediterranean isles, were exchanged, dimly and discreetly, ever so guardedly, but all expressively, imperceptible lingering looks." If the archly designated addressee of these fondly remembered expressive looks was none other than Henry James, then he is thereby integrated into a community of knowledge and truthfulness from which the so-called "master" is excluded.

The final curiosity I have for pointing out is that in the *Notebooks* James traced the origin of the story not to any personal anecdote from his experience, but to Daudet's novel, *Numa Roumestan* (the editors try to explain this discrepancy without casting any doubt on James's literal veracity). This is the story of a politician from Provence, a genial man whose unkept promises cause suffering to those who believe in them and whose lying provokes his wife's contempt and temporary estrangement, to be resolved at the end only through a death and a birth. In his 1882 essay on Daudet, James singles out this work as best mirorring this author's own personality:

> The weak points in the man of the South, in M. Daudet's view, are the desire to please at any cost, and as a natural result of this, a brilliant indifference to the truth. There is a good deal of all this, in its less damaging aspects, in the author of *Numa Roumestan*.30

May it be a fault in a writer of fiction to be very fond of fiction? In this case it seems to me that James is distinctly culpable. Fondness of fiction—in its less damaging aspects?—manifested itself not only in his fictions. In misrepresenting the source of "The Liar," did the Master forget himself to assume a liar's role? Or was he, as Leo Bersani avers, "so utterly released from the superstition of truth?"31 Did he not know how well-read he could be? I cannot, I'd better not, say that I know.

HEBREW UNIVERSITY, JERUSALEM

28. Ibid., 178.
29. In "The Liar" Lyon keeps everybody waiting before dinner and then, it is said, "There was no delay to introduce him to a lady, for he went out unimportant and in a group of unmated men" (314).
30. *Literary Reviews and Essays*, ed. A. Morell (New York: Twayne Publishers, 1957), 184.
31. Bersani, op. cit., 155.

ANSELM HAVERKAMP

Error in Mourning—A Crux in Hölderlin: "dem gleich fehlet die Trauer" ("Mnemosyne)[1]

Am Feigenbaum ist mein
Achilles mir gestorben,
Und Ajax liegt
An den Grotten der See,
An Bächen, benachbart dem Skamandros.
An Schläfen Sausen einst, nach
Der unbewegten Salamis steter
Gewohnheit, in der Fremd', ist gross
Ajax gestorben
Patroklos aber in des Königes Harnisch. Und es starben
Noch andere viel. Am Kithäron aber lag
Elevterä, der Mnemosyne Stadt. Der auch als
Ablegte den Mantel Gott, das abendliche nachher löste
die Loken. Himmlische nemlich sind
Unwillig, wenn einer nicht die Seele schonend sich
Zusammengenommen, aber er muss doch; dem
Gleich fehlet die Trauer.

  Beside the fig-tree
My Achilles has died and is lost to me,
And Ajax lies
Beside the grottoes of the sea,
Beside brooks that neighbour Scamandros.
Of a rushing noise in his temples once,
According to the changeless custom of
Unmoved Salamis, in foreign parts
Great Ajax died,
Not so Patroclus, dead in the King's own armour.
And many others died. But by Cithaeron there stood
Eleutherae, Mnemosyne's town. From her also
When God laid down his festive cloak, soon after did
The powers of Evening sever a lock of hair. For the Heavenly, when
Someone has failed to collect his soul, to spare it,
Are angry, for still he must; like him
Here mourning is at fault.

[Hamburger's translation]

---

1. Friedrich Hölderlin, "Mnemosyne" (third version), *Sämtliche Werke*, 1–7 (Grosse Stuttgarter Ausgabe), ed. Friedrich Beissner (Stuttgart: Kohlhammer/Cotta, 1943–72), 2: 198.

True "mourning" is less deluded.

—Paul de Man[2]

I   Error;
II   Parataxis;
III Anthropomorphism;
IV   Melancholy;
V   Cruxes.

I

Hölderlin's last line has not been much of a crux so far. All professional readers of "Mnemosyne" agree that mourning is not simply missing in this line: "Here mourning is at fault" (Hamburger's translation); "likewise, mourning is in error" (Sieburth's).[3] Since Beissner first edited the poem in the Hölderlin Jahrbuch of 1948–49, his first reading has remained almost unquestioned. "Fehlen" here means "fehlgehen": "Mourning . . . errs like the one who failed to restrain himself and roused the anger of the Heavenly. Mourning commits the same error as this one in that it also lets itself slip without resistance into death."[4] Even Sattler, who seldom misses an opportunity to object to Beissner's edition, wants to make sure no unsuspecting reader mistakes a sentence that could mean only one thing for the experienced Hölderlinian: "According to ordinary language 'gleich' could be misunderstood as 'sofort' [immediately] and 'fehlt' as 'nicht vorhanden' [not present]. The mourning for the deceased thus corresponds to the 'sin' of the wish to die."[5] Finally, however, after the difficult grammar of this poem and the many attempts to come to terms with it, nothing seems simpler than the conclusion: "Mourning is just missing" for the one who, "failing to collect his soul," must die ("for still he must"). The unanimity of Hölderlin interpreters, not satisfied with mere "lack" and insisting on the weightier "erring" of mourning, gives evidence of a peculiar blindness that confirms the questionable state of affairs ex negativo, in the denial.

---

2. Paul de Man, "Anthropomorphism and Trope in the Lyric," The Rhetoric of Romanticism (New York: Columbia University Press, 1984), 262. Subsequently abbreviated as RR.

3. Friedrich Hölderlin, Poems and Fragments, trans. Michael Hamburger (London: Routledge and Kegan Paul, 1966), 501; Hymns and Fragments, trans. Richard Sieburth (Princeton, N.J.: Princeton University Press, 1984), 119. All subsequent quotations will follow Hamburger's translation or, in consultation with Sieburth, occasionally diverge therefrom. See Paul de Man's review "The Riddle of Hölderlin," The New York Times Review of Books 15:9 (19 Nov. 1970), 47–52.

4. Friedrich Beissner, "Hölderlins letzte Hymne" (1948), Hölderlin—Reden und Aufsätze, 2nd ed. (Köln/Wien: Böhlau, 1969), 211–46; quoted in the "Erläuterungen" of the "Grosse Stuttgarter Ausgabe," 2: commentary of "Mnemosyne" ll. 50–51, 830.

5. Friedrich Hölderlin, Sämtliche Werke (Frankfurter Ausgabe), ed. Dietrich E. Sattler: Einleitung (Frankfurt: Roter Stern, 1975), commentary of ll. 52, 69.

Paul de Man, who dealt with "Mnemosyne" more than once, ends two closely related essays on Hölderlin with its final strophe only to break off the quotation each time before the last sentence. The second time, though, he risks a paraphrase that leaves no further insight to be wished: "die Trauigen (die griechischen Helden) müssen doch (sterben), aber die Trauer (des Dichters) *fehlet.*"[6] True to the letter ("buchstabengetreu"), he holds firmly to Hölderlin's text: "fehlet" is the crucial word that defies paraphrase. The problem, which is carefully preserved down to the phonetic representation of de Man's paraphrase, moveover cannot be reproduced in translation. Mindful of Hölderlin research, the English translator of de Man's text not surprisingly follows the pattern of established interpretation, especially when it sounds so familiar from this author's mouth: "the mournful ones (the Greek heroes) must nonetheless (die) but the mourning (of the poet) is in *error.*"[7]

Error, however, cannot be the last word. A closer look into de Man's text shows that he does not corroborate the previous interpretations of "Mnemosyne" but rather unsettles them. While these interpreters may feel secure in their readings of this poem, his paraphrase arouses the suspicion: how else, if not by its absence, could "fehlen" err? Such a question does not overleap the semantics of the passage but presupposes it. Only with this presupposition can that other, Hölderlinian meaning acquire significance. One may say more precisely that what is essential to the development of this significance is Hölderlin's preference for the etymological origins of language rather than its ordinary uses. Mourning's error is grounded in the absence of mourning and consists in nothing but its lack. In a movement adapted almost mimetically to the syntax of the text, de Man sharpens the evident ambiguity of the crucial word to an undecidability of the whole sentence.

Certainly, this supplementary remark of "Mnemosyne"—"dem/Gleich fehlet die Trauer"—seems to carry the burden of the poem as little for him as for Hölderlin. The poet adds an afterthought, separated by a semicolon, that is well suited to overwhelm surreptitiously (*hinterrücks*) the central thought. The subject concerned, though not the subject of this valedictory sentence, is the insisting force of the afterthought, the poet. De Man, who sees the poet's concern with the self-protecting act "to collect his soul," follows the poet's mimetic remembrance of the heroes, "the mournfulness of which almost draws him on to a similar dying," but finally acknowledges the poet's separation from the heroes "through his care for preserving memory." "The poet and the historian," he concludes in a formulation owing to "The Rhetoric of Temporality," "converge in this essential point ["grounded less in a personal than in a historical experience"] to the extent that they both speak of an action that precedes them but that exists for consciousness only because of their interven-

---

6. Paul de Man, "Wordsworth und Hölderlin," *Schweizer Monatshefte*, 45 (1966), 1141–55: 1154.

7. "Wordsworth and Hölderlin," trans. Timothy Bahti, *RR*; 64.

tion."[8] In both Sattler's compact summary and Beissner's commentary, the phrase "dem/Gleich" has no such temporal implications but rather signifies a pure correspondence in error: the one who fails to collect his soul mourns in vain. What is striking about this excessive, if crude, equation is the exemplary conclusion that sees "mourning at fault." The coda of the poem appears to be an intensification of a statement whose performative force puts the poem itself into question.

II

"By the figtree/My Achilles has died (and is lost to me)." Beissner designates these two lines "the germ of the poem."[9] Even if the genetic argument is fallacious, it provides a useful myth that reconciles the poetics of "Mnemosyne" with its origination and permits it, provisionally, to appropriate its last strophe for its own purposes. Like the last sentence ("dem/Gleich fehlet die Trauer"), the last strophe of "Mnemosyne" also recasts the preceding verses, retrospectively setting the end at the beginning by showing the beginning as the end. This is the movement of the myth that is remembered, the beginning that returns at the end: the homeric epic of the wrath of Achilles. Thus the question that ends the second strophe—"In wrath a traveller walks/Distantly divining with/The other, but what is this?"—finds its answer in the third. The critical commonplace of Hölderlin's identification with Achilles, which has been played out on all levels by Hölderlin studies, experiences in this connection an essential modification. The lyrical "I," of which the double use of the personal pronoun reminds us ("mein Achilles mir"), does not merely show, as Beissner phrases it, an "intimate concern for the heroic figure of youth." Rather, it bears witness to an identification through wrath that results at the end of the third strophe in the inability to mourn.

The remembrance of myth is directed towards its "wrathful heroes" ("zorn'gen Helden," as in the ode "Thränen").[10] Even more than the death of Achilles, it pertains to the suicide of Ajax, whose anger had been inflamed by the loss of the "King's own armour" to the cunning Odysseus. The subject here is not the survivor but the death of the "many others." With the prototypical wrath of Achilles and his glorious death the derivative anger of Ajax and his ignominious suicide are brought into tragic perspective. Furthermore, it is not the case that Hölderlin's poem amounts to a cataloguing of traditional details like the figtree, metonymic landmark of the battlefield of Troy, or Salamis, the island of Ajax. This peculiar arbitrariness of detail does not depend on the

---

8. Ibid., 64–65. See "The Rhetoric of Temporality" (1969), *Blindness and Insight*, 2nd ed. (Minneapolis, MN: University of Minnesota Press, 1983), 207. Subsequently abbreviated as *BI* 2.

9. See, besides Beissner's "Erläuterungen," op. cit., Jochen Schmidt, *Hölderlins letzte Hymnen: "Andenken" und "Mnemosyne"* (Tübingen: Niemeyer, 1970), 59–70.

10. See Jochen Schmidt, "Der Begriff des Zorns in Hölderlins Spätwerk," *Hölderlin Jahrbuch* 15 (1967–68), 128–57.

associative connection of names nor does it represent scenes from the epic. Rather, Hölderlin repeats his reading of the heroic myths of classical Greece and does so not in the enumeration of references but in the wording of his own translations. In addition to the figtree from the *Iliad* and Pausanias's reference to the city of Mnemosyne, this passage has to do above all with quotations from Sophocles' *Ajax* and Pindar's second *Nemean Ode*. The form of the tragic monologue and the scheme of heroic eulogy are "mixed" in such a way that Pindar's scheme, that is, the derivation of the hero from his home (Ajax from Salamis), is fulfilled and surpassed by the Sophoclean monologue (in *Ajax*). Pindar writes: "and truly she, the Salamis ["the unmoved Salamis" of "Mnemosyne"] was able to rear a man deadly in battle. Before the walls of Troy, Hektor learned this from Ajax." In Sophocles, however, this same man, calling to his distant Salamis, succumbs to madness and ends in suicide.

In his reconstruction of Hölderlin's theory of the "modulation of tones," Szondi has worked out a progression towards "epicization" in the thesis: "the *perfection* [Vollendung] of the lyric lies in the epic."[11] Yet "Mnemosyne" shows that such an insertion of epic passages into the lyrical poem works in the service not so much of a return of the epic as of its renewed remembrance in precarious circumstances. "The tendency towards the epic in the lyrical as well as in the tragic poem," for which Szondi adduces Pindar's seventh *Olympian Ode* and Sophocles' *Ajax*, becomes in "Mnemosyne" itself historical: Hölderlin cites it as a failed attempt. What Szondi calls, in Hölderlin's phrase, "the epic treatment" of the lyrical poem goes beyond the modulation of tones and lies also outside triadic ("dialectical") construction (which is confirmed by the peculiar self-sufficiency of the third strophe within the so far insufficiently explained construction of "Mnemosyne"). Agreeing with Beissner's hypothesis about the origin of the poem, Szondi calls the "naive" tone of epic style the "germ-cell of the representational mode that characterizes, throughout and ever more exclusively, Hölderlin's late works." Following early remarks by Benjamin, Adorno gave this naive-epic mode of representation in late Hölderlin the name "paratactic," and therein identified in particular its metonymic character. More precise than Jakobson's characterization of narrative in terms of metonomy, Adorno's parataxis signifies a "resistance to synthesis" that rests more on a grammatical than a semantical opposition of the paratactic and the hypotactic. That is what he means when he says that "in Hölderlin the poetic movement upsets for the first time the category of meaning."[12] Parataxis undermines syntax in that it ignores the synthetic possibilities of its paradigm. It is Adorno's contention that, in the paratactic countermovement to the syntactic production of meaning, language does not lead "beyond the subject" but rather speaks "for the subject . . . which can no longer speak (Hölderlin was probably the first whose art had some idea of this) from out of itself."

---

11. Peter Szondi, "Gattungspoetik und Geschichtsphilosophie," *Hölderlin-Studien* (Frankfurt: Suhrkamp, 1967–70), 146.

12. Theodor W. Adorno, "Parataxis—Zur späten Lyrik Hölderlins" (1964), *Noten zur Literatur* 3 (Frankfurt: Suhrkamp, 1965), 156–209: 191–92.

Thus the concept of parataxis has more than the descriptive uses Szondi finds in it. The paratactic sequence of mythic elements in the last strophe of "Mnemosyne" is a case in point. In Benjamin's formulation, on which both Adorno and Szondi rely, "Men, the Heavenly, and princes" seem to "fall headlong out of their old orders into sheer contiguity [zueinander gereiht]."[13] The fall out of the old orders into metonymic arbitrariness, that is, from the syntax of the order of things into the parataxis of a text that no longer represents the order of things, is in "Mnemosyne" no fall of figures and names but of texts whose wreckage results in a ghostly afterimage of that which was once to be epically remembered as myth. Pausanias's description of the ruins of "Elevterä," whose name is superimposed on the "fields of Mnemosyne" as handed down from Hesiod, is the allegory suited to this state of affairs: already in antiquity the "city of Mnemosyne" was a ruin. "Elevterä" ("freedom") signifies with extreme irony what remains to be deciphered as the cultural trace in mythic nature. Of this Benjamin's statement holds true: "On the face of nature 'History' is written in the ciphers of the vanishing past."[14] History itself has become unreadable. Or rather it remains readable only as an allegory of its unreadability.

In one of Hölderlin's fragments, the problematic of which will not be quickly exhausted by our reading, we find first a speculative, then a rhetorical definition of the lyric: "The lyrical and, according to sensuous appearance [dem Schein nach], ideal poem is naive in its meaning. It is a continuous metaphor of *one* feeling."[15] In the rhetorical concept still common in Hölderlin's day (the *continua metaphora* of Quintilian), the lyrical poem is conceived of as an allegory whose coherence guarantees the unity of a single feeling. Since the lyrical poem is, in Hölderlin's definition, the ideal poem according to sensuous appearance and is naive in its meaning, this allegory elevates a naive meaning to the appearance of the ideal. In the tendency of the late hymns, as interpreted by Szondi, the ideal appearance of the "art character" (Kunstcharakter) of the poem turns naive: the lyrical poem becomes epic. The naive "ground" (Grund), however, turns heroic: wrath becomes mourning. Yet this last turn, according to Hölderlin's last verse, fails. The naive meaning of the unity of one feeling of wrath, whose extended metaphor brings about within the allegory of the poem the ideal appearance of epic, refuses to be recast into the heroic meaning of mourning. "Allegories," we read in *Allegories of Reading*, "are always allegories of metaphor and, as such, they are always allegories of the impossibility of reading."[16] In the extended meta-

---

13. Walter Benjamin, "Swei Gedichte von Friedrich Hölderlin" (1920), *Gesammelte Schriften* 1–5 (Frankfurt: Suhrkamp, 1974–82), 2: 112.

14. Benjamin, *Ursprung des deutschen Trauerspiels* (1928), *Gesammelte Schriften*, 1, 353. See Theodor W. Adorno, "Die Idee der Naturgeschichte" (1932), *Gesammelte Schriften 1–22* (Frankfurt: Suhrkamp, 1970–80), 1, 357.

15. "Über den Unterschied der Dichtarten," *Sämtliche Werke* (Grosse Stuttgarter Ausgabe), 4: 266; as quoted by Szondi, *Hölderlin-Studien*, 119; see 158.

16. Paul de Man, *Allegories of Reading* (New Haven, CT: Yale University Press, 1979), 205.

phor developed in "Mnemosyne," the naive "ground" of wrath becomes the allegory of an unreadability whose mourning remains melancholia. The "metaphor" of wrath ("tenor") remains unreadable as metaphor ("vehicle") of the naive "art character" ("epic") and, as such, its lyrical development becomes the allegory of a failure. Mimetic affinity with the anger of the hero ("distantly divining with the other") turns into "mimetic affinity with death," the death of Mnemosyne.[17]

The extreme radicalization of the third version of "Mnemosyne" occurs in the shift from the "wild courage" and "divine force" of heroes, which was the subject of the previous versions, to the death of memory itself, Mnemosyne: "From her also/The powers of evening came to sever a lock of hair." Hölderlin communicates this unheard-of event, which is something entirely his own, in the words in which another modern author, Schiller, translates another ancient author, Virgil. Beissner discovered the wording in the later version of Schiller's "Dido," dating from 1803, the same year as "Mnemosyne." In the context of the story of Dido, the undoing of the tresses ("Lösen der Locken") as well as the laying down of the cloak have romantic overtones that associate the tragic *Liebestod* with the consummation of the love act: "it pounds together," as Empson remarks of Keats's "Ode on Melancholy," "the sensations of joy and sorrow till they combine into sexuality."[18] In "Mnemosyne," this movement is recalled and reversed. Its lyrical tone, through the epicization of the poem from the *Iliad* to the *Aeneid,* is colored "naive" in order to let it fail "sentimentally." The romantic possibility that would draw from melancholy a temporary pleasure (one which Keats pushes to the extreme) is here rejected. The final incapacity of mourning is made manifest by the death of Mnemosyne. The compulsion to die, which in the epic was the necessity of the hero's death (thus the preceding versions from classical texts), confirms after this unheard-of death of Mnemosyne yet another necessity. In de Man's reading, the sentence "but he must nevertheless [die]" "holds just as well for the necessity of the turning back upon oneself."[19] Yet this necessity now lacks possibility: the ability to mourn.

It is interesting that Hölderlin takes the death of Mnemosyne, which cannot be quoted from any text, from the mouth of someone who, for him, was not just another poet. His disillusion with Schiller is followed by his adaptation of Rousseau: "the 'one' designated in these lines ["when someone has failed to recollect himself"] can be none other than Rousseau."[20] The formulation is contradictory, however, for this "one" is no one in the quoted passage

17. See Theodor W. Adorno, *Ästhetische Theorie, Gesammelte Schriften,* 7: 202; "Parataxis," *Noten zur Literatur 3,* 189–90.

18. William Empson, *Seven Types of Ambiguity,* rev. ed. (New York, NY: New Directions, 1966), 214.

19. "Wordsworth and Hölderlin," *RR,* 64.

20. "The Image of Rousseau in the Poetry of Hölderlin" (1965), trans. Andrzej Warminski, *RR,* 45.

and remains none. Even Hölderlin fails in the face of Rousseau's demand. And yet this demand fits no one else but Rousseau. In the phrase "to re-collect oneself" (sich zusammennehmen) "re-collection" happily entails a prior "collection" (Sammlung), which Hölderlin interpreted as "preservation" (Schonung).[21] Hölderlin almost quotes the strophe of his Rhine hymn dedicated to Rousseau: "But he whose soul, like yours, Rousseau,/Ever strong and patient/Became invincible. . . . " This recalls Rousseau's fifth *Rêverie*: "Mais s'il est un état où l'âme trouve une assiette assez solide pour s'y reposer tout entière et rassembler là tout son être, sans avoir besoin de rappeler le passé ni d'enjamber sur l'avenir . . . "[22] There is, indeed, no critique of Rousseau in Hölderlin's adaptation just as there is not so much a critique in his allusion to Schiller as a farewell to lost hopes. But the image of Rousseau survives merely as an image and functions in "Mnemosyne" only as a quotation, as an instance of heavenly anger ("Unwillen") against which there is no appeal. The ability of the Heavenly to be angry is what disqualifies the wrath of the poet. What remains to the poet, who had identified himself with the wrath of Achilles and now faces the destiny of Ajax, is only a final remark, the coda "dem gleich fehlet die Trauer."

The failure of appropriation that manifests itself in the remembrance of the Greeks nevertheless practices a "self-recollection" within the text. The result of this recollection, however, loses that which is collected. "Der Grübler," we read in Benjamin's fragments, "dessen Blick, aufgeschreckt, auf das Bruchstück in seiner Hand fällt, wird zum Allegoriker."[23] Lost in melancholy, the brooder turns allegoric, when all of a sudden he realizes that the piece in his hand is a fragment. Likewise, in epicization Hölderlin's poem suddenly realizes the fragmentary condition of the lyric. Epic parataxis does not reconstitute the epic but rather collects the fragments of its appropriation. The allegorical coherence of "Mnemosyne" consists in this metonymic accumulation of its parts that does not represent the myth itself so much as its loss in the process of appropriation. This poem is itself only in so far as it presents others as itself.

III

"There always are at least two texts, regardless of whether they are actually written out or not," Paul de Man writes in one of his last texts.[24] This other text, which is presupposed and implied by "Mnemosyne," is entitled "An-

---

21. Ibid., 27.
22. As quoted by Bernhard Böschenstein, *Hölderlins Rheinhymne*, 2nd ed. (Zürich: Atlantis, 1968), 91.
23. Benjamin, "Zentralpark," op. cit., 1: fragment 28, 676.
24. "Anthropomorphism and Trope," *RR*, 260–61.

denken." As Baudelaire's "Obsession" can be called a reading of "Correspondences," so Hölderlin's "Mnemosyne" can be called a reading of "Andenken." This reading, though, cannot be conceived of in terms of intertextuality. Neither can it be traced in the text as quotation or allusion. In other words, the one text does not represent the other. Rather, one can say that the one "understands" the other. De Man does not hesitate to use this hermeneutic metaphor of understanding, for it is the metaphor of hermeneutics par excellence. He specifies this relation between texts in terms of the lyric, in which it manifests itself as "specular symmetry along an axis of assertion and negation (to which correspond the generic images of the ode, as celebration, and the elegy, as mourning)." Celebration and mourning, then, are for him the two alternative modes (as far as genres are concerned) of the lyric that itself "is not a genre, but one name among several to designate the defensive motion of understanding, the possibility of a future hermeneutics." "Mnemosyne" thus reads and "understands" "Andenken" in mourning. The death of Mnemosyne exhausts the possibilities of the lyric in that it grounds the impossibility of reading in the inability of mourning. As a motif, this death is not comparable with the vanishing of the muses that made such an excellent pretext for lyrical melancholy from the pastoral to the elegiac odes of Hölderlin's predecessors in the Göttinger Hain.[25] Without memory and the defensive abilities of understanding ("to re-collect oneself"), there is no possibility left for a future hermeneutics.

Hölderlin interpretation, especially under Heidegger's imprimatur, has seen the close relation of "Andenken" and "Mnemosyne" more in terms of celebration than of mourning and has consequently identified in "Mnemosyne" not the anticlimax ("regression") of "Andenken" but its climax ("intensification"). This was possible under the motto "where danger is, salvation also grows": the threatening death of Mnemosyne increases the salvific potential of remembrance.[26] Such may have been a possible interpretation of the earlier versions of Hölderlin's poem, but in the third version the death of Mnemosyne appears always already completed. This prior completion is what Henrich aptly formulated as the difference between Hegel and Hölderlin: "For Hegel, to remember [Erinnern] is always to transform: interiorization [Er-innerung] as the overcoming of the past's being-in-itself. . . . For Hölderlin, on the contrary, memory is a preserving [Bewahren] that stands under the claim to be true to the past and hence seeks and maintains the past in its own right."[27] The mythic organ of interiorization in Hegel is the epic singer whose "pathos is not the stupefying power of nature, but Mnemosyne, recollection [Besinnung] and developed inwardness, the interiorization [Erinnerung] of the once immediate essence."[28] Being true to this no longer immediate essence turns the

25. See Karl Vietor, *Geschichte der deutschen Ode* (München: Drei Masken, 1923), 145–46.

26. See Reinhard Meyer-Kalkus, "Mnemosyne," *Historisches Wörterbuch der Philosophie,* ed. Joachim Ritter & al. (Basel: Schwabe, 1971–84), 5, 1442.

27. Dieter Henrich, *Hegel im Kontext* (Frankfurt: Suhrkamp, 1971), 34.

28. Georg Wilhelm Friedrich Hegel, *Phänomenologie des Geistes*, ed. Johannes Hoffmeister, 6th ed. (Hamburg: Meiner, 1952), 564.

preservation of the past into an impossible endeavor. De Man speaks of a "transformation of trope into anthropomorphism" that defines the lyric "as the instance of represented voice." It is the Nietzschean, deconstructive point of this performance that de Man recognizes: "Anthropomorphism seems to be the illusionary resuscitation of the natural breath of language, frozen into stone by the semantic power of the trope."[29] The frozen allegory—which crumbles under the melancholic gaze of the author into fragments of intertextual references—restores no epic muse. At best, parataxis mimetically recalls epic "naiveté" without yet, in this remembrance of the epic, being able to compensate for the loss of the natural breath of the lyric.

"Why on earth should a 'lyrically' interiorizing recollection [Zurück-denken] culminate in a peak performance [Gipfelwort] like the closing remark of the poem 'Andenken'?" asks Heidegger, who has little interest in mere backwardness:[30] "Was bleibet aber, stiften die Dichter" ["But what is lasting the poets provide"—Hamburger;] ["But poets establish what remains"—Sieburth.] Like the last line of "Mnemosyne," the last line of "Andenken" needs close examination. What remains might be lasting, but the question is where do the poets come in? The answer "Mnemosyne" provides does not establish what Heidegger is thinking of. "For the promise of Heidegger's ontology to be realized," de Man observes, "Hölderlin must be Icarus returned from his flight."[31] Though the myth leaves no doubt that Icarus actually flew, it is equally certain that he never returned. The relation between "Andenken" and "Mnemosyne" displays a perfect symmetry between open "assertion" and complete "negation." "Was bleibet" ("Andenken") remains on account of the poets. What they establish, however, remains doubtful since on and by their own account the mourning is missing: "fehlet die Trauer" ("Mnemosyne"). The remembrance that "Andenken" provides indeed reminds us of Icarus's flight: "memory is engendered as an act of consciousness freed from the restrictions of time and space, but entirely contained in the original, material perception." Commenting further on the opening stanza of "Andenken," de Man refers to another famous line: "Memories originate out of perception 'as flowers originate' ['Brot and Wein']."[32] Like the classical topos of inspiration in the first strophe ("The north-easterly blows,/Of winds the dearest to me"), so also the flower metaphor ("as flowers originate") belongs to tradition—the former to poetic, the latter to rhetorical tradition, the historical coupling of which de Man describes as a relation between anthropomorphism and trope. The north-easterly breeze revitalizes, in an illusionary resuscitation, the natural breath of language, frozen into the semantic flowers of the trope.

In an open critique of Heidegger, de Man characterizes the lyrical illu-

---

29. "Anthropomorphism and Trope," op. cit., 247.

30. Martin Heidegger, "Andenken" (1943), *Erläuterungen zu Hölderlins Dichtung*, 3rd ed. (Frankfurt: Klostermann, 1963), 83.

31. "Heidegger's Exegeses of Hölderlin" (1955), trans. Wlad Godzich, *BI* 2, 255.

32. "Image and Emblem in Yeats," *RR*, 199. See also "Intentional Structure of the Romantic Image" *RR*, 3.

sion as "a temptation . . . to make sense perception . . . into the ontological experience par excellence. . . . [For Hölderlin,] it manifests itself above all as a nostalgia for the world of the Greeks that we conceive (wrongly) as a world founded on the ontological priority of the sensuous object."[33] The philosophical point is perhaps less important than the poetical one stemming from this "fundamental error." Yet neither the anthropomorphism of "Andenken" nor its deconstruction in "Mnemosyne" can be accounted for in terms of error. "How does it happen," we read in a recent essay assessing a similar constellation of authors and texts, "that in such divergent and, indeed, mutually conflicting commentaries as those by Heidegger, Adorno, and Szondi (I deliberately give Benjamin a place apart) the same privilege finds itself attached to the lyric—and, as a consequence, the same interest is shown in the 'last' great poems of Hölderlin—where the critic goes about the task seeking that which is, indeed, inscribed there, that is to say, a thought?"[34] What Lacoue-Labarthe calls "the caesura of the speculative" is exactly what is at stake in the symmetry between "Andenken" and Mnemosyne." What was thought of in "Andenken" as the unmediated origin of remembrance out of perception remains in "Mnemosyne" an inaccessible past that the wanderer, "distantly divining," pursues. The anthropomorphism of the lyric, as "the instance of represented voice," names in "Mnemosyne" yet another anthropomorphism, the voice of which it fails to represent. What *is* represented, however, is the voice of the lyric in its mimetic failure to represent the epic. In this case, the "caesura" in question is not an allegorical self-signification of representation but the melancholy of an allegorical failure.[35]

Once "the melancholy of the muses" in Burton's *Anatomy* had been superseded by the invocation of the "Muse Melancholia," melancholy became the very anthropomorphism of the lyric. Next to irony, which has been taken since Quintilian's double definition as both trope and state of mind (Socrates being its personification), melancholy becomes the predominant anthropomorphism of trope. "Mnemosyne" is not an allegory of the lyric; rather it shows the latter in the state of melancholy. The death of Mnemosyne reduces melancholy to its allegorical denominator. It inscribes, to recall Benjamin's image, "Allegory" on the face of this anthropomorphism. Under the sign of Allegory, reading remains melancholy and does not meet the condition of "true" mourning. The anthropomorphic "tenor" of this allegory proves, as de Man emphasizes, that "the possibility of anthropomorphic (mis)reading is part of the text and part of what is at stake in it."[36]

---

33. "The Image of Rousseau," *RR*, 38–39.

34. Philippe Lacoue-Labarthe, "The Caesura of the Speculative," *Glyph*, 4 (1978), 57–84: 60.

35. See Andrzej Warminski, "Hölderlin in France," *Studies in Romanticism*, 22 (1983), 173–197: 191–2; as well as "Endpapers: Hölderlin's Textual History," *Readings in Interpretation* (Minneapolis, MN: University of Minnesota Press, forthcoming).

36. "Anthropomorphism and Trope," op. cit., 247.

IV

It is not difficult to discern in Benjamin's anatomy of baroque melancholy "the narcissistic type of object choice" that, according to Freud's supposition, influences "the disposition to succumb to melancholia" and makes the rise of modern subjectivity into the story of what Adorno calls the "damaged subject." The damage, which the subject does not simply sustain but experiences in its narcissistic constitution, is part of what "one calls one's character" (Freud). As such, "instincts and their vicissitudes" rearrange the associated commonplaces of "character and fate" (Benjamin).[37] "If the object becomes allegorical under the gaze of melancholy," writes Benjamin, "this gaze lets life flow from it; consequently, it remains as a dead, though eternally secured object lying before the allegorical poet, at the mercy of his grace and disfavor [Gnade und Ungnade]."[38] The psychoanalytical hypothesis of the narcissistic constitution of the subject on the model of internalized objects finds its baroque point in Benjamin's observation that the melancholic gaze presupposes, even entails, the death of the contemplated object in order to save it eternally and thereby achieve salvation for the subject as well. The "realism," in fact, "anthropomorphism" in Freud's concept of narcissism (whose mythical analogue is Lacan's "mirror stage") has its historical paradigm in Benjamin's description of baroque melancholy. Benjamin's claim that the object of melancholic contemplation can be none other than the melancholy man himself corresponds to narcissistic "regression" in which "identification with the object becomes a substitute for the erotic cathexis."[39] The identification here is basically an introjection that interiorizes its objects. Indifferent before the eye of the melancholic, objects are left behind, outside, dead.

One can certainly not say though that Hölderlin, of whose late, almost baroque phase Benjamin speaks, succumbs to baroque melancholy. On the contrary, it is his resistance to melancholy—his mourning, to be more precise—that leads him "beyond the subject." "In the late hymns," Adorno continues in the passage already quoted, "subjectivity is not the absolute and not the ultimate. It is understood rather to commit a sacrilege in which it imposes itself as if it were absolute and ultimate, all the while following an inner logic of self-positing. This is the construction of *hubris* in Hölderlin."[40] The sacrilege of hubristic subjectivity is the anthropomorphism of the lyrical "I" that invokes objects the interiorization (*Erinnerung*) of which follows the logic of melancholic self-positing. "There is no trace of *hubris* in Hölderlin and Keats,"

37. Sigmund Freud, *Das Ich und das Es* (1923), *Studienausgabe*, 1–10 (Frankfurt: Fischer, 1969–79), 3: 296. See Walter Benjamin, "Schicksal und Charakter" (1921), op. cit., 2: 171–79.

38. *Ursprung des deutschen Trauerspiels, Gesammelte Schriften*, 1: 359.

39. "Trauer und Melancholie" (1917), *Studienausgabe*, 3: 203. See Jean Laplanche, *Life and Death in Psychoanalysis*, trans. Jeffrey Mehlman (Baltimore, MD: The Johns Hopkins Press, 1976), 136.

40. Adorno, "Parataxis," *Noten zur Literatur* 3, 202.

de Man maintains: "Both poets could identify themselves with their hero in the first two stages, but not in the last" (the particular reference is to Hölderlin's *Empedockles*)."[41] The third strophe of "Mnemosyne" represents this last stage in which the preceding identification with the hero is interrupted.

The second strophe had opened with a question: "Wie aber Liebes?" ["But how loving?"] The sentence is simpler than the translation permits it to be (both Hamburger and Sieburth miss the point). For here Hölderlin presupposes the syntactic construction of a statement with which the first strophe had ended and which is thus put into question in the second: "es ereignet sich aber/Das Wahre" ["what is true is what is bound to take place"—de Man.][42] With this syntactic construction in mind, the question at the beginning of the second strophe reads as a question of whether love is bound to take place. Where, in the first strophe, we read "das Wahre" as the asserted truth, in the second strophe we read "Liebes" as a loving in question. Under the banner of this question, Hölderlin's wanderer walks along the heights of the Alps, the boundary to the Greek south. "Distantly divining with the other," he identifies with his hero in wrath. In his "Remarks on Oedipus," Hölderlin treated wrath as the moment of identification in tragedy that, as a limitless unification of God and man, inner and outer nature, is to be purified by "limitless separation."[43] The wrath of the wanderer is motivated by the compulsion to achieve such a limitless unification, yet is simultaneously characterized by the futility of this striving. This wrath is no longer the result of a naive identification with the hero but rather is dominated by the failure of this compulsion to imitate. Just as Dante's wanderer succumbs, in a momentary identification, to Francesca's seductive talent, a weakness that completes itself in a mimetic swoon, so Hölderlin's wanderer is overwhelmed by the wrath of his hero Achilles.

The loss of the first figure of identification leaves him with the role of "the second best Achaean," Ajax.[44] For the latter was not only second after Achilles, but moreover was one who already had failed in the attempt to replace Achilles' "actual surrogate and alter ego," Patroklos, who had died "in the King's own armour." Ajax is the negative reflection of Achilles as Patroklos is the positive. He fails to occupy the place of Achilles, both in the role of the first among heroes and in his coveted armor, which he loses to Odysseus. The anger of Ajax, which does not match the wrath of Achilles but remains limited to its imitation, turns into ridiculous madness when he—caricature of the wrathful hero—mistakes a flock of sheep for the enemy army.

41. "Keats and Hölderlin," *Comparative Literature*, 8 (1956), 28–45: 44.
42. "Foreword," Carol Jacobs, *Dissimulating Harmony* (Baltimore, MD: The Johns Hopkins University Press, 1978), xi.
43. "Anmerkungen zum Oedipus," *Sämtliche Werke* (Grosse Stuttgarter Ausgabe), 5: 201; as quoted by Jochen Schmidt, "Der Begriff des Zorns in Hölderlins Spätwerk," *Hölderlin Jahrbuch*, 15 (1967–68), 128–57: 157.
44. Gregory Nagy, *The Best of the Achaeans* (Baltimore, MD: The Johns Hopkins University Press, 1979), 31. See chs. 2 and 6.

At least one further passage from the context of Hölderlin's translation of Sophocles should be mentioned: Beside the "grottoes of the sea," the moribund Ajax imagines, after his death, the hard, relentless complaint of his mother, "when of his sickness,/his madness she hears."[45] The remembrance of his mother motivates his suicide. Indeed, it was more the question of the mother than the father that was crucial for Hölderlin's own fate, which, after Diotima's death, in "Mnemosyne" "expresses a despair beyond despair—that is, that state of mind which, so it seems, allows only for suicide or massive schizophrenic disintegration and retreat."[46] The psychological diagnosis has here a significance that is not external to the text. It draws our attention to a structure similar to a double bind that links the impossible appropriation of the Greeks with their impossible representation and impossible mourning. "Dem gleich fehlet die Trauer" represents this double bind that the reader seeks to circumvent only to succumb to it all the more certainly. While complaining about errors in mourning, the reader lacks its representation to the same extent that he denies it. In this case, the meaning of representation is determined by a repetition "on the receiving end." If there is "a fundamental division in the writer's mind," such as Empson claims for his seventh type of ambiguity, it is represented in the text only to the extent that it is reenacted in the reader's mind.[47] The anthropomorphism of the represented voice has as its echo the anthropomorphism of the reader's response, i.e. his "subjectivity."

V

Melencholia illa heroica, an expression by Melanchthon that Benjamin takes as emblematic, suits Hölderlin even better than Baudelaire.[48] In heroism vis-à-vis melancholy, though not yet to the extent of spleen, Hölderlin is as close to Baudelaire as the difference between "Andenken" ("Remembrance") and "souvenirs" ["memories"] permits. His heroic measure lies not in the identification with the wrath of the hero but in the endurance of an impossible mourning.[49] In the impossibility of this mourning, remembrance reflects the traces of interiorization that the narcissistic erection of the other as hero has left behind. It is marked through mnenic signs the encounter of which triggers vain feelings: "the cross which once was placed/There on the wayside for the dead"

---

45. "Aus dem Ajax des Sophokles," *Sämtliche Werke* (Grosse Stuttgarter Ausgabe), 5: ll. 596–645, *Ajax,* 279.

46. Helm Stierlin, "Creativity and Schizophrenic Psychosis as Reflected in Friedrich Hölderlin's Fate," *Hölderlin—An Early Modern,* ed. Emery E. George (Ann Arbor, MI: University of Michigan Press, 1972), 215.

47. Empson, op. cit., 192. See Paul de Man, "The Dead End of Formalist Criticism" (1956), trans. Wlad Godzich, *BI* 2, 237.

48. "Zentralpark," op. cit., fragment 44, 689.

49. See Jacques Derrida, *Mémoire,* trans. Avital Ronell (New York, NY: Columbia University Press, forthcoming).

arouses the anger of the wanderer in his "distant divination" with the lost other. The equivalent of this cross (*crux*) in the epic is the figtree, in which ancient and Christian tradition (anamnesis and anagogy) intersect in the manner of a chiasmus: the cross stands for the death of this life, while the figtree is the reminder of a promised afterlife (for which various passages in the New Testament could be cited). In the second strophe of "Andenken" the figtree is set apart from the other trees: "But in the courtyard a figtree grows." Sattler, who reads all these trees as memorials (the oak tree for Klopstock, a silver poplar for Heinse), identifies the figtree as Diotima, whose destiny has fulfilled itself in its sign. ("I will be" are her last words in *Hyperion*.)[50]

The examples are problematic in detail, but it is not difficult to derive from them the figtree as a double sign for Achilles and Diotima, hero and beloved. It is noteworthy that in the case of this hero the incommensurable wrath is inflamed by the loss of his beloved (Briseis), at which point his mother comes to his aid (a mother whose absence Hölderlin bewails in the elegy "Achill"). Hence the figtree in "Mnemosyne" seems to stand as echo of that which is remembered in "Andenken" but is in fact the cross. The sign of death is not simply replaced by the sign of promise. On the contrary, this other sign is reminiscent of the failure of another remembrance, but this reminiscence fails as well. If the figtree in "Andenken" triggers recollection, then it stands in "Mnemosyne" also for the impossibility of this recollection (the symmetry of assertion and negation mentioned above). The symbol of the beloved gets absorbed into the sign of the hero whose futile imitation had made her a symbol and caused her death. The promise is cancelled by death; death is not overcome by promise. In representing the failure of interiorization (*Erinnerung*), the figtree signifies mourning. The grave of the failed hero in "Mnemosyne" becomes a sign of mourning for the lost beloved outside the poem. She does not lack mourning, nor is the poet at fault.

"Ein Zeichen sind wir, deutungslos/Schmerzlos sind wir und haben fast/Die Sprache in der Fremde verloren." ["A sign we are, without interpretation/Without pain we are and have nearly/Lost our language in foreign lands."] The third and last version of the third strophe of "Mnemosyne" still presupposes this first strophe of the second version (the third version of the first strophe being of a later date). What remains of our language is signs without interpretation. What the poets establish is not interpretation but the assurance that the signs remain. "Stiften," etymologically, suggests the "stiffening" of the sign.[51] What does *not* remain, what is dismissed, on the other hand, is the anger and pain transmitted by interpretation. The transmission occurs in an echo—mentioned by Hölderlin in the same strophe (second version) as the lines quoted above—an echo that characterizes the relation between mortals

---

50. Dietrich E. Sattler, *Friedrich Hölderlin—144 Fliegende Briefe*, 2 vols. (Darmstadt/Neuwied: Luchterhand, 1981), letter 131, 2:610. See letter 20, 1:103–05.

51. See Rolf Zuberbühler, *Hölderlins Erneuerung der Sprache aus ihren etymologischen Ursprüngen* (Berlin: Erich Schmidt, 1969), 109.

and gods. The echo is the perfect allegory of divine anthropomorphism. It does not answer, but sounds like an answer: it is "a 'delusion' of the signifier."[52] What leads Hölderlin "beyond subjectivity" is the deconstruction of the human as echo, of lyrical subjectivity as anthropomorphism. The death of Mnemosyne, therefore, is no end. The sentence of Hesiod's *Theogony* that calls her the mother of the muses also gives the latter's part of the story. It is the opposite of their mother's name, "lesmosyne": "the forgetting of ills and a cessation of anxieties."[53] The death of *mnemosyne* thus dissolves the effort of *lesmosyne* and brings a return of the repressed: a qualification of signs as symptoms rather than symbols, traces rather than tropes.

CONSTANCE

Translated by Vernon Chadwick in collaboration with the author.
Thanks also to Bill Jewett.

---

52. "Anthropomorphism and Trope," *The Rhetoric of Romanticism,* 248.
53. As translated by Nagy, *The Best of the Achaeans,* 97.

HOWARD FELPERIN

The Anxiety of Deconstruction

> Leopards break into the temple and drink to the dregs what is in
> the sacrificial pitchers; this is repeated over and over again;
> finally it can be calculated in advance, and it becomes a part of
> the ceremony.
>
> —Kafka, *Leopards in the Temple*

That deconstruction has manifested, over the past decade, an uncanny power
to arouse anxiety in the institutions of learning that house and host it, will
come as no surprise to students of the movement. Indeed, the present conference may itself be regarded as the latest, admittedly mild, attack on that
continuing anxiety. Having at last been accepted as a fact of institutional life,
deconstruction now presents us with the problem of how best to live with and
control it, like a recently discovered disease that has proved not to be fatal, as
was first feared, but merely discomforting, and for which there is still no
known cure, though research continues. If we have not yet learned how to stop
worrying altogether and love deconstruction, we have at least passed beyond
the initial shock of its recognition. There are even signs that deconstruction
may prove, in the course of its progress, to be self-deconstructing, i.e. self-
curing, so that those who come down with it may eventually find themselves
diagnosed as normal once again, well and truly able to carry out the institution's business as usual. And if that turns out to be the case—so runs the
argument of this paper—it will be a new and serious occasion for anxiety.

In looking back at the institution's early reaction to deconstruction when
it emerged in the late sixties and early seventies, it is not difficult to identify
the source and account for the strength of the anxiety it produced. Deconstruction was—well—different. "Difference" or *différance* was, after all, its philosophical watchword and principle, and the new terminologies and methodologies with which it invervened in the institutional discourse were certainly different from those the institution, particularly the Anglo-American
institution, was used to. Not only was deconstruction different from the critical and pedogogical practices in place in the sense of being alien and unfamiliar—that, after all, was true of structuralism as well—but deconstruction
appeared to be disturbingly different from itself, maddeningly elusive in the
unpredictable repertoire of terms and procedures then being mounted in rapid
succession under its name: *"différance," "misprision," "aporia,"* "undecidebility," *"mise-en-abyme"* .... What would they think of next? Not
quite or not yet a school or a movement, its reluctance or inability to routinize
itself—as distinct from structuralism's eagerness to do so—rendered it

254

uniquely threatening to any institutional mentality. This potential enemy was doubly dangerous for being at once different and protean, not fully or clearly one thing or the other, indistinctly different. At a time when the older orthodoxies of new and practical criticism were under challenge from several theoretical quarters, deconstruction was sometimes conflated in the general alarm with other heretical movements, mistaken for a version of structuralism or confused with a kind of Marxism, as often by the heretics themselves, anxious for avant-garde reinforcement, as by the defenders of the old faith, undiscriminating in the acuteness of their sense of present danger. Only at a later stage in the ongoing triumph of theory, could it begin to be recognized that deconstruction stands against not only the old new criticism but the methodological novelties of marxism and semiotics as well in mighty and binary opposition.

As its oxymoronic self-appellation suggested from the beginning, deconstruction was always, given its negative understanding of the differential and deferential nature of language and textuality, a practice oppositional to all philosophies of construction, the newer as well as the older, an antimethodical method. Operating from the margins, it exposed and released the anxiety of reference and representation at the only too metaphorical heart of more conventional methods, the anxiety necessarily repressed in the interest of any claim to a positive or systematic knowledge of literary texts on which our academic institutions have traditionally been based. As a form of oppositional practice, deconstruction gained considerable strategic and tactical advantage of its marginal or liminal status—comparable to that of such other liminal phenomena as ghosts, guerillas, or indeed, viruses—over its more clearly—defined, predictable, indeed institutionalized, and therefore vulnerable opponents and would-be allies. With the linguistic resourcefulness and mobility accruing from an extreme language skepticism, deconstruction had the capacity to come in under existing or emerging critical systems at their weakest point, the linguistic bad faith on which they were built. It could thus undermine the extroverted and hypertrophied structuration of semiotics with mole-like persistence, worrying away at its linguistic underpinnings until its Babel-like towers teetered vertiginously before collapsing into the groundlessness of their own pseudoscientific discourse. Or it could take the rhetorical "ground," the historio*graphic* soapbox as it were, out from under the solemn hectoring of Althusserian Marxism, leaving it with a lost sense of direction and the fuddlement of acute aporia. It is hardly necessary to mention in this context the deconstructive subversion, or more accurately, sublation of new criticism itself, in so far as American (as distinct from French) deconstruction carried to an unforeseen flash point some of New Criticism's most cherished principles. By scrutinizing the words on the page harder than New Criticism ever had, deconstruction discovered not their translucent and freestanding autonomy but, in a radical defamiliarization, their dark, even opaque, character as writing, black marks on white paper; not the organic unity that binds together irony, paradox, and ambiguity in a privileged, indeed redeemed and redeeming, language, but unrecuperable rhetorical discontinuity. Little wonder, then, that of the several schools of criticism vying for institutional dominance, deconstruction was, in its difference, the most feared, vilified, and misprized.

Nor is there need, in the present context, to document in any great detail the political and psychological conflicts that no doubt lent added piquancy even at times acrimony, to what might have been quite amicable philosophical differences. We are dealing, after all, with recent institutional history to which most of us have borne witness, and it does not take a Michel Foucault to remind us of the will to power that inheres in any will to knowledge and its institutional discourse. Suffice it to say that considerable power was and still is, at stake, nothing less than that latent in the pedagogical discourse and practice of literary study at all levels, from postgraduate programs down to the school curriculum—more on this shortly—so the anxiety has run high in proportion to the stakes at risk. While the agitation has so far been felt mainly at the top of the pyramid, it is clear to all concerned that the repercussions could be massive and long-term. For those critics concerned not with maintaining the continuity of institutionalized literary study in something like its present historical formalism, but with transforming it into a revolutionary political practice, deconstruction has come to be identified as an elitist cult and a reactionary force. More or less explicit in the work of such marxist or leftward commentators as Hayden White, Frank Lentricchia, Frederic Jameson and Terry Eagleton, is the view of deconstruction as regressive, a throwback not to the Russian formalism of the teens and twenties, as was structuralist poetics, but if anything, to the dandyist aestheticism of the nineties, a displaced religion of art. The ultrahigh formalism of deconstruction, arising from its obsession with linguistic difference and duplicity, returns criticism in such a view, to the idealist metaphysics from which it was supposed to deliver it, while the practitioners of deconstruction become *capi* of a hermeneutic Mafia or the high priests of a new mystery cult. The mark of such a cabal is its style— a frequent target for all opponent sides—or rather, its styles. For even after allowing that deconstruction has many styles, what they have in common is the challenge of difficulty and danger. So much so that charges of a deliberate obscurantism designed to exclude all but an elite—only those who already know will understand and so be saved—are not infrequent.

But the strongest reaction by far to deconstruction, no less allergic but much more alarmist than that of the Marxists, has come from the upper reaches of the literary-critical establishment across the English-speaking world. This is not really surprising, since it has the most to lose. For such figures as René Wellek, M. H. Abrams, and E. D. Hirsch—to confine ourselves for the moment to America—deconstruction poses a fundamental threat to the institutional and pedagogical practices of a long dominant critical and historical humanism going back to the Renaissance. Despite their conscientious pastoral care, that orthodoxy is breaking up, and deconstruction offers no help in holding it together. Quite the opposite: as a theory of language and literary language subversive of the notion that the meanings of literary texts are determinate or determinable, much less, in M. H. Abrams's unfortunate phrase, "obvious and univocal," and hence the notion that the study, not to mention the practice, of literature is a socially meaningful and valuable activity, deconstruction has been rejected as "apocalyptic irrationalism," "cognitive atheism," and "dogmatic relativism."

The fine excess of these phrases, the woundingness or woundedness of these words, should not be underestimated. The self-avowed language skepticism that deconstruction cultivates, indeed flaunts, as its philosophical program (or counterprogram), its self-proclaimed resistance to the imperialistic or totalitarian tendencies toward "positive and exploitative truth" built into any critical system—be it Marxist or semiological, historical or New Critical—obviously have grave institutional consequences. In this respect, deconstruction is a voice (or as we shall see, several distinct voices) crying out not in the desert but amid the superabundance of our overnourished institutions. Or perhaps more precisely, crying out within the desert of that superabundance. How else should the established institution react to a school that must, by its own logic, oppose institutionalization, with its tendencies toward consensus and routine, as yet another manifestation of the original philosophical sins of logocentricity, positivism, and reification? What, after all, is an "establishment" or an "institution" if not something only too pervasively and oppressively present? Worse yet, the rebels who are making these defiant gestures toward existing institutional authority are, it might seem, rebels without a cause, some of the institution's own favorite sons. Harold Bloom is the former student of M. H. Abrams at Cornell; Geoffrey Hartman, of René Wellek at Yale. Even Paul de Man, as a teaching fellow at Harvard, served his time under Reuben Brower in one of the smaller but more fruitful vineyards of "close reading." Yes, there seems to be an element of Oedipal reenactment at work, with the overreaction on both sides, on the part of the fathers as well as the sons. When M. H. Abrams maintains the availability of literature's "obvious and univocal sense," or René Wellek reaffirms the achievements of Yale formalism against the "apocalyptic irrationalism" of its deconstructive successors, these academic patriarchs are insisting, like latter-day Lears, that in our dealings with language, something, even if it lacks the total conviction of ultimate certainty, is preferable to nothing: "Nothing will come of nothing. Speak again." Imagine their shock and dismay to hear their own beloved offspring reply that the something they cherish and affirm is based on and amounts to nothing more than philosophical nostalgia or wishful thinking. What else could the patriarchal reaction be when filiation itself, once conceived as a benign relation through which something precious is based on—be it literary influence or real estate—is put into question. All the more disturbing when those who raise the question are themselves—again like Cordelia—the apples of the patriarchal eye.

From a sense of *lèse-majesté* on behalf of the institutional superstructure, it is a short step to offence on behalf of the affronted subject. What is the subject, after all, except what it is defined to be by those who are officially, i.e. institutionally, appointed to teach it. So that any critique of the institution, a fortiori a critique so radically skeptical, is necessarily construed as a critique, in this case virtually a dissolution or demolition, of the subject itself. In this respect, the reaction to deconstruction is analogous to an early and still persistent reaction to psychoanalysis: an irrational fear that, if this sort of analytical activity is pursued, the subject of it, be it literature, the personality, or even the person himself, will veritably disappear, be analyzed, as it were, out of existence. The fear of self-annihilation in its extreme form, may also be akin to the superstition among some primitive tribes that photography steals the souls of its subjects. From the standpoint of deconstruction, what both fears—that literature or human personality have their very existence imperilled by some ways of scrutinizing them—have in common is a superstitious, magical, or sacramental view of language, within which the relation between signifier and signified is a sacred and inviolate given: words mean exactly what they say. Hence the primal terror aroused in some quarters by the very term "deconstruction"—after all, the word has the same root-meaning as "analysis", a "loosening-up"—quite apart from the actual disintegrative thrust of deconstructionist, indeed of all structuralist and poststructuralist thinking, in which that fundamental relation of language is seen to be problematic.

It is worth pointing out at this stage, however, that this view of deconstruction as a nihilist plot is incompatible with the view of it as an elitist cult. Why would the high priests of a religion of literature want to abolish the source of their status and power? Such a state of affairs would be akin to the Mafia lobbying for the extirpation of opium networks in Southeast Asia, or to the venerable comic routine of a man sawing off the bough on which he sits. Deconstruction cannot, within Aristotelian logic at least, be what each of its chief polemical opponents has claimed—a priestly cult and a nihilist plot—at one and the same time. Or can it? We could reply that within the current institutional politics, deconstruction may well seem elitist and conservative in relation to Marxism, while in relation to our established formalism it may seem utterly radical. But to leave it at that, would be to play into the hands of deconstruction by accepting its extension of the structural linguistic principle that that which has its existence within a system of differences with no positive terms, is in the nature of the case contradictory, perverse, multivocal, mind-boggling, thus leaving the scandalous undecidebility of its institutional position intact.

To leave it at that would also be to let deconstruction off the hook of its own real or potential anxiety, for what I am arguing in this paper is that deconstruction is, or ought to be, not only the cause that anxiety is in the institution, but institutionally anxious in itself. This latter anxiety arises out of its own uncertain potential for institutionalization, the questionable capacity of a practice so profoundly oppositional, skeptical, and antisystematic to turn into a transmissible, teachable program in its own right. For there is great potential for anxiety in deconstruction's apparent desire to destabilize the interpretive structures and conventions through which institutional authority is manifested and perpetuated, while remaining unwilling quite to relinquish any claim to institutional authority for its own practices. In institutional terms, what the new Marxists and the old New Critics have in common is the premise that authority in interpretation is necessary and resides in communal, i.e. institutional, consensus; each is antiauthoritarian only with respect to the other's authority-conferring community. Both are threatened and scandalized by a deconstructive antiauthoritarianism so radically individualistic or solipsistic that it denies the interpretive authority and the communal basis for it, not only of other communities but of its own community—to the extent it can be said to form one—as well, and then has the further audacity to insist on its own institutional pride of place. These conflicting impulses within deconstruction express themselves in the apparent insouciance with which deconstruction transgresses the communal rules of the language game known as literary criticism while continuing to play it, in repeatedly exceeding the rules of the game by introducing an element of free-play deriving from a heightened and everpresent awareness that the rules of the game were arbitrary in the first place. Such a gambit might be tolerable even to other players who are playing more "seriously," i.e. conventionally, that is, who are so caught up in the game, and have so internalized its rules, that they have forgotten or repressed their own awareness (if they ever were aware), of the original arbitrariness or groundlessness of those rules. But it becomes intolerable once it is clear to these honest souls that the deconstructive transgressors, the disintegrated consciousnesses at the table, are not just kibitzing, but playing to win, and have one eye firmly fixed on the institutional stakes. That is having it both ways, or as some would call it, cheating. In either case it is breaking the rules that the community has agreed to play by, the rules that by virtue of this agreement, may be said to constitute the community.

Deconstruction's desire to have it both ways, to be in the community, even in its mainstream or bloodstream, but not *of* it, is more than a matter of wanting institutional prestige and influence, while violating some of the institution's most honored conventions and taboos, like making more puns than is thought seemly, or writing books without footnotes. It is a matter of putting into question the very constitutional and contractual basis, the rationale of social consent, on which the institutionalized interpretive community exists, what may be termed its major premise that there is something which requires and justifies, in social and historical terms, the service it renders, and for the sake of which it structures its activities. That something, that sine qua non and raison d'être, is the presumed existence of literary or poetic, as distinct from ordinary, language. Here we encounter a further paradox that the one deconstructionist for whom, as far as I can tell, this distinctive category does not exist, is also the one who is least subject to, and least the object of, institutional anxiety. For Derrida, as for the late Barthes, the category of literary language has dissolved, through the powerful reagent of *différance*, into writing and textuality in general. The relative absence of anxiety over and in Derrida—this is admittedly hard to measure—may well have to do with the primarily philosophical context of his work. For the institution of philosophical, as distinct from literary, study has long since given away any social or missionary rationale and is to that extent less predisposed, if not quite immune, to institutional anxiety. The idea has been around for some time now among philosophers, particularly Anglo-American philosophers, that theirs is a highly technical language game of only marginal social and practical consequence, and whether or not they accept this view, the reemergence under the name of deconstruction of extreme language skepticism in the mode of play is not likely to carry much shock value for those familiar with the work of Nietzsche, Heidegger, and Wittgenstein. We shall have to return to the marginal standing of philosophy as an institution; for literary deconstruction, as we shall see, continues to propose a dubious merger with it.

It is rather American—specifically Yale—deconstruction, proceeding, as it does, very much upon the humanist premise of literariness, and aware of the increasingly imperilled centrality of its institutionalized study for culture at large, that occasions the anxieties I have been describing. Perhaps the richest irony of the situation is that the definitions of literary language it still feels compelled to produce, ought to be, as the only poststructuralist defense of poetry on offer, the shibboleth of institutional acceptance, indeed, respectability. But that defense is so uncanny and paradoxical that it does not feel to the institution like a defense at all. Rather, it seems more like a surrender of the power of literary language to engage with, let alone enhance, anything beyond itself that might, in turn, lend it privilege, validity, or in the language of the Supreme Court, "redeeming social value," in particular the moral, mimetic, or expressive value conferred on it by traditional poetics:

> For the statement about language, that sign and meaning can never coincide, is what is precisely taken for granted in the kind of language we call literary. Literature, unlike everyday language, begins on the far side of this knowledge. . . . The self-reflecting mirror-effect by means of which a work of fiction asserts, by its very existence, its separation from empirical reality, its divergence, as a sign, from a meaning that depends for its existence on the constitutive activity of this sign, characterizes the work of literature in its essence. It is always against the explicit assertion of the writer that readers degrade the fiction by confusing it with a reality from which it has forever taken leave.[1]

I have selected this definition of literary language from the work of Paul de Man, not because his definition is singularly fugitive or teasing. Definitions

---

1. Paul de Man, *Blindness and Insight* 2nd ed. (Minneapolis: University of Minnesota Press; 1983), 17.

comparably threatening to the institution's sense of cultural mission could be culled from the work of Geoffrey Hartman, for whom art is characterized by the "generic impurity" of being "ambiguously involved with sacred and profane" and "always inauthentic vis-à-vis the purity of the ritual and vis-à-vis a thoroughgoing realism," or even from the work of Harold Bloom, for whom a poem is not a relief or release from, or a resolution or expression of, an anxiety, but itself "an anxiety." I single out de Man's definition because it states in terms more unrecuperable and uncompromising, more austere and demanding if you will, than the others, the deconstructive defense of poetry as a denial of precisely what the institution of literary study has traditionally thought of itself as being about. Literature, for de Man, remains an enlightened mode of language, "the only form of language" he calls it in the same passage, "free from the fallacy of unmediated expression"; but its enlightenment consists precisely in its disclaimer of what is normally claimed for it—its special immediacy or at least its special power to mediate something outside itself and something important to us. The revelation literature offers is that it can never be what the institution of its study blindly takes it to be.

Having brought out into the open, in luminous essay after essay, the anxiety of reference that blinds and vitiates the interpretive labors of the normal humanists who compose the institution, de Man might reasonably be expected to be urging that we write paid to those labors and dismantle the existing institutional support-system that sustains them. Or at least that we radically change the departmental and curricular structures that promote in their *Wissenshaftlich*, systematic way the ongoing misunderstanding of literature as something whose relation to and meaning for society can be ascertained by the historicist and/or formalist methods in place in the academy. It is just such a need for sweeping institutional change, after all, that the Marxists, given their own materialist demystification of bourgeois literary study, increasingly proclaim. They openly aspire to reconstitute the institution anew from the ground up, the ground being a not-so-new version of history and the study of literary forms giving way to the study of ideological formations. That may be, from the deconstructive viewpoint, only another and more intense manifestation of the old anxiety of reference, but at least it has the courage and candor of its conviction or fantasy. Indeed, some younger, self-styled deconstructionists of my acquaintance—none of them at Yale—would like to see the institutional structures that the old historicist and formalist anxiety of reference shores against its ruin give way to more expansive and flexible institutional structures that would bend with what they take to be the new bliss of difference that deconstruction—in its French forms at least—promises. They envision a carnivalization of the institution in which the old divisions between departments of national literature, between departments generally, disappears, and a new free-play reigns, where students are given high marks for making puns and dispensing with footnotes. The logical outcome, in institutional terms of deconstruction would surely have to be some kind of antiinstitution, where the full writerly fluidity of differential intertextuality could flourish without the guilt or anxiety induced and controlled by the oppressive superstructures and restrictive routines of departments, canons, methodologies, and footnotes. Perhaps it was some such academy without walls that the late Roland Barthes had in mind when he answered an interviewer's question about the place of literary study in the university to the effect that "it should be the only subject." After all, if deconstruction stands, as Richard Rorty suggests, in the same relation to "normal" criticism and philosophy as "abnormal" sexuality or science do to their "normal" counterparts—"each lives the other's death and dies the other's life"—should not its chief practitioners outspokenly advocate the legal and constitutional reform of the institution, if not actively attempt to found a new antiinstitution of an unabashedly utopian kind?

In fairness to the Yale deconstructionists, they have braved considerable communal opprobrium by proclaiming, up to a point, the unnegotiability of their differences with the institutional definition of the subject. "A critic must choose," wrote J. Hillis Miller, "either the tradition of presence or the tradition of difference, for their assumptions about language, about literature, about history, and about the mind cannot be made compatible." Yet the cry for large-scale institutional reform that such incompatibility ought logically to issue in has not been forthcoming. However different the deconstructive definition and defense of literature, it seeks neither blissfully to abolish a canon, nor radically to alter it, nor even to rewrite afresh the institutional style sheet of our dealings with it. Yale deconstruction may argue for, may even exemplify, the play of difference in its approach to literature, but there can be no mistaking that in so doing it is *hard* at play. No bliss, no *jouissance*, not even much *plaisir*, here in Puritan New Haven, thank you; we prefer "rigor," "strenuousness," "ruthlessness," anxiety and old-fashioned "hard work." For all its puns and abandonment of footnotes, this free-play turns out to be very hard work after all. The highest compliment Geoffrey Hartman can pay to the work of Paul de Man is to call it "a kind of generalized conscience of the act of reading," and conscience, as students of medieval allegory well know, is no figure of fun, at least not in his work. What prevents Yale deconstruction, unlike its Parisian cousin, from giving itself up to an abandonment of the institutional controls of method and system, and embracing a complete laissez-faire regarding the object of that method and system, is the distinctly Puritan work-anxiety it continues to share with the older institution, whose forms it largely accepts despite its declared differences with the traditional rationale for those forms.

But what, then, is the point of all this sweat and strain? Having relinquished all claim that the strenuous study of literature will confer on its students any positive benefit of cultural or historical identity, moral goodness, psychological wholeness, or even philosophical wisdom—the traditional humanist justifications for the institutionalized study of the canon—Yale deconstruction seems content that the institution continue to exist for the sake of work alone, in so far as its *Aufhebung* of work is also an emptying out of work's former purposes and justifications:

> The whole of literature would respond in similar fashion [i.e., as Proust responds to de Man's deconstruction of his rhetoric], although the techniques and the patterns would have to vary considerably, of course, from author to author. But there is absolutely no reason why analyses of the kind here suggested for Proust would not be applicable, with proper modifications of technique, to Milton or to Dante or to Hölderlin. This will in fact be the task of literary criticism in the coming years.[2]

What is at issue here is not the logic or accuracy of de Man's prediction—his prophecy, uttered more than five years ago, is coming only too true—but its tone of equanimity. Deconstruction is indeed proving thoroughly amenable to routinization at the hands of the institution to whose authority it once seemed to pose such a challenge of incompatibility. More than that, it has all but become the institution, as its life and activity rapidly becomes indistinguishable from the life and activity of the institution at large, as one classic text after another is subjected to moves and reflexes increasingly predictable and programmatic, and the aporias and undecideabilities, the *mises-en-abyme* and impasses, the deferrals and misprisions in the canonical literature are relentlessly unfolded. Deconstruction has made so much work for us all, it hardly seems to matter that, not only do the traditional justifications for that work no longer apply, but no justification other than the technical challenge of the work itself, seems to be offered.

It is at this point that the full anxiety of deconstruction begins to appear. The last thing deconstruction wants to be, or be seen to be, is an empty technology of the text, like its old rival, structuralist poetics. So it now emerges that the traditional humanist justifications of hermeneutics and history, according to de Man himself, may even *reappear*, if the institution only goes one step further in meeting the challenge:

> It would involve a change by which literature, instead of being taught as a historical and humanistic subject, should be taught as a rhetoric and a poetics prior to being taught as a hermeneutics and a history. The institutional resistances to such a move, however, are probably insurmountable. . . .
>
> Yet, with the critical cat now so far out of bag [sic] that one can no longer ignore its existence, those who refuse the crime of theoretical ruthlessness can no longer hope to gain a good conscience. Neither, or [sic] course, can the terrorists—but then, they never laid claim to it in the first place.[3]

De Man's professed skepticism about the full institutionalization of deconstruction is at this point surely rhetorical. The institutional "change" he

---

2. Paul de Man, *Allegories of Reading* (New Haven: Yale University Press, (1979), 16–17.

3. Paul de Man, "The Return to Philology," *The Times Literary Supplement* 4158, 10 December 1983, 1356.

recommends is minimal and moderate—still no call for a full-blooded utopia of differential bliss, but only for more "theoretical ruthlessness." Such a change, in fact, has either already taken place, or soon will, as courses in, conferences on, and centers for the study of methodology and theory not only proliferate, but move from the periphery to the longed-for metaphorical "center" of the discipline.

But even if this change has already occurred, or is about to occur, why would de Man be content to see it happen? Why would deconstruction acquiesce in what, on its own terms, would be a form of self-destruction? How can it accept its own institutional routinization with the same insouciance it once displayed in transgressing the institutional routines by which literature was supposed, by being reduced to law and order, to yield up its truth? If the diverse academic formalizations and normalizations, grammatizations and rhetorizations have been revealed, by de Man's own highly principled practice, *not* to be capable of negotiating the transition from the semiotic to the hermeneutic and historical, that is, from sign to meaning, how is studying them *first*, logically or chronologically, going to help? That nostalgic or desired transition can *never*, by de Man's definition of literary language, be methodically made, no matter what new priority is given to the study of rhetoric and poetics, or with whatever "theoretical ruthlessness" that study of method is pursued.

The "critical cat" is indeed so far out of the bag that its existence cannot be ignored, but why should de Man think, or wish to think, it will find any ground, old or new, to stand on by seeking out departments of philosophy or theory? While the proposed merger of deconstructive criticism with philosophy and theory no doubt identifies an area of hard work shared by deconstruction and the traditional institution, that area would have to be, by de Man's own lights, one of continuing contention rather than newfound accord. For the interests at stake are opposed and incompatible. What has deconstruction taught us if not that there is no theoretical "ground" so long dreamt of by philosophy outside the writerly practice, from which epistemology, ethics, and now writerly practice itself can be positively described? What has Derrida taught us but that the philosophical tradition, including deconstruction, *is* writerly practice. De Man's proposed institutional merger with philosophy and theory—if he means by it the Kantian kind, and what else has poetics proved itself to be?—would be at once regressive and counterproductive. It would be like the managing director of a growing company recommending to its shareholders a merger with an all but bankrupt competitor, whose imminent collapse will give the company a complete monopoly of the market. As Richard Rorty describes those "weak textualists" who think they are adding the prestige of philosophy to their criticism when they discuss a writer's epistemology: "Thus conquering warriors might mistakenly think to impress the populace by wrapping themselves in shabby togas stripped from the local senators." On the other hand, if de Man is recommending merger with what Rorty terms the "abnormal" philosophical tradition, culminating in Derrida and de Man himself, that variously denies the real or potential groundedness of discourse, he is recommending only what has already taken place. Whatever his Yale colleagues may mean by philosophy and theory when they recommend it, de Man is certainly no "weak textualist," and we must give him the benefit of the doubt by assuming it is the latter kind of merger he has in mind, which is to say, more of the same.

But in the very ambiguity of de Man's proposals, we sense the impasse confronting deconstruction as it ponders the possibilities of its institutional future and the full anxiety it quite properly feels in the situation. Too Puritan and conscientious to abandon itself to the textual hedonism of its French counterpart, which in its utopianism could never be institutionalized anyway, Yale deconstruction has only two courses open to it, neither of which it can pursue without anxiety. Either it can continue to attempt its project of opposition, which would now mean to oppose the routinization of its own earlier practice by resisting the cooption of its techniques by the institution, now composed of its own graduate students and disciples, by withholding its blessing from the ongoing deconstruction of the canon by textual techniques now only too familiar and repetitive. It is, of course, an open question whether and how long even such resourceful critical minds as we are dealing with could maintain such an adversary role, could continue to devise new ways of rescuing difference from the authoritative presence they have become in the work of their epigones. Even if they could so maintain the energy of deconstruction, the Puritan dissidence of their dissent, they would have to abandon all hope of institutional detente. That eventuality must be a cause for anxiety. The alternative would be to acquiesce fully in their present institutionalization, to give their blessing to the wholesale routinization of deconstruction now under way. For deconstruction to do that would be for it to cease to be deconstruction, for it to pass into institutional history. That thought too must cause considerable anxiety.

Whether the conscience of deconstruction is good or bad, it certainly exists and is powerful enough to bring upon itself in its current dilemma an acute *malconfort*, an aporia with a vengeance. For Paul de Man was never more clairvoyant than when, more than a decade ago, he foresaw his own present situation:

> All true criticism occurs in the mode of crisis. . . . In periods that are not periods of crisis, or in individuals bent on avoiding crisis at all cost, there can be all kinds of approaches to literature: historical, philological, psychological, etc., but there can be no criticism. . . . Whether authentic criticism is a liability or an asset to literary studies as a whole remains an open question.[4]

This account of the nature of criticism as difference from institutional norm is of course perfectly consistent with de Man's account of the nature of literature, and indeed underwrites deconstruction's own aspiration to literary status.

---

4. *Blindness and Insight*, 8.

Were deconstruction now to avoid crisis by acquiescing in the assimilation of its critical difference, its questionable status as a liability or an asset, by settling down under institutional auspices to the no longer hard but now empty labor of processing the entire literary canon, it would no longer be "true criticism" but just another "approach to literature." For deconstruction will be "true criticism," by its own lights, only as long as whether it can be done at all, and what it means institutionally to do it, remain open questions. Just as a number of critics in the midsixties, among them the present charismocrats of deconstruction, were writing against formalist and historical interpretation and calling, from within the institutional routine that new and practical criticism had become, for different styles of reading, so essays are now beginning to emerge from within theory—the present paper is just one of them—against the institutionalization of theory, including that of deconstructive theory.

Having all but prevailed within the academy and secured its institutional line of succession through the process described by Max Weber as the routinization of charisma, some exponents of deconstructive theory now envision its expansion beyond the walls of departments of English, French, Philosophy, and Comparative Literature. Hillis Miller, for example, sees the time as right for colonizing the pedagogy of the schools. So it was always written. And despite his caveats concerning theory, Geoffrey Hartman aims at nothing less than the repossession in the name of literary theory of the wider cultural discourse by an adventurous band of well-trained, versatile hermeneuts for hire, offering their skills for the decipherment of textuality in law, medicine, and commerce. One cannot help wondering whether they are to be deconstructive textualists, and if so, imagining the sober justices of the Supreme Court listening to their briefs! Yet it was de Man himself who once cautioned that "a literal-minded disciple of . . . Frye—is given license to order and classify the whole of literature into one single thing which, even though circular, would nevertheless be a gigantic cadaver." With its positive and positivist capability, its massive potential for reductive reification, Frye's protostructuralism once seemed the methodological antitype of deconstruction, with its insistence on negative capability, its inbuilt recalcitrance to being turned into "positive and exploitative truth." It was difficult indeed not to concur with Hartman that "to imagine children of the future performing little Anatomies as easily as they now do basic operations in mathematics may not be everyone's Utopia." Fortunately for all of us, Frye's utopia of "sweet science" did not quite come off. Perhaps that means there is still hope we may yet be spared all the potential utopias of deconstructive theory, where little aporias and *mises-en-abyme* are extrapolated from the world's textuality as easily, normally, and literal-mindedly as "close-readings" once were.

MACQUARRIE UNIVERSITY, SIDNEY

ANDRZEJ WARMINSKI

Dreadful Reading: Blanchot on Hegel

No rereading of Blanchot in the 1980s can take place without coming up against what a fragment from "Fragmentaire" calls "the dread of reading" (*l'angoisse de lire*): "The dread of reading: it is that every text, no matter how important and how interesting it may be (and the more it gives the impression of being so), is empty—it does not exist at bottom (*il n'existe pas dans le fond*); it is necessary to clear an abyss, and if you don't jump, you don't understand."[1] If in order to understand (reading and the dread proper to it) we have to clear the abyss of the text's essential non-existence, it may be good to know what this non-existence comes down to. Rather than proceeding directly to the text of Blanchot and its non-existence—and thereby risking too immediate an answer to the question of (the existence or non-existence of) his text—we would take a detour and begin by way of the question of reading: as a pretext, then, Blanchot's reading of Hegel, in particular the *Phenomenology of Spirit*—an apparently existent text if there ever was one. Another fragment from "Fragmentaire" provides us with something like a kit for rereading Hegel through Blanchot: "One cannot 'read' Hegel except by not reading him. To read him, not to read him, to understand him, to misunderstand him, to refuse him, falls under the decision of Hegel, or it does not take place. Only the intensity of this non-place, in the impossibility that there be one, disposes us for a death— death of reading, death of writing—that leaves Hegel living, in the imposture of the finished Sense. (Hegel is the impostor, that is what renders him invincible, crazy for his gravity (*fou de son sérieux*), counterfeiter of Truth.)" On the one hand, this fragment formulates the dread of the reader in the face of Hegel's System: whether you read Hegel or do not read him, you'll regret it because in either case you will have been read *by* Hegel. That is, to read Hegel—the

This paper was delivered at a Special Session ("Re-reading Blanchot in the 1980s") of the 1983 MLA convention in New York. It will appear as an Epilogue to: Andrzej Warminski, *Readings in Interpretation: Hölderlin, Hegel, Heidegger* (Minneapolis: University of Minnesota Press, 1986).

1. Maurice Blanchot, "Fragmentaire," in *A Bram Van Velde* (Montpellier: Fata Morgana, 1975).

Phenomenology of Spirit, for example—means to follow at a distance and immerse oneself in the dialectical movement of knowing's (*das Wissen*) examining itself as the philosophical observer who is both superfluous and necessary, who puts himself in by leaving himself out, the "we" of the text. In short, the reader of Hegel—objective genitive—inscribes himself, is already inscribed, in the *Phenomenology* as the book's own "we" and thereby becomes the reader of *Hegel*—subjective genitive—Hegel's own reader. But even *not* to read Hegel—to misunderstand him, to refuse him, etc.—falls under the decision of Hegel precisely to the extent that it defines and identifies itself as the refusal *of*, or in opposition to, Hegel, the System. That is, the refusal to read Hegel, like all (mere) negations, has a positive content—it is always the negation *of* something, in this case the negation of Hegel and therefore still belongs to him, Hegel's own negation. In short, the familiar work of determinate negation insures that reading or not reading Hegel will not make a difference. And yet, on the other hand—and this would have to be a third, other, hand since both one and two turned out to be the hands of Hegel—the writing of the fragment begins to make an imperceptible difference once we begin reading it. For the text gives us not only the difference between reading Hegel and its negation, but also the difference between reading and "reading"—in quotation marks. However we read this third, other, neuter (*neither* one, reading, *nor* the other, not reading) reading in quotation marks, it is clear that its difference is not easily masterable by a thought whose motor is determinate negation: for "reading"—in quotation marks—cannot be thought as the negation (of reading or not reading), it can only be . . . read. Whatever else it does, such a reading opens up a space for the reading of this fragment and a rewriting of its terms differently, otherwise. For one thing, we can now read the "or" in "or it does not take place" (*ou cela n'a pas lieu*) as meaning not "in other words" but "on the other hand." That is, a reading of Hegel that would not fall under the decision of Hegel would have to be one that did not take place—but in a sense of not taking place different from, other than, the opposition to take place/not to take place. In other words, it would be an other not taking place that is not the negation of taking place—an other negative. It is such an other negative that the fragment introduces by taking advantage of the French idiomatic expression "avoir lieu" (to take place, to happen) to create a non-place (*non-lieu*) which is not the negation of place—a space in which the reading of Hegel in quotation marks (neither reading nor not reading) can take place without taking place. It is necessarily impossible that there *be* such a non-place, for its space (and time) would necessarily be other than that of any dialectical (or onto-) logic. So: a non-happening is turned into an impossible non-place where we are supposed to read, Hegel, in quotation marks—a reading that makes necessary a rewriting of both the "we" and "death" in a different sense, in a sense different from the "finished Sense" (*Sens achevé*) of Hegel. Small wonder, then, that reading—Hegel, for example—is dreadful, for it comes up against a Nothing that does not turn over into Being (nor does it reveal and conceal Being) but rather rereads and rewrites Nothing. (This is perhaps how we should read Hegel's "invincibility." As another fragment from "Fragmentaire" puts it: "The correct critique of the System does not consist of catching it in error (as one often delights in doing) or in the interpreting it as insufficient (this happens even to Heidegger) but of rendering it invincible, uncritiquable, or, as one says, "un-get-around-able." Thus, nothing escaping its omnipresent unity and re-collection of everything, no more place remains for fragmentary writing (*il ne reste plus de place à l'écriture fragmentaire*) except to disengage as the necessary impossible (*sauf à se dégager comme le nécessaire impossible*): that which therefore writes itself in the name of the time outside time, in a suspension that, unreservedly (*sans retenue*), breaks the seal of the unity, precisely in not breaking it, but in leaving it to the side (*de côté*) without one's being able to know it." In other words, the third, other, neuter reading of Hegel is not a dialectical trick—like, say, Hegel's critique of what he calls the bad infinity (an infinity that does not include finitude is finite, limited by the finitude it does not include) or of "absolute difference" (an absolute difference is different from everything, including itself, difference, and therefore turns over into absolute identity)—rendering the System invincible in order to demonstrate that its invincibility is limited by its not containing "vincibility" but rather a rewriting of its seal of invincibility elsewhere, otherwise, on the side.)

Such a rewriting of Hegel's negative in another place, to the side, is what takes place in Blanchot's readings of Hegel in the 1940s—in particular "La littérature et le droit à la mort"[2]—and what accounts for their peculiar "distance" from the text of the *Phenomenology* as formulated in the essay's first footnote: "It should be understood that the remarks which follow are quite remote (*fort loin*) from the text of the *Phenomenology* and make no attempt to illuminate (*éclairer*) it." If we remember this footnote, we will not make the mistake of charging Blanchot with having taken out of context and mixed up specific moments of different dialectics in the *Phenomenology:* the attempt is not to explain Hegel but to rewrite him in an other place. But it is also no answer to dismiss this rewriting as Blanchot's flippant "tendency to allegorize philosophical texts as parables of writing," for the question remains: what does such allegorization mean and do to the reading of the *Phenomenology?* In order to determine the other place, to the side, in which moments of the *Phenomenology* as diverse as Hegel's remarks on death in the Preface, the dialectics of work, of universal freedom and Terror, the unhappy consciousness, master and slave, etc. can all be read as though on the same level and rewritten into parables of writing, we will begin with Blanchot's rewriting of Hegel on (the) work and Hegel on death: what takes place (and where), what difference does it make, when work and death are read as writing? In regard to work, an immediate answer would be: nothing takes place, it makes no difference, for here Blanchot's essay seems to follow Hegel quite closely. Just as in the *Phe-*

---

2. Maurice Blanchot, *La Part du feu* (Paris: Gallimard, 1949).

nomenology the individual (*das Individuum*) who is going to take action finds himself "in a circle in which each moment already presupposes the other"— that is, he can know the end or goal (*Zweck*) of his action only from the act but he can act only if he already has that end or goal—so in Blanchot's essay the writer finds himself in a double bind: "He has no talent until he has written, but he needs talent in order to write (*Il n'a du talent qu'après avoir écrit, mais il lui en faut pour écrire*)." And yet substituting "writer" for "individual" here makes all the difference to the resolution of the double bind, to how one breaks the circle and begins to take action or to write. For the individual, there is an immediate way out, indeed, immediacy *is* the way out: "The individual who is going to act seems, therefore, to find himself in a circle in which each moment already presupposes the other, and thus he seems unable to find a beginning, because he only gets to know his original nature, which must be his End (*Zweck*), *from the deed*, while, in order to act, he must have that End beforehand. But for that very reason he has to start immediately (*unmittelbar*), and, whatever the circumstances, without further scruples about beginning, means (*Mittel*), or End, proceed to action; for his essence and *intrinsic* nature (*ansichseiende Natur*) is beginning, means, and End, all in one."[3] That is, as Hegel continues, the beginning is provided by the given circumstances (*vorgefundene Umstände*) in which the individual finds himself—this is the "in itself" (*an sich*) of the individual—the end is the "interest" (*Interesse*) that the individual posits (*setzt*) for himself—this is the "for itself," *das seinige*, of the individual—and the union and sublation of this opposition (*die Verknüpfung und Aufhebung dieses Gegensatzes*) is the means (*Mittel*). In short, taking immediate (*unmittelbar*) action is the means (*Mittel*) that mediate between the individual's circumstances and interest, what it finds and what it posits, in itself (*an sich*) and for itself (*für sich*), immediacy and mediation. But then what about the writer? Can he break the circle by beginning to write immediately? The writer's circumstances, his given in itself, are that he cannot write until he has written, i.e., that he is not a writer *before* he has written, but that once he has written he is no longer writing, i.e., that he is not a writer *after* he has written: he is always not yet and always no longer a writer writing. (As *Après coup* puts it: "Du 'ne pas encore' au 'ne plus,' tel serait le parcours de ce qu'on nomme l'écrivain . . . ") The writer's interest—the end or goal he posits for himself—is to *be* a writer, and this interest cannot be mediated with the circumstances of his always not yet and always no longer being a writer because the means are lacking. That is, the writer's only means are writing, but writing is not a means, it does not take place immediately, here and now, but always in a different place and a deferred time—not yet, no longer, suspended, interrupted. In short, there is no such thing as beginning to write immediately—writing neither begins nor ends—and hence the writer takes a different

---

3. G. W. F. Hegel, *Phänomenologie des Geistes* (Hamburg: Felix Meiner, 1952), 288. English translation by A. V. Miller: *Phenomenology of Spirit* (Oxford: Oxford University Press, 1977), 240.

way out: he writes (the means) the impossibility (the circumstances) of being (the interest) a writer: a non-synthesis, a non-action, exterior to itself. And yet if writing "must be recognized as the highest form of work"—as Blanchot's essay puts it—then its conditions would necessarily be, on the one hand, the conditions of possibility of all work and, on the other hand, the conditions of *im*possibility of all work in that the condition of writing is the unmediatability of beginnings and ends, circumstances and interest, immediacy and mediation, etc. Hence to substitute the work of the writer for the work of the individual would mean, in the case of the *Phenomenology*, to replace the order of presentation (*Darstellung*) by the order of that which makes the presentation possible—but which needs to be excluded because it also makes it impossible. A good example of the way writing functions as an excluded condition of possibility and impossibility for the work of dialectical mediation is a skit that dramatizes the critique of the immediacy claimed by the first figure of apparent knowing in Hegel's *Phenomenology:* sense-certainty.

The "work" of sense-certainty, what it claims as its truth, is the most immediate kind of apprehension of Being as "the this" under the double aspect of the "Now" and the "Here." After asking sense-certainty "what is the now?" and answering for example "the now is the night," the critique of sense-certainty tests its truth: "To test the truth of this sense-certainty, a simple experiment is sufficient. We write down this truth; a truth can't lose anything by being written down; much less can it lose anything from our preserving it. If we look again at this written down truth *now, this noon,* we shall have to say that it has become stale."[4] Now the critique of sense-certainty's truth hardly requires comment: instead of an immediate, particular now, sense-certainty, as soon as it says anything, is able to say only a mediated, universal now that is indifferent to the particularity of night and day. But more interesting for our purposes here is the work of writing that allows the critique to take place: that is, in spite of the fact that neither sense-certainty nor we can say an immediate, particular, self-identical Now (or Here), our critique of that Now depends on another self-identical Now (and Here), a self-simultaneous moment, in which we were able to read and compare "Now is the night" and "Now is the day." In other words, the very critique of sense-certainty's Now and Here requires another Now—a time of reading—and another Here—a place of writing: it requires, in short, this piece of paper on which I write this and this.[5] But, of course, this piece of paper on which I write and read this is not the particular piece of paper sewn into my copy of the *Phenomenology* and that I can see,

---

4. Hegel, *Phänomenologie*, 81, English 60. Some other "exemplary" readings of Hegel: Andrzej Warminski, "Reading for Example: 'Sense-certainty' in Hegel's *Phenomenology of Spirit*," *Diacritics* (Summer 1981), "Pre-positional By-play," *Glyph 3* (Baltimore: Johns Hopkins University Press, 1978), and "Reading Parentheses: Hegel by Heidegger," *Genre* XVI, Number 4 (Winter 1983), 389–403.

5. Our reading of "this piece of paper" crosses that of: Paul de Man, "Hypogram and Inscription: Michael Riffaterre's Poetics of Reading," *Diacritics* (Winter 1981).

touch, smell, and taste. It is also not the particular piece of manuscript paper preserved in the Hegel archives in Bochum on which Hegel wrote "Now is the day" and "Now is the night" and compared them. To identify it with *that* piece of paper would be to fall back into the position of sense-certainty: the Now of reading and of writing is not one we can see, it can only be written and read. This does not mean that we are talking about an ideal, universal piece of paper, as it were. No, this piece of paper on which I write "Now is the day" and "Now is the night" and read them is the material condition of possibility of the opposition between particular and universal. It is neither the particular, immediate, phenomenal piece of paper available to the senses nor the universal, mediated, intelligible piece of paper available to the mind, but other: a piece of paper that exists in the here and now of writing and reading. It is a piece of paper conditioned by the materiality (as distinguished from phenomenality) of reading and writing. And the necessary exclusion of this conditioning materiality from Hegel's construction and critique of sense-certainty's phenomenality is readable in the text's suppression of the act of reading: when we come back to sense-certainty now, this noon, with the piece of paper on which we had written "Now is the night," we do not *read* it, says the text, but rather look at it (*sehen . . . wieder an*)—when it is only *reading* the inscription that will allow us to compare night and day. This switch from reading to looking—from the materiality of the text to the phenomenality of the book, from something that can only be written or read to something that can be the object of a consciousness's knowledge—is a necessary condition of the *Phenomenology*, what allows it to begin and end by mediating beginning and end. For in order to begin, Hegel, like the individual, has to begin immediately with the given circumstances of immediate knowing and the posited end—absolute knowing, the absolute—a standard against which he can measure all too immediate forms of knowing. But to do so he has to forget the means—writing: the material fact that the Absolute in order to be, i.e., to become, has to have been *not* presupposed and posited (nor, as Heidegger would have it, dis-concealed) but *written.* In short, in order to begin Hegel has to forget the material fact that he has already begun in a way he should not have, in a way that makes all beginning (and all ending) impossible: with an inscription of the Absolute, here and now, i.e., somewhere and sometime else. Without such forgetting the work of the *Phenomenology* would become the impossible work of writing—always not yet and always no longer written. That is, the impossibility of *writing* the *Phenomenology* would become readable: the *presentation* (*Darstellung*) of the *Phenomenology* is possible, its writing, no; the writing of a *text* is possible, the writing of a *work* (like the *Phenomenology*), no. The writing of the text takes place elsewhere in a non-place written by a "Hegel"—in quotation marks— who could not, did not, write the *Phenomenology of Spirit*—a Hegel more like a Nietzsche or a Blanchot. This would be one way to read the non-existence of the text—the *Phenomenology*, for example—at bottom. (It would also be one way of justifying Blanchot's taking different moments of different dialectics

out of context and rewriting them as though they were on the "same level":
they *are* on the same level, for his reading takes place on the level of the *text*,
the space and time not of the dialectical presentation [*Darstellung*], but the
other space and time of the writing (and reading) of the text.)

If Blanchot's reading of work as writing makes work impossible (and yet is
its condition of possibility), then death read as writing makes death impossible
(and yet is its condition of possibility). It is important to distinguish this death
without death—language, literature, writing, the word, as the "life that endures death and maintains itself in it" (*das Leben . . . das ihn erträgt und in
ihm sich erhält*), a phrase that is rewritten several times in "Literature and the
Right to Death"—from the deaths of Hegel. In the "Introduction" to the *Phenomenology* Hegel himself distinguishes between two deaths: that of natural
life and that of consciousness. What is limited to a natural life (*natürliches
Leben*), he says, cannot by itself go beyond its immediate existence, but it is
driven out beyond it by something else, and this something else is its death.
Consciousness, however, is driven out beyond its immediate existence by a
violence it suffers at its own hands: that is, because it is its own concept
(*Begriff*), because it carries its own standard (of the truth of knowing: the
Absolute) within itself, it is constantly dissatisfied with its immediate existence. In short, consciousness is always also self-consciousness, it carries its
own death within itself. And this necessary condition of consciousness—the
fact that it can and has to make its own death an object of (self-)con-
sciousness—is what distinguishes it from mere "natural life." A cat squashed
by a truck does not *die*, properly speaking; its "natural life" is, as it were,
extinguished. But unlike the cat, consciousness can die because it can know its
own death, it can represent its own death to itself—indeed, such self-representation is the "truth" of consciousness, i.e., self-consciousness. In other words,
a condition of consciousness is its having to represent its own death to itself,
but such representation is not possible without a subterfuge, as Bataille would
put it: in order to be "we," we have to die while watching ourselves die. We
require a spectacle, theater, sacrifice, a comedy in which we can represent our
own death to ourselves and survive it. But Blanchot recognizes that this comedy of sacrifice—identifying our own death, ourselves, in the extinguishment of
a cat, say—is a linguistic operation, a matter of (impossible) *signification*
rather than representation, since death is not a something (or a nothing) that
can ever become an object of consciousness's knowing, just as I cannot *experience* death, I can only name it, impose a sense on it (by catachresis, say), give it
a face, eyes, and a point of view (by prosopopoeia, as Hegel does when he speaks
of looking into the face (*Angesicht*) of death). In order to bring death into the
world, we (in order to be "we") bring death into the word. And from the point of
view of what Blanchot calls everyday language, the word "death," like all
words, works—by negation: " . . . for a moment everyday language is right, in
that even if the word excludes the existence of what it designates, it still refers
to it through the thing's nonexistence, which has become its essence. To name

the cat is, if you like, to make it into a non-cat, a cat that has ceased to exist, has ceased to be a living cat, but this does not mean one is making it into a dog, or even a non-dog."[6] Death, in the word, works all right, but, what Blanchot calls literary language, observes that "the word cat is not only the nonexistence of the cat, but a nonexistence made *word,* that is, a completely determined and objective reality." In other words, the word "cat" gives us not only the non-cat, the cat in his non-existence, but also the *word* cat, just as the word death gives us not only a non-death, the negation *of* death that we can put to work in the world, but also an other death in its determinate and objective reality—a linguistic death, the death of the word. And this third, other death—the death without death—falls completely out of the grasp of a consciousness or a self or a subject. When I say "I die" I suffer the death of the impossibility of dying: on the one hand, saying "I die" is the condition of possibility of any "I" what-soever; on the other hand, "I die" is not anything that can be said *by* an "I" since death can have no, *is* no, subject. At most, I can say "I dies"—in other words, I can never *say* my own death, I can only write (or read) it as the death of an other "I," a linguistic, grammatical subject, someone or something else's. In short, in order to *be* an "I," I have to say "I die" while forgetting that I could never have said it—that in saying it I turn myself into *the* "I" and say "I dies"—while forgetting that I could only have *written* it and thereby had dispossessed myself of my "I" and my own death (death as negation) forever. (So: just as writing was the condition of (im)possibility of the work, so writing is the condition of (im)possibility of death.)

Blanchot's reading of work and death in Hegel as writing is particularly helpful for a rereading of the famous passage in the Preface of the *Phenomenology* quoted repeatedly in "Literature and the Right to Death" and the mas-ter/slave dialectic—one place where work and death are explicitly con-joined—to which that passage points. "The life of Spirit," writes Hegel, "is not the life that shrinks from death and keeps itself untouched by devastation, but rather the life that endures it and maintains itself in it." In the struggle for self-recognition, it would seem to be the master who looks death in the face, who is willing to risk death for the sake of recognition, whereas the slave becomes the slave because he shrinks from death, is not willing to risk his life. But, of course, the master's "victory" is already his loss, for the death he faces is only natural death and the life he risks is only "natural life." That is, the master is willing to give up his life in its immediacy, but because he is willing to give up this immediacy *too immediately,* he falls back into an immediate relation to nature: that is, the slave now satisfies immediately the master's merely appe-titive, natural needs, and the master does not have to work to satisfy them, he does not have to exercise his freedom on nature by appropriating it. It is the slave who, precisely because he was afraid of natural death, because he was not

---

6. Maurice Blanchot, *The Gaze of Orpheus,* trans. Lydia Davis (Barrytown, N.Y.: Stationhill Press, 1981), 44.

willing to give up his natural life, it is the slave who looks the death of consciousness in the face: he give his death a name and a face—master death—and
thereby appropriates, masters, death by working nature, putting (natural) death
to work. This is a familiar dialectic. Blanchot's supplementary insight consists
in noting that the slave's very first work—giving voice to his dumb (*stumm*)
absolute fear of death, naming death as his own negation—brings into the
world still another, third, neuter death, whose excess can never be recovered by
the work of (determinate) negation. It is thanks to this excess of death—death
as written (and read)—that the System works like an invincible impostor.[7]

YALE UNIVERSITY

---

7. Blanchot's supplementary insight would require an extensive rereading of the master/slave
dialectic. We have sketched only the barest outline of a beginning here.

WERNER HAMACHER

The Second of Inversion: Movements of a Figure through Celan's Poetry

Under the sign of its semantic function, to which classical (Aristotelian) doctrine expects language—in its only truthful, that is, its predicative statements—to reduce itself, language appears caught in an aporia that itself admits only of aporetic solution: either it is explained away as an empty gesturing which must evanesce before the power of the factual, or it is granted all the weight of the only certain reality, whose forms (*Typen*) are stamped upon the entire realm of the objective and which alone first constitutes the status of objectivity itself. In the first case, language is destined to be extinguished before the presence of the world of things and their movements; for itself it is nothing, a mere instrument, in the crudest instance one of deixis, a means of reference which is to disappear where the things themselves appear. In the other case, once language is exalted into a schema for all reality, it can confront in reality only itself once again; it employs objects to attest to the efficacy of its figures, straying into a virtually endless process of repeating, without resistance, the forms prestabilized in itself. If in the one case language points to a reality to which it cedes all rights, only to step back from its light as its shadowy reproduction, in the other case reality retains only the rights of language, in whose image it is created. The infinitude of reality in the one model stands confronted with the infinitude of language in the other.

In both cases, language and its inherent epistemological structures are denied the power of being a reality with its own rights and its own structure, a reality which could not be exhausted by any relationship of analogy, of representation, or of characterizing (*typisierung*) other realities. Accordingly, both accounts of language, defining it essentially in terms of its functions as signification and reference, must fall into the paradox that when language finally reaches its destination, it is no longer either signified or referred to. There it would either give way to what it intends, or else it would remain only itself within that which is modelled after it. At the end of any semantic theory of language and of its truth stands the aporetic verdict: language does not speak; it has nothing to signify, being only itself or its disappearance. But this aporia

276

arises only if we grant that reality shows itself merely as objectivity; that this objectivity materializes in its presence; and that, under the condition of its absence, projected in the image of such present objectivity, language is to step in, either as substitute or as prototype, to maintain or to guarantee the possibility of the objective. According to this idea of a transcendental semantics—which organizes not just classical philosophical systems but even the most unreflective linguistic theories of language—language would stand as the proper place of origin for any reality cast as objectivity.

But the view that reality must follow the lead of language, and not the other way around, will necessarily be construed by a naive, by a normal and natural understanding of the world, as hopelessly demanding. In such a view, the world appears topsy-turvy and perverted, stood on its head. So too, in the texts of Kant and Hegel, where theories of absolute subjectivity reach their highest development, metaphors of turning and of the turning point, of wheeling about and of reversal, of upending and of return, make their entrance together with the metaphors of reflection and of speculation, in unprecedented density and profusion. Joining the Platonic figure of *epistrophè* and the evangelical figure of *metanoia*, they assume a compulsory power which was to become for subsequent philosophical and literary texts, virtually mythical. Kant's "intellectual revolution" attempts, still as it were experimentally, and with express reference to the Copernican turn, to make it plausible that a knowledge a priori of objects must before all else stamp upon them the forms in which we are to know them. In such a knowing the subject gives its objects the rule, as the form of presentation, which alone permits them to be objects of knowledge. The inversion of accepted ways of thinking that Kant set in motion thus secures access to reality by assigning to knowledge the form of objectivity, thereby bringing the whole of the given under the epistemological premises of subjectivity. The *ordo inversus* engineered by Kant's critique—which of course does not begin to exhaust it—is the figure of totalized subjectivity.

In this matter, Hegel appointed himself executor of the Kantian legacy, by viewing not just the natural world, with Kant, but equally the world of history, as ordered under the principle of the representing and thinking spirit. The *locus classicus* among his corresponding formulations refers once again to a revolution, the French Revolution, in a significant turn of phrase whose fragility would merit a full-length analysis. It is to be found in his *Lectures on the Philosophy of History:* "Never since the sun had stood in the firmament and the planets revolved around it had man been seen to center himself on his head (*sich auf den Kopf . . . stellen*), i.e. in thought, and to construct reality according to it. . . . This was like a glorious dawn."[1] When the light of reason first

---

1. G. W. F. Hegel, *Werke in zwanzig Bänden* (Theorie Werkausgabe), ed. Eva Moldenhauer and Karl Markus Michel, (Frankfurt am Main: Suhrkamp Verlag, 1970), v. 12, 529. Translation adapted from George Wilhelm Friedrich Hegel, *The Philosophy of History*, trans. J. Sibree (New York: Dover Publications, Inc., 1956), 447.

rises, as soon as man stands himself and his reality on his head (*auf den Kopf stellt*), it is because his life and his history then first find a stable foundation for their significance in the head (*auf dem Kopf*). Reality, with its historical process, first comes to itself in thought, and has taken its first true stance—the standing of its truth, in which nothing alien any longer stands against it; in which, rather, the Other turns out to be the other of its *self*—in a headstand. In taking its stand on the principle of subjectivity, historical reality sets itself aright: it demonstrates thereby that the infinitude of subjective spirit's self-reference is already inherent in the objectivity of finite spirit.

Hegel's speculative inversion does not stop with bringing the objective reality of history to itself, and hence to reason. The inversion of the Hegelian style performs its greatest feat—contrary to the deepest intentions of the Kantian inversion—with nonreality, with death as the abstract negation of entities (in general). Spirit shows itself as substantial subjectivity in converting its own nonreality, its dismemberment and its absence, into being. In the Preface to the *Phenomenology of Spirit*, Hegel writes: "Death, if that is what we want to call this non-reality, is of all things the most dreadful, and to hold fast what is dead requires the greatest strength." Spirit is the power of finding itself in absolute dismemberment, "only insofar as it looks the negative in the face and tarries with it. This tarrying with the negative is the magical power that converts it into being. This power is identical with what we earlier called the subject, . . . authentic substance, . . . whose mediation is not outside of it but which is this mediation itself."[2] Death, "if that is what we want to call this non-reality," can only be held fast, looked in the face and converted, if it is transformed from death into something dead; from a nonreality, by prosopopoeia, into a face; from the negation of the I into the pure energy of the I. It can only be converted once it has been allotted its place within the circle of speculative inversion. This is not to carp at a *petitio principii*— though this *petitio*, this *petitio principii* is perhaps *the* problem of philosophy—but rather to make it plain that the life of spirit can only convert the nonreality that is death into objective reality because its absence cannot come into view except as the hollow mold of its contour (*Gestalt*), as a death in the image of life, as a negative after the pattern of "absolute position or positing," as Kant defines being. Meaning can only be affixed to a death to which subjectivity has lent an aspect, a countenance, a face, tracing the outline of its own contour. The process of prosopopoeia—that is, the bestowal of a face or a mask—and with it, the root of the possible significance of finite life, is still problematic for Kant (most pointedly in the paragraphs on the Analytic of the Sublime in the Third Critique), but also still for Hegel (in those regions of his thought he himself regarded as peripheral to the system). The master trope of Hegelian philosophy—negation of negation, speculative inversion—holds sway over a territory already shel-

---

2. G. W. F. Hegel, Phänomenologie des Geistes. (Berlin: Ullstein, 1973), 29. Translation adapted from G. W. F. Hegel, *Phenomenology of Spirit*, trans. A. V. Miller (New York: Oxford University Press, 1977), 19.

tered by the principle of subjectivity from the absolute shapelessness of death—"if that is what we want to call this non-reality." Only because nothingness, as Hegel writes in his critique of skepticism, always figures as the "nothingness of something," only therefore because it has already assumed the figure of objective being, can the figure of inversion be brought to bear on it, to convert (*umkehren*) it into being. With this conversion, the subject's being has mediated itself with its nonbeing, and it is itself nothing other than the movement of this mediation with its other as with itself.

By virtue of this ability of the substantial subject to mediate and to convert (*Verkehren*), a meaning binds itself with each of the linguistic signs it posits. We certainly do "want to call" that nonreality, even if after a certain hesitation, death. Such a meaning remains indispensable for the correspondance (*Verkehr*) between the sign and what it signifies, as for the communicative interaction (*Verkehr*) between various speakers, because the signified is itself always already inserted as a moment of mediation into the form of subjectivity. To the extent that whatever falls within the realm of language becomes, through the movement of mediation, a means of language's semiocentric inversion, it also—at least according to Hegel's intention—moves to the center of its own meaning. It no longer signifies, but is itself the process of signification; it no longer refers to something absent, but is itself the process of its realization and its coming into presence: the pure energy of self-realizing, self-presencing subjectivity.

One could demonstrate the efficacy and the determining power of the figure of inversion, here sketched only with reference to two standard philosophical texts, over the philosophical and literary texts of the Romantic and the Classical periods, of Feuerbachian and Marxian materialism, and of so-called poetic realism up to Neoromanticism; one could demonstrate its effect on the macrostructure of the *Bildungsroman* as well as in the syntactical detail of the lyric.[3] However diverse the intentions controlling this figure may be, the inversion remains—with the great exception of Hölderlin, who sets the opacity of finite linguistic materials against the universalizing of their semantic energy.[4] Inversion remains the dominant rhetorical and epistemological figure for the consolidation of meaning and the universalizing of subjectivity. To this extent it is also the canonical form of the lyric. It reaches its

---

3. Manfred Frank and Gerhard Kurz have already carried out a portion of this task, though not with uniform persuasiveness, in "Ordo Inversus: Zu einer Reflexionsfigur bei Novalis, Hölderlin, Kleist und Kafka," *Geist und Zeichen: Festschrift für Arthur Henkel* (Heidelberg: Carl Winter Verlag, 1977), 75–97.

4. These thoughts are given theoretical formulation in a series of notes bearing the title *Reflexion*, in F. Hölderlin, *Sämtliche Werke*, ed. Fr. Beissner, (Stuttgart: Verlag W. Kehlhammer, 1961), v. 4, 233–36. Here one finds the sentence: "Man hat Inversionen in der Periode. Grösser und wirksamer muss aber dann auch die Inversion der Perioden selbst sein." ("We have inversions in periods. But the inversion of the period itself must be still greater and more effective.")

culmination in Rilke's *Neue Gedichte.*[5] In *Archaischer Torso Apollos*[6]—
which is placed at the head of the second part, as though as its emblem, and so
occupies roughly the center of the book—what still survives of Greek plastic
art changes into precisely what time has taken away from it: into eyesight
(*Augenlicht*). *Wir kannten nicht sein unerhörtes Haupt,/darin die Augenäpfel
reiften. Aber/sein Torso glüht noch wie ein Kandelaber . . .* ["We did not
know its unheard-of head,/in which the pupils ripened. But/still its torso
glowed like a candelabrum. . . ."] Contrary to the impression given by the
prosaic temporality of "still," the torso's dazzling gleam does not shine as
something left over of the originally integral form; it comes forth only by
means of that form's fragmentation. Only because eyesight is lacking to this
god of phenomenality does what is absent wander into its torso, bringing its
mutilated body to appearance as something extinguished, making the stone
(*Stein*) into a star (*Stern*), the material darkness into the ground of the phenomenal world of objectivity and the poetic world of sound, in whose place
Rilke's poem presents itself, in its melodic perfection. Just as the beholder
standing before the torso of Apollo becomes something seen, because this torso
itself has become its missing "unheard-of head"—"denn da ist keine Stelle,/
die dich nicht sieht" ["for there is no place in it/that does not see you"]—so
this "unheard-of head" becomes in the poem something heard. In its place the
poem states the imperative of the glance that falls from the torso onto the
reader: "Du musst dein Leben ändern" ["You must change your life."] But how
else change than according to the measure of that inversion which the reader,
who has moved under the imperative of art, has experienced in the shape of
Apollo, brought to appearance and sound by fragmentation? The poem's language and its object have interpenetrated one another so deeply that the one, in
a further inversion, has stepped into the place of the other: the object itself has
become the poem, the poem its object. "You must change your life." Change
your life you must—and here the imperative is at the same time a constative of
necessity, because the resounding glance of the poem itself has become the
subject of a life mutilated in its finitude, and turns its finitude into the fulfilled
perfection of sound and form. The poem is imperative because it is, by virtue of
the figure of inversion it describes and runs through, *necessary* in the strict
sense of *not-wendig*, deflecting need. It transforms the necessity of being mere
fragments into the virtue of ordaining the law of the whole. Only where the
artwork falls to pieces can its sheer form, *ordine inverso*, come forth. The
poem's ethical mandate for living is also delivered in this turnabout, for the life
of what is seen (apostrophized in the *Du*) already stands, as finite, under the law
the poem lays down for its object: having to be, as a fragment, already an other,

5. Quoted from R. M. Rilke, *Sämtliche Werke*, ed. Ernst Zinn (Frankfurt am Main: Insel
Verlag, 1955), v. 1, 557. A translation into English verse may be found in *New Poems*, trans. J. B.
Leishman (New York: New Directions, 1964).

6. Paul de Man has shown this in his text on Rilke in *Allegories of Reading* (New Haven: Yale
University Press, 1979); the following interpretation is indebted to him in various respects.

namely the production of the whole. Thus, the imperative, stating the necessary consequence of the figure of inversion, is also the *restitutio ad integrum* of that center of *Archaischer Torso Apollos*, "jener Mitte, die die Zeugung trug" ["that center that bore the procreation."] The fact that it was once there, though as little known as the "unheard-of head," and that all that remains now is a smile the torso directs at the place that *bore* it, lends the whole text a nostalgic trait. But the fact that this center secures undistorted hearing in the imperative of the production of the whole, and guarantees the entire energy of a subjectivity become sound and appearance precisely as something absent, lends Rilke's inversion poem the pathos of a finitude that shows itself capable of virtually infinite reproduction. The phallic substratum of subjectivity emerges in it with an almost compelling force. The archaic torso of Apollo is the *archē* of a *whole* generation of art. Rilke's latest poems are the first to turn toward a finitude that no longer admits pathos, an absence which does not submit to inversion into pure presence, which resists its transformation into form and resounding signification.

Paul Celan, whose exact acquaintance with Rilke's poetry has been copiously documented, adheres to this tradition. Scarcely any figure in his early and middle lyrics asserts itself with such open urgency as the figure of inversion. But it is characteristic of the position of these lyrics in the history of philosophy—if it is still possible to speak in an unmodified way, with reference to Celan, of history, of philosophy, and of position—that they radicalize this figure to abstract purity, no longer tolerating any ornamental gleam, but seeking ultimately to surpass and to abandon the figure by means of a procedure that is only inadequately designated by the formulation "inversion of inversion." In the early collection of aphorisms and parables Celan published in 1949, in the Zurich *Die Tat*, under the progammatic title *Gegenlicht* ["Antilight"], the judgment that "The embrace lasts only as long as love despairs of it" takes up a position, against the mere concept of unification, in behalf of its concrete realization, which has the potential of pushing its general concept into doubt and into division. In the sentence "The Day of Judgment had come, and in the quest for the foulest of deeds, the cross was nailed to Christ," the apocalypse appears as the very turnabout in which the cross, mere instrument of desecration, becomes itself the object of violation and man becomes irredeemably devalued through his own instrumentalizing. Further, the dictum of Heraclitus is turned against itself in the sentence: " 'Everything flows away': even this thought, and does it not bring everything back to a standstill?" If everything flows away, then so does this thought, which is now on this account already something other, and it can only maintain the flux of all things if it also stands still for them. This dictum can therefore be a universal proposition only when its performance denies the universality of its constative aspect. In this as in the other inversions *Gegenlicht* exhibits, the possibility and the persistence of general judgments and concepts—in which a truth, an insight, or even only a stable signification is expected to be contained—is cast into doubt by its own inner logic. If murder and movement present themselves as negations of existence and dignity, then Celan's inversions negate the remainder of a positive which inhabits its negativity, thereby preventing any harmonizing mediation. In this respect, these are also in no way inversions of inversion in the sense of a dialectical setting aright of the inverted world (*verkehrte Welt*), not a return to its authentic form. Celan's world, as is apparent in the thought of the cross nailed to Christ, is one of perfect ignominy, and the light his texts cast on it is one that is indebted to this very world. It is light only as antilight, and that is the same as darkness. In a reflection that reminds one of the Kabbalistic theory of *zimzum*, the self-enfolding of nothingness, Celan writes: "Don't fool yourself: not even this last lamp gives off light anymore—the darkness round about has been absorbed into itself."[7] If there is still a light and if there is still a language in which this light is imparted, it is not as positive phenomenality and not as the remains of an original logos, but as the empty brightness and the dried-up word that first find space when darkness is absorbed by itself. There is no light that would not be, in this sense, contrary to the ordinary representations of naive consciousness, even of dialectic, merely the lack of darkness. Linguistic signs are not acts of reference adjoined to the representations of autonomous subjects; nor are they the self-realization of their objectivity. In the ellipse of Celan's inversions they are only the barren space cleared by a muteness lost in itself. Like the place of language, so its presence—itself what is apocalyptic in its last moment—is not a primary fact of reason, but the secondary effect of a self-contraction of absence.

The second to last cycle in Celan's second volume of poems, *Mohn und Gedächtnis*, bears the title "Gegenlicht," like the early collection of aphorisms. The last poem in this cycle, a love poem, treats the place of the language of love:

> Der Tauben weisseste flog auf: ich darf dich lieben!
> Im leisen Fenster schwankt die leise Tür.
> Der stille Baum trat in die stille Stube.
> Du bist so nah, als weiltest du nicht hier.

---

7. Celan's texts are cited from the five volume *Gesammelte Werke*, ed. Beda Allemann (Frankfurt am Main: Suhrkamp Verlag, 1983). The first numeral refers to the volume, the second number to the page number. Translations from Celan are more or less original throughout; translations already existing in English and French have provided indispensable guidance. For "Stimmen," cf. *Speech-Grille and Selected Poems*, trans. Joachim Neugroschel (New York: E. P. Dutton & Co., 1971), 81; and *Prose Writings and Selected Poems*, trans. Walter Billeter and Jerry Glenn (Carlton, Vic: Paper Castle, 1977). For "Der Reisekamarad," cf. *Paul Celan: Poems*, trans. Michael Hamburger (New York: Persea Books, 1980), 63; and *Chicago Review* 29:3 (1978), 45. For *Radix, Matrix*, cf. Cid Corman, "18 Poems," *Caterpillar* 8–9 (1969), 16; *La Rose de personne*, trans. Martine Broda (Paris: Le Nouveau Commerce, 1979), 65 and *Poems*, 153–55. For "Ein Wurfholz," cf. *La Rose de personne*, 93. For "*A la pointe acérée,*" cf. *La Rose de personne*, 83–85; and *Poems*, 161.

Aus meiner Hand nimmst du die grosse Blume:
sie ist nicht weiss, nicht rot, nicht blau—doch nimmst du sie.
Wo sie nie war, da wird sie immer bleiben.
Wir waren nie, so bleiben wir bei ihr. [1, 61]

The whitest of doves ascended in flight: I could love you!
In the soft window swings the soft door.
The still tree stepped into the still room.
You are as close as if you were not lingering here.

From my hand you take the large flower:
it is not white, not red, not blue—still, you take it.
Where it was not, there will it ever remain.
We never were; so we remain with it.

The poem, relatively classical and almost didactic in its construction, describes a linear progression of interwoven formations. In accord with the seemingly late romantic metaphor of elevation, that of the ascending dove, it brings together—most likely in reference to the reflected image in the windowpane—first two openings of space, window and door, and then outer and inner spaces, nearness and distance, so as to address (in the last line of the first stanza) the nearness of the beloved as the appearance of a distance: "You are as close as if you were not lingering here." The law of inversion—the greater the distance, the closer the shape—finds similar formulation in *Die Niemandsrose*. In *Chymisch* ["Chymous"] the large, gray sister-shape is said to be "wie alles Verlorene nahe" ["near as all that is lost"] (1, 277); in *Stumme Herbstgerüche* ["Mute Autumn Smells"], the second stanza runs: *Eine fremde Verlorenheit war/gestalthaft zugegen, du hättest/beinah/gelebt*. (1, 223) ["A strange lostness/attended in bodily shape; you might/almost/have lived."] While a tonal severity is produced in these later texts by the abstracta, by the attempt, by the adversative connotation of *zugegen* and the simple *beinah* of the living shape—a tone announcing a shift in the figure of inversion itself—in the text from "Gegenlicht," the harsh distance is dissolved in the seductive *melos* of the smooth language. To be sure, the flower that the beloved receives from the hand of the speaker already becomes, in its attributes (negative throughout), a flower of nothing and no one. The inversion of distance into proximity is radicalized in it to that of absence into presence, which becomes manifest in the line "Where it never was, there will it ever remain," even if it appears softened by the tense shift between "was" and "remain." The poem reaches the extreme of radicality in its last line, where it states the nonexistence of the "we" and draws from it, according to the logic of inversion, the consequence that we remain with that flower which remains forever; that the empty "we," in analogy to that empty flower, has changed into eternally lingering subsistance: "We never were; so we remain with it."

If the "blaue Blume" of Novalis was still a symbol of the universal poeticization of the world, so this early flower of Celan's—which is not blue and
also bears no other color, but shines nonetheless, in its absence, like none but
the flowers of Mallarmé—is no less a symbol: that of the poeticization of lack.
In the best symbolic tradition, the lingering presence of poetry and the unification of I and you in We emerges from this *flos rhetoricus negativum* and comes
to the surface. In the language of this flower, which is certainly not metaphorical in any traditional sense, but surely rather meta-metaphorical, which lays
bare in its extremity imagistic language's mechanism of translation—trope,
turning and reversal par excellence—in the language of this flower, what is
divided has been reassembled and what never was has been reversed into subsisting being, because this language itself is brought from a nothingness to the
status of something that remains. But this transformation depends on the
categorical certainty of being perceived, received, and retained; and only in this
perception [*Vernehmen*], which establishes the unity of giver and receiver, is
the gift of nothing transformed into substantial being: "From my hand you
take the large flower: it is not white, not red, not blue—still, you take it." Were
this taking-up to fail to come about, were the gift not to arrive at its destination, there would be no language, no transformation, no remaining. The inversion of nothingness into being would be impossible. This possibility of its
denial in the face of nonbeing, this possibility of the impossibility of its own
existence opens in Celan's poem only in the dash before "*doch*," in the interruption of the language of tropes, in the mute hesitation of receiving and
perceiving. This graphic pause—Celan later found for such a moment the word
Verhoffen [a state of expectancy, as that of an animal startled at perceiving a
hunter]—opens in the poetic speaking a hole which the logic of inversion is
powerless to close. It opens a spacing that cannot be reversed into nearness, a
difference that cannot be turned into unity, a deaf place that cannot be reversed
into the topos of a corresponding signification. This place is that of an absence,
a place that must remain unattainable for an absence which would allow itself
to be transformed into our own, into the presence of our own language.

As small as this hole in the tropological system of Celan's poem may be, it
makes clear a danger that threatens many of his early texts: that of rendering
nothingness positive, of letting in absence merely as the negative of presence,
of wanting to transform it into everlasting being by the power of language.
However doubtingly and sneeringly even these texts sometimes deny the possibility of such a reversal, they still remain unquestionably committed to its
idea. The emphatic closing lines of *Spät und Tief* ["Late and Deep"] show this:
*es komme . . . /der geharnischte Windstoss der Umkehr, der mitternächtige
Tag,/es komme, was niemals noch war!//Es komme ein Mensch aus dem
Grabe* (1, 36). [let come . . . /the stinging gust of reversal,/the midnight
day,/let come what never was!//Let a man come forth from the tomb.] It is
shown in the oxymora of "rust-born knives" (1, 68), of the lapidated stone (1,
51), and of the "bloom of withered hours" (1, 55). All these oxymora, paradoxes

and inversions take as their subject the movement of time, and in this they also take up in a radical way the problems of the philosophy of subjectivity and of the great literature since Romanticism. Time, as the formal unity of contradictory predicates, supplies the transcendental-esthetic ground for the figure of inversion. The rhetoric of inversion is the rhetoric of temporality, to the extent that the latter is also represented as the unity of what is differentiated within it. The lyrics of the young Celan are shot through with this concept of time, even where they push it to its utmost limit.

Under the Nietzschean title *Praise of Distance,* Celan collected a whole network of antinomian formulations, whose intention is not simply the presentation of unity, but, dialectically, that of the unity of unity and division: *"Abtrünnig, erst bin ich treu./Ich bin du, wenn ich ich bin"* ["In apostasy only am I faithful./I am you, if I am I."] And: *"Ein Garn fing ein Garn ein:/wir scheiden umschlungen.//Im Quell deiner Augen/erwürgt ein Gehenkter den Strang"* (1,33). ["A net caught a net:/we part entangled.//In the source of your eyes/a hanged man strangles the halter."] Only apostasy, betrayal and schism joined together, only the dynamic of difference gives the power of uniting, and the differentiated come together only in the separation of time. *"Im Quell deiner Augen/hält das Meer sein Versprechen"* ["In the source of your eyes/ the sea keeps its promise"]: the promise, given over to its redemption in temporal distance, is already "held" by the sea in the eyes of the beloved, it is already fulfilled and is the—oxymoronically—fulfilled speaking of the poem in which what is temporally dissociated stands together in the form of negative unity. Celan's poetry attempts to speak out of the negativity of time itself; but from a negativity that, as much as it buries the marks of transitoriness from what is said and disfigures it as a bare allegory of speaking, still remains the center of the mediation between source and sea, presence and pastness, I and you, the promise and its redemption in the poem. The promise is held because transitoriness and presence are held together by the thread that runs through them, the thread of time, which pulls them apart. Because time, by means of its negativity and not in spite of it, is the strongest power of synthesis, it is also the ground of all the inversion-figures collected together in Celan's early volumes, in greatest concentration in *Mohn und Gedächtnis.* For inversion is nothing other than the negativizing of the negative, and by the power of its negativity, the strict linkage of what is disjoined: it is the movement of time itself, to the extent that this—as in Hegel, but not for him alone—is determined as the continuum of negativity referred to itself and furthermore as the negative unity of the differentiated. The language of inversion is the language of a time represented as a continuum of negativity. In it I becomes you at the very moment it renounces its trust in you, parts I from you in the very moment that they embrace one another. I and you, in their connection to each other and in their self-relation, are conceived as temporal moments, as moments of time for which a positive unity is unattainable, and for which the negative of its parting is all the more compelling. This same negativity is also stamped upon the speaking that the poem helps attain expression. In it, a promise is first held in such a way that the corresponding oath is broken: *"Hier werf ich/ . . .von mir . . . den Glanz eines Schwures"* ["Here I cast/ . . . /from me . . . the gleam of an oath."] Only apostasy from the word that has been given can fulfill it; only the broken is the kept promise. And thus one might also read the central metaphor of *Garne der Fischer der Irrsee* ["Nets of the Fisherman of Err Sea"], which organizes the whole texture of the poem, as the spinning out of the metaphor of the seaman's yarn, a colloquial turn of phrase that refers to falsehood, deceit, and fantastical fabrication. The promise Celan's poem speaks of, which Celan's poem also itself makes, is a ruse, a promise leading, like the sea of errancy, into errancy, a promise that is fulfilled only in revealing itself as a ruse.

The language of time is not that of a simple refering that could, as itself something subsisting, relate or refer to stable and durable existences. Nor is it the language of deception, which permits one to hold on to the illusion of a realm free of deception. The language of time is the one that denies for itself the denial of its truth-content,[8] that fulfills the false promise through its breach. Thus it is the language of a temporality that is enabled, by virtue of the negation it can potentially repeat to infinity and by virtue of its related continuity, to speak the truth under the conditions of delusion and to speak enduringly under the conditions of disappearance: the endurance of time and of its language. To become one with the movement of time and of negativity, in such a way as to become itself the continuum of time belongs to the deepest intentions of Celan's language in *Mohn und Gedächtnis.* The loving unification of time and language can come about only on account of the fact that both, by dint of their negativity, are energies of unification. The expired, the neglected, the buried: "blind wie der Blick, den wir tauschen,/küsst es die Zeit auf den Mund" [blind as the glance we exchange,/it kisses time on the mouth."] (1, 57). It is time itself that sings and speaks; it is no longer an object of discourse but the subject that delivers it: "Die Zeit, aus feinem Sande, singt in meinem Armen:/ . . . . . . /noch einmal mit dem Tod im Chor die Welt herübersingen,/ . . . " (1, 69) ["Time, from fine sand, sings in my arms:/ . . . . . . /once again in chorus with death to sing the world hither."] The imago of the beloved projected by Celan's poems bears the features of time as much as all the other subjects that find a way into his texts. But this temporal structure befits them only because time is the subject [*Subjekt*] and form of the process of that language in which these subjects [*Sujets*] are presented: " . . . ein Wort, von Sensen gesprochen, . . . " (1, 70) [" . . . a word spoken by scythes"]. Not only does time pass away for the thing, with every word that intends that thing; the word—or the name—is itself the cut by which time does away with the stable existence of ideas.

---

8. Cf. also Paul de Man's groundlaying work *"The Rhetoric of Temporality,"* reprinted in *Blindness and Insight: Essays in the Rhetoric of Contemporary Criticism,* second edition, revised (Minneapolis: University of Minnesota Press, 1983), 187–229.

Nonetheless, in its negativity the language of time is essentially positive: it brings what is said into the finite world and into earthly life. The death effected by the word belongs to the conditions of living: "Aus Herzen und Hirnen/spiressen die Halme der Nacht,/und ein Wort, von Sensen gesprochen,/neigt sie ins Leben." (1, 70) ["Out of hearts and brains/shoot the stalks of night,/and a word, spoken by scythes,/bends them into life.")] The semantic potential of the language that can refer to objects and objective relations in the world of experience is indebteded to its temporalizing as much as is this experienced world itself. Even before its signifying function, what is proper to language is a function of temporization and of temporalization. What Kant says of time is no less valid for temporal language in Celan: it is the formal condition a priori of representation in general. To this degree, Celan's poems—transcendental as only those of Hölderlin, and to a lesser extent Rilke's—speak of the conditions of their own possibility. They do not denominate something determined, but rather bring to language the ground for the determination of speaking itself: its property of temporization (*Zeitigungscharakter*). But in a significant difference from Kant, temporizing language in Celan is not the form of ideational representation that makes it possible to project images of the world and individual ideas, but the very form of alteration that makes the subjects themselves figures of time, thereby robbing them of the possibility of acting as stable subjects of language for the world and its appearances: "Stumm wie . . . (die Halme der Nacht)/wehn wir der Welt entgegen:/ . . . " ["Mute as . . . (the stalks of night)/we waft towards the world:/. . . . "] We *have* no language which we could utilize as an instrument, but *are* only what has been spoken, wafted into a world by the cutting of language, into a world where we must remain mute because there too time takes the word out of our mouths. "Was wir jetzt sind,/schenken die Stunden der Zeit.//Munden wir ihr? Kein Laut und kein Licht/schlüpft zwischen uns, es zu sagen." [" . . . What we are now,/the hours of time grant.//Does it savor us? No sound and no light slips between us to say so"] (1, 70). The word of time does not refer to objective givens or to abstract meanings, it *is* only as the withdrawal of objectivity and meaning. The language of finitude is the chronic withdrawal of language's referential and semantic functions, since with each of its words that bend ideas into life, the world and the being of such spoken things are brought to the point of vanishing. In addressing its own ground, Celan's poetry can state the condition of its own possibility only as the condition of the impossibility of its stable, subsisting semantic content: it opens onto the abyss of its futility. "Poetry," as Celan later formulates it in the *Meridian* speech, "poetry, ladies and gentlemen: this pronouncement of the infinitude of sheer mortality and vanity!" (3, 200).

The standing of the subject and the stability of its discourse, which should still have been assured by the transcendental turn, are shaken by the temporalizing of language and of everything that can enter its realm. The *ordo inversus* which was to have founded the order of subjectivity, and which already fell into difficulties in Kant, with the philosophical discovery of finitude and of a merely finite faculty of human presentation, no longer offers any dependable guarantee for the presentation and linguistic fixation of a world and its possible meaning, when it can be said and must be thought that the scythe—this allegorical prop of death and of time—wields language. The only unity and the only continuum we can speak of henceforth is that of disappearance, of a negativity with no center and no sublation. All the same, the lyrics in Celan's *Mohn und Gedächtnis* still recover their formal unity from this structure of negativity. An inversion-figure like "Blicklos/schweigt nun dein Aug in mein Aug sich" ["Sightless/your eye is now silenced in mine"] (1, 70) still clings, in spite of the negation of language and appearance that is expressed in it, to the close connection between my eye and yours, and maintains, in their intimate unity, the success of communication beyond language and sight. However, while the figure of the inverse order persists, and with it the form of communication, its substance, as pure transitoriness, is consumed, its contents voided, and its ground turned into an abyss. The inverted world is not, as in Hegel, a world stood on the head as its unshakable ground, but one that is held tenaciously in the abyss of temporality, a world become untenable. Celan expresses his perception of the same abyss in a formulation from Büchner's *Lenz* (which like many others in his texts has a anti-Hegelian drift), in a quibbling turn of phrase from the *Meridian* (1961), a turn he imparts to this figure of reversal, which had already become "classical" in Büchner's time. In Büchner it is said of Lenz: "He went on indifferently, nothing lay in his way, now up, now down. He felt no fatigue, except that it was at times annoying that he could not walk on his head."[9] Celan's quite deservedly famous comment on this expression runs: "he who walks on his head, ladies and gentlemen, he who walks on his head has heaven beneath him as an abyss" (3, 195). This abyss—it is not the bottomlessness of the sky and what a run-down philosophy would like to see in it as transcendence, but the untenability of the transcendental forms of our ideation itself—opens up, in ever greater disclosure, in Celan's linguistic techniques and their poetological reflection throughout the late fifties and the sixties.

If language is nothing more than the articulation of the withdrawal of the world, then, no longer capable of designating it as an object, it becomes itself a figure of the plunge. If it is unable to stand the world on the head of its poetic presentation, if it is instead nothing more than the cut and step of a ceaseless passing away, then it is itself drawn into the movement of upending, and it becomes the vertiginous whirl of disfiguration, in which nothing can any longer mean what it says. Just as the signifying functions break down in the face of an "object" such as the abyss, death, nothingness, so too, infected as it were by

---

9. Georg Büchner, *Werke und Briefe,* Gesamtausgabe, ed. F. Bergemann (Weisbaden: Insel Verlag, 1958), 85. Cf. *Complete Plays and Prose,* trans. C. R. Mueller, (New York: Hill and Wang, 1963), 141; or *Leonce and Lena/ Lenz/ Woyzeck,* trans. Michael Hamburger (Chicago: University of Chicago Press, 1972), 37.

this death, the conventionalized units of meaning, the words and the sentences, the strophes—they too are turns—and the unity of the text dissolve, leaving room for an altered form of speech and for the interruption of speech itself. One of the privileged deconstructive figures in Celan is paronomasia.[10] In explicit instances of paronomasia—as when "Zangen" [forceps] is placed alongside "Zungen der Sehnsucht" [tongues of longing], the "Verbrannte" [the incinerated] alongside the "Verbannten" [the exiled], "Schläfe" [temples] alongside "schlaflos" [sleepless], "Erzväter" [the patriarchs] alongside "Erzflitter" [the glitter of ores], "blutende Ohr" [the bloody ear] alongside "blühseligen Botschaft" [blessedly prosperous tidings]—the unity of the word appears to be brought into oscillation by the phonetic proximity of words, in which one affects the other with its semantic potential. In Huhediblu the lines themselves say how they will be and what they will be read as: " . . . du liest,/dies hier, dies:/Dis-/parates—: . . . " [" . . . you read,/this here, this:/dis-/parates—: . . . "] (1, 275–76). They are and are read as disparation: as the diversification and as the disappearance of the monosemic body of the word. In inexplicit instances of paronomasia, another word is produced by a minimal alteration of the phonetic or graphic form of a word that does not itself appear. This other word acts as the distorted echo of the first: thus "rauchdünn" [smoke-thin] replaces hauchdünn [filmy, "thin as breath"] (1, 228), "Morgen-Lot" [morning plummet] stands in for Morgenrot [dawn], "Ferse" [heels] for Verse [verses] (2, 25), "Pestlaken" [plague shroud] for Bettlaken [bedsheet] (2, 153), and "Datteln" [edible dates] for Daten [calendar dates] (2, 134). If in explicit paranomasia the alteration is manifest and the semantic destabilization is confined to the localized zone of the word that actually appears in the text, in the inexplicit paranomasia the corresponding word remains latent, its form uncertain, and exposes every word in the text to the possibility of being an alteration of a lost paradigm resolutely drawing back from rational or divinatory reconstruction. Each of these words presents itself—if not exclusively, then at least primarily—as the disfiguration of something secret, a limine as the translation of something mute. What Celan writes elsewhere about a forgotten

10. Peter Szondi was probably the first to recognize it as such, in "Poetry of Constancy—Poetik der Beständigkeit," Schriften, ed. Jean Bollack (Frankfurt am Main: Suhrkamp Verlag, 1978), v. 2, esp. 338. Szondi though, not unjustly on the whole, places it as "phonological near-identity" under the rubric of unification and constancy. I read in paronomasia, as it is used by Celan, a mode of the diversification of linguistic unities by means of their own dynamic. Ferdinand de Saussure, in his search for a suitable concept for the principle of construction of "saturnine" verses, finally designated as anagrammatic, considered the term hypogram and made this remark: "Paronomase comes so close with its principle that . . . " Jean Starobinski supplies the following commentary: "It is curious that Saussure . . . should not have fixed his attention more closely upon paronomasia. Perhaps he feared . . . that this 'figure of speech' might imperil the aspect of discovery which for him was attached to the theory of anagrams." Les Mots sous les mots (Paris: Gallimard, 1971), 32. Words Upon Words: The Anagrams of Ferdinand de Saussure, trans. Olivia Emmet (New Haven: Yale University Press, 1979), 19. Paul de Man has extensively commented and expanded Saussure's considerations on the hypogram in "Hypogram and Inscription," Diacritics 11:4 (1981).

word is true of these: "Dies ist ein Wort, das neben den Worten einherging,/ein Wort nach dem Bilde des Schweigens, . . ." (1, 92). ["This is a word that entered next to the words,/a word in the image of silence"].

In the *Meridian* speech, Celan cited, as a parallel to the abyssal maxim drawn from Büchner's *Lenz*, the second section ("Come on your hands to us") from the programmatic opening sequence of *Sprachgitter*. Its first text reads:

> *Stimmen*, ins Grün
> der Wasserfläche geritzt.
> Wenn der Eisvogel taucht,
> sirrt die Sekunde:
>
> Was zu dir stand
> an jedem der Ufer,
> es tritt
> gemäht in ein anderes Bild. [1, 147]
>
> Voices, nicked in
> the green of the watery reach.
> When the kingfisher dives,
> the second buzzes:
>
> What stood to you
> on each of the banks,
> it steps
> mowed into another image.

The figure of inversion, imaged explicitly in the text that follows sequentially, is also latent in this one. The objective world of the embankment, its image helpfully turned toward the "you" who is addressed, enters the water-mirror's image—like the voices, which are nicked, averted and untrusted, in the watery reach—upended and stood on its head. This transformation—a metamorphosis like the one Alcyone undergoes when she is changed into a "kingfisher" as she dives after her drowned husband[11]—is occasioned by a cutting. What is trusted and familiar steps "mowed" into another image: mowed, that is, by the cut of *Sekunde,* here understood in its etymological sense—by the *secare* of time. Time changes the voices into the writing of the water-mirror, changes the familiar images of the objective world into the averted, upended, and afflicted images of the literary text. The text offers them no ground beyond that of an *unda* in which they sink away and, following a later paronomasia, sing away. The same displacement underlies the language in which the poem articulates this transformation of a stable image into one that is upended. Not only

---

11. Cf. Ovid, *Metamorphoses*, 11, 720–48. In this connection one also thinks of Celan's remark from September 1966, that naming occurs in the depths of language, that *taufen* and *tauchen* stand in an intimate relation to one another. Reported by Dietlind Meinecke in *Wort und Name bei Paul Celan* (Bad Homvurg: Verlag Gehlen, 1970), 189.

is the metaphor of reaping drawn from the metaphor sleeping in a foreign word (in the *secare* of *Sekunde*)—a practice Celan follows to abundance;[12] this word, *die Sekunde* [the second or the moment], is itself to be cut and read as *diese Kunde* [this message, information, impartment].[13] This possibility is suggested in the phonetic combination of *s* and *i* in *sirrt*, which provokes a corresponding contamination of the *ie* and *Se* that follow; it is also suggested by the colon after *Sekunde*, which allows the second quatrain to appear as the content of this message. *Die Sekunde—diese Kunde*, the second—this impartment: it is time, as something which cuts, that informs the inversion of the imaged world. But this temporal information effects the inversion only by also subjecting the second, the temporal atom, to its own principle of fission, by splitting the unity of its impartment. What stands on separate banks—"on each of the banks"—is brought together by the very principle of sundering which begets an "other image." *DieSeKunde* is not just a metamorphosis but also metaphor in its strict sense; it is the motion of metaphorizing itself: stepping across and carrying over. Every image and turn in Celan's text follows this alteration, dictated by its excentric center, *dieSeKunde*. They are not

---

12. Cf. for example the valuable studies by Elizabeth Petuchowski, devoted to polylingual wordplay in Celan: "A New Approach to Paul Celan's 'Argumentum e Silentio'" and "Bilingual and Multilingual *Wortspiele* in the Poetry of Paul Celan," both in *Deutsche Vierteljahresschrift für Literaturwissenschaft und Geistesgeschichte*, 52 (1978), 111ff. and 635ff. The young Celan's proclivity for wordplay with inversion is documented in an illuminating piece by Petre Solomon, "Paul Celan's Bukarester Aufenthalt," in *Zeitschrift für Kulturaustausch* (Stuttgart: Institut für Auslandsbeziehungen), 32: 3 (1982), 222–26.

13. One finds a comparable manipulation of words, also in the volume *Sprachgitter*, in *Ein Tag und noch einer* ["A Day and One More"]: the expression "der Ast, rasch an den Himmel geschrieben" ["The branch,/hastily scrawled on the sky"] contains the word *Astra*, written apart and dismembered by the line break and comma. Before it finds in *Leuchter* [candlestick] a relatively unambiguous semantic equivalent, it is repeated in disguise once more: "ein Morgen/sprang ins Gestern hinauf" ["a tomorrow/leapt up unto yesterday"]: that is, *Gestern* can also, in this context and with reference to its "hinauf" ["up"], be read as "Ge-Stern" (the noun *Stern*, "star," prefixed to convey generality. Cf. Celan's pun *per c-aspera ad astra*, reported by Israel Chalfen in *Paul Celan: Eine Biographie seiner Jugend* (Frankfurt am Main: Insel Verlag, 1983), 96.

In a poem from *Fadensonnen*, Celan gave the poetic recipe for the preparation and reading of his texts, and not just his: *Kleide die Worthöhlen aus/ mit Pantherhäuten,//erweitere sie, fellhin und fellher,/sinnhin und sinnher,//gib ihnen Vorhöfe, Kammern, Klappen/und Wildnesse, parietal,//und lausch ihrem zweiten/und jeweils zweiten und zweiten/Ton.* ["Shell the word-caves/with panther skins,//expand them, infur and ecspelt,/adsense and absense,//give them vestibules, chambers, shutters/and jungles, parietal,//and listen for their secondary/and in each case second and second/tone."] Here too we have an inversion of familiar ideas. Aside from the duplicity of the word "auskleiden," which in isolation can mean both "dress" and "undress," the external, the skin of the *panther*, is transferred as sense into the inner space of the word, into the *antre*. The sense is only a—but then a foreign, a second—skin, an inner mask. Sound, as what is always second, is in each case further distanced than the audible second, infinitely secondary, it too a *second*. Celan's later poems are written out of this second and for its sake. They are *dated*, as finite language, upon the second, in a most *profane* sense. The inversion of the secondary into the primary, of the outer into the inner is always effected in them so that they expand the character of the secondary instead of domesticating it. Thus we can only "understand" his texts "from afar." *Auskleiden* is also a metaphor, even one of the possible meanings of *Auslegen* (to interpret). To this extent the poem practices the hermeneutic operation it describes.

metaphors for representation but rather metaphors of metaphorizing; not images of a world, but images of the production of images; not the transcription of voices, but the writing of the nicked voices of poetry itself. They inscribe themselves as the script of alteration, by themselves exposed to this very alteration. They write—they *are dieSekunde:* the incisive changing of words in which the phenomenal and linguistic world is opened onto a caesura which none of the shapes of this world can conjure because these first arise only through it.

The second, this impartment, of Celan's poem is the self-disrupting, self-dispersing and disseminating speaking of language. The immanent paronomasis of its homonymy, its differentiation and redistribution of segments of language does not so much articulate a particular sense or cluster of senses—though it does that too, in expressing the intimate linkage between linguisticality and temporality—nor does it turn toward an original meaning whose representation it would be. Rather, it attends to the conditions of possible meaning in general, meaning it engraves with its segmenting articulation, together with the stigma of its derivation from *dieSeKunde.* The privative *se* of *Sekunde* cuts this impartment (*Kunde*), and so language in general, from the unambiguous meaning it could still claim, as an impartment. The second dictates the law of temporal, logical, and linguistic secondariness—and its own as well. As it opens Celan's poem with an unvoiced bilingual (German-French) inversion—*Stimmen, ins Grün: Stimmen, in vert*—so it opens the speech of the interval, of the second between different languages and of the interval of speaking itself.

This impartment, *ordine inverso*—has nothing to impart. It states nothing else beyond that, how, and why it has nothing to state but its own secession. It is as such the self-revocation of the upending movement of conversion (*Verkehrung*) with which—itself mowed down—it enters into another image that no longer belongs to or admits a "you." Nothing could be more alien; for it is the graven image of a fundamental alteration, the alteration of the ground into groundlessness.

The figure of inversion was to guarantee language's semantic function, under the conditions of finitude. But if the semantic function is suspended by a radicalizing of the inversion which makes language into the image of its own interruption, then language's ability to communicate is also put into question. It can no longer be thought as the exchange between two or more already constituted subjects of a common language; rather, since language can only be language in the first place as the parting of speech from itself, it must be thought as the im-parting of speech (*die Mit-teilung des Sprechens*), through which, unstable as they may be, its subjects are first constituted. The fact that this im-parting[14] can no longer be a mediation in a shared center, can no longer

---

14. Helpful hints for treating the problem of language as an im-parting that precedes any reduction and idealizing of communication, hints however which have yet to be worked out, are

be communication within a common medium; that in it there is no longer a place either for the universalizing of language or for its instrumentalizing as a means, finds expression in *Radix, Matrix*, one of the longer texts of *Die Niemandsrose*. It may be advantageous for the understanding of this very difficult text to recollect that language, for Celan, even in *Mohn und Gedächtnis*—and especially his mother's language, his mother tongue[15]—also had an instrumental character: that of help and protection. He is at his most unreservedly positive in the poem *Der Reisekamarad* ["The Travelling Companion"]:

> Deiner Mutter Seele schwebt voraus.
> Deiner Mutter Seele hilft die Nacht umschiffen, Riff um Riff.
> Deiner Mutter Seele peitscht die Haie vor dir her.   ·
>
> Dieses Wort ist deiner Mutter Mündel.
> Deiner Mutter Mündel teilt dein Lager, Stein um Stein.
> Deiner Mutter Mündel bückt sich nach der Krume Lichts. [1, 66]
>
> Your mother's soul hovers ahead.
> Your mother's soul helps navigate night, reef after reef.
> Your mother's soul whips on the sharks before you.
>
> This word is your mother's ward.
> Your mother's ward shares your couch, stone by stone.
> Your mother's ward stoops for the crumb of light.

The poem—"this word"—stands under the guardianship of the mother who helps it steer clear of the danger of being struck dumb, helps it turn away from darkness and preserve what remains of light. It is one of the most lucid poems Celan wrote. But to the extent that, in accord with the steadfastness of the mother tongue, it repeats one and the same syntactical paradigm with only minimal variation, it is also one of his most spellbound. Precisely this paradigm, the matrix of language which guarantees the strength of coherence and comprehension, is forfeited in *Radix, Matrix*. It is a poem of the loss of the mother tongue, of the median and its ability to mediate.

---

given in Walter Benjamin's essay "Über die Sprache überhaupt und die Sprache des Menschen" (*Gesammelte Werke* [Frankfurt am Main: Suhrkamp Verlag, 1977], 2, 1, 142). Cf. "On Language as such and on the Language of Man," in *Reflections*, ed. Peter Demetz (New York: Harcourt Brace Jovanovitch, 1978), 315–16; in Martin Heidegger, *Sein und Zeit (Being and Time)*, s. 34; and more than hints in the untitled introductory text to Maurice Blanchot's book *l'Entretien infini*. I have offered preliminary suggestions toward this problem in a lecture given in 1982 in New York, "Kurze Beantwortung der Frage: Was ist Textualität?" (published in a Swedish translation by Anders Olson in *KRIS* 28, March 1984; in an English version by David Wellbery in *Stanford Literature Review*, Fall 1985). This concept of "Mit-teilung" is also congenial to the concept of "*partage*" which Jean-Luc Nancy has developed masterfully in *Le Partage des voix* (Paris: Galilée, 1982) and "La Communauté désoeuvrée," *Aléa* 4 (Paris, 1983).

15. Israel Chalfen writes in his biography that for Celan's mother, "the German language was more important, and she was careful her whole life to assure that a correct literary German be spoken in her house. She had no patience with the everyday language of Bukovina" (op. cit. 40). And: "she especially liked to read the German classics, and in later years she would vie with her son Paul in citing from favorite authors" (ibid., 31).

RADIX, MATRIX

Wie man zum Stein spricht, wie	As one speaks to the stone, as
du,	you,
mir vom Abgrund her, von	to me from the abyss, from
einer Heimat her Ver-	a homeland
schwisterte, Zu-	tied by blood,
geschleuderte, du,	hurled toward me, you,
du mir vorzeiten,	you me long ago
du mir im Nichts einer Nacht,	you me in the nothing of a night,
du in der Aber-Nacht Be-	you in the counter-night en-
gegnete, du	countered, you
Aber-Du—:	counter-you—:
Damals, da ich nicht da war,	Then, when I was not there,
damals, da du	then, when you
den Acker abschrittst, allein:	paced off the land, alone:
Wer,	Who,
wer wars, jenes	who was it, that
Geschlecht, jenes gemordete, jenes	race, the murdered one, the one
schwarz in den Himmel stehende:	standing black in the sky:
Rute und Hode—?	rod and ball—?
(Wurzel.	(Root.
Wurzel Abrahams. Wurzel Jesse. Niemandes	Root of Abraham. Root of Jesse. No one's
Wurzel—o	root—o
unser.)	ours.)
Ja,	Yes,
wie man zum Stein spricht, wie	as one speaks to the stone, as
du	you
mit meinen Händen dorthin	with my hands there
und ins Nichts greifst, so	and into nothing grasp, so
ist, was hier ist:	is what is here:
auch dieser	even this
Fruchtboden klafft,	receptacle gapes;
dieses	this
Hinab	descent
ist die eine der wild-	is the one of the wild-
blühenden Kronen.	flourishing crowns.
[1, 239]	

Radix, Matrix describes the figure of an impossible dialogue. The first
clause's attempt to give the speaking a determination, by setting the impersonal "one" in a relation to the inorganic "stone," is already suspended with the
insertion of the second part of the sentence by an almost luxuriating digression
in which the I apostrophizes this "you" in a series of pronominations which

collectively touch on all the forms of relation between the "you" and the I. In this way, I inverts the direction of speaking so that it runs along the line of illocution from the I to that "you," though in the beginning of the second clause it still ran from "you" to some indeterminate addressee. The second clause, "as/you"—and with it, the determination of the addressee of *you*'s discourse—remains open even after the end of the first stanza. The sentence it begins finds no conclusion. One finds only inexplicit hints of the possibility that the I could itself be what the discourse of the other addresses, for the series of apostrophes speaks of this "you," as of something tied by blood, hurled up, and encountered, exclusively in its relation to I. This virtual addressee, I, this virtualized I, is however characterized by its parallelism with the stone—the discourse's other addressee—as something mute, something voiceless and indeterminate [*stimm- und bestimmungsloses*] which could not be the subject talking in the poem. In *Gespräch im Gebirg* ["Conversation in the Mountains"], which may have originated contemporaneously with *Radix, Matrix*, Celan writes of the stone: "It doesn't talk, it speaks, and that which speaks, Cousin, talks to nobody, but speaks, because nobody hears it, nobody and Nobody . . . " (3, 171).

Since the determination of the addressee of *you*'s discourse remains suspended in stanza one, we can read in the second stanza, which jumps as it were into the gap in the first, a reprise of the attempt to determine the I. This attempt states at the same time the reason why I did not become the addressee of *you*'s discourse: "Then, when I was not there,/then, when you/paced off the land, alone: . . . ." The you that paces off the field, following an archaic method of determining measurements, determines its place without any I toward which it could turn its discourse. But the second stanza is as well a continuation of the discourse of the I—an I which states its own absence in a voiceless, or at least an indeterminate voice (*unbestimmte Stimme*)—as it is, opened with the colon at the end of the first stanza, the discourse of the you which "at that time . . . was not there" and which I, in its attempt at determination, left alone. This double character of discourse (being both continuation and change) and of the colon (signaling both continuity and disruption) has as its consequence not just the errancy and, on top of that, the diffusion of the you and the I in this text; it also leads to an unsublatable indeterminancy in the structure of speech. This indeterminacy, that of the discourse of the text itself, involves its subject and its addressees as much as its illocutionary character. Nothing is any longer certain in this discourse, nothing is any longer susceptible of determination according to the rules of logic or of its linguistic correlates, if the reciprocal determination of "you" and "I" (as it appeared to classical metaphysics, and even still to dialogics, to be possible as an intersubjective event) is referred back, by means of interruption and immanent muteness, to its lack of an object. The irreconcilable ambiguity of Celan's formulation—in which the absence of the you suspends the I, that of the I suspends the you, and along with it discourse itself is suspended—realizes on the level of composition what the apostrophe says of the you, borrowing from a dialogical terminology: that it is what is "in the nothing of a night . . . encountered." But this "nothing" is as well the space in which the you encounters the I, as it is that which as the you encounters the I—: nothing encounters. Nothing speaks, and it speaks—for the I is also a form of that you—to nothing. As one speaks to the stone, so speaks the stone: to nobody and nothing. The poem, a texture of interrupted illocutionary acts and muteness, thus becomes itself the mute discourse of a stone, a nothing encountered.

In this most radical version of inversion, language no longer converts its own nothingness into the substantial being of appearance, sound, and consciousness, as with Hegel and Rilke. Rather, it converts its literary being, compositionally and semantically, into nothing. This inversion is grounded in the third stanza's questioning after the murdered race (*Geschlecht*). This question too, opened by the colon of the preceding stanza, can pertain just as well to a you asking the I or asking after an I, as it can be I's questioning the you and asking after a you. This question questions undecidably from both to both, and asks for the ground of their commonality. It questions that *Geschlecht*, in which the familial, the geneological, the societal, the sexual and the linguistic unity too would be given and together with this unity the reciprocal determination of speaking subjects in a dialogue, the determination of speaking and language itself. But this qustion is undecidable not just in the sense that it cannot choose either its subject or its addressee, it is also undecidable in the sense of being an impossible, unanswerable question—for it asks after the essence of a race that stands in the heavens, murdered, annihilated, brought to nothing, "black" as "the nothingness of a night." The question itself responds to the indeterminacy of its object, to its own virtual lack of an object, in that it leads (once more after a colon—"who was it, that race . . . :") into an explicative apposition to the question which could be just as much a putting into question of a tentative answer: "rod and ball—?" Rod and ball isolate the sexual aspect of *Geschlecht*, but not, as might appear, its phallic aspect. For *Rute* is the word for *radix*, which stands in Latin not just for the vegetable root, for origin, source, firm ground and soil, but also (as *radix virilis*) for the masculine member. *Hode*, on the other hand, comes from the Latin *cunnus*, the pudenda, and in this respect corresponds to *matrix*, which just as much as *radix* means source, origin, and stem, but in its feminine aspect: ancestress, womb, and uterus. First together, as rod *and* ball, then brought still closer, as in the asyndeton of the title *Radix, Matrix*, as the linking of masculine and feminine sexes, do they become "that *Geschlecht*, the murdered one, the one/standing black in the sky." Only in this linking do they trace the figure of immanent inversion exhibited in the erected abyss.

The question directed at this *Geschlecht*, at this joining of *Geschlechter*—and it is not to be inferred from the text of the poem whether this joining is not itself the murder of it—permits no answer because it lacks an object, because the murdered race it asks after is not the object of a possible representation, even though it and it alone calls for representation. For language would first acquire in the *radix, matrix* not only an object and an addressee but its own ground, its origin and its source, its heritage and the possibility of a future. And only in the race, by virtue of the communality concealed within it, could there be a dialogical mediation between I and you—could there be a communicatory, a determined and determining language. In asking after *radix, matrix*, the poem asks after its own ground. In presenting its question as objectless, it delivers itself up to the abyss of possible meaninglessness, indeterminacy, and incomprehensibility. With a question that is open, not accidentally but structurally, that which questions—"I" or "you," and the language of both—places itself in question and opens up within that which could have counted as a ground: opens itself as an abyss. In the open question, the poem makes itself into an abyss renouncing any possible communality of language, of the race, and announcing nothing more than this renouncing. The language of the poem is *die Sekunde des Geschlechtes*, in which it—cut, murdered—no longer communicates and mediates itself with, but im-parts that which is cut along with it in its nothingness. It is itself the stigma of castration, and in its historical, its most unacceptable form, the stigma of the murder of European Jewry in the extermination camps of the Nazi regime. If, according to Adorno's dictum, "After Auschwitz it became impossible to write poems,"[16] and if Szondi specifies: "After Auschwitz no poem is any longer possible except on the basis of Auschwitz"[17]—then in view of *Radix, Matrix* it is necessary to add that this ground of the poem is an abyss, that it is not the condition of its possibility but rather that of its impossibility, and that the poem is only still capable of speaking because it exposes itself to the impossibility of its speaking. It no longer speaks the language of a race that could be a ground, center, origin, father and mother. Rather, it speaks—uprooted, orphaned (*deradiziert, dematernisiert*)—the language of the murdered. On this account Auschwitz, a name for innumerable unnamables, can never become for it a historically bound fact. Murder cannot become the univocal object of its speaking; it can only be the projection of a questioning that recognizes itself as objectless and mute, and therein as itself a victim of the murder.

Nor does the fourth stanza offer an answer. It stands outside the discourse, as the parentheses fencing it off indicate. It is the discourse of the eradicated root, itself retracted and curtailed in its signification and determinacy by means of its parentheses. "No one's/root—o/ours." What is no one's root is not a root at all, yet by the same stroke, is the root of personal nonexistence. In this root's doubleness—being a root of nothing and itself nothing—the doubleness of *radix* and *matrix* is refracted and so is the doubleness of the nothing

---

16. Theodor W. Adorno, "Kulturkritik und Gesellschaft," in *Prismen* (Frankfurt am Main: Suhrkamp Verlag, 1955), 31; cf. the English translation by Samuel and Shierry Weber, *Prisms* (Cambridge, Mass.: The MIT Press, 1981), 34: "To write poetry after Auschwitz is barbaric."

17. Peter Szondi, "Durch die Enge geführt," *Schriften*, v. 2, 384.

of night, which is a counter-night [*Aber-Nacht*], of the you that is a counter-you [*Aber-Du*]: a re-you and an anti-you, a you and not a you. As the immanent revocation of its name, of its concept and its linguistic sign, the nothingness of language's root announces itself within language, but against it and its semantic function. As the you always doubles and reduces itself into a counter-you for the I, so the root is our own only to the extent that it is no one's, no one's root only to the extent that it is ours. The commonality of I and you that first finds its word—*ours*—in this (parenthetical) locus; this commonality, which is that of the sexes, is first attained in passing back through the bereavement of personal, generic, sexual, and historical existence. Only in their separation from one another and from the race, as the reassuring ground of being and of stable communication, can they be and be open to one another; only in the dispersal, dismemberment, and destruction of language's historical continuity and of the race's homogeneity does it—abandoned to its finitude, to its nothingness—impart.

This im-parting no longer underlies the figure of inversion, however little it can renounce it; for the latter is itself subject to parting. "(Root./Root of Abraham. Root of Jesse. No one's/root—o/ours.)" The terse genealogical catalogue, containing an infinite geneological promise, is after "Jesse" no longer subjected only to a chiasmus, to an inversion of syntagmatic elements that sets a "no one" in the place of "root." This chiasmus is itself subjected, in the line break, to an interruption which opens in the place of "root" an empty space—a "pause," a "hiatus," a "lacuna."[18] This pause is as little devoid of semantic function as it is the "graphic" image of the root's nothingness. It is the pause in the signification of the race's language, no longer allowing of characterization by morphological oppositions. But linguistic signs and their signification can be generated only by means of such morphological oppositions. One could characterize this pause (with reference to Jakobson's concept) as a zero-opposition; that is, as a linguistic event distinguished by presenting no opposition to a previously established linguistic form, and (this against Jakobson's own use of the concept)[19] by refusing nonetheless to neutralize itself with it. The lacuna between "no one's" and "root" cannot be brought down on either side of the opposition between meaning and meaninglessness. It maintains itself between the poles of the opposition as it maintains itself between the negative pronoun "no one's" and the substantive "root," which, in a remarkable convergence between the formal and the semantic structure of this line, designates the root of meaningfulness as such. Engaged neither semantically nor asemantically, the lacuna—and not just here—holds open the space between negation and the

---

18. Pause, lacuna, and hiatus (*Pause, Wortlücke, und Leerstelle*) are concepts employed by Celan in "Gespräch im Gebirg": " . . . the stick is silenced, the stone is silenced; and the silence is no silencing, no word is struck dumb there, nor any sentence; it is only a pause, a lacuna, a hiatus, you see all syllables stand about . . . " (3, 170).

19. Cf. Roman Jakobson, "Signe Zéro," in *Selected Writings* (The Hague, Paris: Mouton, 1971), v. 2, 219.

negated, holds it open for their relation and at the same time for the possibility of their non-relation. Thus, the pause between "no one's" and "root" stands between, on the one hand, that nothingness of the race's language which can still be stated and thereby become this language's negative referent, and on the other hand its sheer absence: between simple muteness and the possibility of saying or writing "mute." In the pause stands nothing, and not Nothing. It is "the weight holding back the vacuum," as the text that precedes *Radix, Matrix* puts it: arresting it and detaining it, checking and proscribing it, suspending it—for the second of reading and writing —its arrival and its departure. In the second of the vacuum, the inversion of the genealogical discourse of "Radix, Matrix" is interrupted and held back. The "root" is withheld in such a manner that it disappears neither *into* the discourse of origins not *out* of it. It is root, the root of the *Geschlect* and of its language, only in traversing its pause—therefore only in suspension. Only as split from itself by this lacuna and gap does language impart as our own; as communal, only as what is withheld by the silencing of communication.

Once this mode of commonality is articulated in the suspension of commonality, discourse's attempt at determination—interrupted in the second line of *Radix, Matrix*—is again taken up in a paradoxical amplification: that just as one speaks to a stone, so "you/with my hands there/and into nothing grasp." Speaking is a grasping with the hands. In his letter to Hans Bender, Celan wrote of poetry as a hand-clasping,[20] thereby awakening to new life the dead metaphor of grasping a concept, of making oneself capable of being grasped and understood. The stone, [*Stein*], in its parallelism with nothingness [*Nichts*], turns out to be its nearly anagrammatic inversion: *Niets*. And just as the language of the murdered race gropes into nothing and says nothing to no one, *so* "is what is here." What is articulated here, in the *hic et nunc* of the poem, is neither the locus of the sheer *nihil negativum* nor the scene of its reversal into the plenitude of being in a language of presence, but rather that mode of being in language (and being *is* only under the condition of such a negative modality) in which language reaches out to its own nothingness, to the nothingness of its own reference, its signification and its determination. It relates to it as to its own no-more; it is—and this is its *so*, its mode, its genre and its *Geschlecht*—the already-there of its no-more, the relation to its nothingness in which it withdraws from itself the relation that makes it language. But as the withdrawal of relation, it keeps relating to the possibility of its own impossibility: as the already-there of its no-more, it is the still-there of its no-more.

The cleft it opens in itself as that of its nothingness is thus at the same time—in keeping open the *possibility* of this impossibility—the gaping of the vegetative receptacle. The plunge of the poem into the abyss of its impos-

---

20. "Only true hands write true poetry. I see no difference in principle between handclasping and poetry." (Letter to Hans Bender, May 18, 1960: 3, 177).

sibility is the *summum* of the possibilities of its speaking. Cut as by a caesura, speaking with the gaps between its words as its impossible you and its impossible I, the poem imparts—uprooted and torn from the matrix of its determinations, without a ground and with no law that would stand over it—as "one of the wild-/flourishing crowns."

> even this
> receptacle gapes;
> this
> descent
> is the one of the wild-
> flourishing crowns.

This high pathetic metaphor, perfectly discreet in its content, may have had two impetuses. One is Psalm 132:18—"His [David's] enemies will I clothe with shame: but upon himself shall his crown flourish." The other is a formulation from the Book of Bahir, possibly known to Celan through Scholem's book on the Kabbalah and its symbolism, according to which "holy Israel" is imagined as *crowning* the tree of the world and of God.[21] From the same work of Scholem it emerges that, according to the teaching of the Book of Sohar, with which Celan must have been quite intimate, the "root of all roots" from which that tree nourishes itself is a nothingness surrounding *en-sof*, the nonground and abyss of God, as its aura.[22] However great an influence these biblical and Kabbalistic metaphors may have had on *Radix, Matrix*, they enter Celan's text only in transformation. There one no longer finds any root of which it could positively be said that it is nothing, for nothingness appears only in a form which is broken by the pause, as a counter-nothing (*Aber-Nichts*), a non-nothing and a double-nothing, as the vacancy and the withholding of its linguistic presentation. The crown which the psalm proclaims for David and his house (*Geschlecht*) is here no longer a crown that flourishes over him or that could be bestowed upon him from outside. The poem itself—"what is here . . . this/descent"—is the one of the wild-flourishing crowns—but just one, not the only one. As such it is subject to no rule dictated from above, nor does it spring from any underlying substratum.

Where no matrix remains, there is also no longer any poem that could claim the privilege of articulating the gaps that open its destruction, for no longer can any one of the gaps stand alone at the end of the attempt to determine it. Speech itself steps forth, altered, where the support it could find in its object or its own figures is lost. The poem is not organized by any end, by any object—not even one defined negatively—or by any subject, not even an absent one—but only by what it, here, *is;* a path, a movement of *descent*, without

---

21. Cf. Gershom Scholem, *Zur Kabbala und ihrer Symbolik* (Frankfurt am Main: Suhrkamp, 1973), 124; *On the Kabbalah and its Symbolism*, trans. Ralph Manheim (New York: Schocken Books, 1965), 92.

22. Cf. Ibid., 138; English translation, 103.

direction or destination (*Bestimmung*). This descent *without* a ground is the crown. But where the ground fails—even the ground of *a* nothingness that is objectified, that appears determined—there one no longer finds the one, no longer *the* crown and no longer *the* poem that would be able to correspond to this failure. Not only the subject and the figure of speech, but even this speaking itself loses its power to determine. Inversion—no longer just a rhetorical figure which this speaking would use to represent its objects, but now the very form of development that should safeguard its own possibility—is defused. There is no longer a one and only, *the* inversion, by which the poem's indeterminate descent could be turned over into acumen, by which its objectless questioning after the race could be upended into its highest pronouncement.

The turning the poem runs through is the one of the inversions: one of two. Just as the grasp of the you, "with my hands," blossoms as a crown into the nothingness of the I and of its *Geschlect*, so the other blossoms in the grip of the I, with your hands, into the nothingness of the you. I and you, supposedly constituting one another reciprocally (if one follows dialogical theories), here deconstitute one another in the chiasmus, it too an inversion, of their crossed attempts to get a grip on themselves and to make themselves capable of being grasped. In this deconstitution they become figures of an encounter with nothing. Each encounters in the other its own nothing, and the discourse of the other opens itself to each only as the abyss of that which is its own. So "what is here" does not just mean the poem in which "you/with my hands there/and into nothing grasp," nor is it simply the chiasmic crossing of I and you in the failing and (by its failure) blooming grasp after the commonality of the race. "What is here" acknowledges itself, in the almost imperceptibly minor detail of the expression "die *eine der* Kronen" ["the *one of the* crowns"], to be the partial discourse of the I. The poem remains tied to the delusive primacy of the I. "What is here" thus refers at the same time to the missing complement that would be the *other* one of the crowns: the one that does not blossom *here*, nor out of the I. The inversion does not offer itself as complete. "Crown of roots:/ with a part"—the movement expressed here is thus presented in extreme condensation by a later text from *Fadensonnen* (2, 196). The one of the crowns remains separated from the others because there is no you for whom the I would not be once again a you, an other whose strangeness interdicts the poem from speaking in its place. The one of the crowns does not represent the other. Its alterity cannot be sublated by an inversion. Only what is rootless, lacking even the root of the one nothing, can be a crown. And only the other for whom even this crown is no root, is a crown itself. There are always, at least, two crowns. They do not permit of inclusion, by means of any inversion, within a common matrix.

The inversion that was, throughout a long period of Celan's lyric production, the very form of movement with which the I and its language could claim to mediate whatever eluded their grasp, has ceased to be its rhetorical and epsitemological matrix. It no longer establishes the commonality in the race's one language, but—itself merely one of two, hence partial—only the commonality in the reciprocal indeterminacy of an I and a you which fail to connect with one another. Being with one another is a standing apart (*Klaffen*), of the abyss and of the receptacle at the same stroke. It rips open the cleft (*Klaffen*) between self and its inversion into its thematic you. The partitioning, the part between two crowns that holds them together and apart no longer finds any positive form in the poem, but splits its thematic field as the parting of the I into stone and nothing, as the parting of the you into you and counter-you. As a thoroughgoing break in all compositional positions, it rends its formal layout, rends it movement as the im-parting of its speaking. The poem is the movement in which I and you im-part, without being able to gather into the one crown that is the positive shape of *this* poem. The poem, and with it the logic of inversion, im-parts: im-parts to and from that which (it) cannot be. The "encounter" with the otherness of the you, which is at the same time its alteration, comes about only as this im-parting and this partitioning of the speech in which it exposes itself and in which it breaks off (*in der es [sich] aussetzt*). It enunciates itself as the movement of alteration, and ceases therein to be simply this poem or simply a poem.[23] Carrying out the differentiation between itself and the other, it is no longer spoken with the voice of subjectivity. Carrying out the differentiation between its being and its nonbeing, it is no longer written from the standpoint of objective being. Carrying out the differentiation between its determinacy in the one *Geschlecht* and the indetermination that the nothing of the *Geschlecht* bestows upon it, it can no longer be affixed to the arche-teleological line of communication. And as the carrying out of the differentiation between its meaning and the inability to mean in the face of nothing, it is a poem that withdraws from the schematisms of semantics and attains its specific gravity only by virtue of its parasemic character. *Radix, Matrix* is a poem which parts ways with every radix and matrix of whatever provenance, a poem that takes leave of itself. Only as the movement of its uprooting and orphaning (*Deradizierung, Dematrizierung*) can it be a speaking that is subordinate to nothing. It is the experience of liberation from even its own language. And only in relinquishing the grounding figure that organizes its movement—inversion—by placing its own trope under erasure, is it on a path uncontrolled by its figure. The radicalizing of inversion leads to the renunciation of inversion as of a matrix.

Since the time of the transcendental turn in philosophy and literature (at the latest), the figure of inversion has been tied to the idea of the turning back, the return, and the restitution of the self. In this scheme, the subject is to take up once again its authentic form and recover an undistorted understanding with itself and its language only in the immanent reversal of a history seen as a process of dissolution. Inversion can be characterized, within this framework,

---

23. Bernard Böschenstein's fine judgment on *Sperrtonnensprache* points in a similar direction: "The poem has outlived itself." In *Leuchttürme* (Frankfurt am Main: Insel Verlag, 1977), 305.

as the figure of the historical, aesthetic, and hermeneutic relation of the subject to itself, and thus as the privileged trope of subjectivity. In this figure, language does not merely relate to itself; in it, and as it, language *is* for the first time actual. Peter Szondi has spelled out the consequences of this theory of subjectivity for one part of Celan's lyric production, though of course without appealing to it himself. In "Poetry of Constancy—Poetik der Beständigkeit," at the end of his analysis of Celan's translation of a Shakespeare sonnet, he writes that Celan has "set, in the place of the traditional symbolist poem that deals with itself and takes itself as its object, a poem that no longer treats of itself but *is* itself."[24] Szondi's formulations have the merit of insisting on a strand in Celan's lyrics that threatens to become hidden by the theories of negativity advanced by the majority of literature on Celan. They have the disadvantage of neglecting, for the sake of the affirmation of self-being, the specific contour of this being that these poems are trying to sketch. Celan's texts do not dismiss subjectivity by devoting themselves to the sphere of the sheer objectivity of their linguistic being, in order to find a new resting place and a guarantee of their own constancy—as so-called concrete poetry tries to do with the technical organization of language's raw materials. They move away from subjectivity rather by articulating the structure of self-reference as that of the speech act which, once released from its ties to the self and the logic of its positing, attains an altered relation to itself in the very movement of being released.

Language is not posited but projected. Following a graphic paronomasia, a parographism which corresponds to the one in Greek between *logos* and *logche* [word and javelin], the word (*Wort*) is a boomerang (*Wurf*holz)—a projectile with the property of turning on itself and returning to its place of departure if thrown in the proper manner. In Celan's poem *Ein Wurfholz*, which describes the movement of the word to itself, its point of departure is no longer a topic— as it was in the poem *Aber*, from *Sprachgitter*, which with reference to the classical poetic emblem of the swan, has the boomerang with which it is compared whiz "from the void":

> die Schwäne
> in Genf, ich sah's nicht, flogen, es war,
> als schwirrte, vom Nichts her, ein Wurfholz
> ins Ziel einer Seele: . . . [1, 182]

> the swans
> in Geneva, I didn't see it, flew, it was
> as if, from the void, a boomerang were whizzing
> into a soul's target: . . .

In the later text from *Die Niemandsrose* (1, 258), the reference to this initial void appears first at the place where the word arrives, in its reference to itself.

---

24. Szondi, *Schriften*, v. 2, 344.

EIN WURFHOLZ, auf Atemwegen,
so wanderts, das Flügel-
mächtige, das
Wahre. Auf
Sternen-
bahnen, von Welten-
splittern geküsst, von Zeit-
körnern genarbt, von Zeitstaub, mit-
verwaisend mit euch,
Lapilli, ver-
zwergt, verwinzigt, ver-
nichtet,
verbracht und verworfen,
sich selber der Reim,—
so kommt es
geflogen, so kommts
wieder und heim,
einen Herzschlag, ein Tausendjahr lang
innezuhalten als
einziger Zeiger im Rund,
das eine Seele,
das seine
Seele
beschrieb,
das eine
Seele
beziffert.

A BOOMERANG, on paths of breath,
so it wanders, the wing-
powered, the
true. On
astral
orbits, by world-
shards kissed, by time-
kernals pitted, by dust of time, co-
abandoning with you,
Lapilli,
dwarfed, diminished, an-
nihilated,
deported and abject,
of itself the rhyme,—
thus it comes
in flight, thus it comes
back and comes home,
for a heartbeat, for a millennium
to stall as
the solitary hand on the dial
a soul
described,
its soul,
which one
soul
figured.

A boomerang, this word, is, thrown, already on its way with the first word of the poem. It is therefore not at home, but grasped in the flight of its displacements and transformations, "on paths of breath." It is underway along not one but several elliptical or circular paths, which traverse the realms of the living (*Atemwegen* means also "respiratory ducts"), the mythical ("the wing-powered" comprises as much an allusion to Hermes, the winged messenger-god from Greek mythology, as to angels, the messengers of God in Judaic and Christian mythology), and the cosmic ("astral orbits"). Wandering through these realms, it becomes an other: from having collided with the shards of the world and of time, to which it must submit on these orbits, it contracts progressively—"dwarfed, diminished," finally to be "an-/nihilated." Only thus, "an-/nihilated,/deported and abject"—and in such a manner that it is brought to the point of disappearing, diverted from the path of living breath, deported, despised, not taken up in knowing and, thrown badly, not delivered to the target for which it was destined—does it come, "come back and come home." The *Wurfholz* "comes/in flight, . . . comes back and comes home" not by corresponding to something else, to another *word (Wort)* or another *call (Ruf)*;

not by reaching either the intention bound up with its throw, or the addressee intended by it; but rather by corresponding to nothing and to nobody, in speaking to nothing and to nobody, as to itself; by being therefore only "of itself the rhyme," as in the poem's central line. It does not come to itself as a given, objective Being, but rather, annihilated, as a nothing—whose place is neither the grounding place where its movement commences nor the target of its meaning but rather the false, the failed, the place of failure (Fehl-Ort) reached only in the displacement of the topography of intention, in its deportation and its dislocation. This is not the place of a positive nothing. Ver-/nichtet does not mean vernichtet; but rather, since the severing of the ver- brings out its intensifying as well as its digressive and dissimilative connotations (as in verschreiben, "miswrite," or versetzen, "displace") it means at the same time the failure of this annihilation. Rather, it is the place of a nothing that does not coincide with itself. The place where the word, the cry, the topos comes back and comes home, is the u-topos that is found where it does not itself arrive as word, cry, and topos. The word comes to itself as to nothing. In Deine Augen im Arm ["Your eyes in the arm"], from Fadensonnen (2, 123), Celan makes it clear that the negation of where (wo) is just as much the negation and the silencing of the word, (Wort), when he writes negation with the negative and privative prefix: entwo.[25] The poem—itself this word, "A Boomerang"—does not write this coming-to-itself by positing itself as an entity that would be like an object maintaining itself in its presence-at-hand, but by exposing and expositing itself as the movement of its disappearance. It abandons itself to destruction, rejection, annihilation; it abandons itself, in exposing itself to the removal of its determination and the proscription of its form. It ex-posits its discourse, in each of its line- and word-breaks, in each shift of image. It does so in its central line in such a way as to characterize its linguistic self-reference not as identity but as paronomasia, as "rhyme," and to concretize this result in the "heim" ["home"] that follows as an agreement in a meaningless "eim." Moreover, this pivotal line is interrupted with a dash which lets the discourse itself, precisely where it comes to itself, come to a stop. Celan's poem, instead of being itself, is the rhyme, the paronomasia of its nothingness. The word—the poem—abandons its being. "La poésie," as it is said in the sole French maxim of Celan that has been handed down to us—"La poésie ne s'impose plus, elle s'expose" [poetry no longer imposes, but exposes itself.][26]

The return and homecoming of the word to itself, traditionally thought as the actualizing of potencies buried within conventional usage or as the "metapoetic" reflection of its contents (and thus, once again, as an inversion that sets things aright), takes a disturbing turn in Celan's poem insofar as it returns not in restituted form to its own property and proper place, but rather in its scarred,

---

25. Cf. Winfried Menninghaus's analysis in Paul Celan: Magie der Form (Frankfurt am Main: Suhrkamp Verlag, 1980), 62–67.
26. Ibid., 181.

dismembered and finally an-/nihilated form, to that which is not its own and in which it itself is not. And it does not signify itself any more than it still *is* itself here. The word refers (*verweist*) only in abandoning (*indem es verwaist*). It separates itself from its derivation and the intentions bound up with it, mortifies what is meant in it and what is addressed by it, and in this it becomes the movement of infinite singularization. The sole interdependence it maintains is—expressed in lapidary fashion, like everything in Celan—the link with what is likewise orphaning: "co-/abandoning with you,/Lapilli." This *Lapilli*, the only apostrophe in this poem, evokes the whole series of stones and rock formations with which Celan's texts, true lithographs, calculate. It evokes the alchemical philosopher's stone (*Stein der Weisen*) and that of the orphans (*den der Waisen*) (2, 283). It evokes the white stone of the apocalypse that resembles the hidden manna and in which a new name is written, which no man knoweth saving he that receiveth it (Rev. 2:17). It evokes the white stones of Hänsel and Gretel that failed to show them the way home, and the stones of Mandel'shtam's first volume of poetry; it evokes the pebble which— like "language," the "three-year-land of your mother" and the "bud on their breast"—"your thoughts carried to Prague,/to the grave, to graves, into life" (1, 285).[27] It calls forth along with these and so many other memorials and headstones, also the black ballot-pebbles called *Lapilli*, from the fifteenth book of Ovid's *Metamorphoses*,[28] which condemned Myscelus to death and which later, having been changed to white by the influence of Hercules, released him and allowed him to leave his fatherland to found a new one at the place designated by God, at the grave of Croton. This absolving and expatriating trait of Ovid's *Lapilli* is sharpened in Celan's poem to the extent that the orphaning of his *Lapilli* knows neither a God nor a homeland except its own nothingness.

Following the syntactical ambiguity of the lines "by time-/kernals pitted, by dust of time, co-/abandoning with you,/Lapilli,/dwarfed. . . , " this abandoning can just as well be abandoning *by* the boomerang as an abandoning whose object is the boomerang. It becomes a kernal of time: the smallest segment of time and the seed of time, isolated as the "solitary hand on the dial" which points, as the linguistic or graphic atom of the passing of time (and the form of the boomerang in effect resembles that of the hour-hand). It points to, it becomes an index, a script and a cipher for time and history, marking its own passage. (The crooked figure of the boomerang represents, in the shape of the *C*, not only a Roman numeral but also the first letter of Celan's name: one can read the entire poem as a *C élan*, as a hypogram, a signature and an auto-

---

27. Cf. Chalfen, 30.
28. *Mos erat antiquus neveis atrisque lapillis,/his damnare peos, illis absolvere culpa.* [It was the practice, in days of old, to condemn prisoners with black pebbles, to acquit them with white.] Ovid, *Metamorphoses*, trans. Mary M. Innes (New York: Penguin Books, 1955), 15, ll. 41–42; 336.

biographical stenogram.)[29] The word, this poem, is, as self-orphaning, *the second* in which it separates itself from itself. As an orphaning that is itself orphaned, it lacks any semantic or communicative reference. Its coming to itself, its homecoming and its return, stands, as an orphaned, objectless, and selfless orphaning, under the sign of the impossibility of arriving.

The boomerang comes to itself, comes to speech—but, orphaned by itself, it never arrives. Only because and as long as it does not arrive, is it coming home. Its homecoming and its return is this: not arriving. Being, being-oneself and being-with-another, is a coming with no arrival. "A Boomerang," as much as it turns on itself and describes its trajectory as a circle, is not itself and cannot signify itself, metapoetically. It refers (*verweist*) to itself, out of the distance necessary for this, as the distancing referal (*Verweisung*) that can never reach home as its proper sense—the intended meaning, the thing meant, and the desired word—without confronting therein that distance, confronting the orphaning the abandoning (*Verwaisung*), confronting its not being present in it. The reversion to itself of any act of referal [*der Bezug jeder Verweisung auf sich*] signs itself necessarily—and so the "boomerang" is not called true, but "the/true"—as the spatiotemporal desevering of a referal and as its self-withdrawal. As language without a language. Its reflection is the second and this impartment, in which it divides itself from itself and is near to itself, as to the difference. Its being—being is abandoning. Its inversion is the trope which, crossing itself, gapes.[30]

---

29. Among the palimpsests, the polypsests of "EIN WURFHOLZ" may be the "Speech of Christ, after Death, from the Cosmos, that there is no God," the "First Flower-piece" from the *Siebenkäs* of Jean Paul, whom Celan held in high esteem. Its central theme is the atheist as orphan—"No one is so much alone in the universe as a denier of God; he mourns with an orphaned heart that has lost the greatest father" (270)—and the fatherlessness of the son of God, who thus ceases to be "himself"— " 'We are all orphans, you and I, we are without a father' " (273). The path the dead Christ traverses in search of his father is not unlike the one taken by the boomerang: " 'I traversed the worlds, I ascended into the suns and flew with the milky ways through the wildernesses of the heavens; but there is no God' " (273). The I finds itself destroyed, in "frozen, dumb nothingness" (274). It is the fate of the isolated poetic figures in Jean Paul's "Speech", like that of the boomerang, to announce their own dissociation and destruction: they signify the nonbeing of what they present. The nearness and the distance between Jean Paul's "Speech" and Paul Celan's poem emerge most pointedly in the fact that, in Celan's Democritean universe, orphaning no longer refers to a God, but only to itself, thereby annulling its own presentation (*Zeigen*); in the fact that the "dial" which the boomerang—"its/soul"—"described," and whose "solitary hand" it is, displays the same O, the same untimely conditioning of time and of the sign, as does the "dialplate of eternity" in Jean Paul: "Aloft, on the church-dome, stood the dial-plate of *eternity*; but no number was to be seen upon it, and it was its own index (*Zeiger*, hand); only a black finger pointed to it, and the dead wished to read the *time* upon it" (273; the page numbers refer to Norbert Miller's edition of Jean Paul's *Werke*, v. 2, Munich 1971; cf. *Flower, Fruit and Thorn Pieces*, E. H. Noel, trans., Leipzig 1871).

30. At the end of the *Meridian* speech, Celan writes: "I find something, like language, immaterial yet earthly, terrestrial; something circular, returning to itself over both poles, thereby—fortunately—even traversing the tropics. I find . . . a meridian" (3, 202). Marlies Janz has stressed the possibility that the discourse on the "meridian" could present a greeting to Adorno, who refers to a meridian (if only very casually) at the outset of his essay "Valérys Abweichungen" ["Valéry's

With reference to *"A la pointe acérée"* (1, 251–52), Celan reported in conversation[31] that he borrowed this text's title from a note by Baudelaire, cited in Hofmannsthal's journal under the date June 29, 1917[32]: "There are certain delicious sensations whose indefiniteness in no way precludes intensity, and no point is sharper than the Infinite." Celan's poem—as its ambivalent title suggests—is written *on* this point of the Infinite, as well as *with* it. Immediately preceding this citation from Baudelaire in Hofmannsthal's notes is a second, from Paul Claudel's *Les Muses*, which runs as follows: "A poem is not made of these letters which I plant like nails, but of the white (*blanc*) remaining on the paper." Hofmannsthal adds to the remark: "Here is the very image of the void that has haunted me." After the citation follows a stylistic appreciation of Claudel's "highly unusual prose," which concludes by affirming that he reins in the sway of the sentence by means of "a sudden freezing." In Celan's poem it is not the flow of language but "the white remaining on the paper" that crystalizes. It is the "unwritten" that petrifies as language, as in that other maxim of Hofmannsthal's, the conclusion of Death in *Der Tor und der Tod*, according to which men are the beings "that explain the inexplicable,/that read what was never written."[33] In the opening lines of his poem, Celan (with Hofmannsthal's help) reads Baudelaire's *"pointe acérée de l'Infini"* as Claudel's *"clous plantés de ces lettres."* Against the latter's intention, therefore, he also reads it as the point in which the unwritten, instead of remaining outside writing, contracts into writing. Writing contracts the *blanc*.

The infinite void crystallizing into language remains operative, in language and through it, as the intermittent movement of laying bare and setting free.

> Es liegen die Erze bloss, die Kristalle,
> die Drusen.
> Ungeschriebenes, zu
> Sprache verhärtet, legt
> einen Himmel frei.

Aberrations"], published in 1960 and dedicated to Celan in gratitude for his *Gespräch im Gebirg*. One could venture, on equally if not more pertinent grounds, the conjecture that the discourse of the "meridian" refers to Heidegger's piece *Zur Seinsfrage*—first published, as a response to Ernst Jünger's *Über die Linie*, with the title *Über "Die Linie"*. This piece followed Jünger in characterizing this "line" as the prime meridian (*Nullmeridian*). The references are not mutually exclusive, they may rather point toward a point of convergence in the thought of Heidegger and Adorno. As far as I know, the only serious discussion devoted to the problem of Celan's relation to Heidegger is in Phillippe Lacoue-Labarthe's "Deux Poèmes de Paul Celan," *Aléa* 5 (Paris, 1984), 65 ff.

31. With Dietland Meinecke; cf. loc. cit., 229ff.

32. Hugo von Hofmannsthal, *Aufzeichnungen*, ed. H. Steiner (Frankfurt am Main: S. Fischer, 1959), 181.

33. Hugo von Hofmannsthal, *Gesammelte Werke*, ed. Bernd Schoeller (Frankfurt am Main: Fischer-Taschenbuck Verlag, 1979), v. 1 (*Gedichte und Dramen*, 1), 297–98. Cf. "Death and the Fool," in *Three Plays*, trans. Alfred Schwarz (Detroit: Wayne State University Press, 1966), 65.

(Nach oben verworfen, zutage,
überquer, so
liegen auch wir.

The ores are laid bare, the crystals,
the geodes.
The unwritten, into
language hardened, sets
free a sky.

(Thrown upward, into the light,
crossways, so
we too are lying. . . .

No matter how much Celan's poetry is quoting in these lines—and not just in these—it always quotes only the unwritten, the empty, the gaping, the *blanc*. No topos, not even the topoi it employs, determines the poem's place; none of its tropes determine its movement; no method determines the path it takes. The *loci communes* of "ore" and "crystals" open up, in the hollow of "geodes," onto a void that no writing, however hardened, can capture except in circumscription and transcription. The metaphor of petrifying the unwritten into language, being itself written, brings to light the fact that it misses the unwritten. The "ways to that place. . . , alongside the spluttering wheeltrack (*Radspur*)" are, by paronomasia, the trace of a discourse (*Spur einer Rede*) that lays bare, in the explosion of its own voicing, something thus far hidden in it. These are the ways of the poem—"spluttering ways to that place." Something is underway along them, not to come into language but to lay open what must remain vacant in its petrification, unwritten in the poem and unattainable in its progress toward "the unrepeatable." It is underway to what has not come into language. It is underway, alongside a track, toward the indeterminable, as something that reads [*lesendes*].

Auf-	Col-
gelesene	lected
kleine, klaffende	small, gaping
Buchecker: schwärzliches	beechnuts: blackish
Offen, von	open, by
Fingergedanken befragt	finger thoughts questioned
nach——	about——
wonach?	about what?

The seed capsule gathered (*Auf-/gelesene*) from a beech (*einer Buche*)—from a book (*aus einem Buche*)—is, parasemically, in respect to its "open," that which is read open (*offen-gelesene*). Explication is setting free; reading is not so much a gathering and sublating as rather an opening of language onto what remained unsaid in it, onto what indicates itself in it of the unrepeatably bygone, onto what only announces itself as what is to come.

This reading open is the questioning movement of thought along a path which, however, cannot lead to the unrepeatable as long as it is a path cleared by the conventions of discourse and of reading. In relating to the unrepeatable, the poem's reading does not give back a pregiven reality; it does not detain any hidden or remote sense within the house of language; rather, it opens onto a coming that no intentional act can bring about. Thus the poem takes a turn in its last stanza, speaking no longer of its own forward mobility (*Gehen*) or that of a reader, but inversely, of a coming.

> Etwas, das gehn kann, grusslos
> wie Herzgewordenes,
> kommt.

> Something that can go, ungreeting
> as all that's turned to heart,
> is coming.

What is coming here can, however, be double. From the viewpoint of the reading that gropes its way, what is coming is the unwritten, that which all reading only attempts to ascertain—the unwritten which must impart from itself to explication through its coming, since it could not otherwise become the object even of the most abstract thought. On the other hand, from the watchtower where the unwritten waits—and the poem refers to this too, with its talk of coming—that which is coming is the poem itself with its questioning reading.

> Etwas, das gehn kann, grusslos
> wie Herzgewordenes,
> kommt.

The poem, as the movement of writing, approaches itself as the unwritten; the unwritten comes to the poem as the experience of the interruption and intermittence of its writing. Its going is the coming of the unrepeatable. It comes as the disfiguration of the figures into which language has conjured that which it has always only talked around. Selfless, it writes itself only in writing the coming of an other—of the poem—in writing itself otherwise and in ascribing itself to another. For the poem, what is coming in its writing is not itself, but that which it does not write. It is always the other that is coming. This two-turned coming—the inversion of writing and the unwritten, of the read and the unreadable, implicit in every poem, in every speaking and reading—is itself the movement of alteration in which even the most hardened self sets out for an other. At that point the "ores" (*Erze*) of the beginning are "turned into hearts" (*Herzgewordenes*).

What is coming, always the other, must be able to set out on a course, to go and also to depart. It is not said that what is coming also arrives. But the conditions of coming—of the poem and of what it does not write, of reading and of what it does not read—include the possible departure of that which is coming. Ungreeting, without a word, in a going that precedes the alternative between coming and going, in the linguistic movement prior to the choice between the word coming and the word going, it is there and away. It writes itself, it reads itself—it comes—free.

FREIE UNIVERSITÄT BERLIN

Translated by William D. Jewett

Bibliography

TOM KEENAN

Bibliography of Texts by Paul de Man

> I would never have by myself undertaken the task of establishing such a collection. . . . Such massive evidence of the failure to make the various individual readings coalesce is a somewhat melancholy spectacle. The fragmentary aspect of the whole is made more obvious still by the hypotactic manner that prevails in each of the essays taken in isolation, by the continued attempt, however ironized, to present a closed and linear argument. This apparent coherence *within* each essay is not matched by a corresponding coherence *between* them. Laid out diachronically in a roughly chronological sequence, they do not evolve in a manner that easily allows for dialectical progression or, ultimately, for historical totalization. Rather, it seems that they always start again from scratch and that their conclusions fail to add up to anything.
> —Paul de Man, "Preface," *The Rhetoric of Romanticism*, viii.

BOOKS

A. *Blindness and Insight: Essays in the Rhetoric of Contemporary Criticism*, New York: Oxford University Press, 1971 [noted here as *BI*]. Second edition, with five additional essays, edited by Wlad Godzich, Minneapolis: University of Minnesota Press, 1983 [noted here as *BI2*].

B. *Allegories of Reading: Figural Language in Rousseau, Nietzsche, Rilke, and Proust*, New Haven: Yale University Press, 1979 [noted here as *AR*].

C. *The Rhetoric of Romanticism*, New York: Columbia University Press, 1984 [noted here as *RR*].

ESSAYS, REVIEWS, TRANSLATIONS

1. Translation of Paul Alverdes, *Le Double Visage* [*Das Zweigesicht*], Brussels and Paris: Editions de la Toison d'Or, 1942.
2. Translation of Filip de Pillecyn [Pillecijn], *Le Soldat Johan*, Brussels: Editions de la Toison d'Or, 1942.
3. *Les Dessins de Paul Valéry*, "texte de P. de Man," Paris: Les Editions Universelles, 1948 [texte: ix–xxxv, dessins: xli–cxi. Authorship not confirmed.]
4. "Jacques Villon," *Konstrevy* 28:3, 1952, 133–38. ["By P. de Man," authorship not confirmed. In Swedish.]
5. "Montaigne et la Transcendance," *Critique* 79, December 1953, 1011–22.

6. "The Inward Generation," *i.e., The Cambridge Review* 1:2, Winter 1955, 41–47.

7. "Le Néant Poétique (commentaire d'un sonnet hermétique de Mallarmé)," *Monde Nouveau* 88, April 1955, 63–75.

8. "Tentation de la permanence," *Monde Nouveau* 93, October 1955, 49–61. Trans. Don Latimer, "The Temptation of Permanence," *Southern Humanities Review* 17:3, Summer 1983, 209–21.

9. "Les Exégèses de Hölderlin par Martin Heidegger," *Critique* 100–01, September–October 1955, 800–19. Translated by Wlad Godzich as "Heidegger's Exegeses of Hölderlin," Chapter 12 in *BI2*, 246–66.

10. "Keats and Hölderlin," *Comparative Literature* 8:1, Winter 1956, 28–45.

11. "Impasse de la critique formaliste," *Critique* 109, June 1956, 483–500. Translated by Wlad Godzich as "The Dead-End of Formalist Criticism," Chapter 11 in *BI2*, 229–45.

12. "Situation de Roman," *Monde Nouveau* 101, June 1956, 57–60.

13. "Le Devenir, la poésie," *Monde Nouveau* 105, November 1956, 110–24.

14. "La Critique thématique devant le Thème de Faust," *Critique* 120, May 1957, 387–404.

15. Translation of Martin Heidegger, "Hölderlin and the Essence of Poetry [Hölderlin und das Wesen des Dichtungs]," *Quarterly Review of Literature* 10:1–2, 1959, 79–94. Reprinted in T. and R. Weiss, ed., *QRL: Special Issues Retrospective* 20: 1–2, 1976, 456–71.

16. *Mallarmé, Yeats and the Post-Romantic Predicament*, Ph.D. dissertation, Harvard University, May 1960, 316 page typescript. One portion excerpted by de Man as "Image and Emblem in Yeats," Chapter 8 in *RR*, 145–238.

17. "Structure intentionelle de l'image romantique," *Revue internationale de philosophie* 51, 1960, 68–84. Translated by de Man, slightly revised, as "Intentional Structure of the Romantic Image," in Harold Bloom, ed., *Romanticism and Consciousness*, New York: Norton, 1970, 65–77. Reprinted in M. H. Abrams, ed., *Wordsworth: A Collection of Critical Essays*, Englewood Cliffs, NJ: Prentice Hall, 1972, 133–144. Reprinted as Chapter 1 in *RR*, 1–17.

18. "A New Vitalism" [review of Harold Bloom, *The Visionary Company*], *The Massachusetts Review* 3:3, Spring 1962, 618–23.

19. "Symbolic Landscape in Wordsworth and Yeats," in Richard Poirier and Reuben Brower, ed., *In Defense of Reading*, New York: Dutton, 1962, 22–37. Reprinted as Chapter 7 in *RR*, 125–43.

20. "Giraudoux" [review of Jean Giraudoux, *Three Plays*], *The New York Review of Books* 1:7, 28 November 1963, 20–21.

21. "Heidegger Reconsidered" [review of William Barrett, *What is Existentialism?*], *The New York Review of Books* 2:4, 2 April 1964, 14–16.

22. "Spacecritics" [review of J. Hillis Miller, *The Disappearance of God* and Joseph Frank, *The Widening Gyre*], *Partisan Review* 31:4, Fall 1964, 640–50.

23. "Sartre's Confessions" [review of Jean-Paul Sartre, *The Words*], *The New York Review of Books* 3:7 [sic; actual issue is 3:6], 5 November 1964, 10–13.

24. "A Modern Master" [review of Jorge Luis Borges, *Labyrinths* and *Dreamtigers*], *The New York Review of Books* 3:7, 19 November 1964, 8–10.

25. "Whatever Happened to André Gide" [review of André Gide, *Marshlands and Prometheus Misbound* and Wallace Fowlie, *André Gide: His Life and Art*], *The New York Review of Books* 4:7, 6 May 1965, 15–17.

26. "Nihilism" [reply to letter to the editor from Michael P. Scott], *The New York Review of Books* 4:9, 3 June 1965, 26–27.

27. "What is Modern?" [review of Richard Ellman and Charles Feidelson, ed., *The Modern Tradition*], *The New York Review of Books* 5:2, 26 August 1965, 10–13.

28. "The Mask of Albert Camus" [review of Albert Camus, *Notebooks, 1942–1951*], *The New York Review of Books* 5:10, 23 December 1965, 10–13.

29. "L'Image de Rousseau dans la Poésie de Hölderlin," *Deutsche Beiträge zur Geistigen Überlieferung* 5, 1965, 157–83. Translated by Renate Böschenstein-Schäfer as "Hölderlins Rousseaubild," *Hölderlin Jahrbuch* 15, 1967–68, 180–208. Translated by Andrzej Warminski as "The Image of Rousseau in the Poetry of Hölderlin," Chapter 2 in *RR*, 19–45.

30. Entry under "Modern Poetics: French and German," in Alex Preminger, ed., *[Princeton] Encyclopedia of Poetry and Poetics*, Princeton: Princeton University Press, 1965, 518–23.

31. "Introduction" and translation, Gustave Flaubert, *Madame Bovary*, "edited with a substantially new translation by Paul de Man," New York: Norton, 1965, vii–xiii.

32. "Wordsworth und Hölderlin," *Schweizer Monatshefte* 45:12, March 1966, 1141–55. Translated by Timothy Bahti as "Wordsworth and Hölderlin," Chapter 3 in *RR*, 47–65.

33. "The Literature of Nihilism" [review of Erich Heller, *The Artist's Journey into the Interior and Other Essays* and Ronald Gray, *The German Tradition in Literature, 1871–1945*], *The New York Review of Books* 6:11, 23 June 1966, 16–20.

34. "La Circularité de l'interprétation dans l'oeuvre de Maurice Blanchot," *Critique* 229, June 1966, 547–59. Translated by de Man, revised, as "Impersonality in the Criticism of Maurice Blanchot," Chapter 5 in *BI*, 60–78. Reprinted as "Maurice Blanchot" in John K. Simon,

ed., *Modern French Criticism: From Proust to Valéry to Structuralism*, Chicago: University of Chicago Press, 1972, 255–76.

35. "New Criticim et nouvelle critique," *Preuves* 188, October 1966, 29–37. Translated by de Man, revised, as "Form and Intent in the American New Criticism," Chapter 2 in *BI*, 20–35.

36. "Georg Lukács's *Theory of the Novel*," *MLN* 81:5, December 1966, 527–34. Reprinted as Chapter 4 in *BI*, 51–59. Reprinted in Richard Macksey, ed., *Velocities of Change: Critical Essays from MLN*, Baltimore: Johns Hopkins University Press, 1974, 207–14.

37. "Madame de Staël et Jean-Jacques Rousseau," *Preuves* 190, December 1966, 35–40.

38. "Introduction," John Keats, *Selected Poetry*, New York: Signet (New American Library), 1966, ix–xxxvi.

39. "The Crisis of Contemporary Criticism," *Arion* 6:1, Spring 1967, 38–57. Reprinted, revised, as "Criticism and Crisis," Chapter 1 in *BI*, 3–19. Reprinted in Morris Philipson and Paul J. Gudel, ed., *Aesthetics Today*, revised edition, New York: New American Library, 1980, 337–51.

40. "Ludwig Binswanger et le problème du moi poétique," in Jean Ricardou, ed., *Les Chemins actuels de la critique* (Colloque de Cerisy, 2–12 September 1966), Paris: Plon, 1967, 77–103; see also de Man's comments at 54, 121–24. Reprinted in 10/18 edition, Paris, 1968, 43–58, no comments. Reprinted in second 10/18 edition, Paris, 1973, 63–89, comments at 49, 106–09. Translated by de Man as "Ludwig Binswanger and the Sublimation of the Self," Chapter 3 in *BI*, 36–50.

41. "Vérité et méthode dans l'oeuvre de Georges Poulet," *Critique* 266, July 1969, 608–23. Translated by de Man as "The Literary Self As Origin: The Work of Georges Poulet," Chapter 6 in *BI*, 79–101.

42. "The Rhetoric of Temporality," in Charles S. Singleton, ed., *Interpretation: Theory and Practice*, Baltimore: Johns Hopkins University Press, 1969, 173–209. Reprinted as Chapter 10 in *BI2*, 187–228. Part 1 translated by Peter Grotzer as "Allegorie und Symbol in der Europäischen Fruhromantik," in S. Sonderegger, A. Haas, und H. Burger, ed., *Typologica Litterarum* (Festschrift für Max Wehrli), Zürich: Atlantis, 1969, 403–25.

43. "Literary History and Literary Modernity," *Deadalus* 99:2, Spring 1970, 384–404. Reprinted in Morton W. Bloomfield, ed., *In Search of Literary Theory*, Ithaca: Cornell University Press, 1972, 237–67. Reprinted as Chapter 8 in *BI*, 142–65.

44. "The Riddle of Hölderlin" [review of Friedrich Hölderlin, *Poems and Fragments*], *The New York Review of Books* 15:9, 19 November 1970, 47–52.

45. "Lyric and Modernity," in Reuben A. Brower, ed., *Forms of Lyric*, New York: Columbia University Press, 1970, 151–76. Reprinted as Chapter 9 in *BI*, 166–86.

46. "The Rhetoric of Blindness: Jacques Derrida's Reading of Rousseau," Chapter 7 in *BI*, 102–42. Reprinted, substantially revised, as "On Reading Rousseau," *Dialectical Anthropology* 2:1, February 1977, 1–18. First version translated by Jean-Michel Rabaté and Bernard Esmein as "Rhétorique de la cécité," *Poétique* 4, 1970, 455–75.

47. "Foreword," in *BI*, vii–x.

48. Comments, in Richard Macksey and Eugenio Donato, ed., *The Languages of Criticism and the Sciences of Man* [retitled *The Structuralist Controversy*], Baltimore: Johns Hopkins University Press, 1970 [1972], 150, 184–185.

49. Review of Jacques Derrida, *De la grammatologie, Annales de la Société Jean-Jacques Rousseau* 37, 1966–68 [published 1970], 284–88.

50. "Introduction," Rainer Maria Rilke, *Oeuvres 1: Prose*, "édition établie et présentée par Paul de Man," Paris: Editions du Seuil, 1972, 7–8.

51. "Introduction," also "Note sur l'édition," "Note sur les traductions," "Annotation et interprétation," and "Chronologie de la vie de Rainer Maria Rilke," Rainer Maria Rilke, *Oeuvres 2: Poésie*, "édition établie et présentée par Paul de Man," Paris: Editions du Seuil, 1972, 7–42, 43–54. Introduction translated by de Man as "Tropes (Rilke)," Chapter 2 in *AR*, 20–56.

52. "Proust et l'allégorie de la lecture," in *Mouvements premiers* (Etudes critiques offertes à Georges Poulet), Paris: Librairie José Corti, 1972, 231–50. Translated by de Man as "Reading (Proust)," Chapter 3 in *AR*, 57–78.

53. "Literature and Language: A Commentary," *New Literary History* 4:1, Autumn 1972, 181–92. Reprinted as Appendix B in *BI2*, 277–89.

54. "Genesis and Genealogy in Nietzsche's *Birth of Tragedy*," *Diacritics* 2:4, Winter 1972, 44–53. Reprinted as "Genesis and Genealogy (Nietzsche)," Chapter 4 in *AR*, 79–102.

55. "Theory of Metaphor in Rousseau's *Second Discourse*," *Studies in Romanticism* 12:2, Spring 1973, 475–98. Reprinted in David Thorburn and Geoffrey Hartman, ed., *Romanticism: Vistas, Instances, Continuities*, Ithaca: Cornell University Press, 1973, 83–114. Also reprinted as "Metaphor (*Second Discourse*)," Chapter 7 in *AR*, 135–59.

56. "Semiology and Rhetoric," *Diacritics* 3:3, Fall 1973, 27–33. Reprinted as Chapter 1 in *AR*, 3–19. Also reprinted in Josué V. Harari, ed., *Textual Strategies*, Ithaca: Cornell University Press, 1979, 121–40.

57. "Nietzsche's Theory of Rhetoric," *Symposium* 28:1, Spring 1974, 33–51, including question and answer session. Reprinted, without Q & A, as "Rhetoric of Tropes (Nietzsche)," Chapter 5 in *AR*, 103–18.

58. Review of Harold Bloom, *The Anxiety of Influence: A Theory of Poetry, Comparative Literature* 26:3, Summer 1974, 269–75. Reprinted as "Review of Harold Bloom's *Anxiety of Influence*," Appendix A in *BI2*, 267–76.

59. "Action and Identity in Nietzsche," *Yale French Studies* 52, 1975, 16–30. Reprinted as "Action and identity in Nietzsche," *Nuova Corrente* 68–69, 1975–76, 570–84. Also reprinted in Robert Young, ed., *Untying the Text: A Post-Structuralist Reader*, Boston: Routledge and Kegan Paul, 1981, 266–79. Also reprinted as "Rhetoric of Persuasion (Nietzsche)," Chapter 6 in *AR*, 119–31.

60. "The Timid God (A Reading of Rousseau's *Profession de foi du vicaire Savoyard*)," *Georgia Review* 29:3, Fall 1975, 533–58. Reprinted as "Allegory of Reading (*Profession de foi*)," Chapter 10 in *AR*, 221–45.

61. "Political Allegory in Rousseau," *Critical Inquiry* 2:4, Summer 1976, 649–75. Reprinted as "Promises (*Social Contract*)," Chapter 11 in *AR*, 246–77.

62. "The Purloined Ribbon," *Glyph* 1, 1977, 28–49. Reprinted as "Excuses (*Confessions*)," Chapter 12 in *AR*, 278–301.

63. "Forword," Carol Jacobs, *The Dissimulating Harmony*, Baltimore: Johns Hopkins University Press, 1978, vii–xiii.

64. "The Epistemology of Metaphor," *Critical Inquiry* 5:1, Autumn 1978, 13–30. Reprinted in Sheldon Sacks, ed., *On Metaphor*, Chicago: University of Chicago Press, 1979, 11–28. Reprinted in Michael Shapiro, ed., *Language and Politics*, New York: New York University Press, 1984, 195–214. Translated into German by Werner Hamacher as "Epistemologie der Metaphor," in Anselm Haverkamp, ed., *Theorie der Metaphor*, Darmstadt: Wissenschaftliche Buchgesellschaft, 1983, 415–37.

65. "Shelley Disfigured," in Harold Bloom et al., *Deconstruction and Criticism*, New York: Seabury Press, 1979, 39–73. Reprinted as Chapter 6 in *RR*, 93–123.

66. "Introduction" [to special issue titled "The Rhetoric of Romanticism"], *Studies in Romanticism* 18:4, Winter 1979, 495–99.

67. "Autobiography as De-facement," *MLN* 94:5, December 1979, 919–30. Reprinted as Chapter 4 in *RR*, 67–81.

68. "Self (*Pygmalion*)," Chapter 8 in *AR*, 160–87.

69. "Allegory (*Julie*)," Chapter 9 in *AR*, 188–220.

70. "Preface," in *AR*, ix–xi.

71. "Pascal's Allegory of Persuasion," in Stephen Greenblatt, ed., *Allegory and Representation*, Baltimore: Johns Hopkins University Press (English Institute), 1981, 1–25. See also otherwise unpublished re-

marks of de Man quoted in Stephen Greenblatt, "Preface," vii–xiii at viii.

72. "The Resistance to Theory," *Yale French Studies* 63, 1982, 3–20.

73. "Hypogram and Inscription: Michael Riffaterre's Poetics of Reading," *Diacritics* 11:4, Winter 1981, 17–35. Partially reprinted in "Lyric Voice in Contemporary Theory" [see below].

74. "Introduction," Hans Robert Jauss, *Toward an Aesthetics of Reception*, trans. Timothy Bahti, Minneapolis: University of Minnesota Press, 1982, vii–xxv. Partially reprinted in "Lyric Voice in Contemporary Theory" [see below].

75. "A Letter from Paul de Man," *Critical Inquiry* 8:3, Spring 1982, 509–13 [response to Stanley Corngold, "Error in Paul de Man," 489–507].

76. "Sign and Symbol in Hegel's *Aesthetics*," *Critical Inquiry* 8:4, Summer 1982, 761–75.

77. "The Return to Philology," *The Times Literary Supplement* 4158, 10 December 1982, 1355–56.

78. "Hommage à Georges Poulet," *MLN* 97:5, December 1982, [vii–viii].

79. "Foreword to Revised, Second Edition," in *BI2*, xi–xii.

80. "Dialogue and Dialogism," *Poetics Today* 4:1, Spring 1983, 99–107.

81. "Hegel on the Sublime," in Mark Krupnik, ed., *Displacement: Derrida and After*, Bloomington: Indiana University Press, 1983, 139–53.

82. "Reply to Raymond Geuss," *Critical Inquiry* 10:2, December 1983, 383–90 [response to Geuss, "A Response to Paul de Man," 375–82; cf. "Sign and Symbol in Hegel's *Aesthetics*"].

83. "Phenomenality and Materiality in Kant," in Gary Shapiro and Alan Sica, ed., *Hermeneutics: Questions and Prospects*, Amherst: University of Massachusetts Press, 1984, 121–44.

84. "Wordsworth and the Victorians," Chapter 5 in *RR*, 83–92.

85. "Anthropomorphism and Trope in the Lyric," Chapter 9 in *RR*,, 239–62. Translated into French by Christian Fournier as "Anthropomorphisme et trope dans la poésie lyrique," Poétique 62, April 1985, 131–45.

86. "Aesthetic Formalization: Kleist's *Über das Marionetten-theater*," Chapter 10 in *RR*, 263–290.

87. "Preface," in *RR*, vii–ix.

88. Maurizio Ferraris and Stephano Rossi, "Da New York: In memoria Paul de Man: L'Ultima intervista," *Alfabeta* 58, March 1984, 12 [transcript of interview with Rossi, 4 March 1983, broadcast on Italian radio, "America Coast to Coast," 1 June 1983].

89. Robert Moynihan, "Interview with Paul de Man," *The Yale Review* 73:4, Summer 1984, 576–602. With an introduction by J. Hillis Miller. Taped in 1980.

90. "Conclusions" on Walter Benjamin's "The Task of the Translator," *Yale French Studies* 69, 1985, 25–46.

91. "Lyrical Voice in Contemporary Theory: Riffaterre and Jauss," in Chaviva Hošek and Patricia Parker, ed., *Lyric Poetry: Beyond New Criticism*, Ithaca: Cornell University Press, 1985, 55–72. Reprints portions of "Hypogram and Inscription" and "Introduction" to Jauss with a brief new introduction.

FORTHCOMING

(1) *The Resistance to Theory*, edited by Wlad Godzich, Minneapolis: University of Minnesota Press, forthcoming 1986. To include essays on Bakhtin, Jauss, Riffaterre, Benjamin, Resistance to Theory, Return to Philology.

(2) *Aesthetic Ideology*, edited by Andrzej Warminski, Minneapolis: University of Minnesota Press, forthcoming 1986. To include essays on Hegel, Kant, Pascal, Epistemology of Metaphor, as well as two previously unpublished lectures entitled "Kant's Materialism" (1981) and "Kant and Schiller" (1983).

(3) *Fugitive Essays*, edited by Lindsay Waters, Minneapolis: University of Minnesota Press, forthcoming 1987. To include previously uncollected essays and reviews.

YALE UNIVERSITY

Appendix: Translations of Pages 13–16 and 17–21

Forgive me for speaking in my own tongue. It's the only one I ever spoke with Paul de Man. It's also the one in which he often taught, wrote and thought. What is more, I haven't the heart today to translate these few words, adding to them the suffering and distance, for you and for me, of a foreign accent. We are speaking today less in order to say something than to assure ourselves, with voice and with music, that we are together in the same thought. We know with what difficulty one finds right and decent words at such a moment when no recourse should be had to common usage since all conventions will seem either intolerable or vain.

If we have, as one says in French, "la mort dans l'âme," death in the soul, it is because from now on we are destined to speak *of* Paul de Man, instead of speaking *to* and *with* him, destined to speak of the teacher and of the friend whom he remains for so many of us, whereas the most vivid desire and the one which, within us, has been most cruelly battered, the most forbidden desire from now on would be to speak, still, to Paul, to hear him and to respond to him. Not just within ourselves (we will continue, I will continue to do that endlessly) but to speak to him and to hear him, himself, speaking to us. That's the impossible and we can no longer even take the measure of this wound.

Speaking is impossible, but so too would be silence or absence or a refusal to share one's sadness. Let me simply ask you to forgive me if today finds me with the strength for only a few very simple words. At a later time, I will try to find better words, and more serene ones, for the friendship that ties me to Paul de Man (it was and remains unique), what I, like so many others, owe to his generosity, to his lucidity, to the ever so gentle force of his thought: since that morning in 1966 when I met him at a breakfast table in Baltimore, during a colloquium, where we spoke, among other things, of Rousseau and the *Essai sur l'origine des langues,* a text which was then seldom read in the university but which we had both been working on, each in his own way, without know-

323

ing it. From then on, nothing has ever come between us, not even a hint of disagreement. It was like the golden rule of an alliance, no doubt that of a trusting and unlimited friendship, but also the seal of a secret affirmation that, still today, I wouldn't know how to circumscribe, to limit, to name (and that is as it should be). As you know, Paul was irony itself and, among all the vivid thoughts he leaves with us and leaves alive in us, there is as well an enigmatic reflection on irony and even, in the words of Schlegel which he had occasion to cite, on "irony of irony." At the heart of my attachment to him, there has also always been a certain beyond-of-irony which cast on his own a softening, generous light, reflecting a smiling compassion on everything he illuminated with his tireless vigilance. His lucidity was sometimes overpowering, making no concession to weakness, but it never gave in to that negative assurance with which the ironic consciousness is sometimes too easily satisfied.

At some later time, then, I will try to find better words for what his friendship brought to all of those who had the good fortune to be his friend, his colleague, his student; but also for his work and especially for the future of his work, undoubtedly one of the most influential of our time.[1] His work, in other words, his teaching and his books, those already published and those soon to appear—because, to the very last and with an admirable strength, enthusiasm and gaiety, he worked on ever new lectures and writing projects, enlarging and enriching still further the perspectives he had already opened up for us. As we know already but as we shall also come to realize more and more, he transformed the field of literary theory, revitalizing all the channels that irrigate it both inside and outside the university, in the United States and in Europe. Besides a new style of interpretation, of reading, of teaching, he brought to bear the necessity of the polylogue and of a plurilinguistic refinement which was his genius—not only that of national languages (Flemish, French, German, English) but also of those idioms which are literature and philosophy, renewing as he did so the reading of Pascal as well as Rilke, of Descartes and Hölderlin, of Hegel and Keats, Rousseau and Shelley, Nietzsche and Kant, Locke and Diderot, Stendahl and Kierkegaard, Coleridge, Kleist, Wordsworth and Baudelaire, Proust, Mallarmé and Blanchot, Austin and Heidegger, Benjamin, Bakhtin and so many others, contemporary or not. Never content merely to present new readings, he led one to think the very possibility of reading—and also sometimes the paradox of its impossibility. His commitment remains henceforth that of his friends and his students who owe it to him and to themselves to pursue what was begun by him and with him.

Beyond the manifest evidence of the published texts—his own as well as those that make reference to his—I, like many others, can attest to what is today the radiance of his thought and his words: in the United States, first of

---

1. Jacques Derrida will soon publish an essay in homage to Paul de Man (Univeristy of Minnesota Press) and a longer work on the oeuvre of Paul de Man (Columbia University Press), the result of conferences held at the University of California at Irvine in April 1984 (editorial note).

all, where so many universities are linked and enlivened by the large community of his disciples, the large family of his former students or colleagues who have remained his friends; but also in Europe at all the universities where I had, as I did here at Yale, the good fortune and the honor to work with him, often at his invitation. I think first of Zurich, where we came together so many times, with Patricia, with Hillis; and naturally I think of Paris where he lived, published and shared editorial or academic responsibilities (for example, for Johns Hopkins or Cornell—and again these were for us the occasion of so many encounters). I also know the impression his passage left on the universities of Constance, Berlin and Stockholm. I will say nothing of Yale because you know this better than anyone and because today my memory is too given over to mourning for all that I have shared with him here during the last ten years, from the most simple day-to-dayness to the most intense moments in the work that allied us with each other and with others, the friends, students and colleagues who grieve for him so close to me here.

I wanted only to *bear witness* as would befit the sort of admiring observer I have also been at his side in the American and European academic world. This is neither the time nor the place to give into indiscreet revelations or too personal memories. I will refrain from speaking of such memories therefore—I have too many of them, as do many of you, and they are so overwhelming that we prefer to be alone with them. But allow me to infringe this law of privacy long enough to evoke two memories, just two among so many others.

The last letter I received from Paul: I still don't know how to read the serenity or the cheerfulness which it displayed. I never knew to what extent he adopted this tone, in a gesture of noble and sovereign discretion, so as to console and spare his friends in their anxiety or their despair; or, on the contrary, to what extent he had succeeded in transfiguring what is still for us the worst. No doubt it was both. Among other things, he wrote what I am going to permit myself to read here because, rightly or wrongly, I received it as a message, confided to me, for his friends in distress. You'll hear a voice and a tone that are familiar to us: "All of this, as I was telling you [on the phone], seems prodigiously interesting to me and I'm enjoying myself a lot. I knew it all along but it is being borne out: death gains a great deal, as they say, when one gets to know it close up—that 'peu profond ruisseau calomnié la mort' [shallow stream caluminated as death]." And after having cited this last line from Mallarmé's "Tombeau for Verlaine," he added: "Anyhow, I prefer that to the brutality of the word 'tumeur'"—which, in fact, is more terrible, more insinuating and menacing in French than in any other language [tumeur/tu meurs: you are dying].

I recall the second memory because it says something about music—and only music today seems to me bearable, consonant, able to give some measure of what unites us in the same thought. I had known for a long time, even though he spoke of it very rarely, that music occupied an important place in Paul's life and thought. On that particular night—it was 1979 and once again the occasion was a colloquium—we were driving through the streets of Chicago after a jazz concert. My older son, who had accompanied me, was talking with Paul about music, more precisely about musical instruments. This they were doing as the experts they both were, as technicians who know how to call things by their name. It was then I realized that Paul had never told me he was an experienced musician and that music had also been a practice with him. The word that let me know this was the word "âme" [soul] when, hearing Pierre, my son, and Paul speak with familiarity of the violin's or the bass's soul, I learned that the "soul" is the name one gives in French to the small and fragile piece of wood—always very exposed, very vulnerable—that is placed within the body of these instruments to support the bridge and assure the resonant communication of the two sounding boards. I didn't know why at that moment I was so strangely moved and unsettled in some dim recess by the conversation I was listening to: no doubt it was due to the word "soul" which always speaks to us at the same time of life and of death and makes us dream of immortality, like the argument of the lyre in the *Phaedo*.

And I will always regret, among so many other things, that I never again spoke of any of this with Paul. How was I to know that one day I would speak of that moment, that music and that soul without him, before you who must forgive me for doing it just now so poorly, so painfully when already everything is painful, so painful?

JACQUES DERRIDA

Translated by Kevin Newmark with the approval of the author.

The first encounter, around 1955, at the Collège de philosophie, led, almost exclusively, by Jean Wahl who was to some extent (or even definitely) our *maître*. The lecture was on "poetry and destiny." I had come because of the subject, but also because it was almost a habit for me in those years, at six o'clock, to be in the rather dusty room of the Institut de géographie, place Saint-Germain-des-Prés, to listen to Massignon or Pierre Jean Jouve, Lévi-Strauss or Georges Bataille.—I had come because of the subject, but I left with a budding friendship which was soon to become admiration and affection.

And for this, this head with the slanted forehead, leaning over an unexpected big smile above which would filter the very blue glance had sufficed; as a word almost whispered which, of important moments, was lowered still more or was interrupted by a little laugh.

This laughter was malicious, somewhat childlike, in any case very youthful: it seemed to suggest that we stop thinking about the idea which had just been proferred, about this preposterous project that a young critic-philosopher (this double choice was still rather rare) had taken on that day, of thinking about poetry. But this was not however a laugh of derision, one in which one feels fright and which anticipates the dogmatism which will follow the instant of doubt. I felt in this abrupt denial of the seriousness of the hour, both the joy of understanding profoundly, and the irony born of the lucid perception of limitations, be they those of philosophy as an enterprise or more immediately the difficulties of a personal thought still fragile, in spite of its magnificent intuitions. And in this playfulness, the nostalgia of those years of play sparkled as well, and the memory, one might surmise, of a sorrow,—already permeated with this detachment, already this serenity of a mind completely dedicated to its work, whatever form his existence had taken, which some of us have seen deepen and mature, become pure irony and wisdom during the rest of his destiny.

Paul de Man. A presence was felt there, with all the mystery which this name evokes; it was on the horizon of a problem which meant a great deal to me, which had sollicited me that day, a region suddenly brighter (not the brightness of an explanation, however, nor even that of a method, but rather that of a fire which is perceived at a distance, on a beach, when one senses that someone down there is repairing his net, and sewing heaven and earth back together). It was a source of happiness for me, two or three years later, when I came to the United States for the first time, to Harvard, for one of those long summers when one wears white as in India in the overwhelming humidity, to find Paul, on the silent grass, in Cambridge. He was then living in Boston, on Beacon Street, in a small apartment under the roof, his daughter was about to be born. I can see him again at our first meeting, approaching across the yard, his head tilted, smiling from afar, the surprising color of his glance already spread around him, under the trees: it was noon, the hour when the shadows disappear. We became accustomed to lunch in the small French restaurants of Harvard Square, or of Berkeley Street in Boston. But it was no longer in order to speak of poetry and destiny, at least in a systematic way, Paul loved poetry too much to refer to it too directly and, by so doing, engage himself in it—he preferred, as in his writing, to evoke poets rather than poetry itself, and critics rather than poets. This manner of marking, cruelly, gently, the underlying limitations of a method or the insufficiencies of a reading, was not distancing himself from the essential, it was practicing, again with this brief and somehow distant laughter which he also turned against himself, an unexpected kind of negative theology.

And above all he spoke to me of Ireland, which he loved, because, he told me once, there one could not distinguish a man from an animal or from a plant (doubtlessly because the language is not separated from the earth, because of its myths and of its admirable popular music), and he evoked Gott Island where I regret having been unable to join him that year or others. The island is off the coast of Maine, with only two or three small houses there in the sunlight. And in the life of Paul de Man, begun again late in America, it was the center which had been missing for so long, the justification, and sometimes the haven: always in any case the proof of the existence, if not of God, at least of this unifying force which, underneath all the sadnesses, the nostalgias, rises again, irresistible for some, in order to lighten their anguish, as water does for the diver.

Paul loved, in fact, passionately loved the natural world as it is, prairies and forests, waves surging among the rocks, this world of the immediate and of the eternal which he never ceased to note, with joy at the most acute point of his anxiety—it was and would remain inaccessible to language and moreover, even to poetry. He who worked on the verbal particle in so intellectualized a manner, one so mediated by culture—let us say, in a word: so "secondary," but it is true that he only touched those fragments of the word already charged with the most intense poetic and metaphysical energy, as if they were the irruption of a spiritual fire as basic and blind as that which impels the stars—, he sought the great deserted beach which extends to the things of nature between usand the light out there in silent evidence. He advanced towards this horizon, in all his moments of solitude, it is from there, when the life of the cities claimed him once more, that he returned with this courage which we admired in him, henceforth capable of that attention, as if cleansed of all care, that he knw how to grant to the most transient student as to the most difficult thoughts. And he of course loved only, and with reason, the works of poetry in which this light appears, or is mediated—lacking sometimes, but painfully acknowledged by the poet. Wordsworth, Hölderlin, Yeats. And Mallarmé, as well. As we know, Paul was drawn to the word which is found in hymns, the last of our religious tradition, or simply in fragments, the signs of our misery, towards that which transcends the word; and which, hurling itself thus, perhaps says something other, in the economy of language, than that which it believes it says. But the gravest error that we could make about Paul de Man would be to think that he loved for themselves, out of a simple taste for truth, those failures of significa-tion, those ruptures which mutely ring in the meaning that great poets have tried to give the world. His eyes followed, at the variegated surface of poetic enunciations, the play of intuitions, of misunderstandings, a mighty swell never broken in which are endlessly exchanged—for whom, we do not know, in the drift of the centuries—reality, so to speak, and dream. In these moments of extreme attention, it was heard at the heart of this Zen monk's laughter that he had always had by premonition that there is no God, even in the very depths of language. But if he so watched the foam appear and disappear around the flotsam which comes from upstream, and slides towards the estuary, it is because that which shines in figures and images when we read them thus in the infinity of their significance in the material of the text, is always the light, the indifferent and holy light. It is because watching the drift enlarges the sky, even if the sky remains empty.

A long series of encounters spaced too far apart, drift—there again—pro-jects, obstacles, occasions suddenly offered and sometimes seized: the flowing of the passing years displacing the places in which we found ourselves, Cam-bridge for a long time, Ithaca, Zurich, Provence, Connecticut, California. A car which stops, very late, in front of the Clark Institute in Williamstown—it is the museum, the place chosen for the meeting, because of the Piero della Francesca—and Paul and Patricia and the children get out, these are vacation days which will go on in this manner, where? Out of time, it now seems to me, out of the world. Another car, incredibly loaded with baggage which, surprised to arrive in this place by an unpaved road, immobilizes itself in front of the Valsaintes house: and the children have grown, ten minutes have not gone by before we are going down in the ravine, in the heat, Patricia always in front because of her light tripping step. It is in Paul's office, in Woodbridge, that a certain little girl, one Sunday, suddenly risked taking her first steps. Fifteen years later, on a beach in New Hampshire, Paul built a big fire of driftwood, putting in it potatoes and meat, it was already night, I defended myself with flaming firebrands against the assault of a similar sword which a little six year old boy shook with the gauche agility of childhood.

And the last time was at Irvine, where I was living for a few weeks in a little house on the dunes which are at the end of the campus, and Paul, who had come to California for a colloquium, came to see again this place where he himself had lived the year before, where he had been happy, I could see. After which there were two or three meetings which were, without our knowing it, the end—here, at the seashore, there at the home of people we did not know, it is evening, there is a dinner outside, we linger to speak in the garden, under the lamps. I had listened to Paul, in the colloquium, evoke Jauss, present his critical thought, but as if at a distance, as if he were in another world than those discussions or that room: he seemed so withdrawn in the analysis of a few words of a poem of Baudelaire that he did not follow them to the limit of their meaning, dreaming this meaning, one might have said, so well that I thought that he spoke there of himself, that he spoke to himself. "I am two distinct beings," he said to me, more or less, upon leaving the lecture. When the visit was over, we drove, John Naughton and myself, our friend, to the little Orange County airport. It was an afternoon, it was very beautiful and very hot, as usual. And at the last minute, or almost, Paul took his suitcase, we did not get out of the car, it was in silence, it was invisibly—as so often—that life turned past in that moment one of those great sets with which it can lull for years our affection, our dream.

YVES BONNEFOY

Translated by Peggy McCracken

Contributors

SHULI BARZILAI was a post-doctoral fellow at Yale University and is now a lecturer of English at the Hebrew University of Jerusalem, where she teaches courses on psychoanalysis and literature and linguistic approaches to literature.

YVES BONNEFOY, France's great lyric poet, holds a chair at the Collège de France. He has been Visiting Professor at Yale University.

PETER BROOKS is Chairman of the Yale French Department and Director of The Whitney Humanities Center. His most recent book is *Reading for the Plot: Design and Intention in Narrative*.

E. S. BURT is Assistant Professor in the Yale French department and is currently working on Rousseau's autobiographies.

VERNON CHADWICK is a graduate student in the Comparative Literature department at Yale University.

JONATHAN CULLER, Director of the Society for the Humanities at Cornell University, is the author of *Structuralist Poetics, On Deconstruction*, and other works of literary theory. A revised edition of his *Flaubert: The Uses of Uncertainty* was published in 1985 by the Cornell University Press.

JACQUES DERRIDA is Directeur d'Etudes at the Ecole des Hautes Etudes en Sciences Sociales (Paris). He is Visiting Professor in the Humanities at Yale University and the Andrew D. White Professor-at-large at Cornell University.

ROBERTO GONZÁLEZ ECHEVARRÍA is chairman of the Department of Spanish and Portuguese and the Latin American Studies Program at Yale University. He is the author of, among other books, *Alejo Carpentier: The Pilgrim at Home*. His *The Voice of the Masters: Writing and Authority in Modern Latin American Literature* will be published by the University of Texas Press this spring.

SHOSHANA FELMAN is Professor of French at Yale University. She is author of *Writing and Madness* (Literature/Philosophie/Psychoanalysis) (Cornell University Press) and *The Literary Speech Act: Don Juan with J. L. Austin* or *Seduction in Two Languages* (Cornell University Press) and Special Editor of *Literature and Madness: The Question of Reading—Otherwise* (The Johns Hopkins University Press). Her latest book, *What Does a Woman Want?*, is forthcoming from the Harvard University Press.

HOWARD FELPERIN has been for several years the Robert Wallace Professor of Modern Literature at the University of Melbourne in Australia. He is about to take up a new chair at Macquarrie University in Sydney. He has published several books on Shakespeare and a new book on Post-Structurist criticism is forthcoming from the Oxford University Press.

HANS-JOST FREY is Professor of Comparative Literature at the University of Zurich. In this country he taught at Cornell and Yale Universities. He is co-author of *Kritik des freien Verses.*

A. BARTLETT GIAMATTI is President of Yale University.

BARBARA JONES GUETTI studied with Paul de Man at Radcliffe College (B.A., 1959) and at Cornell University (Ph.D., 1967). She is currently Visiting Associate Professor of Literary Theory at Hampshire College.

ANSELM HAVERKAMP is Professor of German and Comparative Literature at the University of Constance and was Visiting Professor of Comparative Literature at Yale University.

WERNER HAMACHER, Assistant Professor at the Institute for General and Comparative Literature of the Free University, Berlin, until 1984 is at present Visiting Professor in the Department of German and the Humanities Center at the Johns Hopkins University in 1985. He is the author of publications: G. W. F. Hegel—"Der Geist des Christentums," edited and introduced by a book-length study *"pleroma"—zu Genesis und Struktur einer dialektischen Hermeneutik bei Hegel* (1978); essays on Kant, Fichte, Schlegel, Schleiermacher, Kleist, Nietzsche, Yeats et al. He is preparing a book of essays on literary hermeneutics: *Entferntes Verstehen.*

GEOFFREY H. HARTMAN is the Carl Young Professor of English and Comparative Literature at Yale Univeristy. He is the chairman of the Department of Comparative Literature at Yale. He is also the director of the School of Theory and Criticism. His latest book, *Easy Pieces*, has just been published by the Columbia University Press.

CAROL JACOBS is Professor of English and Comparative Literature at SUNY Buffalo. She is the author of *The Dissimulating Harmony* (Johns Hopkins University Press, 1978) and is currently working on the question of authority in the context of European romanticism.

WILLIAM D. JEWETT is a graduate student in the Comparative Literature department at Yale University.

BARBARA JOHNSON is Professor of Romance languages and literatures at Harvard University. She is author of *Défigurations du langage poétique* and *The Critical Difference*, translator of Jacques Derrida's *Dissemination*, and editor of *The Pedagogical Imperative: Teaching as a Literary Genre*, YFS 61.

THOMAS KEENAN is a graduate student in the Comparative Literature department at Yale University.

ROBERT LIVINGSTON is a graduate student in the Comparative Literature department at Yale University.

J. HILLIS MILLER is the Frederick W. Hilles Professor of English and Comparative Literature at Yale University. His most recent book is *The Linguistic Moment: From Wordsworh to Stevens* (Princeton University Press, 1985).

MINAE MIZUMURA is a Ph.D. candidate in French Literature at Yale University. She is currently in Tokyo writing a thesis on modern Japanese novels.

KEVIN NEWMARK is Assistant Professor in the French Department at Yale University.

MICHAEL RIFFATERRE is University Professor at Columbia Univeristy and Senior Fellow of the School of Criticism and Theory.

MOSHE RON teaches English and Comparative Literature at the Hebrew University in Jerusalem.

ANDRZEJ WARMINSKI is Associate Professor of Comparative Literature at Yale University. His book on Hölderlin, Hegel, and Heidegger is forthcoming from the University of Minnesota Press.

The following issues are still available through the Yale French Studies Office, 315 William L. Harkness Hall, Yale University, New Haven, Conn. 06520.

Add for postage & handling

Single issue, United States $1.00
Each additional issue $ .50

Single issue, foreign countries $1.50
Each additional issue $ .75

- -

YALE FRENCH STUDIES 315 William L. Harkness Hall, Yale University, New Haven, Connecticut 06520

A check made payable to YFS is enclosed. Please send me the following issue(s):

Issue no.   Title   Price

_____   _____   _____
_____   _____   _____
_____   _____   _____

                                          Postage & handling   _____
                                                    Total   _____

Name _____

Number/Street _____

City _____ State _____ Zip _____

The following issues are now available through Kraus Reprint Company, Route 100, Millwood, N.Y. 10546.

36/37 Structuralism has been reprinted by Doubleday as an Anchor Book.

55/56 Literature and Psychoanalysis has been reprinted by Johns Hopkins University Press, and can be ordered through Customer Service, Johns Hopkins University Press, Baltimore, MD 21218.

The following issues are available through Yale University Press, Customer Service Department, 92A Yale Station, New Haven, CT 06520.

63 The Pedagogical Imperative:
    Teaching as a Literary Genre
    (1982) $11.95
64 Montaigne: Essays in Reading
    (1983) $11.95
65 The Language of Difference:
    Writing in QUEBEC(ois)
    (1983) $11.95
66 The Anxiety of Anticipation
    (1984) $11.95

67 Concepts of Closure
    (1984) $11.95
68 Sartre after Sartre
    (1985) $11.95
69 The Lesson of Paul De Man (1985) $11.95
70 Images of Power: Medieval History,
    Discourse Literature (1986)
71 Forthcoming Issue (1986)

Special subscription rates are available on a calendar year basis (2 issues per year):

Individual subscriptions $20.00
Institutional subscriptions $23.90

- -

ORDER FORM   **Yale University Press,** 92A Yale Station, New Haven, CT 06520

Please enter my subscription for the calendar year
☐ 1984   ☐ 1985   ☐ 1986
I would like to purchase the following individual issues:

_____

_____

For individual issues, please add postage and handling:
Single issue, United States $1.00
Each additional issue $ .50
Connecticut residents please add sales tax of 7½%.

Single issue, foreign countries $1.50
Each additional issue $ .75

Payment of $_____ is enclosed (including sales tax if applicable).

Mastercard no. _____

4-digit bank no. _____ Expiration date _____

VISA no. _____ Expiration date _____

Signature _____

SHIP TO: _____

_____

_____

- -

See the next page for ordering issues 1 – 62. **Yale French Studies** is also available through Xerox University Microfilms, 300 North Zeeb Road, Ann Arbor, MI 48106.

Allegories of Reading

Figural Language in Rousseau, Nietzsche, Rilke, and Proust

Paul de Man

"Through elaborate and elegant close readings of poems by Rilke, Proust's *Remembrance*, Nietzsche's philosophical writings and the major works of Rousseau, de Man concludes that all writing concerns itself with its own activity as language, and language, he says, is always unreliable, slippery, impossible. . . . Literary narrative, because it must rely on language, tells the story of its own inability to tell a story. . . . De Man demonstrates, beautifully and convincingly, that language turns back on itself, that rhetoric is untrustworthy."
—Julia Epstein, *Washington Post Book World*

[A] work in the tradition of 'deconstructionist criticism,' . . . [which] begins with the observation that all language is constructed; therefore the task of criticism is to deconstruct it and reveal what lies behind. The title reflects de Man's preoccupation with the unreliability of language. . . . The contributions that the book makes, both in the initial theoretical chapters and in the detailed analyses (or deconstructions) of particular texts, are undeniable." —Caroline D. Eckhardt, *World Literature Today* $8.95 paperbound

Yale University Press

Dept. 126   92A Yale Station   New Haven, CT 06520